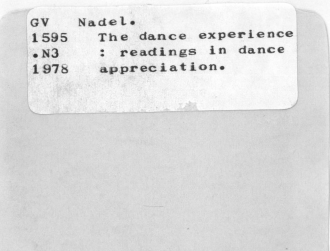

The Dance Experience

The Dance Experience

Readings in Dance Appreciation

Edited by

MYRON HOWARD NADEL

and

CONSTANCE NADEL MILLER

UNIVERSE BOOKS

New York

Published in the United States of America in 1978
by Universe Books
381 Park Avenue South, New York, N.Y. 10016

Library of Congress Catalog Card Number: 77-79939

Cloth edition: ISBN 0-87663-237-1
Paperback edition: ISBN 0-87663-972-4

Printed in the United States of America

To Martha Hill
a visionary in dance education
and a guiding light to our careers

CONTENTS

Part Four: THE LANGUAGE AND LITERATURE OF DANCE

Part Five: DANCE AND THE OTHER ARTS

Part Six: DANCE CRITICISM

Part Seven: THE DANCE ARTIST

Part Eight: PROBLEMS IN DANCE

Part Nine: FACETS OF DANCE EDUCATION

Preface

The Dance Experience has been used by high school, college, and graduate dance courses, but it was originally designed for a two-semester beginning college course, "Introduction to the Art of Dance." The three-credit course contained lectures, films, discussions, and participatory classes in dance technique. For dance, it seemed particularly important to experience the "doing" as well as the "learning about" the art of moving. At the same time, physical participation through dance technique classes is enhanced by an appreciation of dance tradition, history, choreography, aesthetics, and personalities. The course included specific readings on dance history and dance biographies, subjects that we did not cover in *The Dance Experience* because of their ready availability through many books already in print.

Since the late 1960's, when this book was put together, dance has at long last come of age. In the United States, its audience outnumbers those at professional baseball games, and a large percentage of the audience is young. The number of American dance companies has grown from 200 in 1970 to 316 in 1977, and although New York City is still the dance capital of the United States (and the world), more than 300 regional professional companies are performing vigorously throughout the country. (In Canada there are now more than 40 dance companies.) This coming of age of dance reflects what those of us who are professionally involved enthusiastically confirm more people are studying, performing, creating, preserving, reconstructing, working for and writing about dance than ever before!

Most fields of study have specialties of which the beginner is already aware. This is not the case with dance, where students usually do not know that specialities such as Labanotation and even choreography exist as subfields in their own right. We hope that this cross-section of writings will acquaint students with other facets of dance which can provide exciting pursuits and rewarding careers, and help to overcome the prevalent notion among many beginners that dance begins and ends with dancing.

C. N. M.
M. H. N.

1977

ONE

The Nature of Dance

Dance is not a substance that can be felt, lifted, or weighed. It is something that happens when a human entity moves in directed patterns, consciously performing specific movements, and other humans view this phenomenon. Therefore, it is difficult to refer to the art of dance or the work produced as being an artifact or a thing at all. Instead, we must remember that the dance never exists in its totality at any one time but, rather, develops during a segment of measurable time.

That the word "dance" is difficult to define is quite clear, and, for this reason, we should attempt to focus our energies on the art of the dance or on dance as a theatrical experience. It may well be asked why it is necessary for us to dig into the very nature of dance and attempt to dissect an event so fleeting—which should be enjoyed as a fleeting thing. However, most academicians feel that, the more we know about what we are working with, the better we will understand and, therefore, enjoy it. So often at dance concerts we hear that the performance was good but was not understood. Perhaps, this is because audiences are often looking for the same sort of relationships inherent in understanding or knowing people, places, and things. This section includes articles that we feel give a broad-based understanding of the dance as a lived experience.

Those for whom this is the first experience of regarding the nature of dance from an analytical point of view should keep several points in mind:

First, two different roles must come into play before a dance work is presented. The role of the choreographer is to create the concept and movement of the dance work—he is the *creative* artist. The role of the dancer is to perform what is given by the choreographer—the dancer is the *interpretive* artist. Although the choreographer is often also a performer, the two roles must be considered separately.

Second, the articles refer to all kinds of theatrical dance—attempting to show neither the metaphysical connotations of dance nor what dance ought to be but, rather, the art of dance as a creative and controlled phenomenon.

Finally, most dancers and choreographers do not consciously think about their art in such analytical terms or use the language of the following articles while practicing their art. However, they are familiar with, and sensitive to, these same ideas.

The nature of dance as a performing art is worth exploring, because such study fosters one's ability to criticize. Armed with certain basic knowledge, a student of the dance will not waste time dealing with areas where dance is not attempting to enter and cannot enter in pure form. His criticism can then deal with each creative form as it relates to the true nature of dance.

1
A DANCE AESTHETIC

Selma Jeanne Cohen limits her discussion on dance aesthetics to theatrical dancing, the only form that consciously provides an aesthetic experience. She answers many questions basic to an appreciation of dance as an art form.

Dance *does* induce an aesthetic experience, but what is it in dance that induces this experience? Rhythmical movement and expressiveness in themselves do not account for it.

It is pointed out that dance does not seek to portray anything literally—literal movement is more properly in the sphere of the mime. Dance can be movement for its own sake—for the joy of seeing "what wonderfully strange and beautiful things the human body can do." And yet, there has been a symbolism, or stylization, in dance that has evolved from the beginning of theatrical dance in 17th-century France to the present time. This change in stylization is as it should be, for life in the twentieth century has completely different rhythms, lines, and dynamics from the elegant formalized customs that prevailed in the French court of Louis XIV.

Movement of the human body can tell us only so much; it cannot convey facts or ideas as efficiently as words can. Dance movement deals generally with people and perceptions that can be grasped by the eye, such as the qualities of character and emotion.

Cohen develops her aesthetic ideas on dance around subject matter and stylization—those elements that the choreographer uses in the composing of dance. Yet, she does not minimize the importance of the interpreter of the work (the dancer), the expressiveness of movement, form and balance in composition, or the dancer's relationship to the music.

In her book *Modern Dance: Seven Statements of Belief,* Selma Jeanne Cohen presents the philosophies of seven highly individualistic 20th-century choreographers, pointing out that there are no hard and fast rules for creating dances. And if this is so, then the transient nature of dance must be what has hampered any quantity of theoretical consideration of it. However, in the following article, Cohen gives the inexperienced dance audience many things to consider while she promotes an understanding of the nature of the art of dance.

A PROLEGOMENON TO AN
AESTHETICS OF DANCE

Aesthetics is not equally concerned with all kinds of dancing. The ritual, which is designed to ask a favor of the gods, and the social dance, which provides enjoyment for its participants, may—accidentally—give aesthetic pleasure. But this is not their purpose, nor is it the test of their success. The rain dance succeeds when the rain falls. The square dance goes well when the performers have a good time. Only theatrical dancing is designed to provide the observer with an aesthetic experience.

What is the nature of the dancing that induces this experience? It has been defined as rhythmical movement of the human body. But this could be applied to a parade, and any woman will agree that ironing is easiest when done to music. While it is hard to conceive of dancing that is not rhythmical, there is no problem at all to finding forms of rhythmical bodily movement that are not dancing.

Does the distinction lie in the expressiveness of dance movement? The pantomime artist is even more expressive. By watching his movements we know exactly the kind of character he is representing, the emotion he is feeling, even the particular action he is performing, such as opening a door or tying his shoes. We can justify by its literal meaning every one of his motions. We try in vain to do this with a dancer. We watch the great adagio in *Swan Lake* for several minutes, and all we can say in the end is that the boy and girl are in love. We would find it difficult to pinpoint the "meaning" of any one of the ballerina's many *pirouettes*. The dance as a whole has an expressive quality, but this quality does not account for all its parts. It cannot, because its movements are designed for a purpose beyond expressiveness.

Of all the arts to which dance has been likened that of lyric poetry offers the most significant analogies. Like dance, it is both rhythmic and expressive. It makes its statement in a manner that has an important sensuous appeal. In the words of Gerard Manley Hopkins, poetry is "speech framed to be heard for its own sake and interest even above its interest of meaning." Dancing may be thought of as movement framed to be seen for its own sake and interest even above its interest of meaning.

From the *Journal of Aesthetics and Art Criticism*, XXI, No. 1 (Fall, 1962), 19-26. By permission of the American Society for Aesthetics and the *Journal of Aesthetics and Art Criticism*.

The movements of the marchers in the parade are not interesting for their own sake. Almost anyone who can count can march. The precision of the marchers has some interest, but this is a matter of the coordination visible in a large group. An individual performing these actions alone would not attract much of an audience.

The actions of the pantomime artist would seem to be more interesting, because each of them has a meaning. But it is for this very reason that they differ from the movements of the dancer. We watch the mime attentively in order to identify his actions; he is putting on his coat, now he is opening his umbrella. This is movement that has interest of meaning but not interest above meaning. When we fail to understand the movements of the mime, we find no pleasure in his performance.

But we enjoy the movements of the ballerina without feeling the need to define their meaning. We take pleasure in the visual designs made by her body, in the harmony of her balanced poses, in the contrast between straight legs and gently curved arms. We take pleasure in the musicality of her phrasing, which gives emphasis at climactic moments and provides smooth transitions between them. We take pleasure in her control of dynamics, the play of swift, sharp movements against softly flowing ones. We enjoy these patterns for their own sake and interest even above their interest of meaning.

Putting aside for the moment the question of whether the dance has to mean, has to express something, to be a dance, we may ask what kinds of meaning are possible to this art that uses as its medium the movement of the human body.

Certainly there are areas that seem unamenable to expression in dance. A choreographer would find it difficult to compose a dance about the distance of the moon from the earth, or about Kant's categorical imperative. George Balanchine has remarked that there are no mothers-in-law in ballet. And Doris Humphrey has quoted the opening of a rejected dance scenario: "A young man, exhausted, admires the vitality of nature."

None of these will work. The medium of dance is human movement. It deals with people, not with facts or ideas. And it deals with people in motion—not exhausted. We can think very well while sitting very still. We can express the distance of the moon from the earth by gesturing with our fingers, but the matter is better explained in words. We might act out a marriage ceremony to identify the mother-in-law, but it is easier said than done. And what would the poor dancer do with Kant? Neither factual relations nor ideas are promising choreographic material. The area of dance is not that of concepts, which are grasped by the mind by way of words, but of percepts, which are grasped by the eye by way of movement.

What can we tell from movement? We learn two sorts of things about the person who moves. First, he tells us the kind of person he is, his character. He tells us he is confident, shy, vivacious, tough, polite. To see this we need only contrast the walk of a Charlie Chaplin—small steps, chest sunken, shoulders pinched inward—with the walk of the traditional hero: the broad, swinging stride, the chest held high, the shoulders flung backward. Second, the mover tells us his state of feeling at the particular moment. We are familiar with the bowed head of grief, the skip of joy, the clenched fists of anger. Movement gives us sensible images of qualities of character and emotion. These are the proper province of dance.

Within this province, the choreographer's potential range is wide. The degree of particularization may vary greatly. It may come close to that of drama, as in Martha Graham's *Clytemnestra,* in which the individual figures of Greek tragedy relive their sufferings through the patterns of dance. Or it may deal with universals, as in Doris Humphrey's *Day on Earth,* which tells the story of man as the story of mankind—the cycle of birth, love, and death. At a still further remove from drama, the dance may be purely lyrical, like Michael Fokine's *Les Sylphides,* which has no narrative structure at all, but is merely a sequence of dances of serene joy and romantic love as they might be envisioned by a poet, dreaming in a wood by moonlight.

A choreographer cannot make a dance about the moon, but he can make a dance about the way he feels toward the moon—which may inspire him with wonder or joy or nostalgia. He may make a dance about the way he feels toward his mother-in-law because irritation, resentment, exasperation are all feelings expressible by bodily movement. If he could get really excited about the categorical imperative, he might make a dance about that. However, unless he has a feeling for the fact or idea, he has nothing to dance about.

The choreographer deals with images of quality of character and emotion. He must devise movements sufficient and appropriate to their representation.

He may begin with the naturally expressive movement of human gesture. This, however, is only his starting point. Fokine defined dance as "the development and ideal of the sign." Taking gesture, the natural sign of character or emotion, as his base, the choreographer builds from it a movement that has both a visual and an aural design. First he gives the gesture a more definitively perceivable shape in space. He may extend or elaborate its configuration, so that the angry stamp is preceded by a high kick into the air or accompanied by a violent series of turns that send the dancer whirling across the entire stage. Then he gives the movement a pattern in time; prolonging or quickening or repeating it, setting it to a definite rhythm, building it into a phrase. Further, he may enhance the dynamics of the movement, sharpening the contrasts between tension and relaxation, between strong and soft, giving it a more distinctive texture.

Such manipulations, when properly employed, contribute to the "development and ideal of the sign." They do not obliterate the significance of the gesture, but rather they enhance it. Prolongation may emphasize a movement; quickening of tempo may create excitement. Choreographic enhancement, or stylization, extends the emotional expressiveness of the gesture. The dance has not merely added form to the movement; it has intensified the meaning of the movement.

Actually the choreographer may begin not with natural gesture but with dance movements already stylized beyond the form of gesture. That is, he may utilize an established stylistic vocabulary, like that of the ballet or the Spanish dance or the Hindu or jazz. These idioms are products of distinct cultures and represent attitudes toward character and emotion peculiar to those cultures. They are modes of stylization in which comment is implicit. This may involve, as in classical ballet, a polished refining of emotion, for in 17th-century France—where the ballet first developed—decorum of behavior was the ideal. The Spanish dance, on the contrary, especially the flamenco, heightens emotion to passionate intensity. It represents a different attitude toward life.

Modes of stylization change as cultures evolve. The original vocabulary of the ballet derived from the elegant artificiality of the royal court of 17th- and early 18th-century France. In the romantic era, the heroine, once conceived as a gracious though worldly mistress, became an ethereal being, a symbol of unattainable beauty. And women began to dance on *pointe;* that is, on the tips of their toes, which made them appear as if air-borne. The new style came into being because of the new attitude.

Later developments, promoted most notably by Fokine, paved the way for the contemporary psychological ballet exemplified by the works of Antony Tudor. In the 1830s, when Marie Taglioni stepped onto the toes of one foot, her other leg extended behind her, she looked like some heavenly creature about to fly. In 1945, when Nora Kaye first danced Hagar in Tudor's *Pillar of Fire,* she took what was basically the same pose but she looked like an agonized, frustrated woman. Both poses were variations of the balletic stylization, which is the position called *arabesque.* The change came about through a different use of the arms and torso, but even more significantly through the manner of performance—through a distinctive use of dynamic tension, an "attack" unlike any ballet had used before. It altered completely the nature of the choreographer's comment, eliciting reactions not of wonder and admiration but of pity and fear. Neither the classic nor the romantic *arabesque* could have served Tudor's purpose. He had to employ another kind of stylization to embody another kind of image of woman.

The works of men like Tudor are, of course, more than reflections of cultural change; they are products of individual genius that mirror and, in some cases, even anticipate or initiate that change. The choreographer with a fresh image in his mind may feel he must reject existing modes of stylization to create a mode of his own. In 1929 Martha Graham wrote: "Life today is nervous, sharp, zigzag. It often stops in mid-air. It is what I am for in my dances." Her image required an orientation different from anything she found in the dancing of her time. It involved not only the replacement of the flowing, effortless line of ballet with a sharp, percussive thrust, but also the transfer of the source of motor energy from the limbs to the center of the torso. Later in her career, as her approach became more Freudian, she defined the aim of dance as "making visible the interior landscape." Her concept of the image is no longer limited to "life today"; it concerns the whole life of man. Her manner of stylization—now less nervous, somewhat warmer, but still sharp and intense—infuses the image with comment.

The validity of the choreographer's comment is not a strictly aesthetic consideration. From an aesthetic point of view what matters about stylization is its clarity and usefulness to the image. These terms are applicable to both the kind and degree of stylization.

To be clear, the mode of gesture enhancement must be definite and consistent. Otherwise, the nature of the comment appears ambiguous, and the audience is left uncomfortably without a point of reference. If clarity were the sole qualification, however, the choreographer would be always safe in using an established vocabulary, and this would make the art dull and static. In many periods it has done just that. But through the years there have always been some who find that the standard vocabularies, though clear in their own terms, are inadequate to embody the image they want to project. They have dared to expand, to alter, and even to start fresh. They have risked sacrificing immediate clarity to establish a personal comment. For choreography may only seem unclear until audiences are prepared to accept its unfamiliar kind of stylization for the sake of the fresh image it presents to them.

Stylization is useful in kind when it serves the nature of the image. We have seen that different modes of stylization have evolved for this reason. The safety of a ready-made vocabulary has often proved too tempting. But the lure of unmotivated innovation has also been strong. The resulting discrepancies have been both sad and ridiculous. In 1900 Fokine complained about Egyptian slave girls, who flitted about the stage in pink satin toe shoes. We may equally well complain of the use of agonized, so-called modern movements, when they are assigned to a dancer portraying a happy wood-sprite. In either case the intended image is destroyed by an inappropriate kind of stylization.

As regards degree of stylization, we are also concerned with clarity and usefulness. Excessive manipulation obscures the original sign value of the movement. But insufficient enhancement is also a fault. Has the choreographer missed a potential climax by failing to avail himself of devices of stylization? If the movement were still less naturalistic, less literal, would he have achieved a greater effect? Lincoln Kirstein has remarked that dancing on the stage must be "theatrically legible." Stylization makes it so. The purely natural gesture has sufficient meaning for the performer, but for the audience it fails to establish a theatrically perceivable image.

Actually the degree of stylization in dance frequently seems to go beyond the needs of the image. Though it does not interfere with clarity, its positive contribution seems negligible. In terms of the criterion of usefulness, a good part of the great classics would be subject to an editorial red pencil and would never be seen again. Yet we should be wary of hasty condemnation. We have already remarked that dance movement has interest even above its interest of meaning. Sensuous beauty, after all, is one of the great charms of a dance work. Can we deny the art this source of pleasure simply on the grounds that it does not contribute substantially to the image of character or emotion?

The designing of the movement of the human body is the unique property of dance as an art medium. Expressiveness it shares with other arts; even the expressiveness of gesture, for this belongs to pantomime as well. But dance alone has the power—in the words of Théophile Gautier—"of displaying elegant and correctly proportioned shapes [of the body] in various positions favorable to the development of lines." It would seem wasteful to limit the use of this virtue to its expressive function, even though we demand that it should not interfere with that function. If enhancement does not intensify the emotional image, it may still be non-intrusive if it is consistent with the overall mode of stylization and does not demand our attention for such a length of time that the focus of expression is sacrificed.

How strict can we be in our demand for non-interference with the clarity of the sign? No dance is based on a steady flow of stylized gestures. The expressive unit is more often the phrase or even an extended sequence of phrases. The smaller, more literal, unit is characteristic of pantomime. Dance stylization involves the more leisurely use of time and space, the degree of admissible leisure depending on the nature of the work.

In some dances any individual passage (though not any individual step) can be justified by its specific, expressive function. This is the case of José Limon's *The Moor's Pavane,* which is based on the plot of *Othello.* One passage shows Othello's love for Desdemona, another the mounting rage of Iago, another the fears of Desdemona, and so on. All the sequences serve to bring about the final catastrophe.

But when a dance relinquishes plot and deals only with the exploration of the facets of an emotion, the standard of dramatic relevance is superseded by that of lyric relevance. Here more time can be taken to develop sheer intensity of a single feeling as opposed to the sequential definition of successive feelings. Thus, Mr. Limon's

Missa Brevis is constructed as a study of spiritual courage in the aftermath of war. In dramatic terms, the affirmative resolution could have been achieved far earlier than it actually is. There are several scenes that could be labeled as indicative of resignation, where one would seem sufficient. The accumulation cannot be justified in terms of dramatic function. It can, however, be justified as lyrical intensification, and that is proper to this particular dance.

Marius Petipa's three-act *Sleeping Beauty* represents a genre where the overall structure is dramatic, but the story, which requires little emotional intensity, is told at an especially leisurely pace that allows for the insertion of a number of dances that—while consistent with the pervading atmosphere—have no direct bearing on the action. This is not necessarily a weakness. It is a distinction of genre, which demands a distinction of approach.

In the prologue to *The Sleeping Beauty* there are solo dances (we call them variations) for each of seven fairies, who have come to the christening of Princess Aurora. These dances have no dramatic structure in themselves. Yet each has form, a unity of choreographic theme. One is based on fluttering hand movements; another is dominated by tiny running steps on the toes; one is composed of sharp, staccato movements; another of long, legato phrases. This thematic consistency gives a quality of character to each of the dances—they are gentle or spritely or majestic. As a group, they are all rather sweet, and this serves as a foil to what follows: the entry of the wicked Carabosse, who is to utter the fatal curse on Aurora. But their individuality does nothing for the plot. Dramatically, fewer than seven fairies would have served the purpose. We do not, however, object to the superfluous quantity. The dances are varied and charming, and the story is not urgent. Why rush?

Then there is the dance that seems to consist of nothing but dancing. No story. No individual characters. No clear emotional images like love or hate or fear. Just dancing. Yet even in the so-called abstract dance we have a feeling for the presence or absence of consistency of movement quality that suggests quality of human behavior.

The Balanchine-Stravinsky *Agon* is an exploration of energetic momentum, not the momentum of a particular person but of a species of people—jet-age people, perhaps. There is an explosive drive in a dancer's darting burst of action that stops as suddenly as it began. But the dynamic pulse is continued by another dancer, who enters in canonic imitation before the first has finished. The movement is spasmodic, the phrases cut short, transitions eliminated—yet the energy flows without ceasing. A legato passage is introduced when a boy and girl dance quietly together. But the respite is momentary. He stands holding her hand—then suddenly drops to the floor, letting her find her balance where she may. She does not care. The couple have no emotional relation to one another, and in the next scene they are absorbed by the ensemble, never—though without remorse—to touch hands again. There is leisure here, but not for romance.

The emotion is not in the relations of the dancers, but in their attitude toward the movement. *Agon* may be saying that dancing is a marvelously complex and exciting thing that only seems to stop, but perpetually renews itself. Or it may be saying this of life. It makes its comment casually and in a spirit of fun. But it does comment.

Can dance ever be completely devoid of meaning? In recent years some choreographers have tried to create dances that depend entirely on interest of movement for its own sake. They have attempted to obliterate the sign, to divorce gesture from any connection with emotion by isolating it from its customary context, by subjecting movements to artificial, even chance, forms of combination and continuity. But meaning in dance, as we have seen, need not refer to a specific dramatic character or situation, or even to a personal emotion. The choreographer may comment on depersonalized quality of behavior. Even chance continuity, if it is carried out consistently, makes a comment. It may be: "What wonderfully strange and beautiful things the human body can do when it is not trying to say something."

If the dance image could be obliterated, the problems of clarity and usefulness would vanish. Our sole concern would be the interest of the movement itself. Can this be sufficient? Can interest of movement exist in isolation from meaning? We have yet to determine what makes movement interesting.

A child's dancing is interesting when we say: "How wonderful. Susie is only eight." However, the movement is not interesting for its own sake but because it is performed by a child, and in relation to her capacities it is remarkable. Nor is movement intrinsically interesting because it is novel or unusual. This standard is too dependent on the degree of experience of the observer to have validity. We judge movement interest in terms of the elements of movement: space, time, and dynamics.

A dance is usually performed to music, and when we think of the time element of movement, we think of it in relation to music. The relationship must be clearly perceivable, yet not so simple that it offers no challenge to the intelligent observer. In the 1920s Ruth St. Denis experimented with a form she called "music visualization." Each dancer directly mirrored the rhythm and tempo of an instrument of the orchestra and even the melodic line had its parallel, in spatial design. Music visualization did not last. It was not interesting. It said the same thing as the music and nothing more. It made no comment. A dance that moves constantly against the music is almost as dull. The right mean will be judged relatively to other factors, which include the complexity of both the musical score and the movement.

A particularly felicitous example occurs in Doris Humphrey's *New Dance* where the music plays a steady 4/4. A row of dancers follow the phrasing of the music with simple movements, while a series of soloists emerge from the group to do their dances in complex, patterned phrases of 7, 7, and 10, returning to the group on the even count of 24. Since the dance deals with the harmonious relation of the individual to society, the device is good on expressive grounds. But even in a purely formal sense, it possesses the virtues of clarity and challenge.

A special case is the dance performed without music. Jerome Robbins' *Moves* is an experiment in that direction. Many of the phrasings are extremely intricate, and several groups of dancers are sometimes following different rhythmic patterns. They are related, however, by a common pulse, so that a norm is established. Here the choreographer has to supply his own meter. Without it, the effect would be chaotic.

Similar criteria are applicable to spatial design. Groups of dancers in circles and parallel lines are easy to perceive, but they become monotonous. And symmetry is pleasant in a serene kind of way, which is not very stimulating in the theater. Complexity, on the other hand, can be excessive. Two dancers alone on the stage can do quite divergent things without taxing the capacity of the eye of the observer. But imagine what would happen if, at any given moment, each of the Rockettes at Radio City Music Hall had an individual movement pattern. The judgment must be made on a relative basis, as it is for time pattern and as it is also for dynamics—the varying textures of movement effected by degrees of tension.

A balance of clarity and challenge, then, makes movement interesting. But is interesting movement equivalent to an interesting dance?

If the choreographer renounces interest of meaning, he may be accused of the wasteful use of his medium. We have argued that the choreographer should not ignore the unique virtue of dance that is its power to form designs of human movement. While movement expressiveness is not an equally unique virtue of dance, it is nevertheless one of its natural properties because its instrument is a person who not only moves but feels. If we want to deal only with designs of moving shapes, we have no need for human performers. Animated drawings can do the job as well and better, for the graphic artist is not limited to using only those shapes that the human body is capable of assuming. If dance, then, is to realize the full potential of its nature, it will draw on its resources of interest of both meaning and design.

However, the greatest richness of design and the greatest richness of meaning do not necessarily combine to make the greatest work of art. The degree of desirable formal complexity in dance must ultimately be viewed in relation to the species of the work.

Generally, a comparatively abstract dance can bear more intricacy of formal construction than can a predominantly dramatic one, because the latter must beware of the complexity that destroys the sign value of its movements. The less demanding the drama, the further enhancement of gesture can go—providing the humanity of the movement is not lost in the process. Yet the dramatic dance needs stylization, or it degenerates into self-expression, which is fine in its place, but that place is not the theater. Because dancers are people, their movements are naturally expressive. It is their unnatural skills that make their movements interesting.

The very elements of stylization—prolongation, repetition, quickening in time, extension in space—require artificial skills in performance. The child jumps for joy; the dancer soars into the air, his body forming a design of harmonious proportions as he does so. Not even the most gifted person was ever born with such power and control. The long training of the dancer develops his capacities to realize patterns of movement interest. Most of the time the audience is not compelled to special awareness of these skills. They are used constantly as a means to an end, and it is right that we should be conscious only of the final, total effect. The back fall in Martha Graham's technique is an astonishing feat of physical virtuosity. But when Graham does it as the climax of a phrase indicative of grief or guilt, the audience is so overwhelmed with feelings of pity and terror that it has no attention to spare for wonder at her muscular control.

In other kinds of dances the performer may deliberately draw attention to the extravagant physical demands of a movement. Obvious virtuosity has a two-edged impression. On the one hand, the audience is aware of the difficulty of the feat. Otherwise it would lack brilliance and excitement. On the other, the spectator feels that the performer is executing it with ease, for if the obstacles are too apparent, the observer suffers with the dancer. Virtuosity is abused when it becomes an intrusive element. In part this is up to the choreographer. But the dancer can distort an otherwise consistent passage by stepping out of character to perform it with a special dose of personal bravura.

Brilliance and expressiveness need not conflict. In the Rose Adagio of *The Sleeping Beauty* the radiant youth of the princess, just awakening to the conception of the possible joys of love, is shown as she dances with four suitors. She is turned slowly on the toes of one foot by the first partner. She releases his hand to balance alone and is then turned by the next partner. This is done four times. As performed by Margot Fonteyn the duration of the unsupported pose is almost incredible, and when the next suitor comes to her she does not snatch at him in desperation—she graciously allows him to take her hand. The effect, as one musician described it, is like that of a resolution on a tonic chord.

The dancer exploits such virtuoso skills comparatively rarely, reserving them for climactic occasions. His constant task is to clarify, to bring out the meaning of the choreography. He must reveal the quality of the style, the consistency of the overall form of movement enhancement. Classical ballet in its purest manifestations requires great elegance, an assured simplicity of manner, graciousness, and—even in its most expressive moments—a certain aloofness. Some types of modern dance require a sharp, tense attack. Jazz demands one that is freer, more relaxed. Part of this is implicit in the choreography. Much, however, depends on the performer. Considerable realism of dramatic interpretation is commendable in some modern dance works; it is never right in classical ballet. Matters of projection vary accordingly, for individuality of expression is more desirable in some styles than in others. And the analysis can be extremely minute, coming down to matters of phrasing, line, and texture of movement, all of which the dancer uses to illuminate the image of the choreographer as he sees it.

A theatrical dance work contains many more facets than time will permit us to investigate. The relation of dance to music is in itself a area deserving of full and careful consideration. The role played in the dance by costume, décor, and lighting—the whole question of visual spectacle—is of tremendous importance and merits special study. In this art most of the aesthetic problems are as yet not only unsolved, but even unformulated.

The ephemeral nature of dance has discouraged theoretical discussion.   According to Edwin Denby: "Critics have left us as reporters no accurate ballet history, as critics no workable theory of dance emphasis, of dance form, of dance meaning. Dance aesthetics is in a pioneering stage; a pioneer may manage to plant a rose bush in his wilderness, but he's not going to win any prizes in the flower show back in Boston."

2

SPIRITUAL VALUES OF DANCE

The art of dance can hold, in itself, the essence of a spiritual existence. Indeed, from the beginning of time, dance was an important part of religious ceremony. Dance could uplift, generate religious frenzy, and heighten the spiritual mysteries of the unexplainable. During the Middle Ages in the Western world, a great change took place. Dance became associated with sins of the flesh and was frowned upon by the Catholic Church. Later the Puritans also considered dancing sinful.

In our age of growing skepticism about traditional religion, the professional dance artist turns to his art to stimulate spiritual meditation. Inner peace can be found in this art, which requires harmony of mind and body.

THE SPIRIT OF THE DANCE

MYRON HOWARD NADEL

There seems to be a genuine peace of mind (or at least a search for it) among most clergymen and other religious people. Much time is spent in prayer and meditation in a search for inner peace. Through its intensity and discipline, dance training develops analogous powers of reflection and meditation.

The dancer is constantly involved with the imperfections of his human form; through the power of the mind, he attempts to achieve an understanding of himself and his instrument. The thought process can involve picturing the skeleton, working with images or lines of action in the body, lying or standing still picturing the perfect placement, or working out mentally the perfect phrasing for a movement sequence.

Concentration on oneself can become a narcissistic exercise, but this is merely another imperfection to overcome. When the body can be looked at as an object or vehicle for the will of the mind, the narcissistic inclination can be controlled. Meditative thought directed toward the self is vital to the dance.

An example of a specific meditative process is the search for the

15

center of the body (which some teachers refer to as the center of balance) and the central vertical axis in the body (which passes through the center of weight). Both the yoga search for the third eye and various prayer poses in many religions tend toward a symmetry that indicates an attempt at finding a central, balanced composure. The dancer must also search for a center, lest he have no point of reference.

Dance, as an art form, reveals the beauty of the human body and, more important, the beauty of motion. If the body is regarded neither as sinful nor as representing lust, it is seen as a very beautiful instrument, to be shaped by the dancer through disciplined training. It is a most complicated instrument, much more like an orchestra than like any single musical instrument. The task of controlling a complex orchestra, forming it into a unified voice, achieving complex contrapuntal effects, and meeting a variety of other demands is both difficult and time-consuming. The control of so many and so varied factors as are represented by the human body requires a similar discipline, resembling the yogi's control of body functions and, in a strange way, the control of any "base" elements that might be regarded as un-Christian. Naturally, dancers do not perceive the body as evil. To them it is a complex set of factors that must be integrated to realize satisfaction in expressing and glorifying their existence.

Dance pushes the body to the utmost extremes. Such significant use of the most fundamental material thing we possess is as close to the essentials of the mind as use of any material thing can be. The opening of vistas for the body must of necessity expand the possibilities for the mind, and, it follows, for the spirit. Using our own body to the fullest is using our most basic contact with earth to its limit. Indeed, since we are given the body with all its potential, is life really experienced if we do not explore this potential? A dancer begins to experience this richness of life, which, because of the concentration required, is as much a mental as a physical activity.

Most world religions have adopted certain rituals either as essential to their beliefs or as evidence of a spiritual union. Most dance forms, except some of the contemporary schools, have also adopted a ritual, which is designed to produce a good dancer. Ballet has very clear and formalized rituals, slightly altered from school to school but essentially the same. Ballet began in Europe and is practiced all over the world. When the dancer stands at the practice *barre*, he can be certain that the ritual he is about to perform is being observed at the same time in many places. The language of ballet is French and can be understood by dancers in most parts of the world. The universal costume of the dancer consists of leotards, tights, and shirts, with some accouterments and variation, but no one would doubt that, when a dancer has put on his "hat," he is ready for the ritual of self-contemplation, hard physical labor, and the celebration of life.

Although the rituals of the dancer are sometimes executed alone, they are usually done in groups under the guidance of a teacher. Together, the dancers perform the same practice movements, coordinated with music. There is a harmony with others and recognition of a community spirit. The dancer becomes like the rest in ritual in order to achieve his own goals as an artist. These daily activities can compare in many ways to religious services.

The performer is a giver. With his body, he reveals a spirit of life. He cannot be satisfied until the audience accepts him or, more important, his message. The great artist can warn, console, agitate, even seem to purify an audience when it has received the message, even though it is non-verbal. When the audience has responded to the significance of the choreographer's statement and the dancers' interpretation, communication is complete and a sense of satisfaction is achieved. However, the performer does not "take" applause—he first gives of himself; recognition of his work perhaps will follow.

Dance as an art form, as opposed to commercial forms of dance, uses the dancer to propose aesthetic ideals—not to present himself as the central figure. Commercial dance can employ all the same techniques (which are stimulating to watch) but it is devoid of a deeper meaning. Dance does not necessarily have to have a message; it can simply be a statement that movement itself is beautiful. But a dance that is significant is beautiful to some degree, and, if it is beautiful, there is in it celebration of the human spirit.

Is there any merit to the thesis that dance, when entered into with dedication, fervor, and respect for the intellect and spirit of humanity, can take the place of religion?

3
DANCE AS AN INDEPENDENT ART

Susanne Langer agrees with Selma Jeanne Cohen about the ephemeral nature of dance and adds that there is confusion even over what dance *is*. This very confusion, however, has a unique philosophical significance. Langer builds her article on disproving some widely accepted ideas about dance. She analyzes and refutes the concept of dance as visualized music, animated design, or pantomime.

Dancers seem to be unanimous in claiming that dance is a means of self-expression (the emotions of the dancer given vent through movement). How, then, can dance be related to the theory of art as symbolic form? It can, if the reasons for this belief in self-expression are examined. First, the dance gesture is performed in two different senses, which are often confused. The actual gesture is usually employed to create a semblance of self-expression, which then is transformed into "virtual" (or symbolic) gesture. Second, the emotion itself is only imagined feeling, the conception (not the actual experiencing) of which moves the dancer's body to symbolize it.

What, then, is dance? Langer points out that, although dance draws on facets of various arts, it is an independent art. Body movement, the raw material of the dance, is transformed into gesture. However, as Cohen has also pointed out, natural gesture is not dance, it is "vital movement." "Virtual" gesture—that which is apart from the actual emotional situation—can become a dance gesture.

Langer cleverly dispels the notions of an overwhelming majority of theorists that dance somehow has a very special kinship to self-expression. She warns her readers to be wary when the term "self-expression" is used in connection with dance.

VIRTUAL POWERS

SUSANNE K. LANGER

No art suffers more misunderstanding, sentimental judgment, and mystical interpretation than the art of dancing. Its critical literature, or worse yet its uncritical literature, pseudo-ethnological and pseudo-aesthetic, makes weary reading. Yet this very confusion as to what dancing is—what it expresses, what it creates, and how it is related to the other arts, to the artist, and to the actual world—has a philosophical significance of its own. It stems from two fundamental sources: the primary illusion, and the basic abstraction whereby the illusion is created and shaped. The intuitive appreciation of dance is just as direct and natural as the enjoyment of any other art, but to analyze the nature of its artistic effects is peculiarly difficult,. for reasons that will soon be apparent; consequently there are numberless misleading theories about what dancers do and what the doing signifies, which turn the beholder away from simple intuitive understanding and either make him attentive to mechanics and acrobatics or to personal charms and erotic desires, or else make him look for pictures, stories, or music—anything to which his thinking can attach with confidence.

The most widely accepted view is that the essence of dance is musical: the dancer expresses in gesture what he feels as the emotional content of the music which is the efficient and supporting cause of his dance. He reacts as we all would if we were not inhibited; his dance is self-expression, and is beautiful because the stimulus is beautiful. He may really be said to be "dancing the music."

This view of dance as a gestural rendering of musical forms is not merely a popular one, but is held by a great many dancers, and a few—though, indeed, very few—musicians. The music critic who calls himself Jean D'Udine* has written, in his very provocative (not to

*Albert Cozanet.

say maddening) little book, *L'art et le geste:* "The expressive gesticulation of an orchestra conductor is simply a dance. . . . All music is dance—all melody just a series of attitudes, poses."[1] Jaques-Dalcroze, too, who was a musician and not a dancer by training, believed that dance could express in bodily movement the same motion-patterns that music creates for the ear.* But as a rule it is the dancer, choreographer, or dance critic rather than the musician who regards dance as a musical art.[2] On the assumption that all music could be thus "translated," Fokine undertook to dance Beethoven symphonies; Massine has done the same—both, apparently, with indifferent success.

Alexander Sakharoff, in his *Réflexions sur la musique et sur la danse,* carried the "musical" creed to its full length: "We—Clotilde Sakharoff and I—do not dance *to* music, or with musical accompaniment, we dance *the music.*" He reiterates the point several times. The person who taught him to dance not *with* music, but to dance the music itself, he says, was Isadora Duncan.[3] There can be no doubt that she regarded dance as the visible incarnation of music—that for her there was no "dance music," but only pure music rendered as dance. Sakharoff remarked that many critics maintained Isadora did not really understand the music she danced, that she misinterpreted and violated it; he, on the contrary, found that she understood it so perfectly that she could dare to make free interpretations of it.[4] Now, paradoxically, I believe both Sakharoff and the critics were right. Isadora did not understand the music *musically,* but for her purposes she understood it perfectly; she knew what was balletic, † and that was all she knew about it. In fact, it was

* The best known exponent of this view is, of course, Jaques-Dalcroze; but it has received far more systematic statement by L. Bourguès and A. Denéréaz, in *La musique et la vie intérieure* (Paris: F. Alcan, 1921), where we find: "Every musical piece establishes in the organism of the listener a dynamogenic global rhythm, every instant of which is a totality of all its dynamogenic factors, intensity, scope, duration, manner of production, timbres, combined into simultaneous effects and reacting upon the listener according to their succession." (p. 17.)

"If 'cenesthetics' is the soul of feeling, then kinesthetics is after all but the 'soul of gesture.' " (p. 20.)

†"Balletic" is used here in its general sense of *concerning dance,* and not with particular reference to the type of dance known as "ballet." There is no accepted English adjective from a word meaning "dance" that avoids false connotations; in Merle Armitage's admirable collection of essays, *Modern Dance* (New York: E. Weyhe, 1935), the German word "tänzerisch" is translated by "dancistic" (p. 9), but the word sounds unnatural.

so absolutely all she knew that she thought it was all there was to know, and that what she danced was really "the music." Her musical taste as such was undeveloped—not simply poor, but utterly unaccountable. She ranked Ethelbert Nevin's "Narcissus" with Beethoven's C# Minor Sonata, and Mendelssohn's "Spring Song" with some very good Chopin *Etudes* her mother played.

Isadora's lack of musical judgment is interesting in view of the alleged basic identity of music and dance (Sakharoff considers them "as closely related as poetry and prose"—that is, two major forms of one art). Most artists—as we had occasion to note before, in connection with the plastic arts—are competent judges of works in any form and even any mode of their own art: a painter usually has a true feeling for buildings and statues, a pianist for vocal music from plain-song to opera, etc. But dancers are not particularly discerning critics of music, and musicians are very rarely even sympathetic to the dance. There are those, of course, who write for ballet and undoubtedly understand it; but among the hosts of musicians— composers and performers alike—the ones who have a natural proclivity for the dance are so few that it is hard to believe in the twinship of the two arts.

The existence of an intimate relation—identity or near-identity— has indeed been repudiated, vehemently denied, by some dancers and dance enthusiasts who maintain—quite properly—that theirs is an independent art; and those few defenders of the faith have even gone so far as to claim that the world-old union of music and dance is a pure accident or a matter of fashion. Frank Thiess, who has written a book of many remarkable insights and judgments, lets his conviction that dance is not a mode of musical art confuse him utterly about the balletic function of music, which he deprecates as a mere "acoustically ornamented rhythm" running parallel to the independent dance.[5]

There is another interpretation of dance, inspired by the classical ballet and therefore more generally accepted in the past than in our day, that dance is one of the plastic arts, a spectacle of shifting pictures, or animated design, or even statues in motion. Such was the opinion of the great choreographer Noverre who, of course, had never seen actual moving pictures or mobile sculpture.* since these

---

*See his *Lettres sur les arts imitateurs*, in *Collected Works* (St. Petersburg, 1803), reflections on the dance plots appended to Letter XXIV: "That which produces a picture in painting also produces a picture in the dance: the effect of these two arts is similar; they both have the same role to play, they must speak to the heart through the eyes . . . everything that is used in dance is capable of

media have come into existence, the difference between their products and dance is patent. Calder's balanced shapes, moved by the wind, define a truly sculptural volume which they fill with a free and fascinating motion (I am thinking, in particular, of his *Lobster Pot and Fishtail* in the stair well of the Museum of Modern Art in New York), but they certainly are not dancing. The moving picture. has been seriously likened to the dance on the ground that both are "arts of movement,"* yet the hypnotic influence of motion is really all they have in common (unless the film happens to be of a dance performance), and a peculiar psychological effect is not the measure of an art form. A screenplay, a newsreel, a documentary film—all have no artistic similarity to any sort of dance.

Neither musical rhythm nor physical movement is enough to engender a dance. We speak of gnats "dancing" in the air, or balls "dancing" on a fountain that tosses them; but in reality all such patterned motions are *dance motifs,* not dances.

The same thing may be said of a third medium that has sometimes been regarded as the basic element in dance: pantomime. According to the protagonists of this view, dancing is a dramatic art. And of course they have a widely accepted theory, namely, that Greek drama arose from choric dance, to justify their approach. But if one looks candidly at the most elaborate pantomimic dance, it does not appear at all like the action of true drama;† one is far more tempted

---

forming pictures, and anything that can produce a pictorial effect in painting may serve as a model for the dance, as also everything that is rejected by the painter, must be likewise rejected by the ballet master." Compare also his *Lettres sur la danse, et sur les ballets* (New York: Dance Horizons, 1966), Letter XIV: "Pantomime is a bolt which the great passions discharge; it is a multitude of lightning strokes which succeed each other with rapidity; the scenes which result are their play, they last but a moment and immediately give place to others."

*Cf. Borodin, *This Thing Called Ballet* (London: MacDonald & Co., 1945), p. 56: "The basic materials of both the ballet and the film are similar. Both depend upon the presentation of a picture in motion . . . Like the ballet, the film is pattern in movement, a sequence of pictures constantly changing but presented according to an artistic plan—at least in its higher forms. So, too, the ballet. It is, in fact, only that the idiom, the turn of phrase, is different. The difference between ballet and film is very similar to that between two languages having a common origin—as, for example, Italian and Spanish, or Dutch and English. The foundations are almost the same in both cases but the development has in each proceeded along different lines."

†Noverre, accused by certain critics of having violated the dramatic unities of Greek themes in his dances, replied: "But suffice it to say that ballet is not drama, that a production of this kind cannot be subjected to strict Aristotelian

to doubt the venerable origins of acting than to believe in the dramatic ideal of dance motions. For dance that begins in pantomime, as many religious dances do, tends in the course of its subsequent history to become more balletic, not more dramatic.* Pantomime, like pure motion patterns, plastic images, and musical forms, is dance material, something that may become a balletic element, but the dance itself is something else.

The true relationship is well stated by Thiess, who regards pantomime itself as "a bastard of two different arts," namely dance and comedy,† but observes: "To conclude from this fact that it [pantomime] is therefore condemned to eternal sterility, is to misapprehend the nature of some highly important formative processes in art . . . A true dance pantomime may indeed be evolved, purely within the proper confines of the dance . . . a pantomime that is based entirely, from the first measure to the last, on the intrinsic law of the dance: the law of rhythmic motion." As the first master of such truly balletic miming he names Rudolf Laban. "In his work," he says, "as in pure music, the content of an event disappears entirely behind its choreographic form . . . Everything becomes expression, gesture, thrall and liberation of bodies. And by the skillful use of space and color, the balletic pantomime has been evolved, which may underlie the ensemble dance of the future."[6]

What, then, is dance? If it be an independent art, as indeed it seems to be, it must have its own "primary illusion." Rhythmic

---

rules . . . These are the rules of my art; those of the drama are full of shackles; far from conforming to them, I should avoid knowing anything about them, and place myself above these laws that were never made for the dance." (*Lettres sur les arts imitateurs*, Reflection XXIV on the dance plots, pp . 334-36.)

*Evidence for this contention may be found in Curt Sachs, *World History of the Dance* (New York: W.W. Norton, 1937), despite the fact that the author himself believes drama to have arisen from dance that was built on a mythical or historical theme (see pp. 226, 227). In discussing the evolution of animal dances, he says: "From these examples we may see that it has been the fate of the animal dance to grow continually away from nature. The urge to compose the movements into a stylized dance, therefore to make them less real, has taken more and more of the natural from the steps and gestures." (p. 84.)

†Compare Isadora Duncan's comment: "Pantomime to me has never seemed an art. Movement is lyrical and emotional expression, which can have nothing to do with words and in pantomime, people substitute gestures for words, so that it is neither the art of the dancer nor that of the actor, but falls between the two in hopeless sterility." (*My Life* [New York: Boni and Liveright, 1927], p. 33.)

I also consider pantomime not a kind of art at all—but, rather, like myth and fairy tale, a proto-artistic phenomenon that may serve as motif in many different arts—painting, sculpture, drama, dance, film, etc.

motion? That is its actual process, not an illusion. The "primary illusion" of an art is something created, and created at the first touch—in this case, with the first motion, performed or even implied. The motion itself, as a physical reality and therefore "material" in the art, must suffer transformation. Into what?—Thiess, in the passage just quoted, has given the answer: "Everything becomes expression, *gesture* . . . "

All dance motion is gesture, or an element in the exhibition of gesture—perhaps its mechanical contrast and foil, but always motivated by the semblance of an expressive movement. Mary Wigman has said, somewhere: "A meaningless gesture is abhorrent to me." Now a "meaningless gesture" is really a contradiction in terms; but to the great dancer all movement in dance was gesture—that was the only word; a mistake was a "meaningless gesture." The interesting point is that the statement itself might just as well have been made by Isadora Duncan, by Laban, or by Noverre. For, oddly enough, artists who hold the most fantastically diverse theories as to what dancing is—a visible music, a succession of pictures, an unspoken play—all recognize its gestic character. *Gesture* is the basic abstraction whereby the dance illusion is made and organized.

Gesture is vital movement; to the one who performs it, it is known very precisely as a kinetic experience, i.e., as action, and somewhat more vaguely by sight, as an effect. To others it appears as a visible motion, but not a motion of things, sliding or waving or rolling around—it is *seen and understood* as vital movement. So it is always at once subjective and objective, personal and public, willed (or evoked) and perceived.

In actual life, gestures function as signals or symptoms of our desires, intentions, expectations, demands, and feelings. Because they can be consciously controlled, they may also be elaborated, just like vocal sounds, into a system of assigned and combinable *symbols,* a genuine discursive language. People who do not understand each other's speech always resort to this simpler form of discourse to express propositions, questions, judgments. But whether a gesture has linguistic meaning or not, it is always spontaneously expressive, too, by virtue of its form: it is free and big, or nervous and tight, quick or leisurely, etc., according to the psychological condition of the person who makes it. This self-expressive aspect is akin to the tone of voice in speech.

Gesticulation, as part of our actual behavior, is not art. It is simply vital movement. A squirrel, startled, sitting up with its paw against its heart, makes a gesture, and a very expressive one at that. But there is no art in its behavior. It is not dancing. Only when the movement that was a genuine gesture in the squirrel is *imagined*, so it may be performed apart from the squirrel's momentary situation and mentality, does it become an artistic element, a possible dance gesture. Then it becomes a free symbolic form, which may be used to convey *ideas* of emotion, of awareness and premonition, or may be combined with or incorporated in other virtual gestures, to express other physical and mental tensions.

Every being that makes natural gestures is a center of vital force, and its expressive movements are seen by others as signals of its will. But virtual gestures are not signals, they are symbols of will. The spontaneously gestic character of dance motions is illusory, and the vital force they express is illusory; the "powers" (i.e., centers of vital force) in dance are created beings—created by the semblance of gesture.

The primary illusion of dance is a virtual realm of Power—not actual, physically exerted power, but appearances of influence and agency created by virtual gesture.

In watching a collective dance—say, an artistically successful ballet—one does not see *people running around;* one sees the dance driving this way, drawn that way, gathering here, spreading there—fleeing, resting, rising, and so forth; and all the motion seems to spring from powers beyond the performers.* In a *pas de deux* the two dancers appear to magnetize each other; the relation between them is more than a spatial one, it is a relation of forces; but the forces they exercise, that seem to be as physical as those which orient the compass needle toward its pole, really do not exist physically at all. They are dance forces, virtual powers.

The prototype of these purely apparent energies is not the "field of forces" known to physics, but the subjective experience of volition and free agency, and of reluctance to alien, compelling wills. The consciousness of life, the sense of vital power, even of the power to receive impressions, apprehend the environment, and meet changes, is our most immediate self-consciousness. This is the feeling of power; and the play of such "felt" energies is as different from any system of physical forces as psychological time is from clock-time, and psychological space from the space of geometry.

---

*Compare Cyril W. Beaumont's account of a rehearsal of the Alhambra Ballet: "The pianist renders the theme of the movement . . . while the dancers perform evolution after evolution which Nijinska controls and directs with dramatic gestures of her arms. The dancers swirl into long, sinuous lines, melt into one throbbing mass, divide, form circles, revolve and then dash from sight." (Published in *Fanfare*, 1921, and quoted in the same author's *A Miscellany for Dancers* [London: The author, 1934], p. 167.)

The widely popular doctrine that every work of art takes rise from an emotion which agitates the artist, and which is directly "expressed" in the work, may be found in the literature of every art. That is why scholars delve into each famous artist's life history, to learn by discursive study what emotions he must have had while making this or that piece, so that they may "understand" the message of the work.* But there are usually a few philosophical critics—sometimes artists themselves—who realize that the feeling in a work of art is something the artist *conceived* as he created the symbolic form to present it, rather than something he was undergoing and involuntarily venting in an artistic process. There is a Wordsworth who finds that poetry is not a symptom of emotional stress, but an image of it—"emotion recollected in tranquillity"; there is a Riemann who recognizes that music *resembles* feeling, and is its objective symbol rather than its physiological effect;[7] a Mozart who knows from experience that emotional disturbance merely interferes with artistic conception.† Only in the literature of the dance, the claim to direct self-expression is very nearly unanimous. Not only the sentimental Isadora, but such eminent theorists as Merle Armitage and Rudolf Laban, and scholars like Curt Sachs, besides countless dancers judging introspectively, accept the naturalistic doctrine that dance is a free discharge either of surplus energy or of emotional excitement.

Confronted with such evidence, one naturally is led to reconsider the whole theory of art as symbolic form. Is dance an exception? Good theories may have special cases, but not exceptions. Does the whole philosophy break down? Does it simply not "work" in the case of dance, and thereby reveal a fundamental weakness that was merely obscurable in other contexts? Surely no one would have the temerity to claim that *all* the experts on a subject are wrong!

Now there is one curious circumstance, which points the way out of this quandary: namely, that the really great experts—choreographers, dancers, aestheticians and historians—although explicitly they assert the emotive-symptom thesis, implicitly contradict it when they talk about any particular

*Margaret H'Doubler says explicitly: "The only true way of appreciating works of art is by becoming familiar with the conditions and causes which produce them." (*Dance: A Creative Art Experience* [New York: F.S. Crofts, 1940], p. 54.)

†In a letter to his father (dated at Vienna, June 9, 1781), Mozart wrote: "I, who must always be composing, need a clear mind and a quiet heart." And on another occasion (July 27, 1782): "My heart is restless, my mind confused, how can one think and work intelligently in such a state?"

dance or any specified process. No one, to my knowledge, has ever maintained that Pavlova's rendering of slowly ebbing life in *The Dying Swan* was most successful when she actually felt faint and sick, or proposed to put Mary Wigman into the proper mood for her tragic *Evening Dances* by giving her a piece of terrible news a few minutes before she entered on the stage. A good ballet master, wanting a ballerina to register dismay, might say: "Imagine that your boyfriend has just eloped with your most trusted chum!" But he would not say, with apparent seriousness, "Your boyfriend told me to tell you goodby from him, he's not coming to see you any more." Or he might suggest to a sylph rehearsing a "dance of joy" that she should fancy herself on a vacation in California, amid palms and orange groves, but he probably would not remind her of an exciting engagement after the rehearsal, because that would distract her from the dance, perhaps even to the point of inducing false motions.

It is *imagined feeling* that governs the dance, not real emotional conditions. If one passes over the spontaneous emotion theory with which almost every modern book on the dance begins, one quickly comes to the evidence for this contention. Dance gesture is not real gesture, but virtual. The bodily movement, of course, is real enough; but *what makes it emotive gesture*, i.e., its spontaneous origin in what Laban calls a "feeling-thought-motion,"* is illusory, so the movement is "gesture" only within the dance. It is *actual movement*, but *virtual self-expression*.

Herein, I think, lies the source of that peculiar contradiction which haunts the theory of balletic art—the ideal of a behavior at once spontaneous and planned, an activity springing from personal passion but somehow taking the form of a consummate artistic work, spontaneous, emotional, but capable of repetition upon request. Merle Armitage, for instance, says: "... Modern dance is a point of view, not a system ... The principle underlying this point of view is that emotional experience can express itself directly through movement. And as emotional experience varies in each individual, so will the outer expression vary. *But form, complete and adequate, must be the starting point if the modern dance as an art-form is to live.*"⁸ How form can be the starting point of a direct emotional

---

*Rudolf Laban, who constantly insists that gesture springs from *actual* feeling, understands nonetheless that dance begins in a *conception* of feeling, an apprehension of joy or sorrow and its expressive forms: "At a stroke, like lightning, understanding becomes plastic. Suddenly, from some single point, the germ of sorrow or joy unfolds in a person. Conception is everything. All things evolve from the power of gesture, and find their resolution in it."(*Die Welt des Tänzers: Fünf Gedankenreigen* [Stuttgart: W. Seifert, 1922] p. 14.)

reaction remains his secret. George Borodin defines ballet as "the spontaneous expression of emotion through movement, refined and lifted to the highest plane."[9] But he does not explain what lifts it, and why.

The antinomy is most striking in the excellent work of Curt Sachs, *A World History of the Dance*, because the author understands, as few theorists have done, the nature of the dance illusion—the illusion of Powers, human, daemonic or impersonally magical, in a non-physical but symbolically convincing "world"; indeed, he calls dancing "the vivid representation of a world seen and imagined." Yet when he considers the origins of the dance, he admits without hesitation that the erotic displays of birds and the "spinning games" and vaguely rhythmic group antics of apes (reported by Wolfgang Köhler with great reserve as to their interpretation) are genuine dances; and having been led so easily to this premise, he passes to an equally ready conclusion: "The dance of the animals, especially that of the anthropoid apes, proves that the dance of men is in its beginnings a pleasurable motor reaction, a game forcing excess energy into a rhythmic pattern."

The "proof" is, of course, no proof at all, but a mere suggestion; it is at best a corroboration of the general principle discussed in *Philosophy in a New Key,* that the first ingredients of art are usually accidental forms found in the cultural environment, which appeal to the imagination as usuable artistic elements.[10] The sportive movements that are purely casual among apes, the instinctive, but highly articulated and characteristic display-gestures of birds, are obvious *models* for the dancer's art. So are the developed and recognized "correct" postures and gestures of many practical skills—shooting, spear-throwing, wrestling, paddling, lassooing—and of games and gymnastics. Professor Sachs is aware of a connection between such phenomena and genuine art forms, but does not seem to realize—or at least, does not express—the momentousness of the step from one to the other. Like John Dewey, he attributes the serious performance of these play-gestures as dance, to the wish for a serious purpose, a conscientious excuse for expending energy and skill. . . . As soon as a characteristic gesture is strikingly exhibited to someone who is not completely absorbed in its practical purpose—e.g., the gestures of play and free exercise, that have none—it becomes a gestic *form,* and like all articulate forms it tends to assume symbolic functions. But a symbol-seeking mind (rather than a purposive, practical one) must seize upon it.

The reason why the belief in the genuinely self-expressive nature of dance gestures is so widely, if not universally, held is twofold: in the first place, any movement the dancer performs is "gesture" in two different senses, which are systematically confused, and secondly, *feeling* is variously involved in the several sorts of gesture, and its distinct functions are not kept apart. The relationships among actual gestures and virtual ones are really very complex, but perhaps a little patient analysis will make them clear.

"Gesture" is defined in the dictionary as "expressive movement." But "expressive" has two alternative meanings (not to mention minor specializations): it means either "self-expressive," i.e., symptomatic of existing subjective conditions, or "logically expressive," i.e., symbolic of a concept, that may or may not refer to factually given conditions. A sign often functions in both capacities, as symptom and symbol; spoken *words* are quite normally "expressive" in both ways. They convey something the speaker is thinking about, and also betray *that* he is (or sometimes, that he is not!) entertaining the ideas in question, and to some extent his further psycho-physical state.

The same is true of gesture: it may be either self-expressive, or logically expressive, or both. It may indicate demands and intentions, as when people signal to each other, or it may be conventionally symbolic, like the deaf-mute language, but at the same time the *manner* in which a gesture is performed usually indicates the performer's state of mind; it is nervous or calm, violent or gentle, etc. Or it may be purely self-expressive, as speech may be pure exclamation.

Language is primarily symbolic and incidentally symptomatic; exclamation is relatively rare. Gesture, on the contrary, is far more important as an avenue of self-expression than as "word." An expressive word is one that formulates an idea clearly and aptly, but a highly expressive gesture is usually taken to be one that reveals feeling or emotion. It is *spontaneous* movement.

In the dance, the actual and virtual aspects of gesture are mingled in complex ways. The movements, of course, are actual; they spring from an intention, and are in this sense actual gestures; but they are not the gestures they seem to be, because they seem to spring from feeling, as indeed they do not. The dancer's actual gestures are used, to create a semblance of self-expression, and are thereby transformed into virtual spontaneous movement, or virtual gesture. The emotion in which such gesture begins is virtual, a dance element, that turns the whole movement into dance gesture.

But what controls the performance of the actual movement? An actual body feeling, akin to that which controls the production of tones in musical performance—the final articulation of *imagined* feeling in its appropriate physical form. The conception of a feeling disposes the dancer's body to symbolize it.

Virtual gesture may create the semblance of self-expression without anchoring it in the actual personality, which, as the source only of the actual (non-spontaneous) gestures, disappears as they do in the dance. In its place is the created personality, a dance element which figures simply as a psychical, human or superhuman Being. It is this that is expressing itself.

In the so-called modern dance the dancer seems to present his own emotions, i.e., the dance is a self-portrait of the artist. The created personality is given his name. But self-portraiture is a motif, and though it is the most popular motif of solo dancers today, and has become the foundation of a whole school, it is no more indispensable to "creative dancing" than any other motif. Quite as great dance may be achieved by other devices, for instance by simulating necessary connection of movements, i.e., mechanical unity of functions, as in *Petrushka,* or by creating the semblance of alien control, the "marionette" motif in all its varieties and derivatives. This latter device has had at least as great a career as the semblance of personal feeling which is the guiding principle of so-called modern dance. For the appearance of movement as gesture requires only its (apparent) emanation from a center of living force; strangely enough, a mechanism "come to life" intensifies this impression, perhaps by the internal contrast it presents. Similarly, the mystic force that works by remote control, establishing its own subsidiary centers in the bodies of the dancers, is even more effectively *visible power* than the naturalistic appearance of self-expression on the stage.

To keep virtual elements and actual materials separate is not easy for anyone without philosophical training, and is hardest, perhaps, for artists, to whom the created world is more immediately real and important than the factual world. It takes precision of thought not to confuse an imagined feeling, or a precisely conceived emotion that is formulated in a perceptible symbol, with a feeling or emotion actually experienced in response to real events. Indeed, the very notion of feelings and emotions not really felt, but only imagined, is strange to most people.

Yet there are such imaginary effects—in fact, there are several kinds: those which we imagine as our own; those which we impute to actual people on the stage in drama or dance; those which are imputed to fictitious characters in literature, or seem to characterize the beings portrayed in a picture or in sculpture, and are therefore part and parcel of an illusory scene or an illusory self. And all these emotive contents are different from the feelings, moods, or emotions, which are expressed in the work of art as such, and constitute its "vital import"; for the import of a symbol is not something illusory, but something actual that is revealed, articulated, made manifest by the symbol. Everything illusory, and every imagined factor (such as a feeling we imagine ourselves to have) which supports the illusion, belongs to the symbolic form; the feeling of the whole work is the "meaning" of the symbol, the reality which the artist has found in the world and of which he wants to give his fellow men a clear conception.

The almost universal confusion of self-expression with dance expression, personal emotion with balletic emotion, is easy enough to understand if one considers the involved relations that dance really has to feeling and its bodily symptoms. It is, furthermore, not only induced by the popular conception of art as emotional catharsis, but is aggravated by another, equally serious and respected doctrine (which is, I think, untenable on many counts, though it is the theory held by Croce and Bergson), namely, that an artist gives us insight into actualities, that he penetrates to the nature of individual things, and shows us the unique character of such completely individual objects or persons. In so-called modern dance the usual motif is a person expressing her or his feelings. The absolutely individual essence to be revealed would, then, be a human soul. The traditional doctrine of the soul as a true substance, entirely unique, or individual, meets this theory of art more than halfway; and if the person whose joys and pains the dance represents is none other than the dancer, the confusions between feeling *shown* and feeling *represented*, symptom and symbol, motif and created image, are just about inescapable.

The recognition of a true artistic illusion, a realm of "Powers," wherein purely imaginary beings from whom the vital force emanates shape a whole world of dynamic forms by their magnet-like, psycho-physical actions, lifts the concept of Dance out of all its theoretical entanglements with music, painting, comedy and carnival or serious drama, and lets one ask *what belongs to dancing,* and what does not. It determines, furthermore, exactly how other arts are related to the ancient balletic art, and explains why it is so ancient, why it has periods of degeneration, why it is so closely linked with amusement, dressing-up, frivolity, on the one hand and with religion, terror, mysticism and madness on the other. Above all, it upholds the insight that dance, no matter how diverse its phases and how multifarious, perhaps even undignified its uses, is unmistakably and essentially art, and performs the functions of art in worship as in play.

The most important result, however, of recognizing the primary illusion of dance and the basic abstraction—virtual spontaneous gesture—that creates and fills and organizes it, is the new light this recognition sheds on the status, the uses, and the history of dancing. All sorts of puzzling dance forms and practices, origins, connections with other arts, and relations to religion and magic, become clear as soon as one conceives the dance to be neither plastic art nor music, nor a presentation of story, but a play of Powers made visible. From this standpoint one can understand the ecstatic dance and the animal dance, the sentimental waltz and the classical ballet, the mask and the mime and the orgiastic carnival, as well as the solemn funeral round or the tragic dance of a Greek chorus.

4
PHENOMENOLOGY: AN APPROACH TO DANCE

Maxine Sheets looks at dance as a phenomenologist—that is, she employs a philosophical method somewhat akin to "existential" analysis.

Phenomenology is a way of describing an experience—in this case, dance. The phenomenologist looks at dance in a pre-reflective manner, relying on direct intuition of the phenomenon. Thus, he describes dance in terms of a "lived experience." The kinesthetic nature of dance led Sheets to describe closely the two structures that exist in any kinetic phenomenon: time and space.

This look at dance rejects the empirical definition that dance is a force in time and space, for that is not descriptive of the "lived experience" of dance. Dance, as Sheets so simply explains, is a phenomenon that is created. It "does not exist prior to its creation." Note the description of dance as never being but, rather, constantly becoming.

The value of the phenomenological approach to "educational dance" may be that dance can at last be valued for what it is, instead of being prostituted as "an artistic means to a non-artistic end."

PHENOMENOLOGY: AN APPROACH TO DANCE

MAXINE SHEETS

Phenomenology has to do with descriptions of man and the world, not as objectively constituted, not as given structures which we seek to know through controlled studies or experiments, through observable and recordable patterns of behavior, nor yet through a logical analysis or synthesis of known elements. It has to do rather with descriptions of man and the world as man lives in-the-midst-of-the-world, as he experiences himself and the world, keenly and acutely, before any kind of reflection whatsoever takes place. Its concern is with "foundations," as Husserl, the first to propound the method, described this pre-reflective, pre-objective encounter. Instead of reflecting upon experience as the objective relationship of man to the world, the phenomenologist seeks the heart of the experience itself: the immediate and direct consciousness of man in the face of the world. Instead of taking man and the world for granted, each of which is constituted apart from a

From Maxine Sheets, *The Phenomenology of Dance* (Madison: The University of Wisconsin Press; © 1967 by the Regents of the University of Wisconsin), pp. 10-31.

relationship to the other, and assuming the reflected-upon experience to be the fundamental interaction of man with his environment, the phenomenologist's approach is rather to describe the foundation or structures of consciousness and the foundation or structuring of the world on the basis of that consciousness. There is an experience, and the experience must be had in order to be described; the trick is to develop a method of description which takes nothing for granted, and which does not falsify or reduce the effect of the experience itself.

Whether "experience" or any other term constitutes the key to theoretical systems, such systems can only offer a reflection on a reflection. And a reflective judgment of whatever nature—empirical, scientific, logical—upon what has already been constituted as a given—the objective reality of man and the objective reality of the world—is a judgment that in part begs the question at issue in *creative* dance. What constitutes the point of departure for theoretical systems is what constitutes the point of arrival for phenomenology: phenomenologically, the "objectively" given has its roots in the human consciousness, as that consciousness intends, or creates, its own objects.

Phenomenology is not a theoretical system, and insofar as it could be associated with a system at all, it would probably be described as "existential" analysis. The intended distinction is between a system which reflects upon what the man-world relationship is as the convergence of two objective units, and a systematic method which illuminates the lived experiences of man in-the-midst-of-the-world. No actual theory emerges from phenomenology because phenomenology is concerned not with theories about phenomena, but with descriptions of their existence, which is simply the fact that they appear to consciousness. The resultant description is therefore of a phenomenal presence to consciousness. Fundamentally, man is not an objective structure to be known, but a unique existential being, a unity of consciousness-body, which itself knows. Consequently, any conception of man's relationship to the world must be based upon knowledge of his consciousness-body in a *living* context with the world. Phenomenology is hence more method than system, for it engenders a particular point of view rather than a fixed body of beliefs.

For the phenomenologist, any quest for knowledge about a phenomenon begins with the direct intuition of the phenomenon, apart from any prejudice, expectation, or reflection; hence, this direct intuition is *pre-reflective*. The phenomenologist's attitude toward the phenomenon is neither objective nor subjective, but rather an attitude of being present to the phenomenon, fully and wholly, to intuit it as it appears, without preshaping it in any way by prior interpretations or beliefs. He is thus led to describe the "lived experience" of the phenomenon, the essential relationship between consciousness and its world. Through his description of the lived experience, he is able to elucidate *structures* apparent in the phenomenon, forms existing within the total form of life. Thus, if dance is the phenomenon, the phenomenologist describes the immediate encounter with dance, the lived experience of dance, and proceeds from there to describe the analyzable structures, such as temporality and spatiality, inherent in the total experience.

Since the phenomenon is described as it gives itself to consciousness, it is apparent that the phenomenologist looks upon the something happening as an appearance of something, an appearance which indubitably is. Regardless of whether the why or how of the appearance may be factually explained, the fact that something does appear and does exist cannot be called into question. If something appears to consciousness, it is furthermore evident that consciousness is consciousness of something; that is, every consciousness intends an object and is not merely a blind receiver of impressions. The phenomenon gives itself to consciousness only as consciousness is conscious of it, only as there is an immediate, pre-reflective, intuitional awareness. As such, the lived experience engenders a meaning of some order. The pre-reflective, pre-judicative consciousness is not a passive container of impressions, but a consciousness of felt significance, import, or meaning.

The phenomenological method is one of description; yet, as is evident, it is at the same time more than that, for in aiming toward a description of the phenomenon, it reflects backwards toward an elucidation of the structures of consciousness. It bypasses all question of the subject's objectivity or the object's subjectivity by elucidating the immediate world of lived experience, the world as it is immediately and directly known through a pre-reflective consciousness. This initial and direct knowledge constitutes the foundation upon which all future knowledge is built.

Through the foregoing description of phenomenology, we may begin to see how phenomenology relates to a descriptive study of dance. Dance is a phenomenon: it, too, gives itself to consciousness; it appears, and the consciousness of dance is a pre-reflective consciousness. Yet beyond this, it is clear that dance is a particular kind of phenomenon, namely, one which moves, one which is kinetic. A descriptive study of dance must therefore concern itself with an appearance, a phenomenon, which, while moving, remains a totality.

In order to explicate the kinetic nature of the phenomenon of dance, we will pursue the exposition of phenomenology further by describing the phenomenological constructs of two structures which exist within the total lived experience of any kinetic phenomenon: time and space. There are several reasons why such an excursion is both desirable and pertinent. A description of these structures will, of course, illustrate concretely the nature of a phenomenological analysis. But equally, if not more importantly, such a description will provide the foundation for an understanding of how the temporality and spatiality of dance are structures inherent in the kinetic phenomenon of dance itself; and further, how a new terminological-conceptual framework is necessarily generated to describe both the kinetic phenomenon of dance and the lived experience of that phenomenon.

To elaborate on these latter two benefits, it may first be noted that the question, What is dance? has certainly been answered before from an historical, scientific, and educational point of view. The concern here, however, is not with the series of events called dance which have occurred through the ages, with the series of events which are objective correlates of a moving body, nor with the ways in which dance as part of an educational curriculum meets educational standards. The focal point of concern here is precisely that elusive moving form which is created and which appears before us on the stage: the dance as both a formed and performed art. A phenomenological account of time and space as structures within the total lived experience of any kinetic phenomenon will provide the foundation of our understanding of how these structures are integral parts of that elusive moving form.

It may also be noted that the empirical answer which is sometimes given to the question, What is dance? namely, that dance is a force in time and space, is not descriptive of the *lived experience* of dance. When we see a dance, we do not see separate objective factors with no unifying center. What we see is something which perhaps can only be empirically written as forcetimespace; an indivisible wholeness appears before us. Space, time, and force are certainly apparent in dance, but they are not and cannot be objectively apparent. To conceive of them as given objective factors beforehand is to overlook the very quiddity of dance: it is something which is created and which does not exist prior to its creation.

In reference to how a new terminological-conceptual framework is generated, it is evident that if one follows the phenomenological method, one sometimes discovers, within the total structure of the thing presented, new insight into the nature of its appearance. This insight, in turn, leads to new descriptions, and thus sometimes to a new terminology. It is readily apparent that the concepts thus engendered emanate from the primary encounter with the thing in question. In other words, there is first the appearance of the thing, that is, a dance, and second the conceptual framework which is built up in describing it. The new concepts—new only in terms of their being related to dance—which will be presented within the following phenomenological accounts of time and space, are essential to an understanding of dance. They are neither vapid academic reflections upon dance, nor are they concepts which must be artificially grafted onto it; rather, they are descriptive of its immediate phenomenal presence. Specifically, they describe the nature of form in dance, both as it is created and presented. Hence, these new concepts are to be taken neither as intellectual stuffing nor as metaphysical glorifications of dance: they describe the lived experience itself. If the purpose is to elucidate the nature of dance and the structures inherent in dance, then hopefully, the fullness of the lived experience of dance, an experience which we know, should be enriched rather than desiccated by the analysis.

According to recent phenomenologists, temporality and spatiality are inherent structures of human consciousness-body. They are rooted in man's foundational pre-reflective awareness of himself, and not in the more abstractly refined notions of "real" time and "real" space: the immediate lived experience of time and space is epistemologically prior to our notions of objective time and objective space. The specific descriptions which follow are based upon the writings of two eminent and articulate phenomenologists, Jean-Paul Sartre[1] and Maurice Merleau-Ponty.[2] Sartre has elucidated the phenomenological nature of time in his book, *Being and Nothingness*. He has, of course, been heavily influenced by Martin Heidegger.[3] Merleau-Ponty has written extensively on the phenomenological nature of space, centering his phenomenology of perception and behavior on the spatial presence of human consciousness-body.

The phenomenological construct of time describes a complete totality whose substructures, past, present, and future, form distinct but interrelated units. Their interrelationship is internally rather than externally defined: they do not exist as an isolated series of "nows," but as substructures whose meaning derives from their being intrinsic to the whole. If past, present, and future were externally related, their meaning as a disconnected series of "nows," a series of given moments, would be nowhere, for the past was never present and the future will never become present; their non-presence cancels their meaning. Similarly, the present, as an infinitesimal point or "now," is a moment so instantaneous that its meaning is impossible to grasp. Past, present, and future constitute temporality as an *internally* related synthesis whose foundation is within human consciousness-body. Objective time, measurable durations and tempos, is constituted upon this existential foundation. In or understand how foundational temporality is decomposed into objective time, the nature of original or foundational temporality must first be described.

Original temporality is founded upon the *ekstatic** structure of human consciousness-body. Man does not *have* a past since he *is* his past in the mode of not being it; he is always already present. He does not *have* a present, but *is* his present in the mode of not being fixed

*The three temporal dimensions—past, present, future—are described in terms of the three ways man's being stands out (*ek-stasis*) from itself.

in the instant: his present is a flight which projects him into his future. Finally, he does not *have* a future since he *is* his future in the mode of not being it; his future is not yet, but is outlined upon the present out of which he moves toward the future as to a goal. Man comprises temporality within himself, for he is such an *ekstatic* being: he is always at a distance from himself, always in flight. Man negates himself as being past, present, or future while at the same time he apprehends himself as being that temporal totality. He can never apprehend himself as a complete temporal being, existing fully in any given moment, without making himself into an object. Man's apprehension of himself as a temporal totality is a pre-reflective awareness of himself in-the-midst-of-the-world. Hence, consciousness is not explicitly consciousness of itself as it lives, nor of its *ekstatic* structure; such explicit awareness would constitute a reflection upon the lived experience of consciousness. Temporality is founded upon man's pre-reflective awareness of himself as he lives; man only *implicitly* cognizes himself as *ekstatic*, and then only in experiential form.

We may illustrate this implicit awareness of self in the context of everyday life. In crossing a street, a person is neither explicitly aware of himself nor of his *ekstatic* structure: he constitutes himself neither as an object nor as being, fully and wholly, at any one moment, as he crosses the street. He is implicitly aware of himself and his *ekstatic* dimensions, implicitly aware of himself as realizing his intention: "to cross the street." If he were explicitly aware of himself in the act of crossing, he would constitute and apprehend himself as an object, and he would be conscious of himself as transporting this object self at every moment, from "this present now," to "this present now," ad infinitum: and these present "nows" would have no internal relationship. Each step forward would be apprehended as a discrete "now," and the person would be explicitly aware of himself as being that discrete "now" every step of the way. On the contrary, as the lived experience which it usually is, crossing the street is an intentional act which is all of a piece: because it is the "theme" of consciousness, it is a temporal totality. The person crossing the street is implicitly aware of himself as past-present-future, in the mode of not being any one of these at any given moment. The temporal flight of his being is implicitly apprehended in the very act of crossing, which exists for him not as a segmented series of steps but as a totality. The synthesized yet unachieved totality of past, present, and future, which is original temporality, thus exists because human consciousness exists; it is at the foundation a basic structure of the being of human consciousness.

Within the total structure of original temporality are two substructures: static temporality and dynamic temporality. In being implicitly aware of his temporality, man may pre-reflectively apprehend that temporality as a flow from past to future, or from future to past. In static temporality, each instant is apprehended as a separate unit, an independent unit of the succession "before," "now," "after," from past to future. If a temporal flow is to be re-established so that there is unity in such multiplicity, there again must be an internal rather than external relationship between the units. The units are internally related because human consciousness, in its *ekstatic* dimensions, is at the same time a multiple unity and a unified multiplicity. Multiplicity and unity coexist because human consciousness exists as a temporal multiplicity (past, present, future) and a temporal unity (the synthesis of these units). Temporality is thus *diasporatic:* while it is a single cohesive structure, it is a structure whose meaning derives only from the interrelationship of its units. Because human consciousness exists diasporatically, as a temporal cohesion and temporal dispersion of its being, static temporality is likewise diasporatic: it exists both as a multiple unity and a unified multiplicity.

The second substructure of original temporality, dynamic temporality, is a pre-reflective awareness of the flow of time from future to past. We may illustrate this implicit awareness of temporal flow from future to past in the context of everyday life, for any intentional act characterized by an expectant consciousness is a lived experience of temporality from future to past. A person is then implicitly aware of himself as surpassing himself toward his past rather than toward his future. The intentional act may not be "to cross the street" but "to be on the other side"; thus, temporality is lived in reverse to "historical time." The intention, "to be on the other side," is a future which the person "is" only insofar as he surpasses his present and past. The person implicitly apprehends the temporal totality of his being as a backward flow: each step forward is temporally a step backward toward the past until the person reaches his future, until he realizes his intention, "to be on the other side." But the future is no longer the moment it becomes present, that is, the moment the person "is" on the other side. As Sartre has noted, "what I was waiting for—here it is."[4]

Human consciousness attains a permanency in this "backward flow" because it endures as a being perpetually in flight. Just as man never succeeds in overcoming his temporal distance from himself, in effacing the nothingness which separates him from his goal, so he never succeeds in achieving himself as a temporal totality: he is always surpassing the instant as he surpasses himself toward his past. He endures precisely because he never is, completely and wholly, at any given instant.

The reflection which apprehends static or dynamic temporality is a reflection of human consciousness as a unity of succession or as an enduring consciousness, but never a self as object. In such an act of pure reflection, man is at the same time both witness and appearance to himself, both the reflecting consciousness and the consciousness reflected upon. Through such reflection, human consciousness looks for and attempts to found its being, its totality which is always in flight; but such reflection is never wholly successful, because consciousness can neither be totally the reflecting consciousness without its object, nor can it detach itself in order to take a point of view on itself. Pure reflection therefore constitutes immediate knowledge without revelation, for no given emanates from the reflection.

In sum, original temporality is a fundamental structure of human consciousness-body, a structure of which we are implicitly aware until that precise moment in which we reflect upon ourselves as an object. At that precise moment, either the unity of succession, which is static temporality, or the enduring consciousness, which is dynamic temporality, is no longer implicitly apparent. What is apparent is the self as object, a "self-conscious" complete temporal given at every moment. Hence, we move from original temporality to psychic temporality.

Psychic temporality reveals consciousness as a successive order of facts: actions, states, and qualities which are externally linked to one another. Each psychic fact becomes a thing in itself, an appearance, such that human consciousness loses its *ekstatic* structure and becomes a succession of externally related "nows." Since consciousness makes itself into an object and accepts itself as such, any psychic fact presents itself as an objective rather than a lived reality. For example, "I *am* sad." Because I constitute myself as being a given thing in the given moment, temporality dissolves into a series of qualitative befores and afters which are externally unified, and objective time is thereby constituted. It may be noted that deterministic psychologies which outline the history of a person as the sum and sequence of his psychic states and actions are founded upon psychic temporality.

Finally, objective temporality is not only an objectification of self; it is also an objectification of the world by human consciousness, but again, on the foundation of its own original temporality. Man confers temporal values upon objects in the world which would otherwise be atemporal. Human consciousness in its own *ekstatic* dimensions apprehends objects as enduring, complete in their past, present, and future. As Sartre has so gracefully put it, the object transcends the time which flows over it,[5] for it is indifferent to the multiplicity of its appearances which are externally related to one another in time by human consciousness. Objective temporality is, then, a container of all *externally related appearances.* It is made to be by human consciousness which enforces a cohesion upon separate and otherwise atemporal instants. If the object's past were uncreated, it would have no meaning as an appearance in the present because its present would not be apprehended as a present, nor would the future possibilities of its appearances be apprehended as a future. Man organizes time by compressing into blocks of time the separate and dispersed instants in which the object appears. And the object remains totally indifferent to the imposed temporality.

From this brief description of temporality, it is apparent that time exists because human consciousness exists, and it has become clear how temporality is an inherent structure of human consciousness. Our consciousness of time emanates from the immediate awareness we have of our own synthesized yet never achieved totality: my past is yesterday only because I am immediately aware of my presence today and my future tomorrow. Night follows day as an objective temporal succession only because consciousness relates the regular appearances of light and darkness into a meaningful temporal relationship. Consciousness endows the world with a unified temporal structure by relating appearances which are external to one another. But it constitutes this objective time on the basis of its own original temporality.

A pre-reflective awareness of time is thus intrinsic to any lived experience of consciousness-body, for example, crossing a street, kicking a football, waving goodbye; thus, it is intrinsic also to the dancer's lived experience of the dance. A dance, as it is formed and performed, is experienced by the dancer as a perpetually moving form, a unity of succession, whose moments cannot be measured: its past has been created, its present is being created, its future awaits creation. Yet, it is not an externally related series of pasts, presents, futures—befores, nows, and afters; it is truly *ekstatic,* it is in flight, it is in the process of becoming the dance which it is, yet is never the dance at any moment. The dance at any moment is diasporatic, a perpetually moving form whose "moments" are all of a piece.

Just as objective time is founded upon the original temporality of consciousness-body, so objective space is founded upon the original spatiality of consciousness-body. Man in-the-midst-of-the-world is able to endow the world with an objective spatial structure because he is already implicitly aware of himself as a unity of consciousness-body which is spatially present. The unity of consciousness-body, never the object self, but the *lived* self, is nowhere more apparent than in the immediacy and directness with which consciousness "exists" * its body as its spatial presence. Its "hereness" is the existential foundation upon which objective space, measurable distances and relationships, is constituted. Again, we must begin by describing the nature of the foundational structure of human consciousness-body in order to understand how it is

*The verb "exist" is used transitively in the writings of contemporary phenomenologists. The closest synonym is "live": consciousness "exists" or "lives" its body as the inescapable contingency of its being; ". . . the relation of consciousness to the body is an *existential* relation." (Sartre, *Being and Nothingness* [New York: Philosophical Library, 1956], p. 329.)

decomposed; how a lived reality is dissolved into an objective reality.

Any lived experience of the body incorporates a pre-reflective awareness of its spatiality through the bodily schema. Consciousness-body knows itself to be spatially present in-the-midst-of-the-world, not through a factual kinesthetic perception of its parts, but through a pre-reflective awareness of itself as a spatially present totality. To apprehend the totality of the body is to live the body and not to reflect upon it as a given object or as the sum and sequence of kinesthetic sensations. The body's "hereness" is a totality, and not an externally related system of parts. Its "hereness" as a spatial totality, however, is not an isolated and static series of spatial moments, an implicit awareness of "being here," and "being here," and "being here," but rather, a continuous and unified "being hereness": the bodily gestures and movements which are lived kinetic experiences of consciousness-body's spatial presence.

The bodily schema is the foundation of the pre-reflective knowledge of the body's spatiality; it synthesizes all spatial presences of the body. It is, in fact, the bodily schema which allows us to grasp our gestures and movements as a continuous and unified "being hereness." For example, in typing a word, each movement toward a key is not reflected upon separately, nor is all the movement necessary to type the word reflected upon prior to moving. "The corporeal schema . . . summarizes the situation of the body before its tasks";[6] hence, it is a fluid, ever-changing projection of body movement as a *Gestalt*. What is pre-reflectively grasped is not the projected *Gestalt* of body movement, but a knowledge and sense of the body's movements and gestures; the bodily schema does not present us with a projection in the form of an image of our body, but gives us an immediate knowledge and sense of its gestures. In any lived experience, one is neither explicitly aware of bodily movements as a discrete series of parts nor as the sum of a series of parts. It is not a question of being explicitly aware of bodily sensations as we move and judging our spatial reference points in relation to these sensations, for we are already implicitly aware of our spatiality. Because the sensations are already directly meaningful through the bodily schema, our gestures and movements exist for us as a totality.

Consciousness-body moves out toward the world in which it is already implicitly aware of being spatially present. It extends its spatiality toward the world as a means of relating to and communicating with it. We reach out to shake someone's hand, we throw a ball in the air, we travel by various modes from where we are to some place else; we extend our spatiality through the world and toward or away from any situation in which we implicitly know ourselves to be spatially present. It is therefore clear that in any lived experience, consciousness-body is not explicitly aware of its spatial presence as it moves: such awareness would constitute consciousness-body as an object. In any lived experience, consciousness-body is explicitly aware of whatever it constitutes as its object in-the-midst-of-the-world, and it is implicitly aware of its own spatial presence as the meaning of its gestures in relation to that object. The lived experience of spatiality is thus a lived experience of meaningful gestures.

We may illustrate the lived experience of spatiality in-the-midst-of-the-world in the common, everyday movement of reaching. If I reach for a pen which is on the table, it is because I am pre-reflectively aware of my spatial presence in relation to the pen. My immediate "hereness" carries with it a correlative notion of "thereness." Because I apprehend my body in the environment as a spatial presence, I intuitively know the spatial presence and meaning of things in my environment. Its "thereness" exists for me only because my "hereness" exists for me. My spatial presence toward the pen is thus a meaning which my body understands in its gesture toward the pen.

We may note, furthermore, that consciousness takes a point of view on the world only because the body establishes a point of view. I am not suddenly aware of a distance separating me from the pen, for the vision of the pen is already a point of view—already an intuited meaning of my spatial presence. Thus, I do not eke out movement from my body, interpreting its point-to-point progress toward the pen as a fulfillment of my efforts to reach it. I reach the pen because my body understands the meaning of objects as that meaning is intended in the act of seeing those objects. To paraphrase Merleau-Ponty, the body extends its spatiality, that is, grasps its objects, "in one swoop of the intentional arc."[7]

Consciousness-body, through its implicit awareness of its spatial presence, constitutes the spatiality of its environment. At the same time, it knows the meaning of that constituted spatiality in its very point of view upon it. Consciousness experiences its world and itself through its body. If we have conscious experiences, it is because our body moves within the environment as a spatial presence and intuitively knows the meaning of its spatiality.

Through the above example, it has undoubtedly become clear that the spatiality of consciousness-body is *ekstatic*. Its "hereness" does not refer to an objective spatial presence, but to a pre-objective presence, and it furthermore refers not to a static body but to a dynamic body. The spatial being of consciousness-body, its inherent spatiality, is no more apprehended as being at a particular place than is its temporal being apprehended as being at a particular moment. In the above example, the spatial presence, the "hereness," is not referable to the body either as object or as static: my "hereness" in relation to the pen is a spatial *ekstatic,* insofar as I do not apprehend myself as being spatially "here," fully and wholly, at any one point in space as I reach for the pen. In short, a spatial as well as temporal *ekstasis* is an inherent foundational structure of the being of human consciousness-body, and the spatial *ekstasis* like the temporal *ekstasis* dissolves only when consciousness-body apprehends itself reflectively as an object. It is at that point as well as at that moment that the spatial totality of consciousness-body is decomposed and consciousness-body becomes a system of externally related parts.

One cannot speak of being at a temporal moment without speaking at the same time of being at a particular place at that moment. Space and time, whether objectively constituted or as lived, are never actually separate structures. Time does not exist apart from space and space does not exist apart from time; furthermore, both are apprehended in the same way. One cannot be pre-reflectively aware of his temporal totality and at the same time be reflectively aware of himself as a discrete spatial object. Thus, consciousness-body is foundationally not only a spatially and temporally *ekstatic* being, but also a being which is spatially as well as temporally diasporatic. The above example illustrates that the body's moving spatial presence is both a unified multiplicity and a multiple unity: the act of reaching is a projected arc which is a single movement whose particular spatial units characterize the total movement as being this particular movement and none other: I reach the pen without wavering on my course toward it, without over-reaching or under-reaching. Likewise, it is a movement which is uniquely meaningful because each unit within the arc is internally related to all other units: each spatial point, each unit of "being here" and "being here," is unified by the bodily schema, and it is this unification which makes the intentional act of reaching a meaningful gesture--hence, a multiple unity.

In any lived experience, we are always pre-reflectively aware of the spatial-temporal totality of our being because we are never conscious of ourselves as being at any one moment in time or at any one point in space: the spatial-temporal units of our being which constitute our spatial-temporal totality are not explicitly recognized. Because we are implicitly aware of ourselves in any lived experience, we understand the meaning of that lived experience.

Any explicit awareness of the body is perforce an unsuccessful reflection upon the body. The body may never be completely experienced as an object against a background of other objects, because consciousness is able to take a point of view on all things in the world except its own body, which it can only live. When experienced as an incomplete object, the body, from being an ever-changing absolute point of orientation apprehended pre-reflectively, becomes a relative spatial point in the objective world. The reflected-upon body is always an externally related system of parts and never a totality which is lived. As an objective system of parts, the body is often regarded as an instrument of consciousness, an instrument explicitly recognized as carrying out whatever consciousness intends. Such is frequently the situation in learning a new skill, for example, because the body, while it understands the intentional act, is not yet able to coordinate its gestures toward a realization of that act. The skill is had precisely at the point at which the body ceases to be an object manipulated toward a given end and becomes, instead, a lived meaning or a lived experience of meaningful gestures. And it becomes a lived experience of meaningful gestures at the moment the skill is integrated with the bodily schema and one is pre-reflectively aware of his body in the act.

The body's reflective knowledge of itself as an object is the basis upon which objective space is constituted. Insofar as we are reflectively aware of the dimensions of our body as an object, we are aware of the dimensions of other objects in the world. The body becomes a relative point of spatial orientation toward the world and at the same time becomes one object among many objects which are contained in the given space. We circumscribe the given objective space in many ways to correspond to the natural circumscription of our bodies as objects: houses, fences, etc. We make containers within the great objective container and attempt to mark off specific boundaries of ourselves as spatial objects. The body relates to and communicates with the world in extending its spatiality in-the-midst-of-the-world; and in a reverse way, it reflectively asserts itself as a circumscribed object, marking off the limits of its domain and privacy in the objective world. Objective space is thus a container of all things, including consciousness-body, but it. is constituted upon the basis of an original spatiality: man's foundational pre-reflective awareness of his own non-objective spatial presence.

A pre-reflective awareness of space is thus also intrinsic to any lived experience of consciousness-body; hence, intrinsic to the dancer's lived experience of the dance. The foregoing descriptions of temporality and spatiality make clear the fact that any lived experience of the body incorporates a pre-reflective grasp of its temporality and spatiality because these structures are inherent in human consciousness-body. They also make clear the fact that the lived experience of the body is a kinetic phenomenon, e.g., crossing the street, reaching for a pen, creating a dance. Yet, as we shall see, whether the kinetic phenomenon is the movement of our own body, or whether it is the movement of something which appears before us, for example, a dance, a lived experience of the phenomenon incorporates a pre-reflective grasp of its temporality and spatiality.

As we are totally engaged in the experience of any kinetic phenomenon, we are implicitly aware of its inherent spatial-temporal structure. Only when we see the kinetic phenomenon as an object which is moving, when we reflect upon it, separate or distance ourselves from it, are its inherent spatiality and temporality decomposed. The phenomenon then becomes for us an object or a thing which moves within a given space and within a given time. In the immediate encounter with the phenomenon, whether it be the flight of a jet across the sky, the stalking of a cat toward its prey, or a dance, what appears before us is a moving form which exists within its own spatial-temporal structure. It is therefore clear that in our lived experience of dance, we are implicitly aware of the spatiality and temporality of the particular moving form which appears before us. The moving form does not subsist within objective time or objective space, but space and time subsist within the totality of the moving form. Space and time are neither appropriated by the dance as dimensions in which it can occur, nor are they appended to our lived experience of the dance. They are integral parts of an integral whole, structures which are inherent in the total phenomenal presence of dance.

The dance, as it is formed and performed by the dancers, is a unity of succession, a cohesive moving form, and so it is to the audience. What appears before us is not an externally related series of spatial-temporal befores, nows, and afters, but a form which is *ekstatic,* in flight, in the process of becoming the dance which it is, yet never fully the dance at any moment. What appears before us is diasporatic, a perpetually moving form whose "moments" are all of a piece. In short, the dance appears as it has been created: a kinetic phenomenon whose spatiality and temporality are structures created with and inherent in the total global phenomenon itself.

If the phenomenological constructs of time and space have been significant in elucidating the foundational spatial-temporal structures inherent in the total lived experience of any kinetic phenomenon, they have also been significant in emphasizing once again the paramount importance of the lived experience itself, specifically the lived experience of dance. Dance is not only a kinetic phenomenon which appears, which gives itself to consciousness; it is also a living, vital human experience as both a formed and performed art: the experience for both dancer and audience is a *lived* experience. Without returning again and again to this lived experience, one cannot hope to arrive at a valid and meaningful description of dance, the nature of, and structures inherent in, its appearance, creation, and presentation. This emphasis upon the immediate, unreflected-upon experience of dance is necessarily vital to all concerned with dance: critics, choreographers, dancers, audiences, teachers. Yet for educators in dance, it is perhaps most essential, since it is their duty to instruct others, to impart to them a deep and comprehensive knowledge of dance, both practical and conceptual. Because others come explicitly to them in order to learn of dance, and because they undoubtedly influence others, the knowledge which they communicate must be based upon an intimate acquaintance with dance as a formed and performed art. The foregoing descriptions are thus meaningful as a point of departure to explore what the educational implications of a phenomenological approach to dance might be.

A phenomenological approach opens the way toward an understanding of how dance as subject matter relates to education. It offers the opportunity of reevaluating the place of dance in an academic setting by elucidating the nature of dance, to the end that the educational values assigned to it coincide more closely with what it is, or even better, emanate from it. From an educational point of view, dance is sometimes justified in terms of leading to self-realization, individual growth, an appreciation of democratic principles in action, etc. Although the educative potential of dance may certainly include these facets of knowledge, the question may be asked whether such justifications do not exploit dance to the extent that it is no longer an art form, but merely an artistic means to a non-artistic end. It would seem that the problem is to provide an analysis of dance which will elucidate its values for education on the basis of what it is, rather than affix preconstructed educational values upon it. Perhaps other educational values are to be found in dance which might preserve it as an end in itself.

To provide an analysis of dance which might bring to light its intrinsic values for education, one must first answer the question, What is dance? The terms in which the answer is stated will reveal the kind of analysis made, and the kind of analysis made will, in turn, determine the educational values to be found in dance. The tendency, when this question is answered on aesthetic grounds, has been to weight the answer on the side of the dancer (expression of feelings or ideas), on the side of the audience (evocation of feelings or ideas), or to balance both sides equally (communication), without really describing what dance itself is or how it functions, if it does, as a vehicle for expression, evocation, or communication. What is needed is a synthetic view of dance as a formed (dancer point of view) and performed (audience point of view) art. This synthesis is possible through a phenomenological approach to dance, since it perforce recognizes dance as a formed and performed art.

Moreover, if there is any question of bypassing the art of dance within an educational curriculum, it may be because dance has been taken out of movement, and the educational value of dance may be quite different from the educational value of movement. That many colleges and universities are bringing in professional dancers may be a tacit recognition that something is lacking in "educational" dance. If a phenomenological approach to dance can clarify the relationship of movement to dance, it can lay the groundwork for the distinction between dance in education and movement education.

Finally, one of the foremost educational values of a phenomenological approach is that it is open-ended. One's description of the thing in question may not only provide the basis upon which other phenomenological studies may be made, but it may also be further elaborated by others whose experience of the thing goes beyond the original description. This elaboration is possible, however, only insofar as others verify the original description by their own lived experiences of the phenomenon in question, dance, both as it is created and as it is presented. What may come of such elaboration is an on-going literature of the dance, an ever-broadening knowledge and appreciation of what it means to create, present, and experience dance. The value of such an on-going literature for education in dance is notably evident, and not only because it is conspicuously missing: at the least, it would provide a much needed arena for discussion, and at the most, a comprehensive, though thoroughly individualized, approach to the art of dance.

5
DANCE AS SYMBOLIC MOVEMENT

Eleanor Metheny introduces the philosophical concept of the theory of symbolic transformation in movement, in order to examine questions about the meaningfulness of human movement. Three ways of thinking about movement are presented: as a visually perceivable pattern of movement, as a non-verbal symbolic form, and as a perceptual form incorporating *all* sensory perceptions while the movement is being performed.

The difficulty in interpreting kinesymbolic communication is simply stated and is true especially in the dance, where so often the role of the creator of movement (the choreographer) and that of the performing artist are one and the same. This means that the original source for the dance is translated in each instance by the person who designed the total symbolic form. Therefore, since the human body is producing dance and since that person is often also the creator, we may be encouraged to look for literal meaning in movement. However, this is not the point of the article.

The kinestruct, kinecept, and kinesymbol ideas are aids to analyzing the non-verbal communication that exists among choreographer-dancer-audience and are not means to give a verbal translation to each movement or movement phrase.

SYMBOLIC FORMS OF MOVEMENT: DANCE

ELEANOR METHENY (WITH LOIS ELLFELDT)

Is movement meaningful? Dancers believe that it is. An art form is a formulation of meaning; and dancers, as artists, attempt to formulate meaning in movement forms. But what makes a movement form meaningful? How are the meanings of movement expressed and understood? Are tennis-form movements meaningful? Is walking a formulation of meaning in locomotor-form movements?

Our studies are an attempt to answer questions about the meaningfulness of human movement within the philosophical context of the theory of symbolic transformation.

From *Focus on Dance II: An Interdisciplinary Search for Meaning in Movement* (Washington, D.C.: American Association for Health, Physical Education, and Recreation, 1962), pp. 22-24.

Section 1   Within the context of the theory of symbolic transformation we have tested the hypothesis that movement is a symbolic form.

Some understanding of the major premises of the theory of symbolic transformation, particularly as it refers to presentational or non-verbal forms, is essential to an understanding of our analysis. These may be found in brief form in Chapters 1-4 of Susanne Langer's *Philosophy in a New Key,* which is readily available as a Mentor paperback book, M25. Chapters 8 and 10 are also particularly relevant to our analysis.

Very briefly, this theory identifies the mind in operational terms as a process that "makes sense" out of sensory perceptions. The function of the mind, as distinguished from the brain, is to symbolize reality-as-perceived-through-the-senses. Human thought is a process of establishing relationships among these symbolic formulations of experiential reality. Human activities, i.e., activities characterized by human thought, are the expressions of the meanings men find in the thoughts that symbolize their intellectual-emotional comprehension of reality.

As a logically developed theory of epistemology, the theory of symbolic transformation identifies the conditions which appear to govern this operational process of transforming sensory percepts into concepts or symbolic forms of experience. Our studies are an attempt to determine to what extent this process appears to operate in the area of man's movement experiences.

Our initial concern has been with "movement in general" as the generic form out of which specialized forms of movement must develop. The problem of differentiating among the specifics must wait upon the identification of the nature of their common generic source.

Section 2   Movement experiences are observed as dynamic, somatic patterns created by body masses in motion. We have called this visually perceivable form of the movement experience a KINESTRUCT.

As an observer watches another person move he does not see the countless details of the movement. He sees a dynamic pattern created by the changing relationships among the body segments. This dynamic, somatic pattern establishes the identity of the movement as distinguished from other similar or different movements. We have called this dynamic, somatic patterned manifestation of movement which is perceivable as a visual form a *kinestruct. (Kine* is the root of Greek words referring to movement, the concept of form or structure is suggested by the syllable *struct.)* A kinestruct, then, is defined as a visually perceivable dynamic form constructed by body masses in motion.

Section 3   The visually perceived KINESTRUCT is susceptible to meaningful interpretation by the observer. It can be identified as a symbolic form. We have called this symbolic form a KINESYMBOL or a KINESYMBOLIC FORM.

A symbolic form is a formulation of meaning. Its meaning may be "factual"; which is to say that the form denotes or identifies something. Its meaning may be "conventional"; which is to say that the form is a sign for something. What a form denotes or signifies can usually be expressed in words, man's most obvious vehicle for conveying meanings. Words are verbal symbols. Because they can be arranged syntactically in the form of speech or discourse, they are called discursive symbols. The factual and conventional meanings of these verbal symbols can usually be identified with little difficulty, but the connotations a word may have for a person are often too subtle for verbal identification.

Similarly, a symbolic form of the presentational order formulates meanings at several levels. What a picture denotes or signifies can usually be stated in words. But a picture also has connotations or meanings that cannot be fully verbalized. These connotative elements of meaning are "in" the picture as a presentational form, and the mind of the observer deals with these meanings in their own symbolic form even though his tongue cannot give expression to the thoughts in his mind.

The observer who sees a kinestruct can usually "tell in words" what it denotes in terms of "what the person is doing." He can also identify a gesture as a sign and say what it signifies. But words fail him when he tries to describe what is commonly called "the quality of movement" as he sees it in the kinestruct. This "quality" is meaningful to him; he can read it or read into it significant interpretations; but he cannot fully translate those interpretations into language or discourse. Like a picture, a kinestruct formulates its connotations in its own terms, and the essential meaningfulness of those connotations is contained in the form as such.

We may, therefore, identify the kinestruct as a symbolic form. To identify this form in terms of its unique components, we have called it a *kinesymbolic form* or a *kinesymbol.*

Section 4.   Movement experiences are perceived by the mover as dynamic, sensory patterns created by the kinesthetic sensations elicited by the stimulation of sensory receptors that occurs during the act of moving. We have called this kinesthetically perceivable form of the movement experience a KINECEPT.

Except under special circumstances a mover does not see his own kinestructs. His perception of the reality of his own movements is kinesthetic; and what he perceives is "the feel of the movement." Innumerable sensory events are occurring as the proprioceptive nerve endings are stimulated during movement, but the mover does not appear to be aware of these as separate events. Neither does he appear to be aware of the afferent* and efferent† neural interactions that make it possible for him to "make movements" of various kinds. He seems to "feel" the movement as a whole; and he "makes it" as a whole. When he focuses his attention on some part of the movement, e.g., the action of the hand, he still "feels" the movement of the part as a whole.

Kinesthesis is analogous to seeing or hearing. Man perceives a picture or a sight or a sound as an organized form. He is not aware of the countless individual sources of visual or auditory stimulation. He can "look harder" or "listen more intently"—which is to say he can focus his attention on some part of what is perceptually available to him—but he cannot sort out the separate sensory events of that perception. He "sees what he sees" and "hears what he hears" as organized perceptual patterns or forms, and he is not aware of the efferent neural interactions that make this organized perception of sight and sound possible.

Similarly, man "feels what he moves" as an organized, dynamic pattern of sensation, or a perceptual form. Combining the concepts of movement and perception, we have called this perceptual form of movement a *kinecept*. A kinecept is defined as a dynamic, perceptual form that incorporates *all* sensory perceptions associated with a kinestruct during the act of creating it.

Section 5.   The kinesthetically perceived KINECEPT is susceptible to meaningful interpretation by the mover. It can be identified as a symbolic form. We have called this symbolic form, too, a KINESYMBOLIC FORM or KINESYMBOL.

A kinecept may denote something or signify something to the mover. What it denotes, in terms of the movement the mover is making, can usually be "told in words." The mover knows what he means when he makes a gesture or a movement sign; and that meaning can also be verbalized. But the mover is baffled when he attempts to verbalize about "the quality" of his own movements. He is aware of these qualitative differences in his various movements; he can voluntarily alter the quality of his movements. It is also apparent that at times the quality of his movements is related to the intellectual-emotional quality of his "mood." But these connotative, qualitative differences that he perceives as differences in the form of the kinecept cannot be verbalized. Like the connotations of the kinestruct, the connotations of the kinecept are inherent in its

---

*Conveying nerve impulses toward a nerve center.
†Conveying nerve impulses outward.

unique perceptual form. The kinecept may, therefore, also be identified as a symbolic form—a kinesymbolic form or a kinesymbol.

Section 6. The meaning of the KINECEPT is expressed by the KINESTRUCT in KINESYMBOLIC FORM.

The kinestruct and the kinecept have both been identified as kinesymbolic forms. What is the relationship between them? The relationship is similar to that between a picture composed of bits of pigment and the artist's mental conceptualization of the meaning the picture was created to express. The important difference between the picture and the kinestruct is that different physical elements were employed in "making" them. The painter uses pigments; the mover uses his body as a physical object which can be arranged to express meaning in symbolic form.

When a painter finishes arranging his pigments, the symbolic form he has created has become an independent symbolic form, in the sense that it *re*presents the artist's meaning to anyone who looks at it, and it does this without reference to the artist as a person. But the somatic* elements of a kinestruct cannot be separated from the mover's physical being. His being is an essential component of the kinestruct. As he creates a kinestruct, the interaction between the efferent and afferent neurones† at the site of muscle action is so intimate that the kinestruct and the kinecept may be said to "create each other" out of the mover's intent; and neither can "outlive" the other in tangible form. Accordingly there is no tangible *re*presentational form created by the mover. Both the kinestruct and the kinecept are strictly *present*ational forms, each serving to express the meaning of the mover in the moment of their perceivable existence as somatic and sensory realities.

For the mover, the meaning of the movement is conceptualized in the kinesymbolic form of the kinecept. His overt movement is a kinesymbolic expression of that meaning in the form of a kinestruct.

The meanings the mover expresses and the meanings understood by the observer are probably never identical. Each person interprets symbolic forms within his own mental frame of reference. The difficulties in kinesymbolic communication are no different from those inherent in all other forms of attempted communication between human beings.

Section 7. Movement has "intellectual content." Movement experiences may, therefore, be said to be potentially "educational" experiences and may appropriately be identified as "subject matter" in educational curriculums.

---

*Pertaining to the body as differentiated from the mind, brain, or central nervous system.

†A nerve cell with all its processes.

The kinestruct and the kinecept have been identified as kinesymbolic forms. It has been shown that man's movements are intellectually-emotionally meaningful to him, and that he expresses those meanings by moving. As presentational symbolic forms, kinesymbolic forms have been shown to be comparable with the presentational symbolic forms of music and the graphic arts. Movement experiences, or "movement education," would therefore appear to be a "school subject" area comparable with music education and art education in terms of potential contribution to the "fabric of meaning" (Langer) that is identified as liberal education.

Note: In discussing our theory we often encounter the objection that we have not shown *how* kinesthetic neural impulses can be or are transformed into thoughts, concepts, or meanings; and we have not shown *how* the idea of a movement can be or is translated into neural impulses in the motor nerves. Neither have we shown how the proprioceptors* "know" what muscle fibers are under tension, or how the feedback system of proprioception operates to coordinate these tension changes to produce the "desired" movement. We have not overlooked this problem! We are keenly aware that these "mind" and "body" relationships have not been established. But neither have the relationships between the mental and physical manifestations of man as a human being been established in terms of scientifically demonstrable "fact" in any area of man's experiences. Our problem as it relates to the kinestruct-kinecept-kinesymbol relationship is just one of the many subproblems of the nature of man's mind.

*An internal receptor for stimuli originating in the somatic region.

REFERENCES, PART ONE

CHAPTER 3. Dance as an Independent Art

[1] Jean D'Udine (Albert Cozanet), *L'Art et le geste* (Paris, 1910), p. xiv.

[2] See, for example, George Borodin, *This Thing Called Ballet* (London: MacDonald & Co., 1945); Rudolf Sonner, *Musik und Tanz: vom Kulttanz zum Jazz* (Leipzig: Quelle u.Meyer, 1930).

[3] Alexander Sakharoff, *Réflexions sur la musique et sur la danse* (Buenos Aires: Vian, 1943), p. 46.

[4] *Ibid.*, p. 52.

[5] Frank Thiess, *Der Tanz als Kunstwerk* (3rd rev. ed., Munich: Delphin, 1923), pp. 42-43.

[6] *Ibid.*, pp. 44-47.

[7] A statement of Riemann's attitude may be found quoted in Langer, *Philosophy in a New Key* (Cambridge, Mass.: Harvard University Press, 1942), p. 245n. (Mentor ed., p. 199n.).

[8] Rudolf Laban, *Die Welt des Tänzers: Fünf Gedankenreigen* (Stuttgart: W. Seifert, 1922), p. vi.

[9] *Ibid.*, p. xvi.

[10] Langer, *op. cit.*, ch. 9, especially p. 248 (Mentor ed., p. 201).

CHAPTER 4. Phenomenology: An Approach to Dance

[1] Jean-Paul Sartre, *Being and Nothingness*, trans. Hazel Barnes (New York: Philosophical Library, 1956), pp. 107-70, 204-16.

[2] Maurice Merleau-Ponty, *Phénoménologie de la perception* (Paris: Gallimard, 1945), pp. 81-179; Eugene F. Kaelin, *An Existentialist Aesthetic* (Madison, Wisc.: University of Wisconsin Press, 1962), pp. 230-49.

[3] Edith Kern, ed., *Sartre: A Collection of Critical Essays* (Englewood Cliffs, N.J.: Prentice-Hall, 1962), pp. 5-13; Martin Heidegger, *Being and Time*, trans. J. Macquarrie and E. Robinson (London: Student Christian Movement Press, 1962).

[4] Sartre, *op. cit.*, p. 145.

[5] *Ibid.*, p. 205.

[6] Kaelin, *op. cit.*, p. 239.

[7] *Ibid.*, p. 253; cf. Merleau-Ponty, *op. cit.*, p. 164.

The Creative Personality and the Choreographic Process

Elements of the creative personality are very important to understand if we are to grasp the products of creative people. In the realm of dance, where the actual experience has a fleeting existence, the appreciation of the art—especially the new experiments—has a great deal to do with the fundamental nature of those who are giving us these experiences.

A creative personality is not disorganized or undisciplined: For example, an architect must combine the discipline of engineering with the dynamics of the environmental arts. The dancer is most often a highly disciplined person, interested in the inherent logic of the vocabulary of ballet, in the principles of physics, anatomy, and physiology as related to the moving body, in the rigors of physical training, and in concepts of space and time. In addition, the dancer must use this discipline for artistic expression.

When the doors of creative expression are flung open and products are shown that are new and perhaps shocking, as in the performing arts, the appreciative audience must be somewhat sympatico with the personality that makes such products.

We as audience, then, deal with the manner in which a dance can be manufactured or composed. The methods vary greatly from one choreographer to another. Some choreographers are highly aware of the philosophical questions in the creation of a dance, while others are more concerned with the technical aspects of movement. There is no one way to compose dances, but the method of composition often depends on the kind of dance the choreographer intends and the kind of audiences he wishes to see his work.

Choreographers are generally creative people who intend to create a work of art about movement. To appreciate this act of love, it is important to understand both the creator and his process of creating. One should also have an idea of the kinds of training a choreographer may have encountered.

6
THE CREATIVE PERSON

This report of a nationwide study of human creativity answers questions on the character, physiology, and capacity for knowledge and insight that make some people more creative than others. Dancers were not included in the control group, but the findings of the study obviously can be applied to the creative dance artist (the choreographer). Creative people, as one would imagine, were found to be intellectually well above average, but the relationship of creativity to intelligence is not precisely defined.

The artistically creative person has a relative absence of repression mechanisms. He is quite open to his subconscious. This trait carries over to tests on masculinity and femininity, in which the creative males show more of their feminine nature than less creative men. This, however, is not necessarily manifested in a homosexual appearance or behavior pattern. Rather, it denotes an openness in their emotions and a heightened sensitivity and self-perception, indicating as well a broad range of interests.

A great talent of the creative person is the ability to retain many of his experiences, whether pleasant or unpleasant. Thus, he has a great richness of human experience to draw upon and the independence of thought and perception to make his contribution truly individual.

More concerned with the meanings of facts than with details, the creative person delights in the open-ended, which he strives to unify and bring to order. In this light, the choreographer may also be seen as a problem-solver.

WHAT MAKES A PERSON CREATIVE?

DONALD W. MacKINNON

Six years ago, a group of psychologists began a nationwide study of human creativity. They wanted the scientific answers to the mystery of human personality, biology, intelligence, and intuition that makes some persons more creative than others.

Working under a grant by the Carnegie Corporation of New York, the researchers were faced with the usual stereotypes that picture the highly creative person as a genius with an I.Q. far above average; an eccentric not only in thinking but in apppearance, dress, and behavior; a Bohemian, an egghead, a longhair. According to these unproved stereotypes, he was not only introverted but a true neurotic, withdrawn from society, inept in his relations with others, totally unable to carry on a conversation with others less gifted than himself. Still others held that the creative person might be profound but that his intelligence was highly one-sided, in a rather narrow channel and that he was emotionally unstable. Indeed, one of the most commonly held of these images was that he lived just this side of madness.

The psychological researchers who sought a more precise picture of the creative person conducted their investigations on the Berkeley campus of the University of California in the Institute of Personality Assessment and Research. At the Institute, the persons to be studied have been brought together, usually ten at a time, for several days, most often a three-day weekend. There they have been examined by a variety of means—by the broad problem posed by the assessment situation itself, by problem-solving experiments, by tests designed to discover what a person does not know or is unable to reveal about himself, by tests and questionnaires that permit a person to manifest various aspects of his personality and to express his attitudes, interests, and values, by searching interviews.

The professional groups whose creative members were chosen for study were writers, architects, research workers in the physical sciences and engineering, and mathematicians. In no instance did the psychological assessors decide which highly creative persons should be studied. Rather, they were nominated by experts in their own fields; and to insure that the traits found to characterize the highly creative were related to their creativity rather than indigenous to all

From *Saturday Review*, XLV, No. 6 (February 10, 1962), 15-17 & 69. Copyright 1962 Saturday Review, Inc.

members of the profession, a wider, more representative sample of persons in each of the professional groups was also chosen, though for somewhat less intensive study. All told, some 600 persons participated.

As the study has progressed it has become abundantly clear that creative persons seldom represent fully any of the common stereotypes, and yet in some respects and to some degree there are likenesses. It is not that such images of the creative person are fantastic but that they are caricatures rather than characterizations, heightening and sharpening traits and dispositions so as to yield a picture recognizable, yet still out of accord with reality. There are, of course, some stereotypes that reflect only error, but more often the distortion of the reality would seem to be less complete.

As for intellectual capacity, it will come as no surprise that highly creative persons have been found to be, in the main, well above average. But the relation between intelligence and creativity is not as clear-cut as this would suggest, if for no other reason than that intelligence is a many-faceted thing. There is no single psychological process to which the term "intelligence" applies; rather, there are many types of intellective functioning. There is verbal intelligence, and on a well-known test of this factor creative writers on the average score higher than any of the other groups. But there is also spatial intelligence—the capacity to perceive and to deal with spatial arrangements—and on a test of this aspect of intelligence creative writers as a group earn the lowest average score, while creative architects as a group are the star performers. There are, of course, many elements of intelligence in addition to these two.

If for the moment we ignore those patterns of intellective functioning which clearly and most interestingly differentiate one creative group from another, there are some more general observations that may be noted. It is quite apparent that creative persons have an unusual capacity to record and retain and have readily available the experiences of their life history. They are discerning, which is to say that they are observant in a differentiated fashion; they are alert, capable of concentrating attention readily and shifting it appropriately; they are fluent in scanning thoughts and producing those that serve to solve the problems they undertake; and, characteristically, they have a wide range of information at their command. As in the case of any intelligent person, the items of information which creative persons possess may readily enter into combinations, and the number of possible combinations is increased for such persons because of both a greater range of information and a greater fluency of combination. Since true creativity is defined by the adaptiveness of a response as well as its unusualness, it is apparent that intelligence alone will tend to produce creativity. The more combinations that are found, the more likely it is on purely statistical grounds that some of them will be creative.

Yet intelligence alone does not guarantee creativity. On a difficult, high-level test of the more general aspects of intelligence, creative persons score well above average, but their individual scores range widely, and in several of the creative groups the correlation of intelligence as measured by this test and creativity as rated by the experts is essentially zero.

Certainly this does not mean that over the whole range of creative endeavor there is no relation between general intelligence and creativity. No feeble-minded persons appeared in any of the creative groups. Clearly a certain degree of intelligence, and in general a rather high degree, is required for creativity, but above that point the degree of intelligence does not seem to determine the level of one's creativeness. In some fields of endeavor, mathematics and theoretical physics for example, the requisite intelligence for highly creative achievement is obviously high. But it does not follow that the theoretical physicist of very superior I.Q. will necessarily be creative, and in many fields of significant creative endeavor it is not necessary that a person be outstanding in intelligence to be recognized as highly creative, at least as intelligence is measured by intelligence tests.

Regardless of the level of his measured intelligence, what seems to characterize the creative person--and this is especially so for the artistically creative—is a relative absence of repression and suppression as mechanisms for the control of impulse and imagery. Repression operates against creativity, regardless of how intelligent a person may be, because it makes unavailable to the individual large aspects of his own experience, particularly the life of impulse and experience which gets assimilated to the symbols of aggression and sexuality. Dissociated items of experience cannot combine with one another; there are barriers to communication among different systems of experience. The creative person, given to expression rather than suppression or repression, thus has fuller access to his own experience, both conscious and unconscious. Furthermore, because the unconscious operates more by symbols than by logic, the creative person is more open to the perception of complex equivalences in experience, facility in metaphor being one specific consequence of the creative person's greater openness to his own depths.

This openness to experience is one of the most striking characteristics of the highly creative person, and it reveals itself in many forms. It may be observed, for example, in the realm of sexual identifications and interests, where creative males give more expression to the feminine side of their nature than do less creative men. On a number of tests of masculinity-femininity, creative men score relatively high on femininity, and this despite the fact that, as a group, they do not present an effeminate appearance or give evidence of increased homosexual interests or experiences. Their elevated scores on femininity indicate rather an openness to their feelings and emotions, a sensitive intellect and understanding self-awareness, and wide-ranging interests including many which in the American culture are thought of as more feminine, and these traits are observed and confirmed by other techniques of assessment. If one were to use the language of the Swiss psychiatrist C.G. Jung, it might be said that creative persons are not so completely identified with their masculine *persona* roles as to blind themselves to or deny expression to the more feminine traits of the *anima*. For some, of course, the balance between masculine and feminine traits, interests, and identifications is a precarious one, and for several it would appear that their presently achieved reconciliation of these opposites of their nature has been barely achieved and only after considerable psychic stress and turmoil.

It is the creative person's openness to experience and his relative lack of self-defensiveness that make it possible for him to speak frankly and critically about his childhood and family, and equally openly about himself and his problems as an adult.

One gets the impression that by and large those persons who as adults are widely recognized for their creative achievements have had rather favorable early life circumstances, and yet they often recall their childhood as not having been especially happy.

In studying adult creative persons, one is dependent upon their own reports for the picture they give of their early years. Although they may often describe their early family life as less harmonious and happy than that of their peers, one cannot know for certain what the true state of affairs was. In reality the situation in their homes may not have been appreciably different from that of their peers. The differences may reside mainly in their perceptions and memories of childhood experiences, and it seems the more likely since one of the most striking things to be noted about creative persons is their unwillingness to deny or to repress things that are unpleasant or troubling.

The theme of remembered unhappiness in childhood is so recurrent that one is led to speculate about its role in fostering creative potential. In the absence of a sensitive awareness of one's own experience and of the world around one, without considerable development of and attention to one's own inner life, and lacking an interest in ideational, imaginal, and symbolic processes, highly creative responses can hardly be expected to occur. Something less than complete satisfaction with oneself and one's situation in childhood, if not a prerequisite for the development of a rich inner life and a concern for things of the mind and spirit, may nevertheless play an important contributory role.

There is no doubt, too, that some of the highly creative persons had, as children, endured rather cruel treatment at the hands of their fathers. These, to be sure, constitute the minority, but they appear today to be no less creative than those who could more easily identify with their fathers. There is some evidence, however, that those who were harshly treated in childhood have not been so effective or so successful in the financial and business (masculine) aspects of their profession as the others. There is in these persons more than a hint that they have had some difficulty in assuming an aggressive professional role because, through fear of their fathers, their masculine identifications were inhibited.

Both in psychiatric interviews that survey the individual's history and present psychological status, and in clinical tests of personality, creative persons tend to reveal a considerable amount of psychic turbulence. By and large they freely admit the existence of psychological problems and they speak frankly about their symptoms and complaints. But the manner in which they describe their problems is less suggestive of disabling psychopathology than of good intellect, richness and complexity of personality, and a general candor in self-description. They reveal clearly what clinical psychologists have long contended: that personal soundness is not an absence of problems but a way of reacting to them.

We may resort again to Jung's theory of the psychological functions and types of personality as an aid in depicting the psychology of the creative person. According to this view it might be said that whenever a person uses his mind for any purpose he either perceives (becomes aware of something) or he judges (comes to a conclusion about something). Everyone perceives and judges, but the creative person tends to prefer perceiving to judging. Where a judging person emphasizes the control and regulation of experience, the perceptive creative person is inclined to be more interested and curious, more open and receptive, seeking to experience life to the full. Indeed, the more perceptive a person is, the more creative he tends to be.

In his perceptions, both of the outer world and of inner experience, one may focus upon what is presented to his senses, upon the facts as they are, or he may seek to see, through intuition, their deeper meanings and possibilities. One would not expect creative persons in their perceptions to be bound to the presented stimulus or object but rather to be intuitively alert to that which is capable of occurring, to that which is not yet realized; this capacity is, in fact, especially characteristic of the creative person.

One judges or evaluates experience with thought or with feeling, thinking being a logical process aimed at an impersonal analysis of the facts, feeling, on the other hand, being a process of appreciation and evaluation of things which gives them a personal and subjective value. The creative person's preference for thinking or for feeling in his making of judgments is less related to his creativeness as such than it is to the type of material or concepts with which he deals.

Artists, in general, show a preference for feeling, scientists and engineers a preference for thinking, while architects are more divided in their preference for one or the other of these two functions.

Everyone, of course, perceives and judges, senses and intuits, thinks and feels. It is not a matter of using one of the opposed functions to the exclusion of the other. It is rather a question of which of them is preferred, which gets emphasized, and which is most often used. So also is it with introversion and extroversion of interest, but two-thirds or more of each of the creative groups which have participated in the study have shown a rather clear tendency toward introversion. Yet, interestingly enough, extroverts, though they are in the minority in our samples, are rated as high on creativity as the introverts.

Whether introvert or extrovert, the creative individual is an impressive person, and he is so because he has to such a large degree realized his potentialities. He has become in great measure the person he was capable of becoming. Since he is not preoccupied with the impression he makes on others, and is not overconcerned with their opinion of him, he is freer than most to be himself. To say that he is relatively free from conventional restraints and inhibitions might seem to suggest that he is to some degree socially irresponsible. He may seem to be, and in some instances he doubtless is if judged by the conventional standards of society, since his behavior is dictated more by his own set of values and by ethical standards that may not be precisely those of others around him.

The highly creative are not conformists in their ideas, but on the other hand they are not deliberate noncomformists, either. Instead, they are genuinely independent. They are often, in fact, quite conventional in matters and in actions that are not central to their areas of creative endeavor. It is in their creative striving that their independence of thought and autonomy of action are revealed. Indeed, it is characteristic of the highly creative person that he is strongly motivated to achieve in situations in which independence in thought and action are called for, but much less inclined to strive for achievement in situations where conforming behavior is expected or required. Flexibility with respect to means and goals is a striking characteristic of the groups we have studied.

On a test that measures the similarity of a person's expressed interests with the known interests of individuals successful in a variety of occupations and professions, creative persons reveal themselves as having interests similar to those of psychologists, architects, artists, writers, physicists, and musicians, and quite unlike those of purchasing agents, office men, bankers, farmers, carpenters, policemen, and morticians. These similarities and dissimilarities of interest are in themselves less significant than the abstractions and inferences that may be drawn from them. They suggest strongly that creative persons are relatively less interested in small details, in facts as such, and more concerned with their meanings and implications, possessed of considerable cognitive flexibility, verbally skillful, eager to communicate with others with nicety and precision, open to experience, and relatively uninterested in policing either their own impulses and images or those of others.

With respect to philosophical values—the theoretical, economic, aesthetic, social, political, and religious as measured on one of our tests—there are two values most emphasized by all the creative groups. They are the theoretical and aesthetic. One might think that there is some incompatibility and conflict between a cognitive and rational concern with truth and an emotional concern with form and beauty. If this is so, it would appear that the creative person has the capacity to tolerate the tension created in him by opposing strong values, and in his life and work he effects some reconciliation of them. Perhaps a less dramatic and more cautious interpretation of the simultaneous high valuing of the theoretical and the aesthetic would be that for the truly creative person the solution of a problem is not sufficient; there is the further demand that it be elegant. The aesthetic viewpoint permeates all of a creative person's work. He seeks not only truth but also beauty.

Closely allied to his strong theoretical and aesthetic values is another pervasive trait of the creative, his preference for complexity, his delight in the challenging and unfinished, which evoke in him an urge, indeed a need, to discover unifying principles for ordering and integrating multiplicity.

In so brief a report, emphasis has had to be placed upon the generality of research findings. What needs to be equally emphasized is that there are many paths along which persons travel toward the full development and expression of their creative potential, and that there is no single mold into which all who are creative will fit. The full and complete picturing of the creative person will require many images. But if, despite this caution, one still insists on asking what most generally characterizes the creative individual as he has revealed himself in the Berkeley studies, it is his high level of effective intelligence, his openness to experience, his freedom from crippling restraints and impoverishing inhibitions, his aesthetic sensitivity, his cognitive flexibility, his independence in thought and action, his high level of creative energy, his unquestioning commitment to creative endeavor, and his unceasing striving for solutions to the ever more difficult problems that he constantly sets for himself.

7

CREATIVITY AND MENTAL HEALTH

Dr. Benjamin Wolman, a leading psychoanalyst, explains the relationship of psychoses and neuroses to creativity. He stresses that, although several great artists have become mentally disturbed, this occurred only *after* years of productive work. No one has been able to maintain his highest level of creative production while in the last stages of severe mental disturbance.

There is, however, one level where mental disorder and creativity are related, and that is in the access to the subconscious. The difference between them is that the mentally healthy creative artist is able to control his emotions and discipline himself in order to communicate.

The myth that creativity goes hand-in-hand with insanity is effectively destroyed by Dr. Wolman.

CREATIVITY AND MENTAL HEALTH: ARE THEY RELATED?

BENJAMIN B. WOLMAN

The source of creative talent lies deeply buried in the unconscious layers of the human psyche. For a while, psychologists believed that creativity was related to intelligence and tried to assess the I.Q.'s of men like Shakespeare, Dostoevsky, Da Vinci, or Beethoven. These studies, besides being guesswork in regard to the alleged level of intelligence, proved futile in terms of the assessment of creative talent. A spectacular case in point was the highly publicized *Genetic Studies of Genius,* diligently pursued for more than a quarter of a century by Lewis M. Terman in California. Terman's geniuses, however, proved to be merely children with high I.Q.'s.

Apparently, there is not much correlation between the unusual gift of creative art and one's academic success. Creative talent lies deeper than that. It cannot be taught. It is apparently carried by a set of mysterious biological units, genes, in a recessive and unpredictable manner. Though there are a few exceptions, notably the Bach family, the history of art does not know of too many cases which suggest the possible existence of *direct* creative heredity. Practically all creative dancers, choreographers, composers, painters, and poets have had

From *Dance Magazine*, XL, No. 3 (March, 1966), 42-44. Reprinted with permission from *Dance Magazine*.

rather obscure family trees and non-artistic offspring. For instance, there are no special creative talents associated with the ancestors or progeny of Euripides, Phidias, Goethe, Chopin, Didelot, Stanislavsky, or Pavlova.

Creativity and the Life Force

Great men and women of art have been endowed by inherited nature with inspirational forces, unconscious and creative. To put it into Freudian terms, creative talent is a part of the general vital force of life and love, the libido. It exists in the layer of the unconscious. Creativity is biologically the affirmative force of life. In its deepest roots it is related to sexuality, the creative force of life, and the sole source of new life. The Freudian term "libido" encompasses more than sexuality in the usual meaning of the word. It encompasses normal and abnormal sexuality, including the most tender and delicate feelings of affection, tenderness, and kindness, as well as the entire gamut of psycho-sexual perversions and sublimations.

A creative artist must have a rich emotional life. The wealth of his feelings, desires, and passions, normal and abnormal alike, are the main source of his creative work. No matter what he conveys in his dance, music, paintings, plays, or poetry, he always delves into his inner resources. His creative work always reflects some aspect of his personality, of his hopes and frustrations, of his shattered or fulfilled dreams. No artist can run away from his true self.

Emotional wealth is not necessarily related to mental health. Mental health and emotional disorders are not inherited, in contradistinction to creative talent which is inherited but in an arduously remote, and often mysterious way. Whether Borodin, Wilde, Flaubert, Da Vinci, Chaliapin, Sappho, and Gide were homosexual or heterosexual is not related to the *origins* of their creative talents. Libido may be misplaced, and one's total personality structure may go astray, irrespective of one's artistic gifts. No one is born mentally disturbed, except for those affected by a small number of organic diseases. Schopenhauer, Nietzsche, and Van Gogh became mentally disturbed (psychotic) as a result of faulty intra-familial relationships in their childhood. All of them became severely disturbed late in their lives, after years of productive work. It is an indisputable fact that some creative men have been mentally disturbed, but their main creative periods coincided with periods of comparatively balanced mental life. No one has retained his great creative powers in the terminal phase of mental disorder.

Although history and science have discounted it, there still persists a widespread belief that in order to be creative, one must be insane and, if insanity is not a prerequisite for creative talent, that it is at least a great help. This is probably the reason why some men who lack talent hope to become creative by acting crazy, analogous to some teenagers who write in an illegible way hoping thus to become famous scientists or authors. In some cases, "acting crazy" may be used as a publicity gimmick, but it never helps to develop non-existent creative talents.

Art and Insanity: The Common Denominator

However, the connection between creativity and mental disorder cannot be altogether dismissed. There is one common denominator between the two: the access to the unconscious strata. In severe cases of mental disorder unconscious wishes and dreams, primordial scenes and irrational images break through the barriers of conscious controls. Dreams and wishes of normal and mildly disturbed people are usually repressed and appear in a disguised way. Dreams of psychotics are vivid, lively, full of color, and are fraught with powerful emotions. Psychotics, as a rule, have uncanny insight into the hidden content of their dreams. They seem to have an immediate, close, and intuitive knowledge of the unconscious. They often surprise the psychoanalyst with their amazing ability to see through unconscious motivation. Working with psychotics, I rarely if ever interpret their dreams; their insight is often sharper than mine, and the unconscious processes, usually lacking disguise, stand naked in their irrationality.

A great artist must have equal access to his unconscious. A great artist sees things invisible to the eye of an average onlooker. Anyone can report a crime, a clash, an outburst of anger, an act of jealousy, or one of despair. But it takes the creative genius of a Beethoven to communicate the tragedy and despair of human life, as well as its exaltation. It takes the genius of Chopin to bring us sorrow and rapture. It requires the uncanny insight of a Dostoevsky, Kafka, or Proust to grasp the depths of human emotions. A great dancer, poet, or painter can penetrate into repressed areas of human feelings hidden from the average onlooker. Great artists are endowed with the gift of perceiving non-verbal or pre-verbal communication of human hearts. They can hear the mute voices of despair and perceive the subliminal light of hope that others are unable to grasp.

Artist and Analyst

Several years ago, I wrote about the personality of a psychoanalyst. Other factors being equal, including all the degrees, all the training, and all the skills, the quality that differentiates a good analyst from a poor one is his ability to see things beyond the usual grasp and to perceive human feelings even if they are not communicated in the usual way. Certainly, a psychoanalyst must be scientifically trained; but what distinguishes the master from the artisan is the ability to reach beneath the surface of conscious communication. A good psychoanalyst must be able to join his patient on the hazardous journey into the dark seas of the unconscious. He must not, however, remain there, or he will fail as a psychoanalyst. A psychoanalyst must be a good diver, but he must know how to dive into the depths of the unconscious and reemerge again on the surface whenever necessary.

The same gift is required, but to a much greater extent of the creative artist. A creative artist has access into his own unconscious, and into the unconscious life of other people. In his creative work he experiences the joys and storms of the unconscious life. Yet, to be a creative artist, he must be able to reemerge at his desk or in his studio or on the stage exercising full control over his actions. However, if he is mentally disturbed, he may have access to the unconscious, yet be unable to utilize his emotional wealth for creative work.

Disorder Knows No Distinctions

There is also another highly important difference between creative art and mental disorders. Not all mental patients are gifted, and not everyone's unconscious is rich, as not every ocean hides pearls and not every mine contains gold. Mental disorder knows no distinction between bright and dull, gifted and arid. Most mental disorders are caused by early childhood experiences, and misfortune comes to genius and idiot alike.

One of the baffling myths encountered by investigations into the phenomena of mental illness is that of the alleged schizophrenic's creative talent. I have been working with schizophrenics for over two decades. Many of them scribble, draw, mix paints, write verse, or concoct stories. Their aesthetic achievements are never higher—and never lower—than those of other people. The fact that they are seriously disturbed makes them more prone to express their unconscious primary processes, but does not make them more gifted or more artistic than anyone else. In some cases, lack of inhibitions lays bare the poverty of their emotional lives. Their effort to express themselves in words, or colors, or sounds, is often pathetic, for a poor soul remains a poor soul whether normal or disturbed.

Aesthetic values are always related to the creative drive of love, the libido. Although the libido originates in the organism, it may transgress its humble origin. True enough, love starts with sex just as the most beautiful flower starts with underground roots. But a flower is not a root and love is not sex. Creative art may express love of man for woman, or woman for man; it may convey the delicacy and subtlety of human feelings for humanity, for nature, and for God-like beauty of life.

Art and Therapy

In the treatment of severe mental disorders, an analyst may encourage patients to do creative work, not necessarily because he intends to turn his patients into artists, but for therapeutic reasons that deserve some elucidation.

Those patients who fail to create results of aesthetic value fail for several reasons. The main reason is that they are emotionally impoverished. Most people have very little to say. There are, however, people whose emotional life is rich but terribly repressed. Some of them do not trust their own feelings; some suffer from inferiority feelings and don't dare express themselves. I have several creative artists in psychoanalysis who, prior to their analysis, were unable to express all the wealth of their unconscious mind. A neurotic artist may have much to say, but he may be torn by a crippling inner conflict that prevents him from finding the proper avenues for his gifts.

Just as a neurotic is overly inhibited, self-conscious, and constrained, the psychotic is under-inhibited and unable to control his feelings. In neuroses, the ego utilizes a great many defense mechanisms which prevent free expression. In severe psychosis, the ego has failed and the individual is at the mercy of the unconscious, erupting id forces. These conditions give creative expression therapeutic value. A neurotic must learn to express himself more freely, and a psychotic must learn to control his communication and make it accessible to others.

Creative art is an inter-individual issue. It must be communicated to be art. A creative artist digs into the unconscious mines of his personality and gives its treasures to humanity. Humanity is forever indebted to those who give us their precious gifts. Using sound, movement, color, clay, and words creative artists share with us the treasures of their rich souls.

The Artist Is the Great Giver

Thus creative art is a combination of *freedom* and *discipline*. The creative artist must have free access to the mines of his unconscious, but he must exercise maximum self-discipline to make his work communicable. In order to communicate one has to learn a lot. The expression of one's artistic intentions can be improved by learning the fundamentals of communication. No one can become a truly great composer without mastering the principles of harmony and counterpoint as no one can be a truly great poet without mastering language.

Nevertheless, the history of art knows cases where some individuals have acquired a superb skill in communication, and have thereby produced books, paintings, or other art objects while conveying precious little human feeling. Quite often a good technique has been used as a cover-up for emotional hollowness.

Just as there are artists who have nothing to say but say it in a quite accomplished way, there are artists with much to say but who are unable to say it well. This may be due to emotional blocks (neurosis), lack of self-control (psychosis, latent or manifest), poor technical training in the art form adopted, or incomplete mastery of that form. For instance, I believe that Pasternak's *Dr. Zhivago* is unusually rich in tender human feelings and profound ideas on man and history, yet judged purely *as a novel,* it is not very well written. There is one other reason why a piece of creative expression may not seem to communicate: the artist may be, consciously or unconsciously, attempting new concepts which he has not yet developed to full power; in such a case, the relationship between the result and a fully realized work of art is analogous to that between a bud and a flower. It has not infrequently happened that the bud has been mistaken for the flower.

A truly great artist is an individual with a rich emotional life and powerful human feelings. To be able to utilize his enormous emotional wealth, he must have an uncannily sharp perception of unconscious phenomena. He must be able to reach into usually inaccessible psychic processes. He must also have the means to make others respond to his own awareness of all the beauty and depth of human experience. The artist is the Great Giver.

8
CREATING THE PRODUCT

Creating a dance can be an inspired activity or merely a task. For instance, the idea for a dance might occur to a choreographer in a dream or might be forced on him because a concert date must be met. In either instance, the choreographer must have a knowledge of his craft that matches the knowledge of a well-trained musical composer.

It is of utmost importance that the choreographer know as much as possible about his field and related fields and that he be able to ask himself serious questions about the progress of his work and make decisions based on a complete awareness of his materials and procedure. No one method for choreographer is correct.

THE PROCESS OF CREATING A DANCE

MYRON HOWARD NADEL

Dance is both a creative and performing art. It is the job of the choreographer to create the movement patterns and to exercise control over the entire choreographic arena where his piece will be performed. This arena includes—in addition to the dance and the dancers—stage lighting, costuming, music, and any other elements desired. The dancer is expected to attempt to carry out the intentions of the choreographer. Sometimes, this person is one and the same, but, in any case, it is the choreographer who must be totally responsible for the approach to his piece. There is excitement and beauty in choreography; it can be thrilling to fashion an idea and then finally realize that it has a life of its own, sometimes as previously envisioned, at other times different from any original intention. The choreographer prepares his dancers and the production for the performance, during which he can do nothing but allow his creation to be. Creators of live performance all know this. On the opening night, the choreographer is a lonely man, watching his child becoming.

The labors of choreography are difficult, and it takes years of experience to know how to approach the dancer, for each new piece is a new idea, and, because dancers are human beings (rather than pigments or notes), the choreographer's very craft is on public display to his dancers.

A choreographer is not born: His talent is a gift, but his craft is learned. Like any artist, the choreographer, whether consciously or unconsciously, creates from the sum of his experiences. He tries to find "new" subject matter, but he is only what his experiences have made him. Even recognizing this, he must always try to create something new, that is, further attempt to discover his undiscovered. But the choreographer is not simply one who compulsively creates movement patterns for people to follow. He has his method, and this has come from experience. These experiences should have built some awareness of possibilities. Skill in choreography—as in any creative endeavor—is partially the ability to analyze the possibilities; the art is in their proper selection. Because skills can be taught, let us glance at some of the endless possibilities of which potential choreographers can be made aware in a course or through apprenticeship or self-discovery.

Because the material of dance is movement, the craft of choreography clearly must begin with the study of movement. Ideally, the choreographer should have mastered a vast array of dance techniques, or at least be sufficiently capable in one vocabulary of techniques; he should be able to demonstrate those patterns he wishes his dancers to produce. If he is disabled, or for other reasons prefers not to demonstrate, he can indicate movements with other bodies—and, perhaps, build upon the manner in which an individual dancer performs his steps. In this way, it is possible to choreograph for others without possessing great technical proficiency—an important skill to acquire for the choreographer who inspires movement vision but cannot perform the actual movements. Through skillful insight, he must gain the confidence of the dancers with whom he is working.

Even a beginning student can choreograph for himself, and, most assuredly, creating dances is an integral part of learning about dance. Therefore, the materials of composition become important to the choreographer, be he novice or recognized artist. The best way to learn about choreography is to choreograph. Private workshops, college courses, and personal push can provide this chance.

What kinds of things should choreographers learn about movement?

The Materials of Composition

No matter how sophisticated theory of movement becomes, it will always fall into the three broad categories of space, time, and energy, and, no matter how simple a concept in movement becomes, it can never limit itself to any one category without taking in all three. We cannot even exist, let alone *dance,* without filling space, spending time, and using energy.

Several good texts on composition are available, although I feel they become somewhat dogmatic by telling the novice what *should* be done. If all points of view are studied and rules are learned only for the sake of finding one's *own* way, the texts and especially the theories are valid. If he takes the rules too literally, a choreographer may never find himself. Rules smack of tradition, and today's student does not tend to look back. Practically, the choreographer must learn to look back, but artistically he will have to be his own man. In general, the textbooks try to present for consideration the most important materials of composition.

The following list of materials is not complete, yet it suggests the infinite possibilities. Every dance starts with one movement—this thesis is the crux of theory in dance composition. It is the complete knowledge of that first movement that must be recognized if composition is to be taught. The first pose and the first movement can be regarded from many points of view:

Space

1) Which part or parts moved?
2) What are the geometric relationships of body parts in terms of angles?
3) What is the slope of the center line of the body in relation to the floor?
4) What is the shape of the body's profile?
5) What shapes are the negative spaces formed by the masses of the body?
6) What is the range of movement? If large, how large?
7) In what direction are the eyes focused?
8) To what distance do the eyes (or the feeling of the movement) focus?
9) Where are you in relation to the structure of the performing area?
10) Which part seems to (or is meant to) lead? A shoulder? A knee?
11) What shape does the body carve in space?
12) Does a part of the body seem to make a design in space as a chalk drawing on a blackboard does?
13) What level is the movement or position?
14) What is the locus or path of the center of gravity of the body?
15) What is the angle of the body or part of the body to the audience's eye?
16) Does the movement stay in one place or locomote?

Any question that can be asked about space concepts should *be asked.*

Time

1) How much time does the movement take? One second? Five seconds?
2) Do all parts move simultaneously?
3) If parts start at different times, when during the movement do they start?
4) Where is the impulse located?
5) How does the reaction to the impulse relate to the impulse in time?
6) Is there an underlying pulse?
7) Is the pulse regular or irregular?
8) If it is irregular, how much time is there between the irregularly recurring pulses?
9) If it is regular, how is it metered?
10) If it is metered, does the meter change?
11) Is there an upbeat before the impulse?

Any question that can be asked about time concepts should *be asked.*

Energy

1) Is the movement sharp? Is it smooth?
2) How strong is the impulse?
3) Are all parts of the movement at the same energy level?
4) Does the movement give the illusion of strength or weakness?
5) Can the movement be described as bound or free?
6) Can the movement be described as strong or light?
7) Can the movement be described as direct or indirect?
8) If a word such as "bound" can be used, to what degree is the movement bound?
9) What shape or phrasing does the energy level create?
10) Is a noise made? Of what quality is it? How loud is it?
11) Is physical force or psychological tension revealed by the movement?

Any question that can be asked about energy concepts should *be asked.*

After the first movement or even position is analyzed by using the above and other possible questions, we come to the next problem—the second movement. Even defining where a movement actually begins and ends is a theoretical problem that has never been solved or defined satisfactorily to me. But, for the sake of argument, most dancers seem to "know" kinesthetically where and when a movement ends. The point is that, after the most complete analysis of the very first movement (which, in the finished dance, may occur elsewhere instead), an analysis of the possible interrelationships of movements can begin.

For example, as soon as two movements are created, there exists a situation in which the movements will always have a relationship. If we call the first movement *A,* the second movement could be the same, or *A* repeated. The second movement could be different enough to be called *B.* It could be similar enough to be called *A'.* Then there is the space between the movements to consider. How long is that pause? Is the pause significant enough to pursue developmentally? Decisions have to be made; each can and should be analyzed.

We can consider a simple line as a graphic example of the monumental variety of decisions to be made:

It happens to be two inches long and one-sixteenth of an inch thick; it is black; it is horizontal. The next line could be half that size, twice that size, or any variation from infinitesimal (almost invisible) to so large that is goes off the page. It could be the same size but green. It could be vertical. It could be perpendicular to the center of the first line. It could be close or far away. In fact, it could be anywhere, but determining the relationship is the important thing. So it is with the craft of choreography—the understanding of the relationship is important, not the relationship itself (for that is a matter of taste).

As more of the dance is created, the possibilities and complexities can grow to enormous proportions. The choreographer should learn about the proportions; he can then control, organize, or arrange them. The conscious arrangement of the content requires the recognition of form.

Form

As in viewing the basic materials of time and energy, we can only look at some of the possibilities for form; there are no rules. Form in choreography entails placing the parts of the dance into some order, some planned relationship. This relationship is repeatable and from this standpoint meets one of the requirements for a work of art. It is not necessary for the choreographer to develop a method in which he is busy at work arranging movements as systematically as one would program a social security number for a computer, but at some point he should be able to discuss the relationship of the contents. Even dances that *seem* formless could, under computer analysis, be found to have a formula. A choreographer can, of course, create new forms, but there are standard forms that might well suit his intentions.

The choreographer might ask:

Should my piece have a movement theme that I manipulate (that is, invert, repeat, use in retrograde, use in retrograde inversion, halve, quarter, etc.) or should the movement develop (that is, enlarge, diminish, change from one body part to another, contrast itself, repeat with new material, etc.)?

Should I put the movements into clear phrases, some of which end, some of which seem to end?

Should these phrases be repeated to make an almost sentence-like structure, or should I keep contrasting and developing each phrase completely anew?

Should I try to sectionalize the movement so that I have a non-verbal thought that has developed to a degree and come to a sort of conclusion? Should I call that section *A* and contrast it with a section I call *B*? Should I repeat *A* after *B* to make a ternary *ABA* form (a very traditional form)?

Should I pick more complex forms based on the musical forms—rondo, fugue, sonata allegro, and so forth? Should I just follow the form of the music, or should I create a form and *then* worry about music?

Should I just take the first movement's motif and keep developing it into an organic whole without a sense of sectionalization? Or should I attempt the illusion of formlessness, with fragmented, seemingly unrelated ideas—all the while knowing that this, too, is an approach to form.

Any question that can be asked about concepts of form should *be asked.*

Subject Matter

The subject matter is brewing in the artist, and, hopefully, study of the craft of choreography will give him a more direct path for his ultimate expression. The idea that movement in itself is important, beautiful, and compelling provides enough subject matter for many choreographers. Attempting to say which subject areas are fair game for the choreographer is a problem for the philosopher, but he might very well limit the choreographer's scope by defining dance too strictly. On the other hand, it is a good idea to restrict the novice choreographer to the basic problems of composing movement; complex motivations or sources may distract him from discovering, the compositional possibilities.

The moment the choreographer has chosen his subject matter—motion for its own sake, a story line, psychological themes, music, or yet untried gamuts—he will begin choosing movement to elucidate and communicate his (usually non-verbal) ideas.

Style

The character of his approach to the development of the dance in its entirety is style. Style is a very elusive subject for discussion, for, just as all dances have form, it is quite impossible to say that a dance has no style. *Every* dance has a style. Fashions and characteristics of historical periods, societies, and individuals have led us to categorize the stylistic traits of works of art old and new. Therefore, there are styles that have been named, or at least specific characteristics that can be recognized. Styles categorized according to period include: the Primitive, Archaic, Medieval, Renaissance, Mannerist, Baroque, Rococo, Classical, Romantic, Impressionistic, and many 20th-century styles.

Specific characteristics of general period styles can include:

Simple, unsophisticated use of motion, color, light, and sound, or complex embellishments

Use of many dimensions, or limitation to planar concepts

Use of gesture quickly identified as stemming from psychological disturbance or the mechanical nature of machines

Use of imitation, dissonances, consonances, symmetry, asymmetry, unison, canon, ballet movements, acrobatics, etc.

Only an extensive study of art, architecture, dance music, theatre, and world history can open the choreographer's vision to what approaches have been previously tried. The novice choreographer would do well to stylize several dances in the ways in which others have approached their work. There is no reason why the creation of a dance cannot be approached as Bach approached some specific work, as Calder approached a specific mobile, or as Martha Graham approached one of her dances. Exploration of styles is a process by which a choreographer can acquire judgment about which approaches might work best for him.

The styles of others can be studied, but also important is the study of the individual choreographer by himself to discover how and why he moves as he does. An approach can, of course, become apparent with no regard for traditional approaches. One way of promoting such self-discovery is through improvisation. Many choreographers spend hours improvising, sometimes supposedly by just letting things happen, other times by dealing with specific problems. The intense absorption with movement in a free-wheeling or controlled experimental-experiential atmosphere can teach a great deal about the possibilities for movement, can heighten the aptitude for movement, and can, therefore, build a choreographer's awareness of the character of his relation to dance, that is, his style.

For some, creating a dance is a process that flows naturally. For others, it is painstaking work. Those who have danced for years and have been around great choreographers and great works of art may have been educated in the craft of choreography without knowing it.

It is possible, though, to learn the craft without having achieved great success as a dancer. For example, a playwright does not have to be a great actor, nor does a composer have to be a great performing musician. There are many ways to learn about the craft of choreography, but the only way to master choreography is by choreographing.

9
THE PRODUCT

George Beiswanger's interpretation of the choreographic process is unusually acute for a non-dancer. Many people think that a choreographer approaches a piece with almost every gesture worked out beforehand on paper or in his mind, or else that the choreographic process is some kind of spontaneous creation based on the necessity to move from a given motivational source that is then remembered. Although both are possible, it is rare for a professional choreographer to work that way. Sometimes in commercial dance, where time is limited, a choreographer may carefully outline the patterns beforehand. But in the creation of dance as an art, and for its own sake, such a method is seldom used.

Beiswanger, much like Maxine Sheets, alludes to the fact that, in creating a dance, the work is always in the process of becoming—that is, everything in the dance is there for the first time. Choreography is worked out with dancers' bodies, so there is usually only a general idea before the process begins. When the piece is finished, it almost certainly has emerged as a cooperative effort—the choreographer will have used the individuality of certain dancers' styles of movement or will have grasped and built upon nuances of a performed movement phrase.

The point that choreographers do not merely appear—that they move up through the ranks much as apprentices do—is well taken. The progression, however, is hardly automatic. As we have seen in Chapter 6, the *creative* artist (choreographer) must have a certain gift, a very special psychic make-up.

Choreography, as Beiswanger sees it, is not a process of putting invented movement patterns in order. It is, rather, a process of initiating movement, of moulding and delineating it, and making the most of what occurs.

CHANCE AND DESIGN IN CHOREOGRAPHY

GEORGE BEISWANGER

Dances, like other works of art, are composed. To choreograph a dance is to compose it. This means that the materials of which a particular dance consists are shaped up into some kind of ordering design as the dance is being made, a design which comes to reside in the substance and make-up of the entire dance work. Hence to choreograph a dance is to design it in the process of making it, for we can hardly conceive of an art-making process which is not a designing activity as well. Thus designed, when the dance is presented in finished performance its order, its quality of design, makes itself manifest as the very clarity (and ease) with which the dance's shape takes its presence before us. At least this is how it seems to those who come to know the work in its full artistry.

Hence the term *choreography* is also used to designate the design or order which a dance has, "the shapes which are ultimately achieved," and in particular these shapes "as they create one satisfactory artistic or aesthetic pattern,"[1] i.e., as they are gathered into one dance whole. If instead the dance appears haphazard or confused, it is the choreography of the dance which we say is at fault, or perhaps our inability to take in the dance's design.

As products of the choreographic art, well-composed dances are illustrative, therefore, "of the mode by which wholes are designed"[2] in dance; and to this wholeness, this designed unity, a completed dance testifies. But the dance also illustrates the significance for choreography, as for all art-making, of another kind of holes and another sort of hole-ness, if I may be allowed the pun. I am alluding to the holes which mark Henry Moore's sculpture as a pervasive feature of their design but which may be taken here as a vivid example of design's openness to chance, of those absurd and blessed windows through which the stuff of *what is* breaks into art from the realm of the undesigned.

While everything in choreography comes by design, everything designed comes into the choreography by chance. For the designer cannot concretely anticipate that which is to go into a dance until it confronts him in fresh immediacy, requiring him to take it into

From the *Journal of Aesthetics and Art Criticism*, XXI, No. 1 (Fall, 1962), 14-17. By permission of the American Society for Aesthetics and the *Journal of Aesthetics and Art Criticism.*

account. Now this means everything of substance in the dance, since everything in the dance is actually there for the *first* time. To design a work of art is to bring the energy of organizing power upon the freshly given; to have something to design is to stand in open readiness for the given which fortune sends.

Choreography, then, is a creative activity fraught with intention and design but fertilized by the spontaneous and uncalculated. The composing of dances affords an exceptionally instructive example of the rich interplay between the planned and the unexpected out of which form springs. For dance is a performance art and it is a group art as well. Its works come into full being only in public presentation and by means of artists with a wide diversity of talents. The impulses which make for the theatrical and the tensions which fire artistic collaboration, these enter into choreography from the beginning and continue to invigorate the process of designing the work until the opening night. In fact, the curtain may never actually descend, once and for all, on the continued making and remaking of a dance classic.

One is accustomed to think that art-making, especially in its compositional aspect, is the activity of a lone artist, an activity shaped and guided by a single hand from germinal idea to perfected work. We think of the writer and his book, the painter and the finished canvas, the sculptor and the neatly mounted artifact. But the model of isolated art-making and the image of the niched relic will not do when it comes to the making of dances. The typical dance piece bears the impress of many hands, all involved in bringing the work to finished performance.

We have in mind more than the fact that dance, like music and drama, relies upon the interpretive power of skilled performers in order to create the fully realized work. Dances are not merely performed by dancers; they are composed upon the bodies of dancers. Unlike drama and music, dance has yet to develop a practicable notation in which choreographers may create by implicitly manipulating the materials of their medium in the same way that a dramatist writes a play, a composer a score, or for that matter a poet a poem. The choreographer composes by directly disposing his materials, in almost the same way that painters and sculptors work in pigment and clay. If he wishes, a choreographer may design every movement down to the last detail, requiring the dancers to imitate him as he composes on his own body or giving verbal directions for the sequence of the movements which the dancers are to follow. The movements are then corrected as the dancers execute them until the composed passage meets the choreographer's design.

As there is no expeditious method for sketching the outlines of a dance in advance, the act of composing seldom begins in an even rudimentary way until the choreographer confronts the actual materials upon which he is to work. George Balanchine has stated that he comes to the composing of a dance with only "the general idea of what I want, perhaps how the ballet begins and ends—all of this suggested by the music—how many dancers and the costumes, and so forth. But it is not until the dancers are on stage and I am with them that I can begin. Then I can move them around. It's like building a sculpture, you see. You have the clay there, and you work on it, moulding it, changing it, shaping it, until you have what you want."[3]

The analogy with sculpture is illuminating. It suggests, for one thing, that the design of a dance is much more of an overall, plastically moulded thing than we are accustomed to think of and look for, since it is our habit to see dances in terms of individual performers doing this and then that. Yet the sculptural analogy oversimplifies the actual choreographic situation. The sculptor's command over his materials may indeed be approximated by the choreographer but only by virtue of the fact that the dancers whom he is using for his design already share with him a common vocabulary of movement and common ways of making dance. The choreographer takes for granted and builds upon an already established collaboration between designer and dancers that goes back to basic ways of moving and basic units of design in movement which are mutually shared because of a common professional training and experience.

I know of no established, productive choreographer who is not or has not been a professional dancer, who is not engaged in the activity of teaching, training, or coaching dancers, and who is not deeply involved therefore in the dynamically interacting, implicitly creating relationship set up from the start between those who dance and those who design dances. In fact, without this intimate and continuing collaboration, dance-making on anything but a purely individual scale—the composer creating studio pieces for himself alone—would be out of the question. To design dances one must first come to know the simplicities of moving which are the seeds of dance design. These cannot be acquired on the composing floor. Working with dancing bodies as he does, the choreographer is not free to waste and spoil materials as painter and sculptor may do, dashing off one trial sketch after another, discarding, and trying again. Experience and experimentation begin much earlier and from the apprentice side of the fence, in learning to be a dancer, dancing with and under others, then teaching others to dance. Practiced movements thus build into compositional units, exercises extend into études, études develop into rudimentary dances, and the budding choreographer is on his way, taking with him an understanding of dancers as those whose movements are already instinct with dance design, and who can become immediate accomplices in the act of choreography.

This they do. For while the choreographer shows the dancers what he wants and corrects them until he gets it, there is a simultaneous and reciprocal process by which the dancers show the choreographer what to compose and how to compose it. As the dancers copy movement and follow directions, stray inventions and chance fragments of design are struck from them like sparks from the anvil. These the choreographer will seize upon to sharpen and enrich the design. A new aspect of composing resilience appears in which reliance is placed upon inventive and constructive capacities in the dancers themselves as they move in the enlarged liberty of their released talent for dance. Instead of designing with absolute exactness, the choreographer may do little more than indicate the general shape and quality of the dance motif and the general direction in which the passage is to be developed, allowing the detailed filling in to be worked out in joint exploration of the relevant possibilities. The dancers try this and that, together or individually, the choreographer nudging the act of muscular invention by keeping the essential image before the imagination of the dancers. Body figurations are progressively refined; patterns in space develop and are articulated; variations in the gestural components of the growing dance are tried out and incorporated.

Along these lines, the design of a finished dance may actually be the cooperative product of all engaged upon the work. This compositional aspect has been conspicuously developed by the modern dance, especially in its application to education where the group designing of dances is fostered.[4] One hastens to add, however, that individual choreographic genius is by no means unknown to the modern dance and that a great deal more of cooperative designing, at least in implicit form, goes on within the more traditional framework than is openly acknowledged. Here, too, the master choreographer, jealous as he may be of maintaining his complete responsibility for the entire design of a ballet, is nonetheless on the alert for the significant variant in gesture, the enlivening deviation in step, the individual quirk which makes the generality of a composing idea come alive through the concrete particularity of some one dancer's vitality and style. The choreographer thus reaches beyond his dancers' technical and gestural repertory to enlist the inventive capacities they possess for the enrichment of his design. Choreography moulds the dancing material, yet the material in turn shapes the choreography.

But the impress of the performers is not all that enters into the developing structure of a dance. To this must be added all that the musical accompaniment builds into the dance's designs, providing in some cases the dance's initial inspiration and basic framework, adding to others a supplementary, contrapuntal pattern, and affording still others a tonal floor upon which the design's dynamics may securely play. As a theatre piece, there is likewise the space which the dance comes to occupy and invest, a space generated by the idea and design of the dance but requiring nonetheless the collaboration of the visual artist in order that it may be realized in terms of stage set, lighting, and décor.

So complex, then, is the fabric and so closely interwoven are its strands that it eventually becomes impossible to tell from which of the dance's innumerable sources a given feature of the design first came. Nor is it really important to do so, for a well-designed dance is not to be resolved into its fragmented parts. Where the choreographer supremely counts is not in the specific details, for while he invents many of these, he inherits others from his tradition and he embraces still others from his colleagues and collaborators. What the choreographer gives to the dance are the substantive image and idea from which the stuff of the dance is generated, the animating motion from which the design springs and grows, and the sustaining energy upon which the entire work is carried. These make the dance what it is, these keep it going, and these give it a history. For the work does not end with its première performance, its first cast, or even its originating choreographer. Fresh occasions, new performers, remodeling composers are received into the work, as accretions were assimilated into a medieval cathedral, to bring new shapings, new stresses, new values. Versions proliferate—one thinks of the ballet classics in this respect. Dances—if they are large enough in idea and energy—display the characteristics which epic poetry possessed in its preliterate stage when mythic themes were built into towering structures by the composing power of the chanting, performing bard.

Such in brief are the circumstances under which the designing energy operates in an art of movement which is also a group, a performance, and a theatre art. But what specifics of design does choreography exemplify when it comes down to principles and methods? From art to art, the ways of the designer are basically the same. Design in dance originates, develops, and proliferates as it does in the verbal and visual arts. The patterns of dance are rooted in the orders of organic being and in the ordered ways of culture whose regularities and formalities are bequeathed to the choreographer as the gross underlying shape of his composing habits. Dance finds the way to "measure"; it parses the temporal dimension; it develops a prosody. Dances exemplify repetition, emphasis, contrast, proportion, balance, harmony, sequence, or what have you—the so-called principles of form. Such elements appear as point, line, shape, mass, direction, dimension, and space both positive and negative. For dancer and choreographer alike, the medium of movement is as natural a language and as intimate a means of inner communing and outer making as are words for the writer and tones for the composer.

The source of design in all art is the organism in its moving aliveness, the energy of the human creature working within the stuff of the felt world to make something special in glory, clarity, and worth. The arts differ with respect to the particular stuff within which this moving is made to take place. In dance it takes place within movement, that is to say, within the human creature's muscular capacity. Muscular capacity is the physical means by which dances are made. But the means becomes available to the choreographic imagination only through the operation of a metaphor, a metaphor by which a *moving* in the muscular sense takes on the character of a *doing* or *goings-on*. Dance is not just muscular, nor is choreography just the shoving of muscles around. Muscles move in order to create a daring and splendid *to-do*. Strictly speaking, then, dances are not made out of but *upon* movement, movement being the poetic bearer, the persistent metaphor, by which muscular material is made available for the enhanced, meaningful, and designed *goings-on* that are dance.

Now one may wax metaphysical about this metaphor. Paul Weiss has recently written in *Nine Basic Arts* (p. 214): "By living through the dance one lives through a course of vital becoming, a reality whose being consists in its coming to be. The dance teaches us what the import of a world of process is." Such a statement says more than I, for one, am prepared to assert about the larger significance of dance. Nonetheless the statement is not mistaken about the nature of dance in the concrete. Dance does consist of *goings-on* in the act of coming to be.

This tells us something of basic importance, I think, about the choreographer's business, the nature of his ventures in dance design. His work is to see that goings-on in movement come to be. Dancers love to move and to make with movement; they are adept at the movings essential to dance's *goings-on*. But it is the choreographer rather than the dancer who possesses the secret of the metaphor; it is he who knows that you have to take chances with movement if you are going to make dance's *goings-on* come to be. The audacity of the choreographer is exactly that of setting dancers in motion in order that a new *goings-on* may come to pass.

Such a conception, however, is not in line with our customary notion of what the choreographer is up to. We think of choreography not as putting dancers in motion but as taking dance movement and putting it in order. Composing is supposed to be a process by which dance steps are invented and assembled, a process in which well-defined rules of order are applied to well-defined bits of material in order to construct a work of art. We have, in short, a *post facto* view of the composing process in terms of the finished products which come out of it. We see the order in perfected art and we think of the choreographer as primarily engaged in putting it there. But to the choreographer the overwhelming fact, when he begins to work, is that he has no order to put there. Order does come out of the process, but composing itself is not a process of taking things and putting them in order, as one would arrange objects in a room (something which any of us can do). Instead, composing is the process of getting movement going—of moulding, shaping it—so that it has the order of the metaphor evoking it.

Any choreographer will tell you that dance-making is at its best, its most fertile and inspired, when movement freshly flows to unfold an order never before known, in material never dealt with before. Not that all of a dance comes this freely. Composing does have to be pieced out with conscious invention, when the going falters and already codified ordering procedures step into the breach. But the genius of choreography, without which nothing gets going at all, remains in a curious way that of taking movement as it comes and making the most of it.

One understands why the choreographer reaches out so avidly for anything which may get him started, why his sensitivity is open to the chance idea from which a new *goings-on* gets underway. Not being choreographers ourselves, we take for granted that the artist works by taking directly that which he already knows and has felt in order to give it form. This, I have come to believe, is not so, not in any direct way. What the artist makes into art is that which comes at him afresh, which he has not already figured out and possessed. It is the mass of the *just-met,* the *now-confronted,* into which the artist thrusts the creative gesture. In so doing, the artist eventually brings to bear all that is relevant from his known, his funded, experience. But this he can use only as he launches out into the world of immediate encounter, grasping what comes so that *its* order may be made manifest. That the order thus *manifested* is likewise the order which the choreographer *makes*—this may worry the logician. But it merely proves to the choreographer that he knows his business—and that the gods are with him.

REFERENCES, PART TWO

CHAPTER 9. The Product

[1] Professor Herbert M. Schueller, Wayne State University, in a letter to the writer.

[2] *Ibid.*

[3] Quoted by *Dance Magazine*, XXV, 10 (Oct., 1961), 42, from an interview with George Balanchine by Ivan Nabokov and Elizabeth Carmichael, which appeared in *Horizon: A Magazine of the Arts*, Vol. III, No. 3 (1961).

[4] The Paper was read at the annual meeting of the American Society for Aesthetics in Detroit (Oct., 1961).

THREE

Forms of Dance

The development of an aware dance audience is complicated by the many types of dance that can be seen simply by purchasing a ticket. It is further complicated because labels that seem to mean a great deal have been given to these varied types or forms, but, after a close examination, the labels tell us very little. However, studying any subject matter calls for a certain amount of categorization, and, indeed, a good deal of the learning process is based on it.

In this section, therefore, various writers describe some ideas under easily recognizable headings that will foster a clearer concept of the formal possibilities in the dance arts. Although jazz, tap, and musical comedy dance are all widely seen, they have been purposely avoided here, because, more often than not, they appear less as concert dance than as products of the commercial theatre. This does not imply that these forms have not contributed to concert dance or that great artists have not created worthwhile works within the framework of commercial dance.

The forms described and discussed here remain in the world of concert dance. Three broad categories emerge: ballet, modern, and ethnic. The last is essentially a presentation of cultural or folk dances that can provide a stimulating theatrical experience when redesigned for theatre. The first is the most popular. Modern dance remains the most highly individualized concert approach.

The most popular form among the dance arts is ballet. Although the term is used a great deal, and allegedly denotes a distinct form of dance, its meaning has been distorted over the years because of developments in dance history. The origin of the word "ballet" is from *ballo,* meaning, simply, dance.

Because of our English word "dance," which is related to the German *Tanz,* the adoption of "ballet" from the Italian *ballo* creates what seem to be separate entities. Semantically, "ballet" and "dance" are the same, but, because words pick up a great deal of baggage over the years, it helps us to understand these terms if we study their present connotations. An attempt is made here to re-examine popular adjectives, such as classical and modern, which have been tacked onto the word "ballet" to achieve a clearer view of the relationship of ballet to the establishments that foster the art.

THE BALLET

MYRON HOWARD NADEL

Ballet is the oldest form of Western dance art existing today. The tradition has descended directly from the European ballets of the Romantic era, such as *La Sylphide* and *Giselle,* but the legacy clearly extends back to the entertainments of the Italian court of Catherine de Medici and the beginnings of professional ballet under the reign of Louis XIV of France.

Interest in ballet is partly generated by its connection with tradition. In our society of swiftly changing values, the training and traditional aspects of the art remain essentially unchanged. For those seeking security in formality, excitement in spectacle, and elegance of manners, the old-guard ballet retains these qualities. Similarly, other arts also interest us because of their traditional form—the plays of Shakespeare and Molière, the operas of Verdi and Gluck, the paintings of Rembrandt and Raphael—all couched in formality, spectacle, and period stylization. Along with these masters should be included such men as August Bournonville and Marius Petipa, who represent the old guard in ballet design.

Value judgments are not placed on the term "old guard," because it merely refers to the age and style of the traditional ballet works, not their quality. Certainly, a work of art is not good or bad because it was produced one hundred years ago, nor does the fact that people have desired to preserve any work ensure its quality. The continuous revival or reinstatement of a work often indicates that the piece is or was significant; that is, either it was given great acclaim at its creation, or it achieved notoriety because of certain revolutionary characteristics, or it was rediscovered after being quietly produced initially. Such preserved pieces usually have a content based on universals. A play about specific problems of the New Deal era or a musical piece devoted to characteristics of the French upper class would have to be a solid work of art to attain lasting recognition or be open-ended enough to symbolize basic human experience. A stylistic period can again become fashionable—witness the Baroque in music or Mannerism in painting; shifting tastes, thus, account for revivals in some cases.

The traditional ballet has remained popular, and many versions of the old-guard ballets (produced between 1830 and 1900, roughly), which might be referred to as "romantic" in stylistic connotations, are constantly reproduced. Happily, we are able to see examples of the old through the avant-garde because of the many and varied ballet companies today capable of performing in both historic and modern styles.

The ballet has a language of movement whose elements can be combined in virtually limitless variety. The basic language itself developed from the kinds of movements used in the court ballets of the Renaissance. These movement patterns, in turn, most often had their origin in folk or peasant recreational dances, which were later refined into the spectacle entertainments known as *balletti*. The development of the professional dancers in France, landmarked by the establishment of L'Académie Royale de Musique et Danse (mid-seventeenth century), also signaled recognition of the need for systematic training of the dancers' instrument (the body). It then followed that owing to systematic training, the abilities of the dancer increased to the point where ever more spectacular feats became possible. So the vocabulary of movement ultimately deriving from folk material expanded into an uncluttered classic training designed to develop strength, flexibility, stamina, and, most of all, an aesthetic sensitivity to the body as an instrument for expression.

Most so-called ballet movements appear harmonious; symmetrically designed, with long, unfragmented phrasing resolved by cadential endings, they seem to flow in a consonant way agreeable to the healthy human specimen. As a side note, so-called modern movements call into play both the agreeable and disagreeable, styles in and out of any set vocabulary, dissonant as well as consonant—in fact, *any* movement. But the modern dance has come to know its own "systems" or schools of training too, and ballet has by no means excluded whole areas of human movement.

The Technique

"Classic" refers to the dancer's training and basic vocabulary of movements. Such terms as "romantic ballet" and "modern ballet" refer to styles of choreographic works, but these styles utilize the classic training that is fundamental to the ballet. As an aid to understanding the focus of ballet, compare the dancer as an instrument to the piano. First, the normal piano has 88 keys and a rather complex mechanical system in an acoustically good housing. The number of different sounds that can be produced on a piano is enormous, ranging from banging the lid, plucking the strings, and whistling through cracks in the keys to striking the keys with varying energy and fingering. These broad possibilities relate to the dancer's unlimited range of movement possibilities. Our present music system is derived from certain musicocultural developments—as well as mathematical laws relating sounds; certain vertical relationships, or harmonics; and horizontal relationships, or melodies. This system has developed its own aesthetic, on which most Western music from the sixteenth century is based. So the ballet focuses on dance-culture developments as well as on an aesthetic based on limited principles of balance and use of the body. Just as classical music is built on the diatonic scale, the ballet has basic movements and standard positions of feet, arms, and body. Music combines notes in chordal and melodic structure; classic dance has set movement patterns. In each instance the basic vocabulary is systematized, although worlds of sound and motion await to be formed by a composer even within the strict systems. Artistic liberty makes each system a stepping stone, never a prison.

Just as a great deal more should go into the perception of a great musical composition than a cursory knowledge of the scales and harmonic structures, so in ballet we should go far beyond acquainting ourselves with the idea that the essential movement vocabulary has a structure.

Romantic Ballet

The romantic ballet is embodied in ballets with a story based on subject matter from mystical or miraculous occurrences, legends, or fairy tales. Such ballets as *La Sylphide, Coppélia, Giselle, Sleeping Beauty,* and *Swan Lake* fit into this category. Although these ballets were all choreographed before the twentieth century, they are often presented today in new versions. Most companies associated with state-supported theatres, such as the Leningrad-Kirov and the Bolshoi of Russia, the Royal Ballet of England, and the Royal Danish Ballet, are able to present versions quite close to the originals because these companies are scrupulous guardians of tradition, and constant revivals keep them continually in touch with the old ballets. The romantic ballet is very much an art of Western Europe. It reflects the needs and desires, but most of all the escapist dream, of a European society coping with the Industrial Revolution. The romantic ballet idealizes women and is popularly believed to have placed men in a purely supportive role. Although women's parts were indeed built up, there are numerous examples of important male roles in the romantic ballets (many of which have survived). It is common for dance history books to stress that the decline in ballet was due not only to the servile role of the male but also to the growing obscurity of pantomime and to a concentration on technical brilliance. In fact, choreographically, most of the ballets were extremely weak: the same stodgy patterns were transferred from ballet to ballet, with novelty provided solely by a change of costume to give the dancers a different character. No one can deny the near futility of the majority of goings-on; however, the romantic ballet produced a few uncontested masterpieces.

There are some other general characteristics that should be noted. Most romantic ballets are four-act, full-evening spectaculars with a story line. One of the acts is often separately performed in concerts today when a director wants to give greater scope to the repertory or when the full-length version would be too demanding. Toe or point shoes were first adopted by the leading ladies of the romantic ballet. Symbolically, they emphasize the loftiness of the female; technically, they demand greater skill than ordinary ballet shoes. Defined categories developed for the romantic ballet, and, with them, preassigned roles: leads, or heroes and heroines, were always *prima ballerinas* and *premiers danseurs;* principals, or soloists, were sisters, fathers, and other secondary figures; character dancers played villains, old men, or peasants. The *corps de ballet* took shape.

Pantomime plays an important part in advancing the story line (although the broad outlines are generally common knowledge). Interrupting the story thread are dances—sometimes by a large group, sometimes by two, three, or four dancers (*pas de deux, trois, quatre,* and so forth)—that are not intended to advance the plot. The *pas de deux* for male and female often has a set musical and formal exposition of movement material. The duet will open with a grand adagio, with the female supported on point and in lifts by the man. The movements are lyrical and usually expressive of a joyful, loving moment in the ballet's plot. Immediately afterwards, the man will lead his partner aside and return to do a solo variation that displays his technical brilliance. The male variation usually exploits large jumps, *battérie* (beats), and multiple turns. The man exits, and the female variation follows. Her dance highlights the use of the point shoe, body flexibility, and balance, featuring close, fast footwork and brilliant turns. Lastly, in the coda, male and female alternate in brief series of movements. This section is most easily extracted for general viewing—on television, for instance—because the subject matter or context of the dance is secondary to the bravura requirements.

The ballets generally deal with nobility in mythical kingdoms, which allows for grand entrances and exits, rich costuming, lavish stage settings, full orchestration, and general spectacle. The romantic ballet is entertaining and exciting, rather than profound, and far more compelling as a sheer visual, kinesthetic, and auditory experience than as drama.

Modern Ballet

The second category, which includes the majority of ballets in today's repertories, can broadly be referred to as the modern ballet, although, because of the wide range of subject matter, form, and music, it is difficult to pinpoint general characteristics. Therefore, it will help to examine the elements common to all.

The vocabulary that was discussed earlier remains central to any discussion of modern ballet. Dancers are classically trained, and choreographers know the ballet movement vocabulary well. Whereas in the romantic ballet the vocabulary is strictly adhered to, the modern ballet will consider classical training as a point of departure and use pure vocabulary only when it is best suited. The choreography for the modern ballet is frequently far more inventive than a manipulation of existing patterns, and there is freer license for movement development. Ballets can be created around any subject matter with dramatic content, or they can be purely abstraction.

Movement has always been related to the nature of costuming. In the romantic ballets, women's costumes were at least mid-thigh length, heavy, and tight (corsets were worn), and the men's costumes were also bulky. With shorter dresses, corsets discarded, and costuming relevant to the character of a piece, the movement possibilities in modern ballet became far broader. Point shoes can be, and usually are, worn, though not always. The pure formality and manners of classical movement that continue to exist in the classroom are used on stage only when the piece demands such style.

The development of the modern ballet parallels the development of modern dance (early twentieth century to the present). Michael Fokine is given credit for being a revolutionary in the modern ballet field. Isadora Duncan, who nurtured a seed eventually known as the modern dance, was his contemporary. These two people were aware of each other, but their worlds were quite different, symbolizing, in fact, a basic difference between modern dance and modern ballet. The former is revolutionary, anti-establishment, grass roots, and for the most part American. The latter derives from a highly developed form, evolves within established ballet theatre companies, and is mainly Russian and Western European. Modern ballet is an adaptation of the revolutionary spirit of the modern iconoclasts within the framework of ballet establishments.

Ballet companies are expensive to operate, and experimental works can only be a luxury; the "research" is done by small modern companies. For financial reasons, only if the experiments of the moderns become fashionable will they be taken into the repertory of ballet establishments and so disseminated to a wider public. Although there are a handful of chamber ballet groups now, the vast majority of professional ballet is performed by large organizations.

The modern ballet sometimes follows a story line, but more frequently takes another form. The central concern of the modern ballet is movement exposition growing out of a central idea. This exposition will, therefore, be more totally coherent without traditional trappings unrelated to the central idea. Therefore, if the choreographer has completed his exposition, a piece may last twenty minutes instead of encompassing four acts. Modern ballet, like modern dance, is very much concerned with the craft of composition, while the dancers' real—not storybook—identity must serve the piece. Although it was not the purpose of all romantic ballets to act as vehicles for the dancers' special technical skills, this was often the case. This, too, is possible in the modern ballet, but not likely.

To further illustrate the idea of abstraction versus story line, we can look to descriptions of ballets of the romantic era and post-19th-century pieces. A description of the romantic ballet *Giselle,* first produced in 1841 by Jean Coralli, begins as follows:

> Hilarion enters and peers about him as if in search of someone. He gazes at Giselle's cottage with tenderness and at its neighbour with anger. The door of the latter opens mysteriously and Albrecht, disguised as a peasant and calling himself Loys, emerges, accompanied by his squire, Wilfrid. The latter seems to be urging the former to renounce some project, but he is dismissed. Wilfrid bows low and retires.
>
> The game-keeper, astonished to see so splendidly attired a youth making obeisance to a peasant, is filled with suspicion.[1]

One of the first modern ballets by Michael Fokine, *Les Sylphides* (1909), originally *Chopiniana* (and not to be confused with *La Sylphide*), begins with this description:

> When the curtain rises the *corps de ballet,* a shimmering mass of white, are seen grouped against the background in a semi-circle; in the centre are the four dancers who will render the variations.
>
> The dancers are dressed in the traditional ballet skirt of the period of Taglioni, the edge of the skirt reaching mid-way between ankle and knee; their hair is adorned with a little fillet of white

flowers, at the breast there is a tiny posy of forget-me-nots. Silvery wings are attached to the dancers' waists.

The effect of these floating white clouds against the cold atmosphere of the scene reminds one of snowflakes whirled hither and thither by the wind in the moonlight of a winter's eve. At other times they resemble wisps of mist, the surf on a breaking wave, and perhaps best of all a phantom poet and his muses, at play beneath the waning moon in the shadow of a frosted glade.

Apart from the first mazurka, all the dances breathe an intense sadness, save only the last, which is full of rapture, a joy of quick movement; and, just as the spectator feels he must join in to free himself from the intense strain on his emotions, the curtain falls. Then, so torn is he between conflicting emotions of sadness and rapture, that a few moments elapse before he can applaud.

The phantoms, the glade, the moonlight—all have faded away, but an unforgettable memory remains, and a regret that the vision has passed, and so quickly.[2]

It is clear that both pieces are concerned with mystical occurrences or romantic notions, but, while the action of *Giselle* can be described concretely, we find *Les Sylphides* is a one-act piece built purely on movement in a romantic style—connotations are clear, but dramatic situations are not used or developed.

Les Sylphides also marks a milestone in the use of music for ballet, because the short Chopin pieces were brought together by the choreographer for his own purposes. The repertory of music written for the ballet has also been enriched by many composers, the most noted of whom is Igor Stravinsky.

Subject matter for modern ballet is almost limitless, with an important area of exploration being the psyche, reflecting a new-found awareness of psychology. Some of Antony Tudor's most memorable ballets derive from his understanding of human interaction and emotions and his ability to find movements and bring together acting dancers to fulfill his ideas. The Americans Agnes de Mille and Jerome Robbins explored areas of American thematic material within the ballet. The important choreographer George Balanchine achieved a wide choreographic range and has demonstrated his skills in many styles.

After the initial surge of the modern ballet in Russia, the impresario Serge Diaghilev organized the Ballets Russes, which became the most important modern ballet company and was seen all over the world. After the Diaghilev era (he died in 1929), America became the home of modern ballet. The New York City Ballet and the American Ballet Theatre are outstanding products of this transplantation.

The modern ballet is any style suited to the idea of the choreographer, usually conceived and performed within the

establishment of a producing organization. It often obeys the call of
spectacle, but, fundamentally, it is concerned with movement. The
classical training of dancers and choreographer becomes the planting
ground for movement ideas.

New Ballet

Just as the term "modern dance" is weak, so is the term "modern
ballet." Both are futile attempts to categorize a world of possibilities.
Because of this, it is sometimes difficult, and becoming more so, to
isolate the true differences between the two. In fact, the similarities
are becoming so important that it becomes necessary to find a way
to describe them. We might refer to these similarities as the "new
ballet." Today, most professional dancers are the products of both
classical and modern dance training. It is becoming less important to
be modern for modern dancers and more important for the ballet
companies to relate to the "now" society. The philosophy of both
modern dance and ballet is not to create distinct separations but to
be allowed to use any means at one's disposal to create works of art.
These means include scientific technology, an interest in motion for
motion's sake, and a range of movement as broad as our physical
limits can encompass. All seem to be useful in working toward the
same goal—good dance. New important companies such as the
Harkness Ballet, the City Center Joffrey Ballet, and some regional
companies in part represent this enlarged view. Also, today's fast
communications, constant change, and possibility for historical
perspective allow all dance artists to choose the areas of which they
wish to be a part.

The ballet today is generally represented by organizations in
which a variety of dance experiences can take place. On the other
hand, many of the successful modern dance companies are becoming
tightly organized and seem to be banding together. The old terms
"ballet" and "modern dance" are less and less useful, as it becomes
harder and harder to nail down the differences between them.
Perhaps we should say that "ballet" now describes an establishment
for dance under which a vast variety of styles can flourish. This
establishment allows for some experimentation but is not truly adept
at it. Most experimentation is done by individual artists and small
companies or groups, working in a changing artistic
environment—sometimes supported by universities; sometimes, by
government and foundation grants; and sometimes, by gate receipts
and part-time jobs. When the experiments are notable, the
establishment can begin to assimilate them. Perhaps the activities of
the establishment should be called "the ballet" and all others should
be broadly called "the dance."

Folk, ethnic, and character dance are very often confused. They all have much to do with characteristic national origins; the difference lies in their use.

Folk dancing is performed as a social recreational activity in which all can participate. Ethnic dance is more specialized, with highly trained dancers performing before an audience. It may have evolved from the unchanging folk vocabulary, but the stress is on performance virtuosity by trained dancers.

Character dance is yet another step removed from the original folk dance, in that it is a further stylization and is usually performed by ballet dancers. The original music is not used here. Rather, both the choreographer and the composer strive for the flavor of a certain type of folk dance within the traditional vocabulary.

QUESTION AND ANSWER

YOURY AND ELIZABETH YOURLO

Please explain the difference between folk, ethnic, and character dance.

Because not all people use these terms in the same way, this question can easily lead to a lot of verbal confusion. Nevertheless, it is still possible to make some broad, but clear, distinctions—granting that in actual fact the categories may well overlap.

Folk dance is communal dance performed to traditional music. It has its origin in rituals; for example, ceremonies of courtship, marriage, preparation for battle, celebration of the seasons, mourning, etc. However, although a certain amount of these dances are still ritualistic in purpose, most of them have become secularized into forms of social recreation. Thus folk dance is dance, not so much to entertain an audience as to involve its participants. Any member of an ethnic community *can* be a folk dancer, and probably on occasion is. While these dances are dances for everybody, a particularly good dancer is respected in any society, and it is not

From *Dance Magazine*, XL, No. 11 (November, 1966), 18-19. Reprinted with permission from *Dance Magazine*.

unusual for virtuoso competitions to develop. Folk and square dancing (our own Western tradition) are exceedingly popular as a form of pleasurable recreation in the United States right now.

Ethnic dance is also traditional dance done to traditional music, but the essential difference from folk dance is that its performers are especially trained and perform for an audience. The steps are more difficult, there is a complex vocabulary of gesture, and a technical jargon to describe it. Some ethnic dance (Spanish flamenco, for instance) probably evolved as a more complicated form of folk dance. But class distinctions may also determine who may learn certain dances. Thus Japanese emperors put tight restrictions on which families could teach and learn Kabuki. And throughout the Orient and Africa the priestly caste often has had the sole right to perform sacred dances.

Because it is more complicated, ethnic dance is generally more interesting than folk dance to watch. Indeed, it is specifically intended to be watched by someone. But until recently, people weren't very interested in watching other people's ethnic dances. The dance vocabulary was unfamiliar; the symbolism meaningless. Travel has changed that. Now dance is considered a significant way—even by governments—to become familiar with other cultures. In America the Denishawn dancers were among the first to tour a variety of theatricalized ethnic dances, many of them Oriental. Nowadays, it is common for native ethnic soloists and troupes to travel around the world presenting versions of their own dances. In these theatricalized presentations, folk and ethnic materials often overlap. Among the many famous theatricalized folk-ethnic companies are the Ballet Folklorico of Mexico, Inbal of Israel, Bayanihan of the Philippines, and of course, Moiseyev Dance Company of Russia. Because its director, Igor Moiseyev, was for years a Bolshoi ballet choreographer and its dancers all have had classic ballet training, the Moiseyev company also approximates the kind of dancing known as character dancing.

Character dancing, as terminology and as dance, belongs exclusively to the artistic realm of classical ballet. Actually, the term "character dancing" is sometimes applied to two kinds of dancing—both in the context of ballet. Thus we use the term to describe what G.B.L. Wilson in his *Dictionary of Ballet* calls "a dance based on movements inspired by a particular trade, profession, or mode of living."

However, in terms of our present discussion, by "character dancing" we mean the stylization of folk or ethnic dances choreographed according to the traditions of ballet technique and set to music composed or arranged by "serious" composers.

The nineteenth-century choreographers were particularly fond of including a number of character divertissements in their ballets. *Coppélia* introduced the czardas to the ballet stage. *La Sylphide* contains Scotch jigs and reels. *Raymonda* contains a number of Hungarian character dances and even a classical solo for the ballerina with some adroitly added Hungarian touches. *Napoli* contains a lively tarantella. And *Swan Lake,* Act III, has a czardas, a Spanish dance, a Neapolitan dance, and a mazurka.

The Russians and Danes put great stress on character dance and develop specialists in it. While it is always a required part of the curriculum in European state ballet schools, American dancers rarely have an opportunity to study character dance. Some people even claim that Americans are temperamentally unsuited to such dance. But the truth is that Americans *can* do character work with great verve and brilliance—*provided* they have been thoroughly and properly taught.

Certainly, Americans have no difficulty in performing their country's special contribution to character dance—the exhilarating stylizations of American folk dance material (or "Americana" as it is sometimes called) in works by our own choreographers. Agnes de Mille's *Rodeo,* Eugene Loring's *Billy the Kid,* Jerome Robbins' *Fancy Free,* Anna Sokolow's *Opus 65,* and many other works, all use forms of vernacular American dance. Such borrowings continue to be an important means of bringing vitality and variety to theatrical dance.

Doris Humphrey's philosophy is especially interesting because her work is considered an important achievement in the development of modern dance. The following article gives us a good look at modern dance composed before the 1950s.

Modern dancers, in the beginning, attempted to rediscover natural movement; they felt that highly stylized ballet technique was not compatible with their primary purpose—to communicate. The twentieth century needed a dance art that could speak to modern man of his humanity. So a new type of dance—not relying upon spectacle, codified movement, pantomime, or story line—developed. The term "modern dance" refers to this form of dance, as John Martin described it in the early 1930s.

Doris Humphrey's works are frequently reproduced by means of Labanotation and are often seen on college campuses. Also, her many disciples and her excellent text, *The Art of Making Dances,* have brought her ideas into almost every classroom where dance is taught. Many still regard her principles highly, thereby giving her definitions of modern dance much importance.

AMERICA'S MODERN DANCE

DORIS HUMPHREY

The twentieth century has seen the emergence of a new dance, so vitalized by fresh aims, revolutionary movement, and a widened range of subject matter, that it has inevitably been classed as "modern," along with the music, painting, and literature of the new age. Its essential purpose is to reveal something about people, to communicate to each individual some emotional state, idea or situation which he can identify with his own experience. Grasping modern dance should be easy, and the fact that it frequently is not is due to failure on both sides of the footlights. Dancers are sometimes guilty of a variety of sins, of which obscurity is the most unforgivable, and audiences, on their part, come unprepared and tradition-bound. In the interest of clarity, let me state again what

From *Theatre Arts,* XXXIV, No. 9 (September, 1950), 48-50.

modern dance seems to be, and what contribution it has made to the art.

A Theatre Art of Our Time

Pioneers in the field were all professional dancers, who searched in their own souls and bodies for new means of communicating to audiences. Dances were born in the wings of the stage and cradled on the apron. That is to say, literary ideas were not primary, plots were absent, music was secondary, likewise costumes and décor, and the expressiveness of the human body was paramount. Not all dancers with new ideas were consistently devoted to this purpose, yet the main line can be traced from Ruth St. Denis and Isadora Duncan to the present, and if one word were selected to characterize the whole trend, that word would be "subjective." Dancers found that they were people first, with new attitudes and feelings about life in a world of vast sociological, psychological, and historical change. Wrapped in emotion, and suffused with a vision, they spoke to us, not only of themselves, but of a new language of movement which had to be discovered to convey their meaning. The old forms would not do, the resources of the human body had to be enlarged, revitalized, to contain the new dance.

New Means of Communication

Modern dance bases its technique on natural movement, and this includes not only the use of the body in its rhythmic, dynamic, and linear functioning as a highly complex animal, but also an enormous amount of gesture, a ready-made language, repeated by so many millions of people that they have become patterned, crystallized, and recognizable. There are, for instance, endless social gestures, and the collective gestures of crowds, and movements of work, play, and emotional states. All these evidences of behavior have been noted and used before in the stage arts, but it is modern dance which enriches them with a wider range, a subtler and more penetrating understanding which removes them from pantomime, and above all endows them with natural movement. Today it might be difficult to see anything natural in a performance of modern dance, and indeed, only the basis is natural, for the whole product has been put through a process of stylization which not only makes it unique, but art. Stylizing basic behavior so that it amounts to abstraction is one of the outstanding contributions of the new dance to culture, and it is precisely here that audiences should be more sensitized and aware.

As modern dance began to be established, the rest of the stage arts were gradually added. New music was basically saying the same thing as dance, hence was welcome, but was asked to be a different sort of partner. The two elements were considered as separate contributors to a central idea or an emotional texture, and this often led to unusual accompaniment which abandoned traditional music. Whole dances were supported by percussion only, or with new sounds from old instruments, and music was even dispensed with altogether, dancers making a sort of visual sound of their own. So, too, the spoken word was added to an art that had been non-vocal for centuries. Thus it was a short step to a full use of the elements of theatre. Three-dimensional sets appeared, costumes were designed to fit the new freedom of the body, dramatic lighting played a score as moving as music. Two more outstanding changes were apparent. A new approach to choreography had to be discovered to fit the central concept, and lastly the male dancer was brought back to his former eminence as an important person with something to say.

New Subject Matter

Modern dance has been particularly enterprising in searching out new themes. Additions to the world's knowledge about people in the form of psychology was a natural experimental field for an art so subjective to begin with. New revelations about behavior found their way into dance, sometimes as contemporary themes, and sometimes as revaluations of myth and legend. These were not all dark and Freudian either. Some very penetrating dances were done with a light touch, and Terpsichore found herself listening to a rare sound, genuine laughter in a dance theatre.

There were social themes too, many of them valid, but some reaching too far into the field of propaganda. Even if Fannie Brice satirized the whole thing as "Rewolt," the awareness of changing social relationships is important as a contribution to the range of material.

Delving into the riches of modern literature, dancers do not hesitate to translate plays, poems, and novels into plastic terms—as often as not quoting the authors extensively. These forms come close to the lyric theatre, which musicians and playwrights have also been struggling toward. New expression in the theatre was the concern of a great many people and individual effort overlapped at various points.

Two other main streams of subject matter were outstanding. These were the religious and the folk theme, called in this country, "Americana." Folklore has long been the basis for dance, so the material itself is not new, but it must be remembered that movement is the heart of the matter, therefore familiar themes treated with modern technique are modern dances, and, conversely, a ballet straight out of Americana is still a traditional dance if done in a traditional manner. Religious dances, on the other hand, are a new thing in the world, since the lapse of ritual. The awakened consciousness of dancers, stemming from Ruth St. Denis and Ted Shawn, has brought back this most profound experience of the spirit to the church, the school, and the stage.

To illustrate more concretely how a choreographer goes about coordinating the elements which go into a modern dance, I quote a description of three dances on social themes, which I wrote in 1936:

During the recent insurgence of art as conflict, I felt that much of the work produced was completely negative and that some affirmation should be made. My trilogy, composed of *New Dance, With My Red Fires,* and *Theatre Piece,* was conceived under such circumstances as these. In the face of a dance world largely proclaiming, "This is not!" I would say, "This is!"

The first work, *New Dance,* was concerned with social relationships, with a modern brotherhood of man. Since I was conveying an idea and not a concrete program, I built the dance in symphonic form. When it was done, I found a preliminary dance must be composed to show the world as it is today. This work, *Theatre Piece,* gave added force to *New Dance,* which showed an ideal world.

Both of these dances were concerned with large social relationships, and I felt that the picture would not be complete without showing something of the relationship of man and woman within this social scheme. In such a way *With My Red Fires* was composed, using both the abstract movement of the first dance and the dramatic movement of the second.

Each of these dances was planned as to form before it was begun, but how was the first move determined? From the idea . . .

For instance, in the first part of the *New Dance* the theme required a disconnected, unorganized outpouring of desire from a fragment of a group by the remainder of the group. For this, Charles Weidman and I obviously were the central figures broken off from the group, the rest of the dancers, the onlookers. These two sometimes moved together harmoniously, sometimes at variance, but always restlessly as though in search of a new life. This was the mood of discovery which I needed. The setting for the *New Dance* also came from the idea. I needed blocks at the beginning to suggest an arena from which a crowd looks down. These were used later, piled in the center, to emphasize unity, and balanced harmony achieved at the end. The music was especially composed by Wallingford Riegger.

13
DANCE OF THE ABSURD

Faubion Bowers attempts to relate works of Alwin Nikolais, Anna Sokolow, Paul Taylor, Erick Hawkins, and other dance artists to a development known as the "Theatre of the Absurd." "Absurd" does not mean ridiculous but, rather, illogical. A premise is that man applies meanings to things—they do not have meaning in themselves. Absurdism is characterized by lack of logic, order, and predictability. Similar trends can be found in all the arts.

In reading the following article, be cautious about applying Bowers' use of the term "Absurd" to all of the choreographers he mentions. Instead of using illogical composition, Nikolais, Taylor, and Hawkins are trying to use movement for immediacy of expression. In our opinion, they are not so much trying to follow the Absurdist school as they are reaffirming the beauty of motion. Many of Anna Sokolow's dances, set to biting jazz scores, have a highly emotional content.

It is a good academic exercise for the student critic to be aware of such stylistic labels as Classicism, Romanticism, Expressionism, and Absurdism, but the terminology must be used with intelligence, restraint, and knowledge. No matter what the choreographer's own philosophy is (and it should be recognized), the critic may very well be acting as the historian of the day, trying to put the current trends into some perspective and making a logic from what he sees. We have chosen the article not because we agree with the labeling but because the perspective presented has validity.

The choreographers under discussion are considered part of a movement that might be called the "new dance." These contemporary artists are a generation away from those artists considered leaders of the "modern dance."

DANCE: A REVIEW

FAUBION BOWERS

It has become fashionable these days to talk about—and attend—Theatre of the Absurd. Sartre started the phrase and meant something serious, if debatable: man can accept responsibility for his life and acts only when aware of the world's absurdity. A good many plays so designated have nothing to do, really, with this thesis. Any new, off-beat, odd-ball or otherwise unusual happening in the theatre, funny or sad, is Absurd. The term sticks because it is convenient.

In dance, the most orphaned of theatre arts, enough zany and incomprehensible, but enjoyable, performances have now taken place and grown sufficiently popular that dancers need a catch phrase. Perhaps by extension, Dance of the Absurd is as good a designation as any. To those dance-goers who have at last found that their minds can grasp Martha Graham, I have to say that there are yet miles to go in the labyrinth of strange movements, extraordinary ideas, and other departures from ballet or dance as it was when we were younger.

These extreme, new dancers have been appearing more or less regularly, but only recently has word spread to any extent. As a result audiences have increased, and, though the general bafflement remains steadfast, discerning spectators are becoming noticeably hoarser in their approval. One troupe, Alwin Nikolais' young dancers at the Henry Street Settlement Playhouse, appears weekends every other month. Nikolais creates dance sequences called *Imago, Finials* and the like, of exquisitely plotted abstract movements and motions. He couches them in costumes ranging from odd, through fantastic, to the outlandish. One number, well applauded if not wholly appreciated in New York, on tour in the provinces and at Spoleto last year, was *Noumenon.* The several dancers are dressed—perhaps the better description is bundled—in jersey bags of different colors. Sitting on stools, to disconnect the foot from the ground and confuse the human shape, they look like blobs. The dance consists of rhythmic juttings and protrusions illogically appearing from nowhere, anywhere unexpected. At the end, the dancers stand upright on the stools, their concealed hands wrapped around to

From *The Nation,* CXCVII, No. 6 (September 7, 1963), 116-19.

enlarge the headnob. For the first time the audience knows for sure that these mystery cocoons are human.

Nikolais makes a specialty of theatrical accouterment. For one dance he attaches hoops of varying size at the ankles, knees, hips and chest, and covers the dancer's now distorted body with cloth. Like chessmen come alive, the figures bob and sway. In another dance, the costume is long suction pumps for hands, long enough to make a grotesque dance-walk on all fours merely by a slight leaning over. Elsewhere Nikolais' company—this time fully visible and scantily costumed—stands beneath a décor of bits of paper—a constellation of triangles, squares, hexagons. One dancer makes a deep motion to the floor of the stage and an arrow of colored paper follows; a second steps widely back, and another part of the décor descends, minutely following the movement. It takes a short while to figure out that invisible wires tie the dancer to his setting, and that *it* dances along with him. Dances as far out as these require electronic music, and this, too, with its droplets of sounds, jingle-jangles and outer-space whines, is composed and manufactured by Nikolais, the musician-choreographer.

For dance of a different sort, I recommend Mikhail Santoro at the Charles Weidman Theatre of the Expression of the Two Arts. There, any Saturday, Santoro may dance a lecture in calligraphy. Suddenly, while casually talking to the spectators, he will fall to the floor in a dangerous but well-calculated drop, rise again and start talking about lines. He pulls an invisible line from out of the floor, carries it as if it tenderly existed, and then starts painting on a large square of brown wrapping paper. His dance movements dictate the lines he paints in black and white, and as you puzzle out what picture the dance will make, hanging on for life and dear sanity to visible logic, Santoro speaks: "We know this is a man, because here's a hand . . ." He quickly sketches a birdlike claw in the center of the paper—where the clutch destroys the very comprehensibility you have momentarily found. Then, dotting the eyes with two red splotches, the dance is over.

Within Dance of the Absurd there is, of course, the more and the less. Among the less comes Anna Sokolow's recent *Opus 63* (after the year, not the number of works composed) where Jerome Robbins' jazz movements are abstracted and attenuated, that is, twice removed from literalness. One section satirizes the blandness of society, the distance between people and persons except when "twisting." The star of the section is an Amazon—the tallest dancer ever to appear on stage—who, dead-pan, crushes her writhing, sex-tatic partners as she sinks to the ground, until they become feelers or antennae, threadlike spindles of leg, and she becomes a giant insect. At least, that's the way I saw it.

Another of the less strange dancers is the noble and aristocratic Erick Hawkins. Still, he can give you a shock of surprise. In one of his dances, *Pine Tree*, he stands for an interminable length of time on one foot with the other extended at right angle. When you can bear it no longer, he slowly begins to lower his leg, and the accompaniment, composed and played by Lucia Dlugoszewski, strums a single stroke on the wooden ladder-harp. Then Erick Hawkins walks round in a series of identical circles—nine times is about the maximum the audience can take—and disappears in the wings.

Paul Taylor, evolving out of ballet, up from Martha Graham, into himself, is one of the most widely known practitioners in the Absurd field. A few years ago he conceived and rehearsed a dance where, in business suit (was it gray flannel?), he stood motionless while a grim clock ticked off seconds. I doubt if any dance has ever been more condemned, but those exacerbated ones who saw it and suffered under its static silence are still talking about it. *

Dance of the Absurd appears to be more than an aberrational sidetrack. To a new crop of youngsters now coming up this idiomless idiom seems natural. One of the most brilliant evenings of dance—so accorded by the press and soon to be repeated—was given a short while ago by Albert Reid. Still in his early twenties, Reid has already developed amazing technical command, control and ease. He can do virtuoso tricks with his body—stand on his toes, one leg or one hand, endlessly, leap, fall, spin—so that the wary will trust his competence; but more important, despite the coldness of a young dancer just out of training, he shows what he intends with his mind. His distortions and grotesqueries of movement claw at your nerves until a soft moment unexpectedly touches the gentlest of your emotions. Always off balance, harshly angular, unusually extended in series of body stances never seen before, his fleeting seen-before postures come only to startle you.

One of Reid's eye-catching, heart-troubling dances was *Each Time You Carry Me This Way* (a popular tune), performed on the floor by means of slides and slithers. The arms repeated patterns, the upraised knees created symmetrical phrases, and the sporadic uprighting of the body punctuated the concealed purpose. The meaning? It could be the loneliness of the basket-case, or an incapacitated beggar plying his trade. In fact, it is the stylization of the pull exerted upon one human by an (invisible) other.

A Little Talk, the evening's show stopper, is a larger-than-life replica of a simple situation: the boredom when someone talks too much. Reid sits in a kitchen chair, motionless, the eyes staring straight ahead vacantly. The toes wiggle. Then the fingers twiddle. The eyes, slower than slow, wander to their corners and back. He slumps inch by inch until he is supine, then moves into a slow somersault with the chair until the initial, rigid, agonized posture of

*This dance was reviewed by the famous critic-teacher-musician Louis Horst in *Dance Observer* with a blank review.

the beginning is resumed. The only sound is the squeak of the chair.

From the meaningful, Albert Reid turns to the absurdly meaningless. His troupe begins dancing before the curtain is raised. You hear foot sounds. Then the curtain rises a few inches, sinks again, rises again, and you continue to watch a foot-dance with the concentrated attention of a movie camera close-up. Somewhere along the line, imponderable nerves of aesthetic response are touched. When Judy Garland's voice singing "Zing went the strings of my heart" booms out unrelatedly at the end of one dance, something goes zing in the spectator's amazement and admiration.

Out of inexplicable meaninglessness, we somehow learn, in theatre and dance, that something special may be generated. Nerves are touched, and even grated. Hearts are tampered. But what happens ultimately is aesthetic. There's beauty there. Strange, unbelievable, but it is catching us and catching on.

14
THE NEW NEW DANCE

"Modern dance" is only a label under which we can include almost all of the American concert dance of the twentieth century not directly determined by 19th-century ballet philosophy. It is a weak term at best. "New dance" is a good general term for the concert experiments and trends occurring today.

Erica Abeel takes a look at the generation after Humphrey's and points out why some of the things now going on cannot be classified as modern dance. One of the main questions is, in fact, whether much of it is dance at all.

The modern pioneers had something to say—something about the nature of man and about complex 20th-century society—something that could not be said with the traditional ballet vocabulary. Modern dance became an expressive art with its own stylization and symbolic gesture.

The new dance rejects dance movement stemming from a motivational vocabulary. It has been stripped of all extraneous elements and is left with pure movement. Dance, then, is not always recognizable as significant gesture and is having non-dance movements incorporated into its vocabulary. Alwin Nikolais constantly disguises and nearly obliterates the form of the human body. The new dance has become in some cases quite respectable; in fact, some of the new dance is almost too "in" to be new. Thus, we have the notion of the "new new dance."

Up to this time, no one has ever denied the assumption that a performing dancer must be a trained, disciplined technician. In some of the new groups, however, several performers have never had *any* training. Traditional choreographic processes, too, are rejected, and the structuring of the composition is often left to chance, improvisation, or divine inspiration.

This is a movement to be watched closely, one that is very confusing to those who are just beginning to accept modern dance as a legitimate art form along with ballet. A serious doubt arises in many audiences as to the theatrical validity of these far-out, sometimes illogically organized performances of the new new dance. Does this variety of experimentation really belong in front of an audience, or does it fall more properly in the province of the studio?

THE NEW NEW DANCE

ERICA ABEEL

Modern dance is no longer the new dance. Born in the twenties, an infant in comparison with the other arts, it has already become a Tradition, a kind of Academy of concert dance. Some observers, in fact, view the moderns as a case of premature fossilization and have consigned them to a wing in the Museum of Dance next to the Ballet Collection. Others feel that the judgment is more premature than any supposed demise. But what many people fail to realize is that modern dance and new dance are not only two distinct, but two opposed, genres; that new dance is not so much a vigorous shoot on the modernist tree as a totally different species.

New dance has speedily become a storm center of experimental activity in the arts. The branch most representative of these experimental tendencies is the Judson Church group, a child of the sixties, although its roots go back to Merce Cunningham's schism with Graham's great theatre. Alwin Nikolais and Murray Louis are making new dances, too, for they represent a radical departure from the traditional modern idiom, but are less experimental than Judson. Nikolais is working within a fairly rigid, "closed" concept of a total theatre of movement, props, sound, color, and light. He presents finished art works, ready to qualify for Masterpiece status. Judson seems to eschew "finish," presenting bits and parts of things, sections in progress, an abandoned inspiration; taking risks; incorporating accidents; horsing around (which is serious, too); and undermining the very concept of The Masterpiece.

A primary goal of the post Denishawn pioneers was the up-dating of dance, the creation of a medium that, unlike ballet, would express modern times. Dancers were to say, in their movements, "We belong to the twentieth century; we have something to reveal about it in the light of contemporary experience; the dance is an art with fully as much scope as literature and can tell about modern man as authors and poets do."[1] Dance developed into an expressive art; that is, a medium designed to tell about something aside from its own movement content. Compare a typical modern dance sequence with one variety of balletic *pas de deux:* the modern dancers are communicating emotion through movement, the ballet couple is

From *Dance Scope*, II, No. 2 (Fall, 1965), 21-26. Copyright © 1965 by the National Dance Teachers Guild, Inc. Reprinted with permission.

saying nothing beyond the geometrical designs formed by the assumption of a series of standard poses (I am discounting the chivalric male-female relationship implicit in the *pas de deux*). In the Graham idiom, movements "mean something": a turn is the release of pent-up joy, staccato angular gestures express anguish, stillness is contemplation or the marshalling of inner resources. A parable of modern man is set forth, closely paralleling a literary form, but with movements standing in for words.

Common to much of new dance today is the rejection of the motivation-based movement vocabulary. Dance here shares certain preoccupations with painting, in recent times the most vanguardist of the arts, and shows the influence of John Cage. Painting became interested in eliminating all extra-painterly elements, such as a figurative subject, or even the subject of the artist's personality, as it is expressed through the motor-storm of the brush's strokes, dabs, and whorls, and concentrating exclusively on the essence of painting, considered by some to be color. Similarly, choreographers began to explore the possibility of a dance purged of "extraneous" elements such as emotion, story line or even humanity, and pared down to a system of "pure" movement. This goal is violently opposed to traditional dance's aspiration to assume the status of a vital and contemporary art form by competing, as it were, with novels, poems or plays, by saying essentially the same thing as the arts of literature but contributing a special resonance and impact possible only through dance. "Let's not compete any longer," says the new dance. "Let's confine dance to creating something inseparable from the medium of the dance, something that a novel, say, or a play, could never hope to reproduce." John Cage succinctly points up the new attitude in one of his lectures: "We are not, in these dances, saying something. We are simple-minded enough to think that if we were saying something we would use words."

An important strain in modern art is greatly concerned with the ousting of the personality from the art work. One group of painters strives for the universality and order of creation uninflected by a creator's individual temperament. John Cage attempts to make music structured by chance devices, and so freed of the limiting factor of a particular will. Merce Cunningham charts the sequence of movements in his dances by chance, substituting in this way a kind of mystical arbitrariness of Fate for the meaner, less telling arbitrariness of his own taste. What results is a dance indeed "freed" from extraneous controls, irreproachably plotless, cold as a star.

It is a dance especially fresh with regard to music. It is well known that a Cunningham-Cage collaboration has nothing to do with the traditional practice of setting a dance to pre-existing music or commissioning a score to "fit" a dance. Rather, dance and music occur simultaneously onstage, two activities going on at the same time in the same place, with only a certain time structure decided on in advance. What a liberating effect on dance, truly on its own for once! In the past, dance has been subservient to music, deriving an ABA structure from the sonata form or borrowing its shape from the Theme and Variations, bending itself, at any rate, to fit the music, sometimes figuring, ironically, as an accompaniment to the music when the reverse was supposed to be the case! A good example of a score totally overpowering the movement onstage is the arrangement of Doris Humphrey's *Passacaglia and Fugue in C Minor,* in which the dancing, although very moving, is upstaged by the stentorian tones of the organ.

While art can eliminate figurative elements, dance cannot very well do so, unless it would effect a mutation of the human form into a set of masses, hollows and line. But a Cunningham dance has so thoroughly shed any vestiges of emotional derivation that it comes as close to being "abstract" as a medium whose material is the human body can come. By abstract I mean non-referential in human terms. The triumph of the Cunningham idiom is that it broadens and renews the vocabulary of dance by making movement unrecognizable as gesture. It becomes impossible, for example, to relate a contraction to a pang of emotion because the dancer is no longer functioning onstage as a fellow sufferer but as a creator of movements that elude interpretive tags. Any stale identifications on the part of the audience are immediately chastened by the performer's dead-pan, one of the clichés of the avant-garde. Traditionally considered a divine or privileged region of the human anatomy, the head, in Cunningham dance, has no more status than the big toe. Cunningham's company has so successfully stifled personality projection—except for a trace of hauteur in Carolyn Brown's carriage, a hint of animal malice in Cunningham's features—that an ensemble work has the appearance of animated architecture.

Equally preoccupied with the creation of a fresh dance vocabulary are Alwin Nikolais and Murray Louis. A movement sequence in Nikolais is the product of a kind of kinetic determinism or internal necessity generated by the motions themselves. Murray Louis' solos in Nikolais' most recent work, *Galaxy,* are a glorious image of this choreographic method. José Limon's stage charisma has a lot to do with the projection of the self mastering the movement material. Louis' *Galaxy* solos give the opposite impression: it is as if the movements were mastering the dancer, as if the dancer were being danced by a host of Terpsichorean spirits. Louis' body seems a garden of quirks, impulses, seizures, all perfectly logical and necessary, but not a little surprising, especially to Louis! One witnesses the curious spectacle of a current of movement "passing through" the dancer rather than originating in him.

It would be a gross oversimplification to call every moment of a Graham opus dramatic or motivational. While they usually serve to establish an emotional climate, some of the choric passages in the larger Graham pieces have an abstract quality and are admirable simply as studies in moving line and dynamics. But Graham, although never obvious or Instantly Interpretable, is concerned for the most part with human drama, blown to mythic proportions and informed by an archetypal radiance.

Murray Louis, on the other hand, occupies a true inter-polar zone, successfully combining elements of two aesthetics. Not as doctrinaire as Nikolais, the *doyen* of neo-Bauhaus theatre, his movement style still borrows heavily from the master. But this style is often at the service of an emotional image, as in *Antechamber,* in which an unbearable tension is built up and exploded; or of an excursion into the fantastic, as in *A Gothic Tale. Landscapes* uses a brittle, mechanical-toy mode of movement to evoke an inter-stellar climate and intuitions of organic processes on a remote planet. Grounded in kinetic determinism, Louis' dance is nonetheless concerned with poetry.

His dance is not avant-garde, though, if the term is understood to include an experimental spirit, allowance for spontaneous interference from within the choreographic non-structure and from the environmental situation, an intentional raggedness somehow synonymous with hip or cool and a disavowal of "dance-looking" movements. Louis is not experimental to the extent that he is willing to fail theatrically: his dances all work, or try to, and if they don't it is due to a momentary lack of focus, usually adjustable through performance. His movements are at all times stylized, that is, recognizable as dance, whereas Judson, for example, has a special fondness for "dancers" who have never set foot in a class.

Last May a group of dancers, painters and sculptors presented the First New York Theater Rally, a series of dance concerts and Happenings. Painters and dancers have been collaborating since the days of Diaghilev and, more recently, Cunningham, Cage and Rauschenberg have co-authored dances, but significantly, the Theater Rally painters choreographed their own dances, performing in them as well. The focus of works by painters Rauschenberg and Alex Hay and sculptor Bob Morris was probably as far from the traditional conception of dance as anything has ever been. What was involved was a new kind of theatre, based on the free, environmental ideas and sequential illogic of Happenings. But many of the new works by trained dancers are scarcely more movement oriented. Watching well-trained dancers, such as Judith Dunn, hopping, skipping, running and worrying mattresses in Yvonne Rainer's *Parts of Some Sextets,* one has a distinct sense of waste.

If Cunningham has broadened the range of the dance vocabulary by disassociating already familiar dance movements from meaning, resituating them in a new context, some of the Judson choreographers have actually added to the dance vocabulary, and in so doing raised some interesting questions, by the inclusion of non-dance movements. Here there is an obvious link with Pop Art (dance, recently, has closely paralleled developments in the plastic arts) which chooses to set on the pedestal of Art such non-art objects as Campbell's soup cans. Rainer's mattress-worrying is of very limited interest as movement. Its unique value, perhaps, is the fact that it is now being done, and is calling itself dance.

Judith Dunn's *Speed Limit* is a much more interesting exploitation of a non-dance vocabulary because it also utilizes stylization in the form of extreme economy of overall design. Dressed in jump suits, or workmen's overalls (fast becoming another avant-garde cliché), Dunn and Bob Morris manage to convey an entirely absorbing emotional adventure between two individuals (people? pandas? abstractions?) by performing a series of rolls on a mat. When I say "emotional adventure" I am reading in *my* particular response to the work, which may have been about that, or something else, or nothing at all.

There is generally a heavy dose of non-dance in Rainer's group numbers. Some of her solos, though, seem concerned with movement, and when they are, are probably among the more probing new dance experiments. In *New Untitled Partially Improvised* she comes on in leotard and blackened face, stares at the audience, who naturally stare back at her (fun for awhile because it exposes the audience-performer situation, usually taken for granted), and at very wide intervals performs a cluster of rapid, fluid movements—all to a Bach toccata. Although initially irritating—one imagines such titles as *Ego I* or *Megalomania II*—the piece is nonetheless intriguing, for it is playing with the idea of suggesting movement without actually moving. It is as if a motion-fest were going on behind some opacity which, during the still intervals, lies between us and the action. The piece is the first that I know of to deal with the illusion of movement.

Modern dance and new dance are close neighbors in time yet eons apart in spirit. The "missing link" between the two aesthetics is Cunningham, who retains the danciness of traditional dance while pointing to the new approach by freeing movement from psychological associations. The Cunningham break with Graham was an inspired innovation. But today's practice of incorporating non-dance movements is totally disorienting because it erodes the very definition of dance. The problem of the sixties is no longer the forging of a new instrument but the problem of what is and what isn't dance. While theoreticians prepare to hang themselves on the horns of this admitted dilemma, more pragmatic spirits go about making their kind of dances. Dance for them is, after all, a theatre art, and in theatre a much more relevant question is, "Does it work?"

EDITORS' COMMENT

In this age of technology and fast communication, it becomes almost impossible to tag what is happening in dance today and put it in a category. It is very important to note that technology and media are having a great influence on many choreographers from both modern and ballet schools. Although such painters as Robert Rauschenberg and such musicians as John Cage have been associated with the new dance, ballet choreographers have also taken some of the new ideas and applied them within the larger spectacle context of the ballet.

Some exciting experiments have been made with dance and film. Arthur Baumann's *Dialogue* is slowly becoming a classic. This piece seems to be a milestone in the skillful collaboration of a film artist and a choreographer. The combination of film and dance is becoming very popular, and, with today's instant communication, we are even seeing that area become old hat.

Other mixed-media productions have involved the use of materials designed by artists, such as plastic baloons and inflated polyethylene. Objects of this sort have become almost commonplace with the experimenters in modern dance and are often seen in ballets. Gerald Arpino used them in *Clowns,* which is in the repertory of the City Center Joffrey Ballet.

The label that would most accurately describe what is happening in dance today is "dance of change." Whatever is "in" today may very well be "out" tomorrow. Ours is an age of experimentation and quick consumption, reflective of our paper-plate lives. But dance, like all the arts, is keeping pace with the times. And, whereas the forms of dance in the past often reflected either an ideal or an escapist's dream, the dance of today captures the harsh realities of our existence.

Luckily for audiences, they are able to see almost all forms of dance performed today. In the final analysis, there are only two kinds of dance: good and bad.

REFERENCES, PART THREE

CHAPTER 10. The Ballet

[1] Cyril W. Beaumont, *Complete Book of Ballets* (New York: Grosset & Dunlap, 1938), p. 129.
[2] *Ibid.*, pp. 564-65.

CHAPTER 14. The New New Dance

[1] Doris Humphrey, *The Art of Making Dances* (New York: Rinehart & Co., 1959), p. 174.

FOUR

The Language and Literature of Dance

The material of dance, as we have stated, is movement. Therefore, the examination of movement cannot be neglected by anyone involved in dance. Movement is, of course, non-verbal, and so a great deal of the learning of movement takes place without the written or spoken word, as does much of the enjoyment of movement. And yet, we are verbal beings, with a need for expanding ideas inherent in the kinetic symbol. Just as the competent musician has an understanding of the mathematical laws governing sound relationships and can verbalize these laws as well as use the labels that have been given to sound perception, so must a dance person have expanded his perception of movement beyond a Stone Age awareness.

When movement can be first understood at a kinetic level and then reinforced and refined via a vocabulary, it has been well taught and, most likely, well learned. Movement well learned is more apt to be well performed, making the channel for the choreographer's communication more direct and closer to original intention. The methods for symbolizing and analyzing movement (although done meagerly before this century) have increased tremendously in the past fifty years. In addition to the vocabulary of movement based on the kinesiologic and anatomical functions of the human body, several new developments in this century have helped us create other symbolic-verbal and purely symbolic means of analyzing movement. Although proponents of these systems are not always in agreement, it must be recognized that the possible language for movement is large, must satisfy the requirements of both academicians and professionals, and, clearly, demands further study and sophistication.

A language when recorded provides a literature and, therefore, a certain viability for the ideas that are notated. It is largely because of the phenomenological existence of dance that its literature has been very much akin to legend instead of record. The music notation we know is a good deal older than any system of movement notation in use today; therefore, music has a vast literature ready for reproduction. But music is less complex to notate, for only the elements of pitch, time, and energy must be represented. The human body is three-dimensional and more complex than any instrument yet devised, and the movement of the body compounds the difficulty of recording the time and energy patterns. And yet, systems are in use today that are doing this seemingly impossible task.

The developments described in this section are largely responsible for giving dance a concrete footing with the other arts, both artistically and academically, in this century. Although the dance literature is small compared to the recorded heritage in the other arts, it is growing. Attempts were made to notate dances as early as the mid-fifteenth century, but most systems arose and then grew obsolete because they were intended to record only certain specific kinds of dance. The important systems—Labanotation, Benesh Notation, and Effort-Shape—provide the notation for all human movement.

15
THE ANALYSIS AND PRESERVATION
OF MOVEMENT: LABANOTATION

Until recently, dance was an illiterate art, with the result that the dances of the past are only legend. We will never know what they were really like, for dance has had no comprehensive written history. True, since the fifteenth century, systems of notation were devised, but they failed either because of complexity or for lack of the skill necessary for detailed drawing. They also became obsolete because they could not be adapted to further evolution in dance movement.

In this section, several notation systems now in use will be described. However, the system most often endorsed by the Dance Notation Bureau, which studies all systems, is Labanotation.

Developed by Rudolf Laban, Labanotation records movement on a staff by means of symbols. It is guarded against obsolescence by being a system that can record *any* human movement. Everything that occurs can be notated—the movement and its direction in space, the floor pattern, the tempo, rhythm and meter, dynamics and flow. And it works equally well for solo and group works.

Now, at last, a body of literature is being assembled to preserve accurately the creativity of our times. The works of great choreographers can now be studied and reconstructed, much as musical scores and written dramas are studied. Dance is no longer illiterate.

Elizabeth Burtner discusses other uses for Labanotation that, in terms of movement study, are beginning to enrich non-dance areas.

Probably the only valid criticism of Labanotation is that it is such a comprehensive system. Writing it is a time-consuming and difficult task, and there are far too few professional notators at present.

DANCE NOTATION MAKES LEGEND INTO HISTORY

ELIZABETH BURTNER

Our heritage in the arts is a rich one and since the arts express how man thinks, feels, moves, and has his being, they are fraught with significance for us. Of all the recording of art forms of the past, that of the dance, which has movement for its medium of expression, comes off least well; in fact, hardly at all.

In the Greek drama alone, this has caused much conjecture. What was the ecstatic dance of the maenads in honor of Dionysus like with its wild running, whirling, shouting, tossing of hair and of torches and thyrsi, as suggested in the *Bacchae* of Euripides; or the mystic "lyreless" dance of the Furies in the *Eumenides* of Aeschylus? *The Birds* of Aristophanes implies a dance chorus of animal mummers, but do we really know, and if so, was the movement literal . . . or abstract? The Egyptians danced to orchestras of lyres and choral chanting. Did the dancers really turn their hands and feet sideways and tense their fingers in extension, or was this simply a stylized conventional technique of depicting the human body in line and color? There are references to the dance in the Bible. In the 105th Psalm, the dance joins other forms of communication in praising the lord for his mighty acts and according to his excellent greatness. *"Praise him with the timbrel and dance; praise him with stringed instruments and organs."* Was this dance improvisional? It is fascinating to read about the mid-summer Morris pageant where Robin Hood was honored with dance around a flower-crowned pole. What were those original ritual folk dances like? The jig, a song and dance act, rose to great popularity during the Elizabethan era. Baskerville and others have written scholarly works about this form of presentation. Exact music and words of the songs are available. Not so the exact movement of the dance. The actual movement of the court dances of the fifteenth and sixteenth centuries, the pavane, the sarabande, the bourree, the chaconne, passacaglia and others, is largely a matter of putting two and two together. There is information to be gleaned from posed pictures; graphs depicting floor patterns, sketches showing the holding of the hand and the flexion of the wrist; and verbal descriptions of steps, all of which leads to variations in interpretations. · We can read Noverre's book, *Lettres sur la danse*

From *GW:* The George Washington University Magazine, Spring, 1967.

(1760). It is considered a classic and it contains his theories on dramatic dance which were innovations of great consequence to the advancement of dance. His choreographed works, which were evidence of the application of his theories, are extinct. *Extinct! Extinct!* is an epitaph which can be applied equally well to great works of dance art in the past and to ethnic forms of dance. In fact, dance has been termed an illiterate art by people of the dance world such as John Martin, author of books on dance, first dance critic in the United States and, until recently, dance critic for *The New York Times.*

Today the picture is rapidly changing. In the United States this is being brought about largely by the work of the Dance Notation Bureau, New York City. Notators and teachers are being highly trained to qualify for accreditation. A library of notated works including those of Balanchine, Doris Humphrey, Charles Weidman, and Hanya Holm are available for reconstruction and performance. Currently, *Les Noces* (Jerome Robbins) and either or both *Pillar of Fire* and *Undertow* (Antony Tudor) are being notated.

Courses in dance notation are part of the curriculum of study in many colleges and universities including George Washington University. Nadia Chilkovsky Nahumck, director of the Philadelphia Dance Academy, is now working with a grant from the Office of Education to develop a comprehensive graded curriculum for dance. The emphasis in this curriculum is not to teach dance but rather to learn about cultures and social groups by transmitting accumulated knowledge about all dance: ballet, modern, ethnic, and social. The thread running through this whole program is notation. Students and cooperating teachers are learning to read through notation much as they may already have learned to read music. The reconstruction of obsolete dances, archeochoreography, substitutes the study of sculpture, painting, and documentary description for actual observation of the dances, as, for example, in the book *Dances of Anahuac, the Choreography and Music of Precortesian Dances* by Kurath and Marti. In this book fragments of movement gleaned from varied sources of information are reconstructed and notated. Currently research projects on Renaissance and Ghanaian dances are under way. At the University of Southern Illinois, the services of a notator on the dance faculty are being used to notate the movements of the jumping spider mating dance as part of a research project in biological sciences.

The system of dance notation taught and used for the notation of works by the Dance Notation Bureau and most prevalent in the United States is Labanotation. Other systems include: the Benesh Notation, or choreology, used by the Royal Ballet of England and by ballet and opera companies in other parts of the world; Choroscript, Alwin Nikolais' system; Kineseography, used by Eugene Loring; Jay Notation; Scoreography; and others.

Anyone can invent his own system of movement notation. The problem is to come forth with one which can be for dance what the alphabet is for literature and what music notation is for music. Because dance is a space-time art it presents greater problems in notation than literature or music. Also, the movement of the human body in space with its infinite possibilities is difficult to record on a two-dimensional piece of paper. This problem accounts for dance being termed an illiterate art. This has also been a constant challenge for a breakthrough of a "way" to record movement which would be efficient, comprehensive, and practical. From the middle of the fifteenth century, nine centuries later than the advent of music notation, all the numerous systems devised have failed. They were either too complicated, required ability to draw, or became obsolete because they were limited to current dances of the day without any thought of an evolving of movement techniques, theories of movement, and forms of expression.

Rudolf Laban, in devising his system of notation, avoided the probability of his system's becoming obsolete by making his approach a movement notation adaptable to any human motion whether dance, swimming, or chopping wood. Laban published his first book on notation in 1928, making dance notation jump a few centuries ahead of where it had been and bringing it closer in development to the present state of music notation. Since then, Laban's system has undergone certain changes. Contributions to the system have been made by numerous people in various parts of the world who have tested the system through use. Revisions made by American and European colleagues as a result of recent international conferences are producing greater clarity, precision, and common meeting grounds. The goal, says Muriel Topaz, compiler and editor of *Changes and New Developments in Labanotation,* used for the first time at the Fifth National Notation Conference last June, is "a commitment to a system internationally developed and practiced as a universal instrument of movement communication." Further evidence of constant revision is the fact that the two major texts on this system, *Labanotation* by Ann Hutchinson, 1954, and *Handbook of Kinetography Laban* by Albrecht Knust, 1956, are being revised and scheduled for republication in the near future.

What are the outstanding characteristics of the Laban system of notation? To quote Ann Hutchinson, "Labanotation is a means of recording movement by means of symbols." Basic principles for recording are as follows: that simple, natural movement is written in the most simple and direct way; that everything that occurs is recorded; that movement is the result of the release of energy through muscular response to a stimulus (inner or outer); that this response produces a visual result in space which is recorded with symbols.

In order to record movement there must be a statement of exactly what occurs: the *use of space*—what direction?—forward, backward, sideward, diagonal and at what level?—low, high, or degrees in between; the *time aspects*—what tempo, length of time in slow, fast, even and uneven intervals; *the dynamics*—texture of movement such as strong or light; and the *pattern* or *flow* in movement—bound or free.

As in music, a staff is used upon which is recorded the movement symbols. This staff consists of three vertical lines

making vertical columns. The center line of the staff represents a line drawn through the middle of the body dividing it into right and left halves.

Additional lines are added as needed.

One reads from the bottom up. Time aspects such as beats grouped into measures are indicated by short and longer horizontal lines on the vertical staff. The symbol for meter, as in music, is a fraction and occurs in the beginning of the notation and wherever else necessary.

A basic symbol, the rectangle, ⊔ placed in a particular column, shows what part of the body is represented. Modifications of the shape of the rectangle mean a specific direction in space. Shading refers to the level of movement in space, while size or length of the rectangle refers to time value.

high
middle
low

One of the most valuable contributions notation makes to the student, other than the discipline of clarity and precision of the execution of movement in space and time, is the knowledge resulting from the study of the works of outstanding choreographers of the past and present. The culminating project of the dance notation course taught for the first time at George Washington University in 1965-66 was the reconstruction from the notated score of Doris Humphrey's *Partita V,* music by Johann Sebastian Bach, Opus 1 in G Major. This work was premiered in 1942 and notated as taught by Miss Humphrey in 1950. For Doris Humphrey and Johann Sebastian Bach the inspiration and source material were the court dances of the fifteenth and sixteenth centuries during which time music was ofttimes commissioned to be composed for dance by a wealthy patron, king, queen, or duke, and at which time dance was a favorite activity of royalty. *Partita V,* as notated by Els Grelinger of the Dance Bureau, includes:

> the *Courante,* for six dancers; a favorite of Queen Elizabeth's.
>
> the *Minuet,* a solo. "Life is like a Minuet—a few turns are made in order to curtsey in the same spot from which we started" (Senac de Meilhan).
>
> the *Passepied,* an ensemble of seven dancers. To quote Louis Horst, "originally danced by the Breton peasants, it found great favor in court circles during the reign of Louis XV when pastoral entertainments *(paysanneries)* were given at every opportunity."
>
> the *Gigue,* done by the ensemble, and again to quote Louis Horst, "the quickest and most hasty of all the pre-classic court forms." Shakespeare refers to it as "hot and hasty like a Scotch jigge."

Doris Humphrey took the qualities of these pre-classic forms and, in the idiom of the movement of the modern dance, choreographed a work which when experienced by students through reconstruction from a notated score gave them practically a first-hand contact with the style of one of the three "greats" who started the American modern dance, the other two being Martha Graham and Charles Weidman. The style of Doris Humphrey's choreography is the result of her own theoretical approach to dance movement. She conceived movement for the dancer's purpose to be basically one of equilibrium. This, to her, meant more than a mere business of keeping one's balance which is a muscular and structural problem. Falling and recovering is the very stuff of movement and it involves the whole scale of the body's reaction to gravity. Its implications for her effected the rhythm, the dynamics, and the design of movement. Miss Humphrey's theories have been a distinct addition to the body of knowledge of dance movement. Few people make such contributions. The present and succeeding generations of dancers do and will move and choreograph differently because of them. One can read about theories and that is good. They come to life, however, in the art product made possible through the reconstruction from the notated score.

The reconstruction of *Partita V* at the University led to bringing the dance up to performance pitch, "a getting it ready," so to speak, for the move from the studio to the theatre and a sharing of it with an audience. *Partita V* was presented at Gallaudet College, the world's only college for the deaf, in a program of dance which included presentations by American, Maryland, and Howard Universities as well as Gallaudet College. It was featured at the 1966 dance concert by George Washington's Dance Production Groups. Dance notation was the subject for a discussion and performance before 200 senior high school students from the Humanities Seminar of three Arlington County, Va., high schools.

A roll call of the students taking the notation course when it was given in 1965-66 included a candidate for the master's degree in drama at Catholic University. She took the course for credit toward her degree through the Washington, D.C., Consortium of Universities.

One student reported, "I try out the symbols for walking, jumping, running, leaping, hopping on my five- and seven-year-old daughters. It's a wonderful way to make them conscious of space-time concepts of movement. I plan to use it in teaching children."

The work being done in dance notation is a great beginning for a dance literature of works of dance. As one of the students said, "It's exciting to be in on it."

Still another student reported, "I like knowing that I can get, in addition to scores for choreographed dances, scores which include studies by Hanya Holm, techniques of Charles Weidman, a syllabus on ballet technique, jazz works by Alvin Ailey and by Peter Gennaro and folk dances. Even the 'twist' has been notated for the sake of posterity. Things are not so ephemeral any more. Hanya Holm has copyrighted the notated scores of her choreography which she did for the Broadway musical productions of *Kiss Me Kate* and *My Fair Lady*."

The notation course will be offered a second time during the fall and spring terms 1967-68. It will include an introduction to Laban's "Effort-Shape" theories and inferences of the implications of these theories for dance, acting, developmental research, geriatrics, psychology, anthropology, and physical therapy. A culmination project will again be the reconstruction of an outstanding choreographic work from the growing literature of notated choreography. This will be done under the direction of a guest-artist notator from the Dance Notation Bureau in collaboration with the teacher of the course.

Movement notation is a fast evolving profession in the field of dance. Performers in dance are now studying their roles from the dance score, as in drama and music, and come to rehearsals knowing their parts. Teachers of History of Dance supplement audio-visual material by actually presenting and having students not only read but work out excerpts of choreography taken from scores. Studies of ethnic dance representative of cultures all over the world can be made. Can one not get all this from film and photographs? One can get a suggestion of the style of a finished product and the general overall visual picture and staging or setting. The camera, however, does not record a composition but rather a performance complete with individual shortcomings and interpretations. A dance film is comparable to the phonographic recording of music. As John Martin says, "Nobody would advocate abolishing musical scores in favor of mechanical recordings."

The long view toward the future indicates that dance as an art cannot fail to profit by building up a literature of its own for study, for stylistic comparison and deduction, for cultural stability and continuity. Non-dance areas: computer science, biology, the behavioral sciences, the realm of sports, provide enormous potentials for use of the notating system. Finally, to quote John Martin again, "Notation has come of age just in time to save our own richly creative period from passing into the limbo of illiteracy. As Doris Humphrey remarked when she saw some of her own compositions on paper: 'Now these works are no longer legend; they are history.'"

16
THE ANALYSIS AND PRESERVATION
OF MOVEMENT: BENESH NOTATION

The other important system of notation today is Benesh Notation. Developed in England under Rudolf and Joan Benesh, this system has gained a world reputation because of its usefulness and the relative ease with which it is executed and read—especially in the ballet world. The system is more visual than Labanotation. It attempts to relate its symbols more to the visual realities of movement than to pure abstract symbolism.

It is too early to determine which system—Laban's or the Beneshes'—will be universally accepted, but it can be safely said that the Benesh system has made its greatest gains in ballet companies, while Labanotation has closer ties with the modern dance and is taught and used in many of the American and European institutions of higher learning where dance is a major field. As indicated by some recent dialogues in *Dance Magazine* on the benefits of each system, a contest seems to be developing. Basically, proponents of Benesh Notation maintain their system to be relatively quick, complete enough, and accurate, while the Labanotation people argue that a system that emphasizes speed must, by definition, lose accuracy and that Benesh Notation assumes that the reader has a thorough knowledge of ballet technique. It seems that most relevant to the argument is the question of whether the systems can and will be used. Both are gaining recognition; both deserve thorough study.

BENESH NOTATION AND CHOREOLOGY

FERNAU HALL

It is not difficult to invent a system of movement notation, and in fact a good many have been invented in the last few centuries. But it is a very different matter to invent a notation which is efficient in use—as efficient operationally as, say, the alphabet and music notation. The trouble is that the amount of information needed to give an accurate, detailed and unambiguous record, on two-dimensional paper, of the movements and salient positions of each part of the body in three dimensions of space and one of time,

From *Dance Scope*, III, No. 1 (Fall, 1966), 30-36. Copyright © 1966 by the National Dance Guild, Inc. Reprinted by permission.

is greater by at least two orders of magnitude than that needed to record speech and music. That is why the art of the dance had to develop for hundreds of years without the support of a generally utilized notation; the need was felt, very keenly, but the solutions proposed did not begin to tackle the problems; in fact it was only in recent decades, with the development of ergonomics, cybernetics and operational research, that it became possible even to take the measure of the problem.

Le Corbusier has said that "to ask the right questions is to get the right answers." When, in 1947, Rudolf Benesh was faced by his fiancée with a request that he invent a dance notation (which she found she needed for choreography) he asked himself the crucial question: What qualities must a dance notation have if it is to do its job under tough real-life conditions? The answers he found daunting, for they seemed to conflict with each other.

On the one hand such a notation must be complete, extremely accurate and universal, recording the finest details of position and movement of each part of the body, no matter what the technique in use (even no technique at all), and no matter how strange and original the choreography. This seemed to demand a great proliferation of symbols. At the same time, however, he saw that an efficient notation must be fast and economic (demanding a minimum of time and paper) and basically very simple (so that a full score recording of a large-scale work with many dancers moving in complex evolutions would still be easily legible). This clearly ruled out any proliferation of symbols.

He was helped in resolving this apparently insoluble dilemma by the fact that he had been trained both as a painter and a musician, and was able to draw on hundreds of years of development in both perspective drawing and music notation. At the same time he was passionately interested in the dance: his mother was a dancer, he liked above all to draw and paint dancers in action, and he was engaged to a dancer-choreographer; moreover, a strong bent for science had brought him in touch with the new ideas in ergonomics, cybernetics and operational research which were just then becoming part of the scientific *zeitgeist*. All the qualities of temperament and background were in fact crucial to his task.

Benesh saw quickly that the only way to resolve the fundamental notational dilemma, recording an astronomic quantity of information simply and economically, was to make the notation completely visual, using simple marks on a matrix; and he was happy to find that the five line staff of music notation provides an ideal matrix for the human body. In fact the five lines intersect the body at its major divisions—top of the head, shoulders, waist, knees and feet (Fig. 1). Moreover he knew that this staff is ergonomically sound, providing the eye with just the amount of guidance it needs: more lines would be confusing, fewer would not provide the necessary accuracy. And the use of this staff facilitates integration of movement and music: written horizontally, in measures, from left to right, the movements could easily be tied to the notes of music, or indeed written words and any other notation which conform to this natural movement of hand and eye.

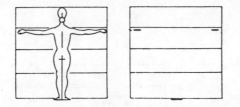

Figure 1. The five-line stave as a matrix for the human figure.

He imagined the dancer, seen from behind, standing against the five-line staff, as if it were a wall. On this five-line matrix he marked the positions occupied by hands and feet, using dashes. This gave a complete record of a pose, so long as the limbs remained in the plane of the "wall" (Fig. 1). To record positions of limbs extending away from the "wall," he used two further signs—a dot and a vertical stroke. These he used to mark the projection of the positions of hands and feet on the wall (Fig. 2). He now had three basic signs:

Level (with the body)   —
In front (of the body) |
Behind (the body)   •

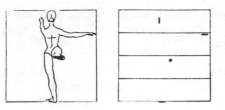

Figure 2. Arabesque, *with left arm extending to the front and right leg to the back.*

This gave a very precise record of the positions of the limbs if these were straight, to cope with bent limbs he used three other signs (derived from those for hands and feet) to mark positions of elbows and knees, as shown below (Fig. 3).

Level

In front

Behind

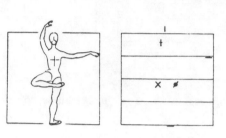

Figure 3. Attitude. *The left hand and elbow are held slightly in front of the body, so are marked with a vertical line. A tick is put through the dot for the left foot because this crosses over to the right-hand side of the square.*

As it stood, this notation represented a great advance on its predecessors; it had all the necessary qualities, resolving the apparently insoluble conflict between accuracy and universality on the one hand, and speed, economy and simplicity on the other. But Rudolf Benesh saw that it was still not sufficiently economic; it still could not make a record as simple and legible as the alphabet or music notation out of the fantastic complexity of movement in three dimensions. The trouble was that movement is continuous, not discrete like music and speech (which are made up of a limited number of notes and phonemes), and so needs a very large number of records of salient positions to cope with all its potential complexities.

Benesh then developed two further revolutionary innovations which gave the notation the necessary speed, economy and simplicity without any sacrifice of accuracy and universality. One was the use of movement lines; he traced the path of movement of a hand or foot between salient positions, thereby summarizing an infinite number of intermediate positions. Written plain these movement lines showed movement in the plane of the dancer's body; if the line moved outside this plane this was indicated by vertical dashes or dots on the line, a logical development from the signs for salient positions in front of and behind the "wall" (Fig. 4).

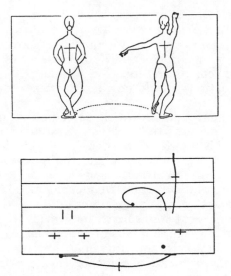

Figure 4. Sissonne. *The dancer jumps forward, extending her left arm up and to the front, to the side, and to the back and down, while her right arm goes in front and up. The curved line under the stave indicates a jump. Short lines crossing the movement lines of the arms and the jump line indicate a forward movement.*

His other innovation can best be understood as an application of the concept of redundancy, familiar in information theory (a branch of cybernetics): in fact he eliminated a great mass of redundancy from the record by showing positions *only when they changed* (Fig. 5). This did not eliminate all redundancy: a certain small amount was retained, enough to make possible checking for errors and their correction (as is often done with computer inputs and programs).

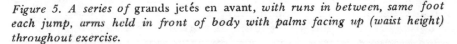

Figure 5. *A series of* grands jetés en avant, *with runs in between, same foot each jump, arms held in front of body with palms facing up (waist height) throughout exercise.*

Here, at last, was operationally efficient notation, incorporating the most rigorous ergonomic and cybernetic principles, and suited to the recording of all forms of human movement. To anyone familiar with older notations, it looks, at first glance, impossibly simple. One tends to feel that there must be a catch somewhere, nothing as simple as this could possibly cope with the infinite complexities of human movement. But there is no catch; this extreme simplicity of the basic system is in fact essential: otherwise a full score (recording all nuances of movement and location of a large number of dancers in simultaneous action) would be too complex and cumbersome to read.

A great deal of development work, spread over a number of years, was needed to perfect the system. Rudolf and Joan Benesh collaborated in this work, developing methods for recording, in precise detail and at each moment, the position of the head shoulders, sections of the trunk, hands, fingers, and feet, location, direction of facing and direction of movement of each dancer, the intricacies of contact and support in *pas de deux;* rhythm, phrasing, dynamics and quality of movement; movement of groups, showing stage patterns and also keeping tabs on individuals.

By this time they were moving in a new world, often finding themselves tackling problems of which even the existence had never before been realized because no notation had been developed in this rigorously operational way. In all of this development work they held fast to two basic principles: each new aspect had to be (a) completely visual and (b) logically consistent with all other parts of the system. (This preserved simplicity and economy, avoiding any proliferation of symbols.)

At this time Joan Benesh was a soloist in the Royal Ballet, and she tested each new development on a variety of choreographic works, making sure that it was efficient under tough professional conditions. (Fortunately the repertoire included a wide variety of styles and techniques of dancing, ranging from pure classicism to character dancing and choreography much influenced by modern dance.) This work culminated in the production of full scores of ballets which were just as succinct, legible, precise and complete as music scores, and like scores they could be used for reproduction of ballets with complete fidelity by choreologists (highly trained notators) who had never seen the originals. What was no less important, the choreography could be written down with speed and accuracy while the ballets were being rehearsed, without making special provision for the need of the choreologist.

This provided professional companies with something they badly needed—a really workable notation—and so, for the first time in the history of the dance, companies began to adopt a notation for use as an integral part of day-to-day administration. The savings in rehearsal time were very marked: instead of the interminable arguments about exactly what happened at certain points, the choreologist went smoothly ahead with the work of teaching the choreography, while the producer (i.e., the choreographer himself or a ballet-master) concentrated on production. At the same time the notation was taught to all dancers in the company school, to prepare for the time when parts could be handed out (as in music and drama).

The notation was first taken up by the Royal Ballet (both companies and both sections of the school); then it was adopted by another British company, the Ballet Rambert, and by a series of companies in a widening circle of other countries: the Turkish National Ballet, the National Ballet of Canada, the Zurich Opera Ballet, the Illinois Civic Ballet, the Württemberg State Ballet (Stuttgart), the Australian Ballet, the Royal Danish Ballet, the National Ballet of the Netherlands.

Directors of dance companies are invariably hard-headed, practical people; they have to be. In fact, the rapid international spread of the notation came about for the same reason as the spread of such inventions as penicillin and the jet engine: it worked. One factor which facilitated this spread was the technique developed by the Royal Ballet for "exporting" ballets from its repertoire to other companies by sending out a team consisting of a choreologist (with full score) and a producer. Working together, they staged ballets with a speed and precision which was overwhelmingly impressive to the directors of the recipient companies, who then invariably decided that they too must have a choreologist on their staff.

The precision in revivals brought about by the use of notation is of course very important artistically, preserving the choreography from the degeneration which is the norm when transmission depends on fallible human memories. Another major artistic gain derived from the use of notation is the great freedom which it gives the choreographer working with a choreologist at his elbow: he can push on as rapidly as he likes (without worrying about whether he or the dancers remember what has been set), and can try out as many variations as he likes, returning if he likes to an earlier variation which he has forgotten but which the choreologist has preserved in a notebook. Norman Morrice was so struck with the advantages of this method of composition when he choreographed *The Tribute* for the Royal Ballet that he swore he never wanted to work in any other way; and he was delighted, when he arrived in Israel to work with the Batsheva modern dance company early in 1966, to find in the company a highly trained notator (Amira Mayroz) who was able to give him the same support he had had in England.

Experience has shown that the notation is just as well suited to American modern dance as it is to ballet or any other style. The fact is that in the highly developed American modern dance of today, precision of line is just as important as it is in any other style, and the notation records it with the necessary precision, along with other essential details at each moment such as rhythm, phrasing, dynamics, and quality of movement. (Figure 6 shows typical American modern dance movements.)

Figure 6. Modern dance phrase of movement. It begins with the dancer lying prone, elbows on ground in front of body, top of body raised. Dancer lifts her right leg to a bent position behind the body and turns onto left side. The dancer completes a half-turn, placing right leg on ground with knee in front of chest in sitting position, left hand on floor. Dancer raises body and bends back, supported by feet and left hand, right hand extended above head. She sits again and returns to original position, going through the same positions in reverse order.

Because of the visual nature of the notation, it facilitates the analytical and comparative study of the dance, and this has brought into existence a new field of study: choreology, the scientific and aesthetic study of movement through notation. When working on the full score of *Petrushka,* for example, Joan Benesh discovered aspects of Fokine's choreography which had never been suspected before, because they could only emerge when the polychory (choreographic counterpoint) was spread out on a page in synchronism with the music.

The development of research in choreography was one of many things which made the formation of an Institute of Choreology essential. Others were the demand for choreologists; the necessity for establishing copyright in choreographic works; the need for a library of choreographic scores; the development of research work in fields such as educational movement, work study and neurology; and the awarding of diplomas.

The Institute of Choreology moved into its own premises in June 1965, and the following September saw the start of the first regular course for choreologists. These may be required to undertake a wide variety of work—including recording and reviving ballets and modern dances, research of all kinds and teaching at all levels—and so their training is correspondingly wide: theoretical and practical work in ballet, modern, character, ethnic (including Indian classical), historical, composition and mime, as well as studies in anatomy, kineseology, history of theatrical dance, and so on.

The Institute has a section concerned with educational dance and other forms of educational movement (such as gymnastics, athletics) in schools, training colleges and universities. It organizes notation training at all levels, coordinates research, and provides the necessary literature. Experience has shown that the same qualities which fit the notation for use under difficult conditions in the world of professional dance are of equally vital importance in the field of education. Because of its simplicity and visuality, the notation—taught as part of training in educational movement—strengthens space awareness, the kinesthetic sense and understanding of movement; because of its logical structure, it lends itself well to integration into a progressive scheme of work. As a scientific recording tool, not based on any system of classification or theory of movement, it provides precise neutral data which can then be used in any required way, including the experimental testing of hypotheses.

It is of great value in speeding up the mastery of skills because it provides a clear and simple analysis of movement patterns, no matter how complex these may be—something of great importance both in professional dance training and in educational movement of all kinds. When a dance movement is based on a specific technique, the notation is normally written in a way which assumes that the reader is familiar with the technique, leaving out things which such a reader would take for granted (e.g. a *plié* after a leap). But the notation can easily analyze a movement in the greatest detail, and this is of the utmost value in teaching technique—showing the proper sequence of movements, and also analyzing mistakes. Figure 7 shows a *glissade*—first written in the normal way, and then analyzed in detail.

Figure 7. Glissade. *(a) As normally written. (b) Written out in full detail showing technique of execution.*

The notation is also of great value in fostering creative work, whether this is based on a highly developed technique or uses non-formalized movements; in fact, composition training forms an essential part of notation training in every style of dance. Among other things it proves that the student really understands what he is doing. Because of the simplicity, economy and visuality of the notation, dancers find it easy and exciting to compose on paper; and it is also of great value to the teacher-choreographer working on large-scale projects.

Because music notation is not well suited to distinguishing between nuances of dance-rhythm, a special rhythm notation has been developed as part of the Benesh Notation, analyzing rhythm into beats and fractions of beats. Phrasing is shown as in music. Dynamics are shown as in music by a scale of six degrees of effort, ranging from fff to ppp. *Sf* shows the movement equivalent of *sforzando*—a movement with the quality of a punch or kick. Other qualities of movement are shown by adapting the immense international music vocabulary of Italian words: e.g. *allegro* (gay), *staccato* (quick, broken, stabbing), and so on.

Separate rhythms and phrases of different parts of the body can be shown—by selection of appropriate salient positions, and (if necessary) by writing, above the staff, phrase marks referring to specific parts of the body. In Indian classical dancing, for example, recording the independent rhythms of feet, hands, head and eyes is essential (Fig. 8).

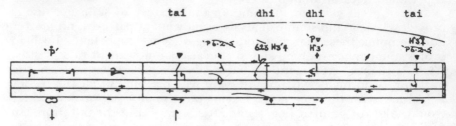

Figure 8. Part of Bharata Natyam Adavu, *showing movements of different parts of the body, including* mudras, *stamping of feet, and movement of arms, hands, eyes and fingers. The words at the top are* solukattu, *spoken syllables giving the rhythm.*

Because the notation is completely visual and objective, it can be used to reproduce even the most exotic images by someone who has not seen the originals, and so helps to establish bridges of communication from region to region and country to country. When the Bolshoi Ballet revived *Petrushka* a few years ago, most of the choreography was reconstituted from the memories of old dancers living in Russia, but there was one dance which could not be revived in this way—Petrushka's dance in his cell, which no one in Russia could remember because it is composed entirely of original dance-images rather than standard steps. The ballet-master appealed to London for help: a score of this dance was sent by the Institute of Choreology to Natalia Roslavleva, a correspondence student of the notation in Moscow; she "read" this to the ballet-master, who was thus able to complete his work.

17
THE ANALYSIS AND PRESERVATION
OF MOVEMENT: CHOROSCRIPT

Alwin Nikolais wrote the following article in 1948, after spending years developing his system. He had certain complaints about the system of Labanotation, although, since 1948 and the founding of the Dance Notation Bureau, Labanotation has been widely adopted. Benesh Notation also has acquired a large following. Nikolais' system is not a well-known one. However, the processes and problems through which one must go in order to translate the visual and dynamic elements of movement into a symbolic language that can later be understood in visual and dynamic terms are much the same for anyone attempting to notate movement.

A NEW METHOD OF DANCE NOTATION

ALWIN NIKOLAIS

The history of dance is tradition. There is virtually no written record or exact knowledge of what dance has been in the past. It has failed to store its accomplishments; its library is meagre, almost non-existent.

In music we have access through printed scores to the accumulated wealth of nearly every period from early counterpoint to present-day atonality. In painting thousands of galleries and museums provide storehouses for original works and good reproductions. But dance knows its past only from occasional sketches, paintings and photographs, statically showing one posture from a composition that originally consisted of hundreds, and from word pictures which are appreciative rather than technically precise. Each performance of a dance is a swan song, unrecorded and lost to posterity except in the undependable memory of those who participated or attended.

In recent years a good many motion pictures of dancing have been made. These, however, are no more a storing up of the actual creation than a phonograph record is a recording of a composition in and of itself; each is an account of a particular performance or interpretation. And the dance film suffers from the reduction of

From *Theatre Arts*, XXXII, No. 2 (February, 1948), 63-66.

three-dimensional movement to a two-dimensional area, much as recorded music suffers from the loss of auditory perspective. Thus any dance film frequently distorts the original action except when that action is specifically conceived in terms of the limitations of the cinema medium. The importance of the dance film to the enthusiast is obvious, but the professional dancer or student of dancing needs a detailed score of some kind, just as the conductor needs the score of a symphony.

By reducing a composition into the skeletal, impersonal form of a score, musical notation demands a new interpretation and a new vitality each time the work is read, a re-creation of the piece through the particular artistic concepts of the individual performer. Any attempt merely to reproduce the composition from an already interpreted source inevitably results in sterility. The intermediary interpretation rather than the original creation becomes the source of understanding. Like the musician, the dancer should be able to go to the original text in order to derive his personal interpretation from it. But he cannot, for no original is available to him.

Before the time of Isadora Duncan methods of notating dance were devised which served to record the limited and standardized dance movements of the day. None of these systems, however, was enlarged to serve the wide, free range of action introduced by Isadora. After her contributions had become a part of general dance vocabulary, any system, to be inclusive, had to account for the full movement possibilities of the human body. It was Rudolf Laban who made the most exhaustive analysis toward that end. Having devised a science of movement, he also devised a method of writing equally as inclusive. Although his system of notation gained more ground than any other, for several reasons it is used comparatively little. The symbols he chose are cumbersome; their inflexibility and bulk make a formidable picture. Furthermore the exponents of his system have not progressed along a path that provokes its widespread use. Yet Laban's research constituted a significant advance in that it looked upon movement as a science capable of being recorded. This science, given dramatic and dance life mainly by Mary Wigman in Europe and Hanya Holm in this country, has provided us with an analytic knowledge that assists greatly in any effort to make dance literate.

It is, of course, impossible to compensate for the neglect of centuries, but with our present knowledge there is no reason why we cannot use some system of writing in order to begin to create a library of choreographic records of our own day. To accomplish this we need to accept a workable system of notation and make it the standard equipment of every dancer, choreographer and dance educator, regardless of the style, school or idiom he favors. This article outlines such a system of dance notation. Used intelligently, the system can provide the means of starting a library for study and performance.

Choroscript, as the system is called, is a method of notating body action on the two-dimensional surface of a sheet of paper in a way which permits its reinterpretation into movement without distortion or loss of the choreographer's intention. The method makes use of symbols representing actions and attitudes of the human body. Much as a motion picture creates the illusion of motion by flashing quickly consecutive still pictures, so this notation in written symbols shows body movement arrested at similar fixed points. The nature of activity in time and space is indicated in such a way that all aspects of the three-dimensional action are laid out on a two-dimensional surface. In other words, Choroscript represents the freezing of action at certain points so selected and so indicated that the symbols, read consecutively, give a clear and complete account of the movement.

The action of the human body rests upon four basic factors, all of which are integral and inseparable: (1) the nature of the body as a moving entity; (2) the space in which the body exists and moves; (3) the time in which the movement takes place; (4) the dynamic energies behind the movement. Choroscript provides a pattern of these factors—a standardized measurement and analysis of the kinetic body and of space, time and dynamics, enabling everyone to derive a uniform meaning from the written symbols representing any action.

The body itself is capable of movement either in its entirety or in isolated components. It must first be analyzed in terms of its various movable units before the totality of its movement can be understood. These units fall into two main groups: the trunk (pelvis, chest, right shoulder and left shoulder) and the extremities (head, arms and legs, and their various minor parts). All these units, in varying degrees, are capable of both independent and coordinated action. Choroscript provides a line graph representing these units. Upon this graph symbols are written to designate the action or nonaction of the unit concerned.

Body action is predominantly axial in character because all body components are attached at joints. Because of their hinge-like or ball-and-socket structure these joints create centers or axles in relation to which or around which the various units move. Since the joints are not all alike, the movement possibilities are different in each case. Knee and elbow joints, for example, permit only hinge-like action, while shoulder and hip axles permit rotation as well. The spine provides a series of axles one upon another, allowing other variations of action. Upon this structural basis movement may be classified in three categories. In *peripheral* movement the body member attached at one end by its joint extends out from that center like the radius of an imaginary sphere, the outward end describing the circumference. *Rotary* movement is the action of the body or body unit rotating within its own space. *Locomotor* movement is a complete shift to a new space. Walking and running are locomotor movements by which the body achieves a new position in space. The chest, pelvis and head are also capable of shifting actions which, though limited, may properly be classified as locomotor.

The symbols representing these three kinds of action incorporate the time element. They are similar to musical notes, for the same system of time indication is used. These symbols, placed on the graph in the section representing a given body unit, thus indicate both the nature of the movement to be performed by the unit and the length of time the unit takes for the action.

It is also necessary to indicate where a given action is intended to occur, and to establish a space scale around the body so that we can determine the relation of the body to space. Because body movement is predominantly axial, maintaining a center in relation to which the body members move, space is symbolized in Choroscript by imaginary rays extending from the central point or axis. These rays act as definite spatial stations comparable to definite pitches in music. There are four groups of rays:

1) Eight horizontal rays emanate from the joint (or on the floor from the weight point in the case of full body actions)—forward, backward, sideward right, sideward left, diagonally forward right, diagonally forward left, diagonally backward right and diagonally backward left. These form a simple compass clarifying the horizontal directions.

2) From the center of this eight-pointed compass, a straight upward ray and a straight downward ray are added.

3) A slanting ray is placed exactly midway between each horizontal and straight upward ray, thus adding eight upward slanting rays. These duplicate the directions of the horizontal pattern but project obliquely upward instead of horizontally.

4) Similarly eight downward slanting rays are added between the horizontals and the straight downward ray.

These 26 rays define the basic spatial stations or directional itineraries. By means of them the definite location and direction of each action may be indicated.

The stem of each note symbol indicates the spatial aspect, according to the graphs shown in the lower section of the illustration. If the action is locomotor the stem is drawn from the center of the ball of the note. Rotary action takes its inception in one of the radial stations, and is shown as progressing clockwise or counterclockwise, with the stem of the note symbol curved accordingly. A designated spot on each body component serves as a pointer, for example, the tip of the elbow on the arm. A small written indicator shows the movement rotating to a certain "o'clock" point. The clock face is visualized as being at the end of the body unit, facing the joint. In all vertical rotations the clock face is on the floor with twelve o'clock forward.

When a composite note symbol is placed on the body graph the movement picture is completed, since the space in which the symbol occurs shows which body unit moves. Each symbol on the graph therefore indicates the time consumed in the movement, the nature of the movement (peripheral, rotary or locomotor) and the radial station to which, in which or through which the unit moves. The staff is read from the bottom upward. Actions occurring simultaneously are written horizontally in relation to one another.

The analysis of the remaining basic factor—dynamics—is complex. Certain dynamic elements are inherent in the body-space-time relationship. The bulk of the body unit in motion, together with the amount of space to be traveled in a specified period of time, dictates the degree of force needed for the accomplishment. Because in such actions the contributing factors are already written, separate dynamic indication would be superfluous. Many other force factors are possible, however, such as momentum and variations of resistance to or release from gravity.

The simplest exposition in Choroscript, and the one most used, is provided in the weight columns of the extremity staff. Here two special spaces permit a record of the activity of the feet as they hold or transfer weight in locomotion (standing, walking, running, leaping, jumping, skipping). The standard note symbol is used for this rather than its locomotor variation. The *pedal locomotion* example at the right side of the illustration shows how the note symbols denote such actions. One symbol not included is the musical rest written on the center line of the extremity staff to indicate air activity. In this context the rest shows the length of time the body is completely in air. Elsewhere rests in the space column simply denote a pause.

Many complexities of movement have been omitted from this introductory explanation. Among these are body orientation to performing space, touching, sliding and weight transfer to other body units. Choroscript provides for these and still other actions, deriving simple and appropriate graphic symbols from fundamental analysis.

The method of analyzing flexions and extensions in Choroscript permits many short cuts in recording. Symbol writing is reduced to a minimum, and complicated body positions are shown by two or three symbols.

Since Choroscript gives a written exposition of all the factors involved in the form of movement, it can also ultimately represent the form of an entire dance composition, not only in its larger features but also in all the necessary detail. The body in action must have discipline and logic in its activity in time and space, or dance creation is not possible. Dance notation must accurately represent this discipline and logic, for only a wholly logical system of movement analysis and writing can promote clear understanding of the language of the body. But neither Choroscript nor any other method of dance notation can be more than a skeletal indication of orderly bodily action. It requires interpretation, just as musical notation does. The performer must imbue it with his own spirit and understanding.

Movement notation is still in its infancy. Its vast potentialities have only begun to be explored. It is difficult to estimate what such a record can do for dance as an art. At the very least it can preserve the products of artistic creation for the enjoyment of future generations. And by clarifying the logical processes of composition it may help to assure the dance of a permanent position as a distinguished member of the family of the fine arts.

Irmgard Bartenieff is one of the world's foremost authorities on Effort Notation. Also developed by Rudolf Laban, the Effort system has had great influence not only in extending the bounds of movement analysis but also in the study of the psychophysical relationships of movement. This important development has increased the uses of movement notation beyond dance into other academic fields such as psychology and anthropology.

Effort is a very important part of dance movement. Thus, the notation of this element is essential to any complete system. Often, elements of dynamics have been welded into the choreography. The notation of effort helps us notate and re-create the essential style of a dance work.

Because of Effort analysis, dance teachers have been able to expand their verbal vocabulary to explain movements more precisely and to isolate component parts for study at an educational level.

EFFORT: AN INTRODUCTION

IRMGARD BARTENIEFF

Effort Notation is a latecomer in Laban's research into the nature of movement. The necessity for another system of graphic symbols arose after the system of Labanotation had crystallized; it became apparent that even after structural and rhythmical details clearly recorded the way in which a movement was performed, the quality of movement had not been fully captured. This became particularly important in studying exertion in work movement where small details in performance had to be differentiated and evaluated for effectiveness. It is the factors used in controlling the discharge of energy which makes for the greater or less effectiveness and makes for greater or lesser fatigue. The study of Effort, therefore, is one of recognizing and interpreting characteristic patterns of handling the movement energy components observable in the work activity of a person as well as in his general movement behavior.

When speaking with or observing people, one sees numerous small movements which have no special meaning until the study of Effort

Reprinted by permission of Dance Notation Bureau, Inc., Center for Movement Research and Analysis, New York City.

elements sensitizes one to its content. This "shadow" language may reinforce or contradict a verbal statement. To the average person this awareness can lead to better understanding of human behavior. It has in psychiatry and psychology aroused interest leading to research into non-verbal behavior of patients and therapy based on Effort-Shape analysis. In this field attempts have been made to formulate a system capable of analyzing the expressive contents of movement. However, none of these systems has survived because in their emphasis on the shape aspect of movement they have failed to include the discharging of energy which we call effort.

The graphic system used to record Effort-Shape observation was invented by Rudolf Laban and elaborated by his co-worker Warren Lamb in the late forties in England.* One quite often hears remarks about the complexity of this system. The complexity, however, is not one of elaborate use of symbols but one of accurate observation of the many extreme and subtle shades of movement expression. There are just 16 symbols to be memorized, eight contrasting Effort elements and eight contrasting Shape elements represented by varying combinations of horizontal, vertical, single and double diagonal lines. In addition, there are some indicators for part of the body, taken from the joint signs of Labanotation.

In our highly specialized industrial age, so many of the possible variations of Effort qualities in work movements have vanished out of our daily visual, tactile and kinesthetic experience that even the dancer's and physical educator's training today has in many cases put new emphasis on retraining this basic sensitivity to feeling and seeing shades of movement. Furthermore, this loss in physical sensitivity has to some degree also dulled the awareness of the non-verbal or movement communication that constantly accompanies verbal expression and interaction between people. Thus, if Effort-Shape is to be used for recording the dynamics of movement behavior and assessing the functional and expressive vocabulary of people, Effort training will have to include physical sensing of movement as well as visual observation.

Warren Lamb in London has worked as an industrial consultant for the past fifteen years using Effort-Shape assessment as the basis for managerial aptitude. His assessments have served not only to place the right man in the right job, but also to balance the various aptitudes of an entire executive staff.

Further research and observation of efficiency and fatigue amongst industrial workers showed that efficiency did not always depend on strength and flexibility or streamlining the number of actions used, but that a balanced use of efforts was essential to forestall fatigue and increase output. Thus too, a number of physical

*Ed.'s note: This was first described in Rudolf Laban and F. C. Lawrence, *Effort* (London: Macdonald & Evans, 1947).

problems occurring among dancers can often be attributed to an imbalance of Effort-Shape elements.

Effort-Shape has been developed in this country for use in research in anthropology and psychology and for practical use in dance therapy; it is being applied increasingly to supplement the training of dancers and actors, and for research in theatre.

FIVE

Dance and the Other Arts

The arts are related on several planes, from the philosophical to the practical. No artist can function in a vacuum; the stimuli received in our world will eventually affect the work of art, and all artists are bombarded in similar ways. Even when one of the disciplines attempts to limit its scope, the very process of creating a work of art depends on ideas that are highly similar for all the arts. More difficult than discussing how the arts relate is discussing their differences.

Each art has a material with which it is primarily concerned; it is in the shaping of that material that the similarity lies. The material of graphic or plastic art is pigment, clay, stone, etc.; the material of music is sound; the material of dance is movement. It is generally recognized that each art form is interested in the movement or the allusion of movement between its parts. Dance, therefore, shapes a very basic material for its exposition. Even though the process of shaping motion occurs to some extent in all the arts, a choreographer will, of necessity, have a deep understanding of the most fundamental material in the arts—motion.

It is interesting to note that a definition of rhythm is the flow of movement, or motion, which implies that we often use these words interchangeably. To say that a piece of art has no rhythm is sheer nonsense, because, if the piece had no concept of rhythm or motion it would not exist as art at all. This is not to say that motion cannot be implied or that a sense of stasis is not a legitimate possibility in any art work, but there must be consciousness of its degree of motion, or the piece has not had its most fundamental shaping.

A more complete description of rhythm might be "the pulsing flow of force in time or space." This definition brings out many broad concepts but really is no better a definition than "rhythm is motion." In the arts, there are very few "truths," so to speak. Things are not simply good or bad but are generally judged on the basis of taste and the awareness, or level of consciousness, of the artist. That is, the *kind* of rhythm cannot be judged, only that there is an *awareness* of the kind of rhythm. That motion flows is self-evident, but that the flow of force or energy occurs gives us the idea that there is a substance involved in rhythm. Without a material or object that flows with force or energy, the definition of rhythm is not complete. The idea that this object can flow in time at any energy level (or seem to flow, as points on a canvas) brings the notion of rhythm to all the arts, whether they deal in time, space, or both. Given that there must be a force, or energy emanation, from an object, rhythm is the most fundamental connection between the arts.

Design, pattern, or sequence is perhaps the next most fundamental notion in the arts, although it unfolds through the use of rhythm. It is certainly clear that a sculptor shapes his material, that a choreographer shapes his movements, that a composer shapes the melodic design. Then, the completed work can be said to have a total design, as well as design patterns within each of its parts. Elements of design can refer to the outlines of a portrait, the contours of a melody, or the sequence of movements. No artist can be oblivious to the demands of design.

It would be possible to compare hundreds of daily tasks common to all artists, possible to show stylistic trends running through all the arts, and certainly possible to show how artists must borrow even basic materials from the realm of another art form. Certainly, a painter focuses more of his time on painting than on writing poetry, but no rules exist that forbid a painter to write a poem in the center of a painting and proceed to develop the shapes of the letters to complete his work. Nothing is *verboten*.

Some artists, by the very nature of their work, must directly use either the talents or the materials of the other arts. For example, film-making relies very much on principles of the graphic arts and on music scores. Opera, as is signified by its very name, is a conglomeration of the arts, and dance, too, relies heavily on the crafts of many.

A dancer must also be a musician; that is, his body must be as musical when dancing as any instrument in an orchestra. A choreographer must have a command of music literature so broad that no music is overlooked for its potential use with dance. He must have a command of the musician's craft so great as to be able to speak to his collaborators with intelligence and to understand the marriage of the two arts that can take place. A choreographer must have a sense for, and skills in, basic design in order to communicate with costumers and set designers. He must know the art and craft of stage lighting in order to control the presentation of his work. A dancer and a choreographer must know acting and directing in order to portray dramatic circumstances when need be and to handle the productions of total theatre. Poetry and literature often provide stimuli for the choreographer's work. All the arts combine in theatre.

IS THE CREATIVE PROCESS SIMILAR IN THE ARTS?

That the creative personality is different from the normal temperament has been recognized for centuries. The creative process is dependent on the unconscious. The arts have been classified in a progression from the emotive arts to those using complex mental and reasoning processes, but the creative inspiration itself remains the same. However, the arts allow for a product that may be fanciful and irrational, while the creative work of an inventor does not have such license.

Artists in all disciplines go through similar processes in developing and giving form to their expression. The process is sometimes slow and labored, sometimes quick and inspired, but there is no evidence to show that one method is better than the next. Michael Fokine created *Les Sylphides* within one day, while other equally great pieces took months to create. But the creative act itself is the same in all the arts.

IS THE CREATIVE PROCESS SIMILAR IN THE ARTS?

JULIUS PORTNOY

The psychological process that takes place in the conception of a work of art is essentially the same, whether it be one art form or another. The creation of fine art, from its inception to the time of its expression, follows a definite behavior pattern. Artists vary in their mediums of expression because of differences in technical aptitudes. These techniques can to a certain degree be acquired and developed as part of a learning process. An artist's medium of expression is what Aristotle would call an accident rather than an attribute of his artistic nature. Artistic creativity cannot be taught or learned—it is basically an emotional phenomenon, even when appearances would seem to deny it. That artists are different from most men in nature and temperament was well known to the ancients and is commonly accepted now as well. But precisely why the artist creates and how is still, in part, unanswerable to this day.

The Greeks considered the artist to be a divinely inspired being who created his art in the same manner that the gods had fashioned

From the *Journal of Aesthetics and Art Criticism*, XIX, No. 2 (Winter, 1960), 191-96. By permission of the American Society for Aesthetics and the *Journal of Aesthetics and Art Criticism.*

the world, after the model of eternal archetypes. One of Homer's many fables is that artists are divinely inspired. Irrational poets rather than rational temple priests are the favorite mortals of the gods. Plato enhanced this Homeric myth with his own belief that the gods take away the minds of the poets and imbue them with a divine frenzy so that when they are in a state of ecstasy they are capable of prophecy and supernatural wisdom. All artists create by the grace of the gods but the gift of the bard is richer than that of any other artist. When Socrates went to the poets and asked them what they had said in their odes, he found that they were unable to give him a rational account of how they had come to create or what their creations meant. The gods had spoken through them, was their contention, and they were not in their right minds when creating. Socrates was poking fun at the poets, as he was at everyone else, but the implication is that the poets were more carried out of themselves when creating than other artists were. Had Socrates talked to artists in other fields about the meaning of their art he would have found that they were not very different from the poets, the favorites of the gods.

The Greeks were not the only ones to compare the artist to gods. The poet Browning likened the creative artist to the God of Christianity. Just as the God of Christendom created the world out of nothing, so the artist performs a lesser miracle in the process of creating something that had not existed before. The musician, like God Himself, transcends natural law—he exceeds even the bounds of mortal creators, Browning believes. That the finger of God has singled out the musician from all the rest is Browning's theme in *Abt Vogler,* but it is questionable whether the finger of God is any more pointed at the musician than it is at the poet and painter.

Kant's classification of the arts gives credence to the notion that because there is a difference between the arts there is also a dissimilarity in the creative process. By placing the more emotive arts at the bottom and the less emotive arts at the top of his hierarchy he gives the impression that art forms which are closer to reason and understanding, like poetry in comparison to music, are produced by a mental process that approaches a philosophic discipline. Hegel practically says the same thing. But Schopenhauer and Nietzsche turn the Kantian hierarchy of values upside down. For them, the emotive arts are higher in importance than those that are able to express concepts. The more irrational the artist is, the greater are his insights, precisely because he is freed from intellectual restraint. To Kant, art born of contemplation is superior to what is produced in the arts by emotive eruptions. To Schopenhauer and Nietzsche, art is an expression of emotion, the animal, the irrational in man, resisting civilization itself.

Our analytic psychologists have gathered an abundant amount of clinical evidence that artistic ideas have their origin in conflicts and repressions of which the artist is not even consciously aware. Rank tells us that the artist strives for immortal recognition by creating something that will live after him. Horace, Shakespeare, and Shelley give poetic expression to Rank's belief that the human craving for immortality is a driving force to create a monument of greater permanence than a fleeting life on earth. Adler is of the conviction that creating art is a means of compensating for organic deficiencies. Beethoven unconsciously compensated for a physical infirmity, Schumann for a mental one, and Chopin for an imaginary one, in musical creation, according to this theory. Freud maintains that creating art is a sublimating process for realizing unfulfilled desires in the form of phantasy. The colorful canvases of Van Gogh and Matisse are an escape from the drab world that most of us know. Jung agrees with Freud as to why artists create but he differs with Freud as to what their creations signify. He not only holds that the creation of art is more than personal wish-fulfillment but is an expression of the collective unconscious, a symbol of eternity expressed in modern form. In the extended line of a Berlioz theme, in the plaintive lament of a religious chant, the voice of the past and present is heard, not just the composer's alone. Bergler obverts the Freudian theory that art is wish-fulfillment with his own belief that the artist creates to hide his actual feelings from us; art is a defense mechanism, not wishful phantasy. The novels of Hardy, Proust and Gide are like protective cloaks behind which these authors hide their actual feelings and guilt. However varied these theories may be, one central theme yet binds them together. Artistic creation is the expression of the unconscious life of man which originates from conflicts and repressions. Artists may create for different reasons but they draw their strength from one source, the unconscious, and then follow a similar mental course in the process of nurturing and expressing their ideas.

It is doubtful whether any one of these theories fully explains why man creates and how. The belief of the analytic school that the unconscious, the storehouse of past experience, hope and frustration, is the never failing source of all art is expanded by Jung to include all human creativity. A song of praise, a poem of hate, a social novel, a religious drama—all have their origin in the unconscious forces, but so do other human activities which are not artistic in nature. Not all creation has its origin in conflicts and repressions either, as the analytic school is apt to stress, but if we peruse the history of art we find that those who have made a lasting contribution have been men who have been burdened with conflicts and tensions, conscious and unconscious in character.

Young people are rarely original, their artistic contribution is mostly technical. They have not lived long enough to experience deep hurts, become embittered and envious. Their psychical disturbances will bring forth a delightful Mozartian Singspiel at best.

Talented young people are virtuosi, master craftmen at an early age. First they must live before they can create.

The ability to create is not the artist's alone. The scientific process of invention and the artistic process of creation are alike. The end product of scientific and artistic creation differs, but the creative process is the same for each. Poincaré's description of the role of the unconscious, the incubation of an idea and the illumination that follows in giving birth to a new mathematical formula could also fit Van Gogh's explanation of the creative process. The scientist relies on knowledge to produce something practical. The artist converts his repressed emotions into something fanciful. The artist may produce sheer nonsense which is something that the scientist cannot afford to do. The psychological process that takes place in a mathematical discovery does not differ from the conception of a new way to depict nature in colors never known before. Working, waiting, and lamenting are common to scientist and artist alike, before their ideas are crystallized. To create is to produce something new, whether it be a concept of a state or a new system of musical sounds. In this paper we are concerned with those who create fine art.

Artists tend to be neurotic personalities. They cannot live with themselves or adjust to others. Even if others were to conform to them, they would not be able to accept the status quo for long. Should their neuroticism become overly severe, they would become unproductive altogether. They are cursed and at the same time blessed with a high degree of sensitivity. On the one hand, this sensitivity creates these very conflicts for them, and on the other hand, because they can resolve these conflicts in such a way that their art gives us a new vision of man, a novel interpretation of the world, they make a contribution to mankind. A man who produces one masterpiece and never another illustrates that the creation of art is not a continuous process. Where there is no strife and tension there is no art, in a pure sense. Scribes and hacks who produce continuously are like parasites living on the ideas of others. They are men of good stability and so they bring forth nothing novel in the arts.

Artists are dedicated people who become so absorbed in what they are doing that they may well shut themselves off from the rest of the world. Still an artist cannot live in isolation for too long a period of time, for then his art will become either symbolic of a vacuous life or it may develop into an overly refined type of expression. It would be as though the artist were saying: "I wish to be as detached from the public in my art as I am separated from the ordinary run of men in my private life."

The stimulus which brings artistic ideas into being may come in response to an inner need, at which time the artist is practically aglow with the fires of creation. At other times in his career he may have a contract to fulfill and the mood to create eludes him. Having learned from past experience that sitting and waiting for the muse will leave him with nothing produced, he will try to evoke a mood which is conducive to creation; that will come with much effort, if at all.

The intrinsic merit of a work of art will have little to do with one method or the other, whether it be spontaneous or labored to meet the terms of a contract. In the spontaneous method, ideas which have long lain dormant will rise to the surface, each part in its proper place, to produce a unified whole. In the more labored method the artist tries to evoke a mood conducive to creation by contemplation and even stimulation, culling from his unconscious fruitful ideas for his needs. In one case, emotion erupts and the work of art emerges, perfect and complete. In the other, emotion is appealed to in order to break through restraint.

Artists draw upon life experiences or imaginary ones for their creations. There is no other source to draw from. They create for the same purpose, in the same way, in terms of psychological relief and unconscious activity. Their methods vary, their personal peculiarities differ, but the creative mechanism is as determined as the flow of blood running through their veins. They have no more control over this process than they have over the direction of a dream. Their art begins in the unconscious, is mulled over, elaborated upon and then comes to the conscious level in response to a personal need, often involuntarily, or in response to some external stimulus. Because artists are controlled by forces they cannot understand, they are as mystified as we are as to how they come by their art and the meaning it conveys. Their descriptions of the creative process cannot be taken seriously. Like art, artists' diaries are written for posterity, a little less fanciful perhaps.

But when we find one dominant tone in all the explanations that artists have left us, however fanciful they may be, there is no brushing it aside. Their malady is the same, one need not be a wise physician to recognize their common symptoms, even when disguised. Consciously or unconsciously they gather material, comb the works of other artists for ideas. They are men of wonder who are impelled to search for what is beyond appearance itself. The material that they accumulate must be assimilated and become part of them. It is this phase of the process during which the artist is particularly restless, irritable, and vexed. Often, a gnawing sensation will not let him rest and then all of a sudden the whole world lights up and everything is clear and bright—with a minimum of effort it arrives, each part relevant, a thoroughly unified work. The same artist may sometimes work in a more arduous way. First he sketches and plans, repeats the process a thousand times, before a half-satisfying work will begin to emerge.

Artists have no qualms about using the forms of other arts when it suits their purpose. Maillol expresses a poem of life in a wistful statuette. Rodin expresses the concept of an architectural monument in the statue of a nude woman. Whitman writes a poem after the model of a musical symphony. Huxley plays one character off against another, in one of his novels, in the same fugal fashion that a Baroque master planned a contrapuntal score. Liszt uses music to create a poetic image. Strauss depicts, as a story teller would, a day of married bliss at one time in his life.

Ancient bards were both poets and musicians; there was no separation between them that far back in time. *Jongleurs* and *trouvères* perpetuated this tradition into the late Middle Ages of Western man. During the Renaissance there were some most exceptional artists who created in several fields without any variance in their creative process. Michelangelo was painter, architect, sculptor, and poet all in one. Leonardo's inventive disposition was just as fertile in scientific endeavors as it was in art itself. In more recent times, Wagner merged practically all the arts into his music drama, as though to belie any lingering belief that there is a difference in the creative process between one art form and another. Picasso works in ceramics, oils, and drawings with a high degree of originality appearing in all three. Modigliani's preoccupation with primitive forms appears in both his paintings and his sculpture. The same idea comes through, be it in stone or in canvas. Eliot's artistic insights are just as evident in his poems as they are in his plays. The material that an artist deals with may be rigid or malleable so that one kind of material may lend itself more easily to the expression of an idea than another. It is also true that artistic ideas that are expressible in one medium can be expressed in another; not as well perhaps, but expressible nevertheless. The psychological mechanism that is involved in creation is the same whatever material the artist may use. Artists resemble the original gods of Greece. Each god created like every other god, but one produced light, another darkness, one love, another war. The only difference is that the gods fashioned the world after eternal archetypes while artists draw their inspiration from a repository of repressed emotion and guilt. Creation is a gift that artists share together, as the gods before them did, and like the gods they contribute according to their specific interests to the making of a new world.

The evidence presented in this paper that artists create alike is surely not conclusive. If it serves as a reminder, however, that in our penchant for specialties and categories we are apt to lose sight of the common denominator in discussing the creative personality, then this paper has served a purpose. In essence, a creative experience may be spontaneous, like a crystallized witticism, condensed and apt for the occasion. It may be labored and drawn out as in the case of a man who works unceasingly until he achieves an effect that pleases him, although he did not know what he wanted or expected before he began his project. There is no evidence that one method has produced art of greater merit than the other.

The source of the artist's creativity has its origin in conflicts and tensions and a host of half-forgotten memories, painful and pleasant alike. It is from this past experience, so much of which has become latent and dormant over the years, that the artist primarily draws his ideas, whatever be his method. Nature's inexorable laws for begetting a work of art are the same for poet, painter, and musician. It is we who devise arbitrary classifications and separate one from the other.

Many choreographers in both ballet and modern dance rely heavily on blending the materials and ideas of other artists into choreographic works. Ballet and painting have been linked for centuries, and early 20th-century ballet, in particular, brought many outstanding painters to great achievement.

This alliance is dwindling in professional dance, partly because of a dance-alone-is-important philosophy and partly because of economic exigencies. But dance, in order to be less a recital form and more a theatre form, must recognize the importance of lighting design, the possibilities for settings and costumes, and the correlation of music. Even when a designer is not available or cannot be afforded, the choreographer should be responsible for the interplay of the theatre arts when building a piece.

MODERN ART AND THE BALLET:
THE TREND IS TOWARD SEPARATION

EMILY GENAUER

List the artists who have been responsible for the settings and costumes of modern ballet and you have a Who's Who of modern art. Picasso, Matisse, Dali, Rouault, Chagall, Léger, Braque, Dufy, Utrillo, Juan Gris, and Marie Laurencin, all would be included. It is no accident that the rise of the one art form coincides with the rise of the other. It is in large part due to the glamor, color, and excitement with which modern art invested it that ballet, which traditionally had been the private amusement of aristocrats, became during the past two or three decades the delight of millions. It is also true that modern art won new converts for itself when an audience, which normally would have little or no personal contact with the new art to be seen then mostly in small galleries, came under the spell of its brilliant fantasy and dazzling color at public ballet performances.

Within the past few years, however, a curious and confounding situation has developed. Despite the fact that modern ballet and modern art have each won for themselves enormous audiences, and

From *Theatre Arts*, XXXV, No. 10 (October, 1951), 16-17.

that ballet particularly owes much of its popularity to the resplendent contribution made to it by top modern painters, the current trend in ballet production is plainly away from the use of distinguished artists as designers of dance settings and costumes. Many of the new ballets are being presented without benefit of settings at all. Others are being mounted by professional scenic designers rather than by fine painters.

There are several obvious explanations for this—but no one of them alone tells the whole story. The first that comes to mind, of course, is economic. The cost of theatrical productions of any kind has risen fabulously within recent years. That of producing a ballet has risen even higher. Sets and costumes are far more elaborate and expensive, and casts are many times larger than one will find in any but the most lavish musical show. Yet a new ballet production is just one more item added to a company's repertoire for presentation only a few times each week. It is that much more baggage to be transported from city to city along with the company's accumulation of elaborate costumes and sets. It necessitates that many more work hours from local stagehands who must erect the sets.

George Balanchine, artistic director of the New York City Ballet Company, and probably the most important choreographer in the country today, estimates that an artist receives about $2,000 per scene sketch, and that it costs about $5,000 to execute it (and many ballets use more than one set); that costume sketches run about $25 each and often as high as $300 for execution. A fair estimate of the cost of mounting any new production, Mr. Balanchine says, is around $15,000, depending, of course, on the number of sets and costumes required. To remount the four-act *Sleeping Beauty* today, he adds, would run around $100,000. With the present financial setup of most companies, he says, that leaves a choice of doing no new ballets at all, or presenting ballets against a plain, painted back-cloth, relying on imaginative lighting to create mood and atmosphere and help project the dancers' movements effectively.

As an inevitable result, choreographers of integrity have lately been devising ballets which do not suffer for lack of settings and may in fact even profit by their absence. Which brings us to the second partial explanation of the new drift away from ballet décor. Mr. Balanchine believes that a ringing virtue has been made of economic necessity. Pure dance, he holds, does not need the crutch offered by elaborate scenery and costumes. Certain ballets, which tell a story or project merely a literary idea or mood, may require décor which immediately fixes time and place for the audience. In others even a ballerina's tutu, he insists, can be a distraction destroying the purity of the dancer's body line. Increasingly he feels that ballets are getting away from literary content, that dance movement itself has become more expressive than reproductive or pantomimic and that its effectiveness in this regard may be impeded by décor and costumes.

Mr. Balanchine goes further. Diaghilev, of course, was alone responsible for the rebirth of ballet in the years from 1909 until his death in 1929. It was his idea to transform ballet from the circumscribed, inert, traditional formula completely isolated from contemporary artistic, musical and intellectual developments which it had become by the end of the nineteenth century, to an integrated expression in which dance, painting and music were fused. But Mr. Balanchine insists that the great Diaghilev actually didn't like dance very much. Moreover, he had very few good dancers to work with, since technical standards have risen enormously since his time. He turned to the great modern artists and composers of Paris and persuaded them to create ballet décor and music for him because he needed them to support his balletically thin productions, to lend their brilliant vitality to performances which could not stand alone. The result was that while the productions profited enormously in visual and aural interest, they also lost what Mr. Balanchine feels was their chief justification, the expression of emotional, intellectual or formal idea through dance itself.

It is a provocative but debatable point of view. There are other dancers and choreographers, no less pure of motive than Mr. Balanchine, no less dedicated to the ideal of expressive dance per se, who disagree with him. Years ago Ruth St. Denis began using scarves and skirts importantly in her dances not, she once told dance critic Walter Terry, because they "look pretty," nor even because the dramatic aspects of her dance characterizations which involved regional and historical associations required them. She used them because a swinging skirt, she said, can be an extension of the curve of a torso in space. She held that it is narrow and limiting of a dancer or choreographer to overlook any of the accouterments of the theatre in the successful projection and realization of a total concept.

Martha Graham, high priestess of pure form and most uncompromising of all dancers where any easy seduction of the public is concerned, has used stage properties in most of her performances since 1933. For the most part they have been done by the noted American sculptor, Isamu Noguchi. Generally they have consisted of unidentifiable constructions which are placed around the stage to establish spatial relationships, and/or serve symbolic purpose. In her famous _Errand into the Maze,_ for example, Miss Graham uses an all but barren stage with only a backdrop painted with three converging lines to imply enclosure. The single physical object on the stage is one large Noguchi form vaguely shaped like a wishbone. Miss Graham, in her dance, climbs over the piece, dances around and with it, establishes a kind of emotional and formal traffic with it. As the dance progresses it becomes apparent that the curtain and the Noguchi form symbolize the threshold of consciousness through which the dancer attempts to reach her subconscious and root out fear. Miss Graham says that her movements take on special meaning in relationship to stage forms. As a matter of fact, she and Noguchi only discuss general ideas, never specific ones. She rarely sees his objects until they are finished and the first performance begins. Then she improvises around them. In this way the "sets" become an integral part of her dance design.

Lincoln Kirstein, general director of the New York City Ballet Company, and himself long a connoisseur and patron of modern art, agrees that the "art artist" (as opposed to the commercial designer) can indeed make a great contribution to ballet. He has himself commissioned many first-rate American artists to execute ballet designs. His own conviction is, however, that such a program is not only enormously expensive but also dangerous. Most easel painters, he insists, are egomaniacs. They visualize a ballet as a one-man art show. They conceive their designs as paintings to be executed on a thirty-by-forty-foot canvas to be observed for an extended period by a captive audience. They refuse to recognize that ballet décor can never be more than one element in an integrated whole incorporating dance, music and décor, with the dance always of paramount importance, and the rest serving merely as accessories. They will not understand, he insists, that a ballet set is a failure if it does not function; that it has no validity except in relationship to the dancers who must move before it. He maintains that even the contributions of the great modern artists commissioned by Diaghilev showed flagrant disregard of dance requirements and stage mechanics. While they succeeded in investing the ballets with that magnificent pictorial interest and visual appeal which were largely responsible for gaining them a wide popular audience, they were at the same time steadily undermining the essential basis of ballet, which is pure dance.

For this reason, says Mr. Kirstein, although he would prefer to employ first-rate easel painters on his ballet productions because of their flair and imagination, he finds that more and more he must turn to professional scenic designers who make up in the functionalism and modest practicability of their concepts what they may lack in imaginative brilliance.

Actually Mr. Kirstein's position, while as valid as Mr. Balanchine's, is also not unassailable. Noguchi is one example of an artist completely cognizant of the totality of a dance projection. There have been many others, among them Matisse, who designed the settings and costumes for *Rouge et Noir,* a ballet choreographed to Shostakovich's first symphony; Tchelitchew, whose successful ballets are too numerous to name; Rouault, who did the sets for *The Prodigal Son;* Chagall, whose originally overpowering backdrops for *Firebird* proved to be brilliantly functional when eventually they received proper lighting; and Rico Lebrun, who handsomely mounted a Spanish ballet for Ballet Theatre only last season.

One of the most interesting of dance-conscious modern painters is Joan Junyer, who once executed a ballet for Mr. Kirstein called

Minotaur. Mr. Junyer not only does not approach the ballet as an art museum but goes so far as to make his set do everything short of actually dance itself. Mr. Junyer rejects backdrops painted on flats, drops and wings with traditional picture perspective. He conceives of dancers not making their entrances and exits from the wings in traditional fashion but appearing from and vanishing into the depths of various shapes and panels projecting onto the stage. Even their costumes are tights broken into various color areas and patterns so conceived that the actual volume of the body appears to change as the dancers move about in different positions.

When a designer goes that far, however, both Mr. Balanchine and Mr. Kirstein agree, he is taking on the prerogative of a choreographer. As Mr. Balanchine says, "Mr. Junyer designs the dance as well as the costumes. All you have left to do is pour the dancers into them."

But there are those who, even as they banish from ballet the artist who allegedly refuses to subordinate his art to its total expressive concept, are quick to defend his reluctance to sacrifice his individuality or integrity. Perhaps they are *too* quick. In their anxiety to preserve the easel painter's purity, they seem to overlook the fact that egomania is not synonymous with integrity. Artists, until the nineteenth century, did the greater part of their work on "order," as it were. They decorated great churches and painted handsome portraits and thereby gave us the world's most precious masterpieces. In executing practically all of them they had constantly to meet physical conditions imposed by a work's purpose and ultimate site, and psychological conditions presented by the authority, importance or ego of their sitters.

Hundreds of fine artists of today have shown themselves no less willing to meet specific conditions than the masters of the past. They do not feel that any loss of integrity is thereby involved.

When Ballet Theatre was organized eleven years ago, its director, Richard Pleasant, inaugurated as part of his project a plan to train prospective scene designers among American easel painters by acquainting them with what their predecessors or European contemporaries had done, and familiarizing them with what ballet looked like both in rehearsal hall and on the stage. With this in mind he invited them to attend performances at the ballet theatre house. They responded with whole-hearted enthusiasm. Artists like Waldo Peirce, Reginald Marsh, Yasuo Kuniyoshi, Grant Wood, and Jon Corbino gave endless time and study to the problem, executing without thought of payment not only ballet painting but possible ballet décors.

Among the American artists who have been given ballet assignments is Raymond Breinin, one of the most respected and imaginative of our younger painters. He did the décor for *Undertow,* to choreography by Antony Tudor. His fee for conceiving and designing both the settings and the costumes, and also executing the major part of the final full-size backdrops, was, he says, "only a small fraction of what was paid to the costumer for very ably executing my costume designs." Despite the fact that "I almost lost my poverty-stricken shirt," and notwithstanding the many heart-breaking and nerve-wracking aspects of the job, he declares, "I have always had a weakness in my heart for the theatrical medium and my *Undertow* venture was somewhat like an answer to a prayer." He would, furthermore, leap at the chance to do another ballet.

One of the reasons why, he admits, is that because of his work on *Undertow,* he already is a member of United Scenic Artists.

Which brings us to the last of the many explanations offered as to why art and ballet appear to be parting company. Before he can execute a ballet setting or costumes, an easel painter has to be admitted to the scenic artists' union. (European décors may be imported along with a complete production as an act of "cultural exchange" between nations.) The financial hurdle is considerable—a $500 initiation fee, regular and fairly high dues, and occasional assessments. These, however, can conceivably be managed.

Money is not the whole story, however. A two-day written and oral exhibition must be passed by all applicants, an examination covering questions as to the characteristics of various types of period furniture and architecture and requiring the solution of hypothetical technical problems and the completion of working blueprints and mechanical drawings. These are requirements which, frankly, only a few easel painters, even those of greatest stature, are prepared to meet, although any architectural student probably could fill them readily.

Horace Bay, president of United Scenic Artists, holds that the test is necessary if scenic designers are to protect the standards of their profession. He insists that it works no hardship on artists possessed of "those technical craft standards of lighting, drafting and shop supervision which should be a prerequisite of theatre designers." Easel painters may have great imagination and style, he admits, but very few of them are equipped to turn out in the limited time normally allowed them by a producer the complete working drawings that are necessary before stage construction can begin. These, he maintains, experience has proven to be of greater value to a producer than imaginative genius.

This, then, is the situation. Ballet impresarios are tending either to dispense with sets or, more in sorrow than in anger, they insist, to commission them from professional designers. And an art form which won its greatest acceptance, everyone admits, chiefly through the visual splendor contributed to it by the greatest of modern artists, is being deprived of this splendor to the point of impoverishment. Perhaps the public has indeed been "educated" to the austere virtues of pure form to the point where it feels that even a starched tutu distracts from its joy in a dancer's motion or interferes with reception of that motion's "message." I doubt it. Most Americans want their dancing to be theatre, in all its richness and complexity, its evocative magic and exaltation. They go to ballet not to find the exposition of a single and pure ideal, but for a total visual and aural experience. American painting today can contribute greatly to that experience.

Helen Tamiris was one of the most outspoken, dynamic, and revolutionary of the modern dance pioneers. She worked in theatre for years, and, besides having a great regard for the dramatic gesture in dance, she also believed that dance, or the art of movement, could strengthen a playwright's and a director's intentions.

Although she mentions musicals as projecting an increased synthesis of acting and dance, she regards the serious theatre as the ultimate direction for this synthesis. Time has proved her correct; we can now see many plays, popular and classical, that rely on the art of movement as an integral part. It used to be an unwritten but practiced rule that a character dancing in a dramatic play or musical was in a state of drugged unconsciousness or, at least, drowsiness. Tamiris' idea of the integrated theatre leans more toward the envelopment of dance by the drama, although it has reverse ramifications.

INTERVIEW

HELEN TAMIRIS

Reporter: When I go to a show I go to have a good time.

Choreographer: Do you take having a good time seriously?

Reporter: If you mean by "seriously" that I want my money back if I don't enjoy myself, sure I take it seriously.

Choreographer: Score one for you! Too bad you can't get your money back, but I didn't mean "seriously" that way. I meant . . .

Reporter: You mean, I am not to be satisfied with just enjoyment, I must look for the higher things in the theatre.

Choreographer: No! No! I'm not making myself clear. Of course you must enjoy yourself. Part of my job as a choreographer is to see that you do. There wouldn't be much theatre left if you didn't. But seriously I . . .

Reporter: I know you choreographers have made changes in the dancing these past few years, not the old line-up with a kick and a one-two-three. The whole style of dance has changed. In many instances the plot is actually told by means of dance, but now what?

Choreographer: I was going to ask—Has the new approach to dance,

From *Theatre Arts*, XXXIV, No. 9 (September, 1950), 50-93.

the use of ballet and creative movement, lessened your enjoyment in the theatre?

Reporter: No, not at all—if you put it that way. But I don't think about "approaches" and "new dance" or anything like that when I'm watching a show.

Choreographer: Of course you don't, and shouldn't. But analyzing the changes and discussing the developments that can still be made is what I mean by taking it seriously.

Reporter. Score one for you this time! Go on.

Choreographer: Don't you realize that a minor revolution is taking place in the theatre? We take for granted music and dance in a musical. That's what musical comedy is. But our legitimate playwrights are beginning to see that they can be as eloquent with the use of music and movement as with the spoken word.

Reporter: Now just a moment! Musical comedy is one thing and legitimate theatre is another . . .

Choreographer: Hold that! I think the wall that separates them is a false one and is breaking down. Slowly, but breaking down. Take Arthur Miller's *Death of a Salesman*. The music is in no way incidental and background. It at times carries the burden of the plot. Remember that terrifying moment—the climax. As the two sons and the mother stand frozen and speechless, the wail of a few musical instruments projects with all its horror the suicide of Willy Loman.

Reporter: Yes, that's true—and you mean like Tennessee Williams. He uses music in *Streetcar* . . .

Choreographer: Yes, very beautifully, but there it is primarily atmospheric. There's a difference.

Reporter: But why are you interested in music? You are a dancer—I mean—choreographer.

Choreographer: Using music imaginatively in a legitimate play is the beginning of that revolution I was talking about. Once in a rare while a playwright will use movement—the dance. But what is interesting and disconcerting at the same time is that on most of these occasions it is brought on by his characters having hallucinations or dreams. The implication is plain. From Ibsen to Hellman everybody is fully dressed and in his right mind. The playwright assumes that "real" people in their sane minds do not dance.

Reporter: Well, except for parties and celebrations people don't dance in real life.

Choreographer: Do you think a play can project the truth and excitement of real life by simply photographic means—naturalism? You admitted the excitement of adding music to legitimate plays. When did you in real life hear a family quarrel accompanied by oboes and clarinets?

Reporter: Score two for you! Now let's get back to dance, or movement as you call it, but let me get all this straightened out before you answer. What you are saying is that the playwright must not only be a writer but a composer and choreographer as well.

Choreographer: Now that is going a bit too far, but in essence that's the idea. However, we do know that few people are endowed with all these talents and crafts, but where music has been used creatively and also in the musical comedy field, specialists are called in. But the writer when working should ask himself: "What will carry my story forward most vividly, honestly, and excitingly—music, dance, speech, or silence?" I believe that once the playwright is consistent with this approach, an extension of the magic of the theatre is opened up. I think the playwright who doesn't recognize this is depriving himself of a wider means of communication. The best musicals are full of important lessons. The writers of these have learned much from the legitimate playwrights in relation to development of plot and characterization, and thereby found the key to the integration of all theatrical elements. So, a good musical is all of a piece, with no interpolations of specialties, imitations, or girls for the sake of girls.

It is now time for the playwrights to recognize that neither subject matter nor the fact that it is tragedy, comedy, satire or farce should prevent him from utilizing any and all media of expression, and particularly one of the most eloquent, the . . .

Reporter: Dance is what you were going to say?

Choreographer: Naturally, the Dance.

USING MOVEMENT FOR THEATRE

Movement is an elemental material of theatre. After the basic techniques of dramatic interpretation, we find the foremost concern of the actor and director is coping with the action in a play. Action implies movement. When movement in a dramatic production is neglected or not shaped, the play remains a read script.

Movement is central to all the arts, but to the dancer and actor the control of expressive gesture is of prime importance to the very act of theatre and to the communication of ideas. Carol Egan alludes to the belief that a major weakness of the American theatre comes from a lack of systematic experience in movement. She feels movement should be integrated into the training of actors and directors in proper proportion to the importance of movement in the theatre experience.

Just as training and experience in the theatre arts and crafts such as acting, directing, lighting, design, and costuming are necessities for the accomplished dance artist, so dance experiences are necessary for the actor. Carol Egan talks about a truly integrated theatre, which is not merely a dream in many parts of the world. The article looks to a special kind of integrated theatre, rather than to the popular concepts embodied in most Broadway and television plays.

MOVEMENT AND THE THEATRE

CAROL EGAN

It is often said that contemporary America is the world leader in many different fields: in technology, the sciences, medicine, and many of the fine arts. Modern painting, music, and dance are certainly flourishing in centers such as New York, San Francisco, Chicago, Los Angeles, and on many university campuses throughout the nation. Unfortunately, the same cannot be said of the American theatre. Several years ago, in the 1950s, with the birth of off-Broadway and regional repertory theatres, the situation seemed more hopeful. For a time it actually looked as though the American theatre would join the other arts in the number and quality of experiments being produced. Within a short time, however, many promising beginnings returned to a safer ground, the traditional and more commercial theatre.

Those of us concerned who are with the theatre find ourselves presently in a rather awkward situation. We are forced to turn to Europe for artistic inspiration. Oddly enough, the one American experimental theatre that may be included among the world's finest has existed in self-imposed exile for several years. I am speaking, of course, of the Living Theatre, whose temporary "homes" of late have included West Berlin, Paris, and other European cities. For the true theatre-lover, the foremost groups of today are to be found scattered around the world. They include the Berliner Ensemble and the Deutsches Theater in East Berlin, the Teatr Laboratorium of Grotowski in Poland, the Piccolo Teatro of Milan, the Living Theatre, and the English groups—Royal Shakespeare, Joan Littlewood's company, and others. The American theatre has almost nothing to offer of an equal caliber.

There is obviously something missing, something essential our theatre continues to overlook. This would certainly include a sense of dedication to the art rather than to success, a willingness to take a chance and perhaps fail, and a search for the original magic in theatre. This last item refers to a return to the more physical and vocal theatre, one based less on text and more on the movements, gestures, and sounds of the actors. Since my field is dance, I shall discuss in more detail the role movement should play in the theatre.

To what extent must today's young actor train his body, as well as his voice and emotions? It is my belief that no actor or actress will achieve greatness without attaining complete control over the physical disciplines. In all great performances throughout the ages, the movement, combined with the text, has distinguished the great actor from the merely proficient. Can anyone who has seen Charlie Chaplin's films deny this? Of course, one may argue that Chaplin was a rare phenomenon—one of the world's finest mimes. I agree. *But,* let us look for a moment at some contemporary theatre ensembles for a brief comparison.

The Berliner Ensemble in East Berlin requires several years' training in various movement techniques for all of its actors. The very roles they must portray necessitate a thorough knowledge of, at the very least, pantomime and acrobatics. When Mackie Messer, as played by Wolf Kaiser, paces his jail cell in impatience, he displays all the ferocity and energy of a tiger. In Brecht's *Coriolan,* this same actor, as Coriolanus' friend Menenius Agrippa, accompanies the victorious warrior back to Rome with the bearing of a true nobleman. Another example from the same company is Ekkahard Schall's brilliant characterization in the role of Arturo Ui. As Ui rises from a small-time gangster to a figure of overwhelming strength and authority, the actor must grow accordingly. One of the most remarkable scenes in the play takes place when the insecure Ui attempts to learn public speaking from an old-time Shakespearean actor. The small, nervous, pidgeon-toed gangster must copy the broad, somewhat theatrical gestures and stances of the pompous actor as the latter recites Antonius' famous speech to the Roman public. It is clear that the problems here are twofold: Ui must retain his natural awkwardness while attempting to superimpose an elegance and grandeur alien to him. While exhibiting the twitches and contortions of an uncontrolled body, the actor must in reality coordinate the smallest, subtlest movements. How many American actors could duplicate the ingenious portrayal that Schall brings to this difficult scene?

The Teatr Laboratorium of Jerzy Grotowski in Wroclaw, Poland, emphasizes the importance of movement, perhaps more than any ensemble in existence today. For this, as for many of his other beliefs, Grotowski is much indebted to the "Theatre of Cruelty" of Antonin Artaud. However, Grotowski calls his own a "poor theatre." The term refers to his attempts to purify the modern theatre, to rid it of the extraneous elements that modern audiences and actors alike have come to regard as necessary to a theatrical presentation. Thus, he relies almost totally upon the barest necessities, that is, the actor and the spectator. Costumes, sets, make-up, lighting effects, incidental music or sounds are, if not completely eliminated, at least reduced to the barest minimum. What is left? The two elements upon which every theatre depends, and without which no theatre could exist—the performer and the spectator. Since the actor is not allowed to depend on technology to help him create his role, he has only himself—his body and voice. He is, so to speak, theatrically stripped. Obviously, this situation demands heightened awareness and discipline from the actor. Grotowski's company members are superbly trained in preparation for this task. Their training includes intensive work in mime, acrobatics, yoga, and, for the voice, special techniques used in the Chinese theatre. During the Teatr Laboratorium's production of *The Constant Prince,* a five-minute monologue is delivered by the Prince (as portrayed by Ryszard Cieslak), in the course of which he very gradually sinks to his knees from an upright position, flagellating himself all the while with a shirt. Let any reader who thinks this to be simple attempt it himself: a hinge to the knees lasting five minutes, chanting all the while, and systematically flaying oneself throughout the exercise! The actors have also developed a unique method of changing their facial characteristics without using make-up. It is based upon a special yoga technique for controlling the individual muscles of the face. With mastery of this technique, the actor can create a "mask" without relying upon Max Factor.

It is not only in Germany and Poland, however, that one finds the movement-oriented actor. Performances by the Piccolo Teatro of Milan are as perfect choreographically as they are theatrically. The actors seem literally to dance their roles. Has one ever seen Sir Laurence Olivier take a "false step"? Every nuance of his gestures gives evidence of years of discipline and training. Could Vanessa Redgrave have danced in the role of Isadora Duncan without a fundamental background in the art of movement?

In most European theatres and drama schools, movement is considered basic to the actor's training. To a great extent, this is due to the system of academies found there. For the American actor, the road is a much more difficult one. The American musical has produced a rare breed of performer, the combination actor-singer-dancer, for which we are admired throughout the world. In *West Side Story,* for instance, most of the roles must be cast with well-trained dancers who have a good knowledge of classical ballet, modern dance, and jazz, and who must also be able to sing and act. Because it takes at least ten years to produce a dancer, we should begin to ask some serious questions. Except in a few universities and private schools, there is little opportunity in the United States for the aspiring actor to achieve a well-rounded training in the various disciplines. Obviously, he must begin to study at an early age, especially dance. He must find a competent teacher in his community (not always a simple matter) and concurrently study voice and acting. Assuming he is sufficiently fortunate (and financially able) to receive the proper training, he will then probably head for New York and the "big time." If he is among the fortunate, he will even pass an audition and find himself employed in a musical or straight play. If the production has a small cast, say, six characters, our young actor will suddenly find himself working with five other actors, all of whom have different theatrical backgrounds. The situation could well be compared to that in a *corps de ballet* comprised of dancers trained in Russian, Italian, and French schools of dance. The results may easily be disastrous.

Is there any possible solution to this problem? Let me offer a few suggestions to the reader. The ensembles cited at the beginning of this essay are groups whose members have studied and performed together over long periods of time. It is no miracle that their productions display a unity of style. Why should the American public continue to patronize a theatre that allows such diverse elements to participate, with the result that the art itself seems perverted? This is not as true in the other arts, even in America. The dance public would never accept a ballet or modern dance performance in which the dancers were not uniformly trained in the style. An orchestra would certainly refuse to play a concerto with a violinist or pianist who is not competent to perform the chosen work. And still we condone a theatre in which, all too often, the only thing binding the actors together is their union contract.

Where do we begin? In my opinion, laboratory theatres are the only answer. These must be formed by small groups of dedicated experimentalists. Certain universities with theatre departments and facilities might prove fertile ground, provided the laboratory theatres were extracurricular activities or included under independent studies and given an absolute free hand in their functions. I am certain there are many faculty members and students who, given the space and sufficient rehearsal time, would be more than willing to dedicate much time and energy to such projects. The results might be not only more meaningful learning experiences for the students but also a step forward in the creation of the new theatre, already being pioneered by the Grotowski ensemble, the Living Theatre, Peter Brook in England, and smaller groups throughout the world. The student revolutions of today exclude no areas of study. And the "cultural revolution" is already affecting all the arts in many ways. Should we not recognize these signs of discontent as valid? Or shall we continue to cultivate our traditional gardens until it is too late?

Assuming that the universities can give a home base to our budding laboratory theatres, where does that leave us in relation to the problem of integrating movement into the actor's training program and professional career? It is to be expected that any theatre department worthy of the name offers some form of movement training for its students. It would be ideal if the dance or movement teacher were included in the laboratory theatre, presuming, of course, he was neither academic nor hopelessly tradition-bound. From its very beginnings, the laboratory theatre should incorporate movement as an inseparable element in the drama. This requires supervision by a trained and probing person.

With such laboratory theatres as a nucleus, who knows what new heights the American theatre might attain? At any rate, now is the time to begin the task.

In opera and musical theatre, dance must be a part of a more complex art work and, therefore, is not necessarily complete on its own.

Antony Tudor traces the long historical association of ballet with opera, ranging from opera ballet as an enlivening interlude that has no connection whatsoever with the plot to the integration of opera and ballet.

Choreographers are called upon to create for many media: concert dance (which is most choreographers' first love), opera, musical comedy, film and drama, and television (particularly variety numbers and commercials). Dance has a place in all these, but it is the concert form that requires the art and craft of dance, while the commercial forms usually use the craft alone. To some choreographers, designing movements for productions other than the concert dance is a job. To a great choreographer like Antony Tudor, it can be a challenge to which he brings his knowledge and taste as an outstanding dance creator.

MOVEMENT IN OPERA

ANTONY TUDOR

Considered as an art form, opera consists more of arts than form. Of the nine Muses, Urania—Muse of astronomy—is the only one not invoked at some time or another in the production of opera. Terpsichore, patroness of the dance, seems to be invited in by the host on various occasions when the party looks as though it might be getting rather dull, in the hope that she may enliven it. At times dancing may even become quite an important factor, and the host wishing to enlist Terpsichore's aid may be one of several people: composer, librettist, stage director, general manager, even an influential patron who admires a shapely thigh or pair of ankles.

In its invocation of the Muses, opera calls upon the talents of musicians, singers, actors, dancers, designers and a multitude of others; but it does not make use of them in any fixed order, and the importance of one or another contributing factor varies according to the work in hand. In some operas, dance plays a major role, in others

From *Opera News*, XXV, No. 14 (February 11, 1961), 8-13. By permission of the publisher, The Metropolitan Opera Guild, Inc.

it figures in a minor but meaningful way, and often it is so inconsequential that members of the audience may wonder how on earth it ever got into the production.

In the earliest operas, song and dance complemented each other; prior to the innovations credited to Gluck, many such musical spectacles consisted more of ballet than of song. There was not much coherence in these productions, and arias from one work could often be transported intact into another without many people being the wiser. Choreographic records show that within the confines of the highly formalized technique then practiced, dances from different productions bear such a startling resemblance that the sole means of distinguishing one from another would seem to lie in the costumes. But in Gluck's operas, the earliest to be found in today's standard repertory, ballet is integrated in such a way that at certain points it *is* the action. The best example of this is the Hades scene in *Orfeo;* in many productions the chorus is banished into near invisibility, or even (as in the recent Metropolitan production) completely into the wings, leaving the stage open for the conflict between the singing Orpheus and the *corps de ballet* monsters.

At this point we might well raise a question: to whom belongs the responsibility for movement in an opera? In the past two decades Broadway has seen entire musical shows entrusted to a choreographer; Jerome Robbins' brilliant *West Side Story* comes particularly to mind. Together with the earlier *On the Town* (also a Bernstein-Robbins collaboration) and *Oklahoma!,* in which Agnes de Mille achieved such a unifying force with her choreography, *West Side Story* adheres to the principles laid down by Gluck about two centuries earlier. Opera has made a move in the same direction; though we have seen very little evidence of this in New York, the European opera houses show many examples. Just this past summer the Orff trilogy *Trionfi* and the new Frank Martin opera *Mystery of the Nativity* were completely staged, respectively, by Heinz Rosen and Margherita Wallmann—both choreographers. England's most eminent choreographer, Frederick Ashton, handled the entire staging of *Orfeo,* as did Hanya Holm on our own continent at the Vancouver Festival. For the most part, however, the stage director dictates the singers' moves, while the choreographer's responsibilities begin and end with the invention of the dance interludes that abound in 19th-century operas.

Of no country is it truer than of France that dance has kept a foremost role in opera. The role of the ballet there was formalized into an obligatory performance during the second act, in which the action of the opera was entirely suspended for as much as half an hour while dancers took over the stage. The balletic interludes of Meyerbeer, Gounod and Massenet can be removed from their operatic contexts and performed as independent entertainments on their own. Outside France, other 19th-century European opera composers used the dance more sparingly, except when they had to conform to the traditional requirements of the Paris Opéra. In most works of this kind, the dancers must bound into action on cue—either in peasant costumes to give local color to the rural scenes, or in ornate ball dresses to prove that stage ballrooms are actually used for dancing as well as for setting off exciting arias, sextets and grand choruses. The other stocks-in-trade of the opera choreographer (or dance arranger, which I personally would prefer as his title) are assorted rituals, orgies and processions, from which he and his dancers can derive only a limited amount of artistic or creative satisfaction. In the usual 19th-century romantic opera, dancing per se is ancillary to almost every other aspect of the production, brought in to brighten things up a little and provide "atmosphere."

Since the stage director must assume overall responsibility for the artistic integrity of the production, one would think that his viewpoint ought to contribute valuable guidance to the choreographer, acting even as a catalyst. But it is rare indeed that the stage director of an opera will discuss with the choreographer the requirements of a particular dance in a particular scene. There is slim satisfaction in devising little dances to fill up the allotted number of bars in fairly lively fashion without hindering the placement of singers or scenery, without obscuring the view of the conductor's baton from other personnel onstage. There exist a variety of opinions whether such interludes should attract attention to themselves; a decision should be arrived at by all the creative participants as to whether a "show-stopper" (away with integrity, if necessary!) or a complete sense of belonging is desirable. My own aims are best satisfied when the production achieves such a sense of theatre that there is no discernible division of labor or effect between the respective contributions of director, designer and choreographer—and we must include the performers, since finally it is they who have to make the synthesis live. Is it so very difficult for opera to achieve this homogeneity, a state where the chorus moves with a grace, a sense of style and a rhythm that could so merge with the dance that neither should give at any moment an impression of belonging in a different frame? The incredible time pressure in putting on a new production militates against such a possibility; so do such essentials as the separation of choral ranks into sopranos, altos, tenors and basses, all of whom must keep the conductor in sight.

We have to admit here that opera appeals to the ear and dance to the eye. Many an opera-lover who attends performances regularly may witness a completely new dance arrangement, even of major proportions, and remain blissfully unaware of it, in the same way that a ballet devotee might attend several operas in which the music sounds much alike to him, the words being unintelligible in a foreign tongue. Consequently, in a production of such harmonious unity that every aspect merged to a degree approaching perfection, we would have to ask for an audience of more than customary discernment to embrace the aural and visual pleasures equally.

The dancer in grand opera is at another disadvantage. The grander the opera, the more lavishly strewn with staircases, boulders, logs, campfires or love seats the stage is likely to be. In the movies, dancers cope with staircases, mountain slopes, ladders, nets, furniture, walls—yes, even ceilings—with a little trickery from the camera and set-builder, but in the theatre we still prefer unobstructed space, with nice, unobstructed ways of getting to and from it. If the dancer is moving fast or has some difficult work with a partner, it is preferable not to be bathed in atmospheric light that makes the running dangerous, the partner hard to find and the dancing all but invisible to people in the upper reaches of the house. The choreographer, being rarely consulted in preproduction conferences, knows little of what lighting is envisioned, or when and how lighting changes will take place. These things all belong in that artistic teamwork that has been esteemed so highly and discarded so lightly in the history of the theatre. Let it be repeated that opera calls for its production upon a host of participants, all of whom should be sensitive to the director's approach, feeling mutual respect for each other's contributory talents and for the work it will be their privilege to present. It must never be forgotten that the hero of the occasion is the composer—even though he often seems to overlook the fact that it takes time to get from one place to another, or that the massing choristers in singing positions onstage from a tight crowding in the wings can be accomplished only by a miracle in four bars of music.

There occasionally appears a stage director whose pronounced sense of designing for his company in space, whose understanding of movement, can be imparted to the performers. Bearing in mind the limitations imposed upon singers so far as their locomotion is concerned (for movement must be minimal while the most exquisite tones are being produced; one senses that parading, trotting, prancing or galloping easily induces a basic sense of insecurity in singers), I do believe that more could regularly be done to improve the stage picture. Even with the principals alone, movements, attitudes and gestures can be worked out that are not only expressive of the situation but becoming to each of the artists involved. A recent noteworthy example was the Metropolitan's production of *Madama Butterfly,* in which both the stage director and his artists brought loving care to their postures and gestures, with enthralling results. But the whole question of *plastique* (i.e., dramatic movement) must be kept fresh and dynamic and not allowed to fall back time and again on a handful of stock gestures and attitudes: Friendship—feet firmly planted on the floor, slightly ajar, left hand raised towards the rafters, right hand firmly placed on the shoulder of friend; Enmity—feet ditto, left hand on hilt of sword, right hand pointing to a spot on floor equidistant between principal and enemy, and happening to hit upon a stray tack that has been inadvertently left there and lies in wait for some unsuspecting dancer. There are no rules of *plastique* that can be applied infallibly, and since all singers are not equally endowed with gifts of grace or bodily proportion, compromise is frequently necessary; this can be brought about by a director whose experience and thinking are oriented around body movement. There are many areas of dance in which dramatic movements have become highly formalized, but in which these elegant, traditional movements are used only in the stylized productions in which they belong. Although it may seem anachronistic to speak of realistic operas—and one must define them largely by the realism of stage gesture and movement involved—even in these it would sometimes be advantageous to make use of the space in a choreographic manner rather than fill it with static hordes. It is demonstrable that a handful of people on the move better suggest a crowd than a clump of fifty standing still.

The choreographic viewpoint is more capable of realization, however, in essentially nonrepresentational, nonrealistic operas such as those of Gluck and Wagner, or formal ones such as those of Handel or Purcell. One cannot do better than quote at length a paragraph from Bernard Shaw's *Music in London* (heartily recommended as most amusing and informative bedside literature) to illustrate this point. "Those who know the score of *Lohengrin* are aware that in the finale of the first act there is a section in which the whole movement is somewhat unexpectedly repeated in a strongly contrasted key, the modulation being unaccountable from a musical point of view, as it is not at all needed as a relief to the principal key. At Bayreuth its meaning is made clear. After the combat with Telramund and the solo for Elsa which serves musically as the exposition of the theme for the finale, the men, greatly excited and enthusiastic over the victory of the strange knight, range themselves in a sort of wheel formation of which Lohengrin is the center, and march round him as they take the finale from Elsa in the principal key. When the modulation comes, the women, in their white robes, break into this triumphal circle, displace the men and march round Elsa in the same way, the striking change of key being thus accompanied by a corresponding striking change on stage, one of the incidents of which is the particularly remarkable kaleidoscoping of the scheme of color produced by the dresses. Here you have a piece of staging of the true Wagnerian kind, combining into one stroke a dramatic effect, a scenic effect and a musical effect, the total result being a popular effect the value of which was proved by the roar of excitement which burst forth as the curtain closed in."

Here must have been an opera director with an eye, an ear, a brain and some knowledge of the emotions. Opera directors who are themselves trained musicians are conscious of subtleties that may elude legitimate-stage directors who take a fling from time to time at staging an opera. In the nineteenth century, opera staging was very much catch-as-catch-can, with the principals doing what they pleased, the chorus fending for itself, the *coryphées* hoping they'd find someone to buy them supper, and any disputes or technical difficulties being resolved by the stage manager. the ballet at that time, bad as it may have been, was nevertheless the only element that had any organized design in its movement. But since then, song came of age in the music-dramas of Wagner and his followers, and dance developed its own form of drama at the hands of many able choreographers. Since these two theatrical art forms can be neither mutually exclusive nor subordinate to one another, their amalgamation is the most hopeful and significant trend in the recent development of opera—as its new composers are demonstrating. And in spite of the fact that not too long ago I saw an interpolated "Pas de Trois" in *La Traviata* that could not have had less to do with its context but dazzled the eye with a series of virtuoso tricks and "brought down the house," I hope that the emergence of the choreographer into the field of opera may take place, that we have outgrown romantic 19th-century clichés and the dance arrangers with them and are entering a new phase with the joint blessings of Euterpe, Muse of lyric poetry, and Terpsichore.

Margaret H'Doubler discusses some historical suggestions that relate the primitive developments of dance, music, and poetry to the same motor impulses. Other writers have said that dance is the central art because it structures movement itself, which is at the core of all the arts. In this respect, the relationship of rhythm in dance and music is of utmost importance. Miss H'Doubler's view centers on primal bonds between music and dance.

DANCE AND MUSIC

MARGARET H'DOUBLER

A discussion of dance would be incomplete without some reference to music. It is quite possible to dance without music, and dance should be recognized and éxperienced as an independent art. But because of the very special and organic relationship of the two arts, much may be gained from building on this relationship and opening the resources of music to the dancer.

Music is said to have come from dance, from the rhythmic impulses of man, and to have taken from dance its rhythmic form and structure. Such an alliance suggests the following development.

The sensations of the varying intensities and stresses and speeds and irregularities of man's powers of locomotion and body exertion must have always delighted and satisfied his inborn sense of rhythm. The agitations of the muscles under strong emotional pressure stimulated the activity of his other natural means of expression. He used his voice; he shouted and yelled and cried. He uttered sounds of joy, sorrow, pain, and fear: the first music. In this stage, music was little more than tone and rhythm. Its rise and fall of pitch, its intensities and accents and tempo, existed as the tonal accompaniment of dance, enhancing and also revealing its emotional expression. Later, man became aware of the power that the sound of his voice had over his emotions, and discovered he could use his voice

From Margaret H'Doubler, *Dance: A Creative Art Experience* (2nd ed.; Madison: University of Wisconsin Press; © 1967 by the Regents of the University of Wisconsin), pp. 153-58.

not only as the language of his feelings but also to arouse an answering state in others, and thus incite to action. As he developed a language, his cries and exclamations became words—thus music grew into song. Because of its new form and completeness as combined in melody and poetry, music severed its connection with dance and became an independent art, leaving dance a free agent of expression. As civilization advanced, words asserted their independence of music, and poetry made its flight into the broad realms of art. Thus three separate arts arose where one had existed. But even though music and poetry have achieved freedom, their rhythmic principles remain those sensed as the motor concomitants of emotional impulses, and as stored kinesthetic memories of past motor experience.

Like all things, music has grown by minute increments. Centuries have faded into the past since the first cry of joy or pain and the first beating of sticks, which marked the rhythms of dance, became fused and elaborated into melody and harmony. It has taken all the resources of man's science and culture to develop the crude rhythms of the first music into the glorious symphonies of the last century. Although dance is older, how young and neglected it seems when compared with the maturity and expansion of music! When man accords to dance the same opportunities and interest he has granted to music, dance too will come into its own and rightly be recognized as an art worthy of sincere effort and study.

Because of its transient phase, music has become associated with movement. And because of the dynamic urge of its rhythmic structure, in addition to its melodic and harmonic qualities, music is the most important of all the partners of the dance. The dancer in his response can translate the sounds he hears back into emotions which will be the substance of a dance. In its purest form, music, like abstract dance, has within its scope only the most generalized emotional situations. It does not depict literally, nor does it require of the listener knowledge of any particular facts. Rather it arouses moods without necessarily arousing associations that impel the mind to make a concrete interpretation. But the listener, if he so desires, may interpret what he hears in concrete imagery.

Although music involves an organization of sound in terms of time and stress values, what is more significant is its melodic and harmonic structure. Rhythmic structure alone has the power of exciting strong feeling states, but it is the melodic and harmonic structures that give music its particular power to express emotions reflecting mental states. In the history of music and dance we find that compositions were written especially to regulate the steps of conventional dances of the period, such as the sarabande, the pavan, the gavotte, and others. In these cases, the form of the dance step determined the meter and form of the composition. But music need not be limited to this one relationship. Its literature is so rich in inspiration that, if wisely and artistically used, it has much more to offer. Of all the arts, perhaps music makes the most direct appeal to the emotions.

Music and dance have rhythm as the basis of their movement, and, because of its temporal phase, music is able to express abstract aspects of action. It can suggest or express ease or difficulty of action, its advance or retreat, its force or weakness, its excitement or repose, its seriousness or gaiety. Through association all degrees and qualities of feeling states are expressed and aroused. Music through tone, and dance through movement, give the feeling tones of ideas, things, or events, not the ideas or things or events themselves.

Music, rightly used, offers a justified guidance to dance creation. Especially is this true for the less experienced dancer, whose motor and ideational vocabulary is not adequate to achieving an independent dance. Through rhythmic structure music may guide the rhythmic form of movement responses and give the setting for a mood or idea. Through its time and tempo and intensity gradations it may exert a control over the range and quality of movement—all aiding in the understanding of the similarity in the structure of the two arts.

When a musical composition is used as the source of inspiration for a dance, its structure will necessarily affect the structure of the dance form related to it. At the same time it arouses associative meanings, and with these come personal and subjective responses. Thus, when music inspires a dance, the result is not an entirely new creation but a reproduction, in a different medium, of something that has existed before. The emotion and the basic form are the same, and both the musical composition and the dance process are creative. The music, carrying a meaning, stimulates to a new creative act. This act is a reinterpretation into the form of another art. Thus a dance inspired by music is like any dance, regardless of the source of its original impulse and structural idea.

To accept aid from music intelligently is, after all, an exercise of knowledge essential to the creation of any dance. The dancer recognizes the sources of help and identifies himself with them and incorporates them in his creative process. It makes no difference whether they are marshaled from the memory of past experience or whether he is reminded of them by objective experience in the outside world.

It is dangerous for dance to follow rules of melody that were never intended for bodily movement, but which may nevertheless give rise to it. If dance is not understood and developed independently of music, it is likely to lean too heavily upon music and lose its own vitality. Too great a dependence on music is often due to lack of ability to respond fully to it. A dance should depend upon the dancer's own concepts to impel and control its movements.

A dance thus related to a musical composition is the interpretation of the dancer's emotional and intellectual responses. It is not limited to the literal translation of note values into activity. Associative meanings put emphasis here and restraint there, molding the whole into an artistic and individual response.

The ideal use of music would be to have it composed for the dance as an accompaniment, as an accompaniment for a violin or for the voice is composed. As an accompaniment, it should bring about a musical analogy to the meaning of the dance, rhythmically and emotionally. It should contribute to the dance rather than detract by obtruding. It must keep its place and not bid for attention. The composer should make his music affirmative, but not let his musical ambition cause him to write music that pleases him intellectually and structurally alone. The music should merge with the dance so that its presence is felt by an enhanced total effect and not by individual achievement. As an accompaniment, the music is a means of helping the observer to sense the dancer's thought and feeling, for it is one more sense perception added to the visual and kinesthetic. Unfortunately, it is not possible for every teacher of dance to have such trained and talented musicians for his accompanists. But, if music is selected wisely and used intelligently, we need not despair, for there is much excellent material to be found in musical literature. The association between dance and music is close and natural, and it will continue. If rightly understood and used, their relationship is of great mutual benefit.

DANCE AND MUSIC: A PRACTICAL MARRIAGE

The relation of music to dance is a very close one. Dance, although the older of the two, went through a long period of subservience to music. Dance experiments with silence have only served to point out that the two arts belong together.

José Limon considers music to be dance's "strongest ally." Music, from the beginning of dance training, affects and demands a kinesthetic response. Indeed, a piece of music is often the inspiration for choreography.

Not all music is meant to be danced. Some is complete in itself and needs no further embellishment. The music for dance should be neither overwhelming nor mere background accompaniment. The combination of dance and music should be a marriage in which one is not complete without the other.

MUSIC IS THE STRONGEST ALLY
TO A DANCER'S WAY OF LIFE

JOSÉ LIMON

Over 25 years of being a dancer have accustomed me to regard the art of music in a very special way. It is not only something to which I can listen and respond with the mind and the emotions and instincts and enjoy or dislike or dismiss casually and indifferently. Music has become more than that, because I hear music with the muscles and bones and blood and nerves: in short, with all the human faculties for movement. The first and inevitable response on hearing a piece of music is: "Can this be danced to? Can I move to it? Does this music say jump, turn, run, reach for the stars or be crushed—do anything, but do not dare to be still in the presence of this sound?"

A young child, still uninhibited by the conventions, will very naturally follow this instinct and move to music. As an adult, I must be circumspect and exercise restraint, but inside there is much dancing. In the imagination there are fulfilled, in the most fantastic manner, all the commands of music.

From *Musical America*, LXXV, No. 4 (February 15, 1965), 10-11. Reprinted from *High Fidelity/Musical America*.

Dancers differ from the sane, ordinary run of humanity in many respects. The dance is not a profession. It is a way of life. Dancers are dedicated people. They accept willingly the rigors of their craft. Their work does not end at five o'clock and is not left in an office or a workshop and forgotten gladly until the next day. In many cases it continues into the night and resumes again, too early the next day, and on Sundays and holidays, with a very tired but indomitable body.

"All Else Is Subservient"

The dancer lives his work. It is not a part of his life, nor even a large part of it. It is his life. All else is subservient and incidental to the dance. From the very start of his training and education as a dancer, in the studio classroom, all exercises are performed to music. Every single movement is accompanied, supported, given impulse and literally enveloped by music. His muscles and muscular responses, his whole being as an instrument for movement has been conditioned to respond to it, so that music is woven inextricably into his very fiber. His response to it is bound to be, in consequence, a kinesthetic one. It is a prime motivator, and the strongest ally to his way of life.

This close relationship between these two arts has in times past led to the unhappy circumstance of reducing the dance to a trivial and servile status. Music has played the role of master and tyrant, rather than that of consort. Curiously, during these periods of degradation, the music used by the dancers has tended to be equally degraded. Certainly it has not been the noblest or most aspiring.

Dancers, in consequence, have essayed the emancipation of their art from what has been called its enslavement to the tyranny of music. They have contended that the dance could never reach the status of a major art, mature and worthy of serious consideration, while this submersion lasted. There have been brave attempts, during a whole recent period, at dance without music, or at least with the minimum of music. Other efforts were made at dancing to percussion instruments only.

This period produced its failures and successes. I remember a number of them: Doris Humphrey in *The Drama of Motion* and *Water Study,* composed in the early 1930s, put into practice her theories that movement had its own inherent phrase apart and distinct from .the chronometric meter of music. She based her work on the "breath phrase." You moved because you breathed. Movement had its origin in the organic, breathing center of the body. The length of the movement phrase was motivated and controlled by the length of the breath phrase, and not by an arbitrary 4/4, 3/4 or 6/8 compass. This created an entirely new concept of the origins of dance movement. The body, in moving to the breath phrase, must recognize other and revolutionary ideas: It had weight; its muscles and bones and organs were subject to the laws of gravity and did not have to move exclusively in seeming denial of these laws, but rather to make use of them and thus add to the dancer's vocabulary. Miss Humphrey experimented with falls and rebounds, or recoveries, from falls and the suspensions of movement that lie in between these. To her the body in all its parts was a constant state of falls and recovery: the heart beat was one such; every gesture in daily life, walking, sitting, kneeling, lifting an arm, the very effort to stand, to breathe, symbolized the drama inherent in the fall and recovery, or in yielding to or suspension away from the pull of gravity.

This led to some superb works, done entirely without music, using only the rhythms inherent in the body. For this reason these were true creations in the art of the dance, since they did not lean nor depend on the resources of a musical composition.

There were other and less notable experiments by less gifted choreographers. But good or bad, they led inevitably to new concepts of the relationship between dance and music.

Significantly enough, Miss Humphrey herself, in discussing this relationship with me one day towards the end of the 1930s, when all this experimentation was done with, observed that her experiments with dance unaccompanied had led her to conclude that the two arts belonged together. The dance had something missing when done to silence—the dance, the oldest of the arts and progenitor of music, must continue to live with it.

But then on a new basis, as I have mentioned, more and more music was being composed for dances. Often the dance was very far along in its composition before the composer was called upon to fit his score to it. Sometimes the creative process was simultaneous. At others the choreographer and musicians worked independently of each other, with only the basic idea in common, and their resultant labors correlated and coordinated at the final stages. This has brought forth many impressive and some great works, which have helped to establish the dance in this country as a major and adult art.

Again, often one just simply hears a piece of music that makes its irresistible command. Miss Humphrey describes this as a true love affair. She has to be "in love" with the music that she uses for her work. This is probably the reason why she can make such magic with music already composed. Her *Day on Earth,* to the Piano Sonata of Aaron Copland, and her *Ruins and Visions,* to Benjamin Britten's string quartets, are fine examples of her indescribable powers. She not only loves the music, she has a profound respect for it, and does not do violence to it by "interpreting" it nor relegating it to an inferior role. Rather, by her uncanny insight into the intent and content of the music, she succeeds in giving it a new dimension, a visual one. She makes a perfect mating between the two arts, so that it is difficult to imagine one without the other.

Often I have observed her method in dealing with music. If in composing to, let us say, an eight-bar phrase of music in 4/4 tempo, she discovers that the choreographic phrase, because of the idea or intent, tends not to conform to the musical one, she stops to develop the dance phrase independently, to let it reach its own logic and conclusion in purely kinesthetic terms, to "let it breathe." Then she calmly superimposes it on the music, and permits it to overlap, and so to create intricacies of accent and dynamics and counterpoint. On the 3/4 tempo of the Bach *Passacaglia and Fugue in C Minor* I have seen her impose choreographic phrases of 8/8, 4/4, 9/8 and 6/8. Only a consummate musician, with a profound knowledge of music and its intent and implications, can take such seemingly audacious liberties. The result is brilliant, inspired, and inspiring choreography. You hear and "see" the music, because movement brings out nuances and dynamics heretofore unsuspected and adds to the spiritual and aesthetic delight.

Not All Music for Dancing

Not all music can or should be danced to. There is much that should be let alone by the dancer, because it is complete by itself and needs nothing from the dance. This seems to me to be true of most symphonies. The art of music has produced some titanic works of such grandeur and stature that any attempt to dance to them would be self-defeating and superfluous. The dance, on the other hand, the parent art, older but not in as advanced a state of development, does need the aid of music. But dancers must guard against selecting music that is not "danceable," that does not have dance inherent in it but is contemplative and philosophical in character.

I cannot conceive of an existence without music, as without dance, for often to me they are inseparable. I have long suspected that composers know this also, because they dance in their music, even when they have not formally titled their music by such choreographic terms as gavotte, minuet, sarabande, allemande, passacaglia, chaconne, etc. I have found much to dance to in Bach (my great favorite), Scarlatti, Purcell, Monteverdi, and Vivaldi. I have had no great desire to dance to, nor great success with, the music of the 19th-century Romantics. When I was younger, I essayed some Chopin, Brahms, and early Scriabin with very mediocre results. It appears that what I have to contribute as a choreographer can better be done with composers of the seventeenth or eighteenth centuries, or with those of the contemporary period. I have found the music of Schönberg and Bartok very exciting to work to; and have had pleasure in working to Samuel Barber's *Capricorn Concerto*. Among the other younger Americans, Norman Lloyd has done some of the most effective theatre-music scores in the repertory of my company, including one of Doris Humphrey's postwar masterpieces, *Lament for Ignacio Sanchez Mejias,* for which he composed some of the most moving music I have ever heard in the theatre. Gunther Schuller with his *Symphony for Brasses* I have found infinitely rewarding for *The Traitor,* a work commissioned last summer for the American Dance Festival by the Connecticut College School of the Dance. In Mexico I have worked to the music of the contemporary Mexicans, Chávez and Revueltas, and the 18th-century Spaniard Antonio Soler, all of which was not only a wonderful experience but helped me in my development as a performer and dance composer.

Need for Music of Our Time

It is the dream of every contemporary dancer's life to dance to the fine music of our time, the creations of our great composers. The sad reality is that these great ones are too busy or too expensive, usually both. I have cherished for a number of years a very exciting idea for a work on a Mexican theme, to be done in collaboration with Cárlos Chávez. I have discussed the idea with him in great detail, both in Mexico and the United States, and he has expressed his desire to undertake it; but even the resources and persuasive powers of the august Juilliard Institute of Music, which is prepared to commission the work, have proven ineffectual in bagging *Don Cárlos.* But one lives in hopes.

If music and its creators are hard to come by, interpreters are yet harder. On our concert tours in this country we must content ourselves with our fine pianists, usually Simon Sadoff or Jules Stein or Russell Sherman. Juilliard gives us its splendid orchestra when we perform for them. Only occasionally do we have an orchestra out of town, such as when we have done concerts with the Erie (Penna.) or Dayton (Ohio) symphonies or in Baltimore or Philadelphia.

Abroad we have played seasons with the National Symphony of Mexico and, during our recent tour of South America, we had a good orchestra in Rio de Janeiro and São Paulo, which played most of our works well, but unfortunately, due to the short time available for rehearsals, could neither perform the Schönberg *Chamber Symphony* nor do justice to the beautiful Barber *Capricorn Concerto.* In Montevideo we had to content ourselves with a minimum of orchestral support or resort to pianos, for the same reason. We have come to the conclusion, therefore, that for extensive touring abroad we will have to carry our own compact and condensed music, consisting of string quartet, two pianos, and percussion.

For over 25 years I have not gone to a concert, nor sat down to listen to a new recording, without a sense of excitement and expectancy, without saying to myself, "Listen carefully and be alert with all of yourself, with your head and your heart, and your legs and arms and your feet, for here perhaps is your new love. Here perhaps is some new magic, and you will belong to each other, and together you will bring beauty into the world."

And to this idyllic and exalted mood, the voice of cold reality adds, "Yes, provided you can persuade the composer to let you use it, provided it is not orchestrated for more musicians than can be paid for by the generosity of Juilliard or be squeezed into the orchestra pit of the auditorium, provided it does not call for 18 brass instruments, and most of all, that it is playable by ordinary mortals."

SIX

Dance Criticism

No one can look at a work of art and not in some way be affected. One certainly cares how he is affected and often cares how others who supposedly know more than he (or, at least, have seen and experienced more) react. Dance criticism, like criticism of any other art, involves taste, judgment, and knowledge of the field.

I have never met a choreographer who was happy after reading his reviews. If the criticisms are unfavorable, the choreographer says the critic either does not understand the field or is prejudiced. If the notice is generally favorable, the choreographer often complains that the critic focused on all the insignificant things because he does not understand the field. With newspaper criticism, the choreographer usually has adequate grounds for suspecting the critic's lack of knowledge. In the dance journals or magazines, we generally find more detailed academic descriptions of dance concerts because the writers have gravitated to the field out of genuine interest and a relevant background.

Although we cannot be pleased at the paltry or non-existent dance background of most newspaper critics, we might examine the function of newspaper criticism. A newspaper critic is generally a reporter who is describing an event for a public that does not necessarily have a deep-rooted interest in the event. The critic is often a person in the community who wishes to promote the field through his own columns. *The New York Times* does not have to use critics of this type. If a newspaper's criticism is presented merely as a report of the concert, we should usually accept it on that ground and remember that even when the critic injects comments and opinions, he is speaking *to* a lay audience and perhaps *for* a lay audience. He does not have to educate the public. The journal and newspaper critics can educate; however, newspaper criticism and field criticism are usually two different animals.

As the audience for dance becomes more knowing and experienced, and as the educated arts audience increases, there may be more demand for serious criticism of dance. Criticism written for those in the field takes on different characteristics, the same exhibited by the discerning audience. Deeper, more penetrating, criticism will lead to a greater enjoyment of dance. Good criticism will be based on an understanding of the field and a strong knowledge of the histories of dance and the other arts. Ideally, the critic should have the openness of a sponge and the communicative power of a poet—nearly impossible requirements for any human.

The dance-viewer should be able to make up his own mind, based on his own constantly growing background, without the aid of a critic. The reading of criticism will then be interesting only to find out what someone else thinks of a certain work, not to help reach conclusions. As audiences for dance become knowledgeable, criticism will inevitably improve or go completely unnoticed. The audience is the ultimate critic.

The most valuable art criticism is based on understanding *and* feeling. The best criticism is evaluative. There is more to art criticism than expressing individual taste, and, at the other end of the scale, more to it than factual observation and analysis.

It is not enough for the critic to state simply whether or not a certain thing pleased him, for such a statement cannot be tested or verified. His immediate response to a work of art is always based on prior experience. Therefore, as one's experience as a viewer grows, his response to pieces will change and become more mature and discerning.

Good and bad taste are not inborn. Good taste is educated taste—tolerant but discriminating. The critic reveals his feelings about a certain piece in terms of aesthetic value. A dance protesting U.S. involvement in a foreign war is not good merely because the viewer agrees with its creator's viewpoint—the piece must be looked at in terms of the special aesthetics of dance.

Jessup implies that the uninitiated in the art of dance should *not* criticize dance works, because their supposed "good taste" will always be judged unfavorably in relation to recognized tastes. There are no substitutes for experience and exposure as prerequisites for the making of aesthetic judgments.

TASTE AND JUDGMENT
IN AESTHETIC EXPERIENCE

BERTRAM JESSUP

Concerning the distinction in function between aesthetics and art criticism it has been said that "The critic aims *to sharpen an image,* the philosopher *to define a sphere.*"[1] If on the philosophical side we understand, as was intended, an inclusion of detailed analysis of what constitutes a given aesthetic sphere, such as the sphere of criticism itself, this is, I think, a good summary statement of the philosopher's role in the common task of explaining aesthetic experience. On the other side, that respecting the critic, it is a good partial statement,

From the *Journal of Aesthetics and Art Criticism,* XXIX, No. 1 (Fall, 1960), 53-59. By permission of the American Society for Aesthetics and the *Journal of Aesthetics and Art Criticism.*

but only a partial statement. Something is left out. The total task of criticism is not completed in merely sharpening the image because the consummatory phase of art experience is not reached if the activity of criticism stops there, with the image.

What is reached by way of sharpening the image is the work of art as fact; what is wanted beyond that is the work of art as value. The value, of course, lies in the fact and cannot be realized without it; but it does not lie in the fact simply as known but rather as known and felt. In aesthetic experience as distinguished from cognitive experience we see something and we find satisfaction in *what* we see and not merely in seeing truly or clearly. What we factually see if our image is sharp and our understanding informed is the work of art as physical, symbolic, or iconic thing; what we feel is the value in the thing. In aesthetic experience we find satisfaction in the thing known but not determinantly in the knowing itself. The aesthetic experience is not finished in saying, so it is; but rather in saying, so it is and thus it moves me. Whatever in criticism contributes to sharpening the image, that is, to perceiving and understanding the work of art is thus aesthetically necessary and justified only as it eventuates in or supports evaluation.

There are thus two clearly distinguishable tasks of criticism to be performed, two spheres of criticism to be defined and analyzed. The one aims to explicate, to "sharpen the image." The other aims to evaluate. The sphere to which my discussion is directed is the latter, that in which value-directed acts and expressions of taste and judgment are the defining characteristics. I wish to define these two activities and the expression of them in art criticism.

But though I distinguish in theory two spheres of art criticism, there is in practice (at least ideally) rather a single, though hyphenated, sphere of criticism, that directed to understanding-feeling. The work of art is a value object, and without a feeling response to it there is no *aesthetic* experience of it. But without understanding there is no relevant object at all. To find value in a work of art you must first know it factually.

Concerning the experience of art, which it is the function of criticism to explain and guide, two errors prevail. One is the error of the ignorant, the other the error of the learned. The first supposes that knowledge is superfluous, the second that knowledge is enough. The former, at least in its downright form, is too gross to deserve much answer. It is expressed familiarly in the pronouncement "I may not know what art is, but I know what I like," with the stubborn implication that knowing, beyond effortless acquaintance, is no matter, that all that counts is how I alone feel. But correction of this crassness does not lie at the other extreme, that which holds that knowledge is all, that responsible criticism ends with factual explication. This is the sophistical error of the learned. It is expressed with typical intellectual intemperance in Ezra Pound's "Damn your taste, I would like if possible to sharpen your perception, after which your taste can take care of itself." The obvious implications are, first, that only fact is open to disciplined and responsible judgment, and, second, that once fact is established, individual taste is sovereign, that again there is no disputing. On this view the task of criticism is complete in factual understanding.

Actually, in the practice of criticism there is always a major premise, expressed or suppressed, that the fact is value. If the critical analysis is aesthetic at all, it must support or lead to or presuppose value judgment. The major premise of every art criticism is always: This object which commands my attention and labors deserves yours; it *is* a work of art, that is, an object of aesthetic value. The value judgment, even when explicit, need not and usually is not baldly stated, as it is, for instance, in Maillol's forthright statement "I do not like Donatello . . . he displeases me as much as Praxiteles."[2] It may rather, though still direct, be joined with a descriptive statement as in Wilenski's "With this lightness of touch Gainsborough gave us frequently the most *charming* orchestration of colour"[3] (italics mine). Or it may be conveyed in ostensibly descriptive adjectives which carry evaluative force; for example, in such statements as that in which a scholar says of a piece of primitive Northwest sculpture in the form of a pestle that "The curve of the shallow cranium and the great proportionate width of the face are admirably controlled by the shape of the handle."[4] Another example of the same method is given when a critic speaking of certain works of Rouault writes, "All three paintings have a grandeur which comes in large part from their condensation, their obsessional force as images seen repeatedly in the artist's dreams."[5]

However communicated, whether as direct and explicit value judgment, or as approval or disapproval partly concealed in semantically double-use words and phrases like "grandeur," "strong," "personal statement," "astonishingly integrated design," etc., that is, in expressions at once informative and evaluative, or in general tone of importance conveyed in statements of basically factual analysis, the evaluative component of criticism is seldom, if ever, absent in writings about art.

Nonetheless, there is a persistent persuasion, both professional and popular, which took its ancient flight, verbally at least, from the Horatian *De gustibus non disputandum*, that evaluation has nothing to do with responsible and supportable criticism, that prizing and disprizing a work of art is an unarguable matter of individual taste, like liking or disliking green olives or caviar, and that expressions of taste are therefore no proper part of criticism. Criticism in practice, however, does not follow this persuasion. It does make value judgments in which assertions of taste, that is feeling responses, are implicit. This practice I wish to analyze and justify.

The experience of art, which it is the business of the critic or, allowing for division of labor, of the collective critical discipline to instruct, to guide and to foster, has two phases, understanding and appreciation (feeling). They are genuinely phases and not alternative and self-complete ways of having art experience. The art object to be felt in appreciation must be understood, and the understanding to be aesthetically significant must lead to a felt appreciation. About this I should suppose there could be no disagreement.

With the first mentioned phase, that of understanding, and the critical task directed to it, I have said, I am not here concerned. My present interest is in the second, that of felt appreciation and the expression of it in criticism.

The components of appreciation, the consummatory experience of art, are taste and judgment, or acts of liking and acts of valuing. Both are at least verbally evident and distinct in much writing and speaking on art. We do sometimes say, "I like it," sometimes "it is good," and sometimes ambiguously, "it is admirable." But the question can be raised whether the distinction is only verbal, whether there really are two components of appreciation. Both aesthetics in philosophy and theory in criticism have insistently brought forth the view that this distinction is indeed verbal only. On this view experiences and assertions of taste are the total content of consummatory art experience and its communications. A feeling respective to an object is the sole content of an appreciative art experience. Report of feeling may be varied in statements such as "it pleases me," "it satisfies me," "it delights me," etc. And such statements may be grammatically garbed in object language, "it is good," and then called judgments. Or they may be suppressed in favor of a seemingly pure factual statement—"In the work of Praxiteles all traces of rigidity have gone."[6] But whatever the verbal form, communications of taste (feelings) are not on this view genuine judgments in the sense that they may be tested or verified by anything beyond the occurrent feeling itself. An aesthetic judgment so-called is then simply a statement of feeling content which grammatically and deceptively takes on the judgmental garb of "it is aesthetically good, or beautiful, etc."

Now this view, the radically subjective, is in one important particular wholly correct, but in another, equally important, completely wrong. The truth and falsity of the view both turn on the maxim *De gustibus non disputandum.* In taking that maxim as a principle they are right who hold that aesthetic judgments are always and solely validated by taste, but they are wrong in thinking that taste is logically and psychologically anarchic and incorrigible. Whatever its original intent, the *de gustibus* principle is factually supportable only in the sense in which it is understood to mean that taste or human affective response is the sole ground in which a judgment of worth can be humanly verified. If, however, it be understood in the sense that no particular or individual taste can be disputed, that it is impossible for anyone ever to be demonstrably wrong in his taste or preference, it cannot be defended either in fact or language usage. Aesthetic judgment is referential to taste but not without limit to tastes. If the latter were true, there could indeed be no such thing as judgment.

If judgment is expressive of taste, then the distinction between correct judgment and wrong judgment rests squarely on the distinction between good and bad taste. The question thus arises, what is good taste? Aesthetic taste may to begin with be understood to be cognate in meaning to literal, that is, gustatory taste. A gustatory taste is what we immediately have in sensation and affective quality when something is placed in our mouth so as to stimulate our taste buds. It is something which happens. No reflection or deliberation is involved. No decision is made. We do not ponder or decide whether something tastes good or not. It just does or doesn't. And as it is with, say, a bite of cheese or a sip of wine, so is it also with a look or a sound of a work of art. We do not decide whether a painting upon which we now turn our eyes pleases us or not. It just does or doesn't. And whatever happens, it is our taste then and there. About that there can be no disputing.

I am not arguing that this, the indisputable occurrent taste, completes the aesthetic experience, that aesthetic experience begins and ends in isolated, self-sufficient acts of taste. I am saying rather that the act of taste is the indisputable terminus of whatever in the aesthetic experience comes before and the essential referent of whatever comes after. What comes before is the total individual experience and the collective affective history of the cultural society in which the individual exists. What comes after is a review of the act of taste in the light of that experience and that history. It is within these contexts that the taste in question is determined as good or bad.

Taste, I am maintaining, is the final referent and sanction of judgment. I am also maintaining that taste is subject *to* judgment, that it, the taste itself, can be judged good or bad and its pronouncements, therefore, right or wrong. This may appear to be contradictory or circular, but it isn't. The seeming circularity lies in an ambiguity of the phrase "judgment of taste." The phrase can mean (1) a judgment in which expression of taste respecting an object (i.e., a work of art) is the essential content, or (2) a judgment in which the nature and quality of a particular taste is the object of reference and appraisal. Both are value judgments but not of the same kind of thing. The first is an aesthetic judgment; the second is a judgment *of* aesthetic judgment. The first means to evaluate a work of art; the second to evaluate ways in which works of art are evaluated. There is an essential difference.

The second kind of judgment attempts to answer the question, what is good taste? The answer which I shall propose, as anyone familiar with the literature of the subject and who is mindful of common usage respecting it will recognize, is not original. It is intended to be reportive of common usage, to set forth what we do in fact commonly mean by "good taste"; that is, I abstract from the data of common usage what seem to me to be the intentional defining characteristics of the term as actually employed.

Good taste, it has often been said,* is rooted in but not guaranteed by native sensory equipment—good eyes, good ears, an alert mind, etc. We are, if normally endowed, born with the faculty of or capacity for good taste, but not with good taste itself. Good taste is not innate or ready-made. For a good taste besides being a keen taste is an educated taste; it is informed, experienced, and cultivated. In its operations it is discriminating, broad, tolerant, and unconfused. In its articulations it is sincere and honest. Finally, it is a taste which is refined but at the same time robust, not so over-refined that it loses its gusto and becomes finicky in the presence of the simple quality and unvarnished fact. Its interest in the orchid must not dull it to the primrose and the dandelion.

Conversely and more briefly, "bad taste" in common usage means besides a taste which is insensitive because of impaired sense faculties or dullness of mind or emotions, a taste which is ignorant, uninformed, inexperienced, narrow, intolerant, provincial, confused, or over-sophisticated. To predicate any one of these characteristics of an act of taste is in common usage to predicate a deficiency and in so far forth a badness of taste. But one deficiency does not entail all the others. A person of narrow taste may, for example, be informed, experienced, and sensitive to whatever he reacts to within the range of his interests. But still to call a taste "narrow" is to subtract something from it qualitatively.

A few illustrations will serve to enforce these characterizations. Good taste is discriminating. A person of good taste in respect to a complex object like a work of art will not react, for example, in a single lump of indiscriminate feeling to John Bunyan's *Grace Abounding* because he meets there an uncongenial theological doctrine; he will rather note that fact as an unpalatable ingredient and then go on to feel pleasantly the charm of innumerable little incidents told by the way and enjoy the admirable honesty and excellence of the simple English prose style.

A person of good taste is tolerant in his responses. He is not quick

---

*Cf., for example, Ingres, "Fine and delicate taste is the fruit of education and experience. All that we receive at birth is the faculty for creating such taste in ourselves and for cultivating it, just as we are born with a disposition for receiving the laws of society and for conforming to their usages. It is up to this point, and no further, that one may say that taste is natural to us." In Robert Goldwater and Marco Treves (eds.), *Artists on Art* (New York: Pantheon Books, 1945), p. 216.

to feel displeasure in the presence of a work of art or kind of art with which he is unfamiliar, of which he does not have experience and about which he does not have understanding. He will not feel antipathy out of hand to dadaist design because it answers to nothing in his previous experience in painting. He will not break into derisive guffaws at a native south African dance because it isn't European ballet. On the ground of spontaneity in occurrent taste response he may not positively like the unfamiliar but also he will not positively dislike it. The spontaneous reaction towards the unfamiliar will in the way of good taste be rather a feeling of surprise and tentative interest.

Good taste is broad. It is a various taste. Many kinds of objects engage its interest and command its approval. It will warm not only. to modern art but to classical too. It will like not only classical music but swing and jazz also. It will enjoy the novel as good reading but not to the exclusion of poetry. It is not provincial. Artistic merits being equal, it will find pleasure in a Japanese landscape as much as in a typical homeland scene. It is not one-sided. It will not exalt purely formal beauties above those of content, nor those of thought above those of sensuous surface. Good taste in the arts in respect to its largeness or fullness is like the taste of the gourmet in respect to liquors, as described, for instance, in a *Liquor Intelligencer,* which puts it this way:

> Every liquor has a charm of its own, from a rare Romanee-Conti 1921 to rough, country applejack picked up in some back road in the Adirondacks. The gourmet takes each in its own terms and enjoys it for what it is. Refinement of taste lies more in the beholder than in the beheld. The man who can drink *only* Scotch, or drink *only* Champagne is like a man who can only love a woman with a mole on her shoulder.[7]

These are in fair sample some of the characteristics which are recognized in common usage as applicable to the idea of "good taste." I do not think, however, that a clearly defined or workable concept of "good taste" results from merely adding them together as defining characteristics. Some among them are disputable in relation to others and will on occasion have to give way. Broadness or extensity of taste may, for example, be questioned or qualified in terms of depth or intensity of feeling response. Nonetheless the field of "good taste" is sufficiently well marked off by such features as these named and a workable or applicable concept can be elicited from that field. I suggest that the following may be offered as defining characteristics, some if not all:

Aesthetic taste to be good must (1) be really aesthetic, (2) be adequately perceptive, and (3) fall within the range of normality. A few words of explanation of each follow:

1) By converse application of the principle of added determinants

a taste is not good aesthetic taste if it is not aesthetic taste at all. If a poem is liked because it is convincing in respect to truth or congenial in moral sentiment, it is not valued poetically. If a building impresses because of its cost, it is not valued architecturally. If a painting is favorably received because of its religious or irreligious attitudes, it is not valued as art. And if a work is found interesting because it throws light on a page of history, it is a cognitive and not an aesthetic interest which is satisfied. And so on.

Whenever some value other than the aesthetic determines the felt interest, then that felt interest and the felt satisfaction which follow it are not aesthetic. The non-aesthetic interest may, of course, be perfectly worthy and by itself it does not result in bad aesthetic taste. But when aesthetic worth is imputed in feeling to the total object on the basis of a separately considered, non-aesthetic ingredient in it, then confusion of value and in that sense "bad taste" does occur. When, for example, a thing of great cost or much labor is deemed *ipso facto* a thing of high aesthetic value the corruption of taste which in one of its meanings is called "vulgar taste" sets in.

The argument against confusion of values does not imply that the presence of values other than aesthetic in the aesthetic object are irrelevant or misplaced nor that the recognition of them there in appreciation is corruptive of good taste. This would be to argue an aesthetic theory of pure form. I am not maintaining such a theory. Aesthetic facts, that is, works of art, are built out of other facts, aesthetic values out of other values. These other facts and other values are then the aesthetic materials, and there is no limit to the materials, physical, ideational, or emotional, which may serve. Stone, concrete, iron, wood, or plastics may be made into statues; sensations, ideas, conflicts, attitudes, or beliefs may be made into poems. But the statue is not the stone or the wood, and the poem is not the idea or the attitude. Concrete by itself may be considered dull, marble beautiful; a belief by itself may be judged true or false, and an attitude as such may be approved or disapproved. Confusion and resulting failure of taste occur not when the material is taken into account but when it is made to account for everything.

An analogy with another kind of value, the cognitive, may help to clarify and enforce the point. In questions of fact or truth there is no limit as to the object which may be known truly, but truth is not determined by any consideration other than fact. We do not deem a statement true because it is beautifully phrased or because it is comforting. An ugly or unpleasant truth or an awkwardly stated truth is just as true as the pleasant and felicitously worded truth. To suppose the opposite is to corrupt the sense of truth and to disable the cognitive pursuit. Similarly with the aesthetic sense; its health and integrity lie not in ignoring other than supposedly "pure" aesthetic facts and values, but rather in taking them aesthetically.

2) Aesthetic taste to be good must be adequately perceptive. This

means simply that what is responded to must be really there in the work and that what is really there must be responded to. To be adequately perceptive is to be fully and relevantly perceptive. The work of art must be seen or heard in whole and not merely in part. Correct response is total response. My previous example of making short shrift of Bunyan's *Grace Abounding* because of the uncongenial theological doctrine which it contains illustrates the point.

Inadequate response may also be described as failure to respond to the work as object and to use it rather as a trigger to set off memories, feelings, and sentiments which are related to the object only by psychological privacies or eccentricities of the individual beholder. In that case the taste is directed not upon the object but upon the recalled and outside incidents and interests of the beholder's life. If, for example, in reading Shakespeare's

> All the world's a stage
> And all the men and women merely players,

he feels confirmed in his own conviction that all is vanity and if he stops there in the satisfied feeling of being confirmed by Shakespeare, then he has not arrived at an adequate perception of Shakespeare's play, nor even of the lines themselves. He is responding to the thought and its value (cognitive) rather than through the thought to the character who is made to utter it and is thereby perceptually defined. He has failed to see that Shakespeare does not make the assertion, but that he *uses* it, that is, that he makes something *of* it. His perception has failed and his taste has been misdirected. A misdirected taste is a bad taste.

3) A taste to be good must be in the range of normality. "Good taste" to be a meaningful concept at all must mean more than my taste and your taste and any taste. It must mean a certain kind of taste or a certain range of taste. A general criterion which I think accords with common usage is that of normality of response based on normality of capacity to respond. In terms of capacity, a good taste is then one which is able to see what sharp eyes can see, to hear what good ears can hear, and to take in what a good mind can encompass. It is also one which is able to feel what an emotionally sensitive nervous system arouses. In terms of actual response, good taste is then the actual full possession and exercising of these capacities. If there is organic deficiency or impairment, lapses in taste result. Thus, for example, Dr. Samuel Johnson's hardness of hearing is correctly inferred to account in part at least not only for his lack of enjoyment of music, but also for his critically unfavorable appraisals of certain poems in which tonal excellence is fundamental.

If the foregoing account of taste is correct, what then is judgment, and what is the relation of taste and judgment in aesthetic experience? A judgment is basically a review and a comparison of acts of taste. It cannot go beyond taste or appeal to anything outside it, but it can challenge or approve individual acts of taste. And it can be rendered in terms of thing language as well as response language. That is, judgments can be of works of art, as they usually are, as well as of appreciations of works of art. This is so because works of art are themselves enactments of taste. The artist paints his taste. The viewer in his response agrees or disagrees.

If the viewer is a critic, he reasons his agreement or disagreement by comparing his response to the work under review with his responses to other works in his experience or by judging (measuring) it by generalized criteria derived from other responses. Even if the work in question is highly original and the point of approval is the unique quality, the "personal impact," it is still the case that the approving taste when used to validate a judgment comes by comparison and generalization. Uniqueness or originality is not a descriptively positive characteristic which can be detected in isolation. It exists and can be recognized and felt only in comparison.

Judgment in the foregoing way is at once reportive and evaluative. To identify a taste which occurs in a *de facto* response (one's own or another's) or which is embodied in a work of art is also implicitly to show it as good or bad. But judgment is also formative and corrective of taste. Part of what is meant by an educated taste is that it is a taste which has been brought under review and which is thereby confirmed in its adequacies or instructed in its inadequacies. In this way a taste is strengthened or amended. A particular taste is strengthened when it is found to be in agreement with other tastes; it is shown to be in need of amendment when it is in disagreement with other tastes, i.e., when it does not fit into one's own system of settled taste, or into the community of taste.

That is to say that the judgment which can confirm or amend a taste must itself be validated by a previous or another taste. And this is not to conclude that a judgment is not really a judgment. To say that judgment is really only an expression of taste does not mean there is no such thing as judgment unless it be further proved that there is no logic of taste whereby tastes may be compared and shown in some meaningful stipulation to be different. Where there are differences in anything factually, there can also be and normally are differences in preferences or value. To say that tastes cannot be good or bad but only different is unwarranted. It is to say that it is impossible to give a meaning to the phrase "good taste" such that it will apply to anything in experience. I have tried to show that it is possible to give a meaning which is not only consistent but also derives from established usage and serves the purposes of communication of aesthetic experience.

There is a logic of taste in the sense that the nature of taste allows an analysis which makes it possible to distinguish some tastes from others and to call the former "good" and the latter "bad." And on this distinction it is possible to maintain that a judgment of taste is really a judgment. A judgment is a measurement, and all measurement is in terms of criteria or units chosen on grounds of convenience from the kind of thing which is to be measured. Thus, for example, when we measure boards or timbers, lengths are measured by lengths, that is by other boards or their equivalents. There is no going outside the material, but it is genuinely measurement which takes place. Likewise, when we judge aesthetic experience, tastes are measured by tastes. But the measuring is not the lengths and the judgments are not the tastes.

27
ADVICE TO THE UNINITIATED DANCE AUDIENCE

Erick Hawkins gives the lay dance audience a sound point of view for watching its first dance concert. Briefly, he asks spectators to come with no preconceptions, to trust the reactions of their senses to the movement, and to enter into the experience fully.

This seems simple, but American audiences, as Hawkins points out, have two big problems that interfere with his advice to relax and enjoy it. The biggest problem is the Puritan tradition that (usually unconsciously) regards movement of the body as suspect and immoral and often leads us to distrust any sensual reaction we may have to it. The second problem is the penchant for analyzation—the inability of many to enjoy a work of art unless they know what it means. The fact is that with the use of abstractionism all the arts have two levels on which to work. In other words, in many dances there is nothing to understand—no message, no story line—simply movement in all its beauty of design, fluidity, and exciting dynamics.

Perhaps the audience should be warned via program notes of what to expect and what to look for in viewing each work.

ERICK HAWKINS ADDRESSES
A NEW-TO-DANCE AUDIENCE

ERICK HAWKINS

If I were going to speak about dance to a group of people I hadn't met before, I would begin by wanting to share with them what my life has been and to share with them, too, what you might call a vision.

One of the saddest things I have experienced in my life in America at this point in history has been seeing and feeling the great separation which exists between those people who value the arts and the general public. One of the reasons for this gap is a Puritanism which, in some form or another, has manifested itself throughout much of Western history. Our ancestors brought this Puritan spirit

From *Dance Magazine*, XVI, No. 6 (June, 1967), 42 & 44. Reprinted with permission from *Dance Magazine*.

with them to America and carried it across the country as they were making the towns, making the cities, making the roads, even making this college. Everyone in America, Protestant and Catholic alike, is part of this Puritan tradition.

It is a tradition which has led us to distrust the senses. And because we distrust the senses, we distrust the fine arts, for the arts deal with the sensuous materials of the world—with colors, shapes, movements, sounds, even tastes. This state of affairs is one of the damndest, saddest things in our history, because art does something for the human soul, when it is used rightly, that nothing else does.

During my own lifetime, I've seen the beginning of a tremendous change of consciousness in America. More and more people are realizing that not to use art is to dry up physically and spiritually. To trust the senses is to see the world poetically; to see the color of a tree; to hear the sound of rain; to feel the shape of something; to see the extraordinary patterning on animals; to see what men can do when they make a form in time, in rhythm, and in dynamics; to hear the extraordinary suchness of all of the kinds of sounds that can be made—how wonderful it all is!

Because it is wonderful, I believe that I as an artist do not have to apologize for my profession to the governor of any state, the president of any college, to any scientist, or anyone else at all. When I'm up on the stage dancing I know that I am making a statement about the beauty of what men and women can be. And nothing is more important than that.

Some people think that dancing for men is an unworthy occupation. I will not allow anyone to say that—because I know that when I dance I am upholding an image of man. That is what good dancing can do. Of course, if you regard something only in a negative way, you will get nothing but negative results. If you say the body is dirty, then you will get moral dirt and all sorts of asinine attitudes which will ultimately lead to great human suffering.

But after you have found how free and rhythmic and flowing the human body can be, then you truly realize that sensuousness does not mean paltriness or evil. I don't know what people are talking about when they say the body is evil. Why *evil*? We're all born from the union of the bodies of our fathers and mothers. That is life and creativity. Then why should we regard the body as evil? When people in the Western world have distrusted dance, I think it's because they've misconstrued the very meaning of a beautiful person or a beautiful human society. Dancing *can* become vulgar at the drop of a hat—that is, if your spirit is vulgar.

I would like you, as you watch the concert tonight, even if you've never seen anything like it before, to try and enter into it fully. It is not necessary for you to have any previous knowledge about dance. Watch closely and react as you wish. If we have performed truly, then you should be able to react to our sensibility. Dancing is meant to be shared.

Now I would like to convey to you what I think is the most important aesthetic formulation of Western thought.

I think it might give you new insight—if you haven't discovered it already—into all kinds of art. The concept comes from a man I think is just about the brightest philosopher of our time, F. S. C. Northrup of Yale. He's a scientific philosopher, but he's also much more than that. The first big statement of his ideas is in a book titled *The Meeting of East and West.*

In it, Northrup shows that art can be roughly divided into two aspects: what he calls art in its first function and art in its second function.

Northrup shows that in art you can first use colors, shapes, sounds, and movements in and for their own sake. Much of what we call abstract art today does this. Abstract? That's a very difficult term, difficult to define exactly. But in general we apply it to such things as the way contemporary painting, for instance, uses colors and shapes, not·to tell us something about the outside world, but just for the pleasure of lines and shapes and colors on a flat surface. That's what Northrup means by art in its first function.

The opposite side of the coin is what Northrup calls art in its second function: when you use the colors, the shapes, the sounds, the movements to tell you something else about human experience, something other than what you see just in the material itself. Thus I could do a movement and make it into something which expressed fear or exhaustion, or had a specific utilitarian purpose, and that would be dance movement in its second function. Or I could do the same movement just because that movement itself was beautiful, and that would be dance in its first function.

Art in its first function and art in its second function are equally good. One of the reasons people sometimes argue about certain works of art is that they are trying to see them on a different level from what the artist intended. If you brought your grandmother to an exhibition of certain kinds of painting I bet she would say, "But what does it mean? I don't understand it." But perhaps all the artist wanted was to create some beautiful shapes and colors just for the sake of creating beautiful shapes and colors. In that case, there would be nothing to "mean."

So many times when people see dances they say, "Well, what does it mean? What does it represent? What story are you telling?" But I say in dance too that it is not necessary to make the movements mean anything. They can simply be movements for the sake of their own beauty, skill, and loveliness of form. Tonight, for example, the last dance, *Early Floating,* is almost entirely movement for its own sake.

On the other hand, the second dance you'll see tonight is an example of art in its second function, because in this dance I chose a theme. It's a dance called *John Brown* and it is a dance about that character from American history. It uses a brilliant poetic text written by Robert Richman, head of the Institute of Contemporary Arts in Washington, and I speak the lines of John Brown while Kelly Holt, a dancer in my company, speaks the lines of the interlocutor. It has a very handsome set by the sculptor Noguchi, and every movement in the dance is telling you, in some way, something about John Brown's feelings. At no time do I make a movement just for the sake of movement. If I jump or turn or do something else, it is to convey a feeling or emotion of John Brown.

These two dances—*Early Floating* and *John Brown*—represent the poles of art in its first function and art in its second. But between art in its first function, where you are concerned just with the material of the art, and art in its second function, when you want to use the material to tell something, there are many intermediary positions.

The other two dances on the program are examples of such "in-between" dances. In *Geography of Noon* the dancers are four butterflies. But they in no way tell you any information about real butterflies. The dance just uses the metaphor of the butterfly, and then makes beautiful movement with it.

The fourth dance, *They Snowing,* is a little poetic metaphor of two people dancing "snow." It's part of a long suite of dances called *8 Clear Places*. We were at the University of Oregon about two years ago and did this dance. A professor of psychology came to the concert and brought his three sons. The one who was seven, although his parents hadn't told him and he hadn't read the program, guessed which dance in the suite was about snow and which one was about rain.

That incident taught me something important. It taught me that if only somebody can be as innocent as a child and simply see what is in front of him, he can then respond to any work of art. So I would be pleased tonight, if after you saw the dances and heard the music—and I have a remarkable composer with me who can create some remarkable sounds—if after you've seen and heard it all, I'd be terribly pleased if you said, "Well, I've never seen anything like it before." I'd be pleased because for me the fun has been, not just to repeat the forms of the past, but to see what I could find *here and now*. I firmly believe we will have a healthy life and a healthy society when audiences can simply come to a concert and say, "Okay, let's look."

28

THE DANCE AUDIENCE, THE CHOREOGRAPHER, AND VALID EXPERIMENTATION

As suggested in the preceding articles in this section, the audience has a responsibility in judging and criticizing the dance. This article goes one step beyond in saying that, especially in experimental works, the choreographer, too, has a responsibility to present the audience with a valid work. The composition, no matter how tradition-defying, should spring from an apprenticeship in the traditional dance forms, so that the audience is not skeptical of the choreographer's background. Picasso's most abstract work is accepted without question because skill in the more traditional, realistic styles is there.

THE AUDIENCE AND THE CHOREOGRAPHER: A SENSE OF RESPONSIBILITY

MYRON HOWARD NADEL

For the first time in the history of the arts, dance has become a leader! No longer does the choreographer have to rely on developments in music, literature, art, and the out-of-date trends seen in many ballet scenarios. Now he can state that he exists in a modern, complex world, propelled by rapid change—and he can be a leader in that change. The result is that audiences are not always given pleasing and traditional concepts of beauty, but are often challenged to accept bold and sometimes shocking presentations. A choreographer today must assume his new responsibility and still keep in mind that the audience, which has paid admission, must feel that it is seeing something of value. This is possibly where the audience and some choreographers today come to blows—on the question of value. Will an audience be satisfied to see dance that negates movement, that seems to say that no movement and "non-dance" movement is still dance?

If, in the new dance, the choreographer works with the idea of negative dance movement, he must somewhere show that he values some aspect of life in a positive way. The choreographer does not have to work with dramatic ideas or with traditional movement concepts of beauty and grace, but he should, I feel, recognize that an audience must be given some kind of stimulation. This is done by the great avant-gardists—Alwin Nikolais, Murray Louis, Merce Cunningham, Paul Taylor, and others. These people are trained in the art of dance, including the art of theatrical presentation—for dance *is* theatre.

There are other groups that include "dancers" who have never seen a dance studio or been a member of any company. They are negating and defying traditions, not because they are bored by tradition, but because they are novices in the field, with less technical ability than a freshman dance student. Therefore, an audience's next question may be whether the choreographer is stating his ideas because he has chosen this particular path for his present development, or whether the trend has chosen him because he is incompetent of following any other. Theatrically, the audience must feel the choreographer is being different, negative, or whatever because he wills it. At least then the spectators, even when disagreeing with the product, will be able to admit that the presentation was consciously controlled, and that content and movement were chosen and executed with the knowledge that only training and experience will bring.

On the other hand, the audience must prepare itself for bold, shocking statements and not expect to be pampered into happiness. The viewer must look at the new dance in a new way, remembering that upon first tasting fine Scotch or Limburger cheese he probably wasn't pleased (and certainly couldn't tell one Limburger from another). First, the audience should allow itself to see the dance as a whole. It should take in the general style and do an analysis of possible meanings afterwards. It should not applaud tricks or search for subtle verbal meaning. Taste in the arts grows with experience, and selectivity should come only after one has seen enough to select from. If one is making decisions as to his tastes in dance after seeing five or six concerts, he had better stop for fear of looking foolish. My advice is to swallow the avant-garde (like the Limburger), sense a reaction in your body, examine its texture and flavor, and compare it to other life experiences—let it settle. After the tenth concert or so, one may be able to say that he prefers one style over another, but he still shouldn't make rash decisions. An analysis of what he saw can perhaps be discussed to some extent.

I feel the avant-garde experiments are important, necessary, usually dynamic, and generally charged with the emotion of belief. Audiences should accept experimentation and consider themselves involved. The choreographer must return this acceptance by being learned in the arts—his own especially—and by believing that what he is doing is of value; otherwise, he shouldn't do it. The viewer should react to this concession with the concession that no judgment shall be made until he has some awareness of the field—a minimum of ten concerts. Spectators can help themselves enjoy the latest developments in dance by relating the performance to personal experiences in the other arts. It wouldn't harm an audience to relate the performance to its personal experience, but one should wait for a sufficient amount of exposure before expounding one's likes and dislikes on the new dance. The viewer should discipline himself to gather experience; he may then demand a sense of responsibility from the choreographer.

With this small problem of choreographer-audience rapport with the new dance, we can easily see the need for educating audiences as well as choreographers in dance—a total art field with a long history and varied philosophies and academic disciplines. Audiences gain an understanding of music and art through the general availability of introductory course work in these areas. Laymen should be introduced to dance, not as exercise but as an enrichment of their lives.

29

THE PROFESSIONAL CRITIC

The realm of the professional dance critic is examined in this article. His profession arose in a society in which the arts have become a commodity and the artist must sell himself or starve. Gone are the days of patronage. The critic, then, is a judge for the public—he examines the value of a newly created work of art.

Mr. Sorell points out that the dance, being both a visual and kinetic art, is very difficult to describe in words no matter what one's reaction to a performance is.

The artist asks the critic to come to the experience without prejudice, with a love and concern for the art, with a sixth sense to catch the artist's intention, and then to discuss the experience in an enlightened manner. This is a tall order, and critics, being ordinary mortals with undeniable likes, dislikes, and preferences, often produce conflicting reviews.

If the student is expected to "be able to discuss" (the origin of the word *criticize*) a dance concert, he can be guided by looking for thematic material, ways in which the choreographer develops the material, unity of style, the subject matter (if any), the integration of light, color, fabric, and music, the flavor of the movement chosen, and the formal design and its relationship to current trends or its place in the history of dance. This type of analysis can be accomplished without making value judgments for which the student is not usually equipped.

TO BE A CRITIC

WALTER SORELL

For it is much more easie to find Faults than it is to discern Beauties.
To do the first requires but Common Sense, but to do the last a Man
must have Genius.

—Dennis
(The Impartial Critick)

First was the creation in its explosive abundance, its burst of beauty
and waste of wisdom. Then, and much later, the critic came down
from Mount Olympus with his commandments, codes and credos.
Only in a moment of creative despair, of doubt in himself as an
artist, could the artist in man have provoked the appearance of a
policeman, prosecutor and judge who called himself critic. He
cleverly chose this epithet from the Greek *kritikos* whose meaning is
"able to discuss."

In the beginning he must have been a teacher who had the ability
to discern and verbalize his impressions and thoughts. In our age,
however, in which art has lost its hallowed purpose of being an act of
gratitude toward God for our heightened awareness of being and has
become a commercial commodity between a producing craftsman
and a consuming humanity, the critic turned into a middleman who
lives on supply and demand which he helps stimulate. He may put on
the hood of the historian to explore the present through the eyes of
the past; he may rush from a performance to his newspaper to get his
copy ready by midnight; or he may talk shop in a trade paper.
Essentially, he is a one-way interpreter who tries to explain the
language of the artist to the understanding of the reader.

Although criticism is considered a secondary art as its existence
depends on the existence of a creative act preceding it, one cannot
exclude the possibility that it may be superior as a piece of
craftsmanship to the creation it criticizes. As no artist can function if
his critical faculties do not play their proper part in his creative
process, no critic can put to paper his viewpoints successfully if not
endowed with the sensitivity and sensibility of an artist.

This is said in full awareness of the ailing condition of most
professional dance criticism which often lacks the necessary

From *Dance Scope*, I, No. 1 (Winter, 1965), 3-9. Copyright © The National
Dance Teachers Guild, Inc. Reprinted with permission.

understanding of one or the other disciplines which are part of the critic's requisite. Moreover, those familiar with the tricky task of translating one language into another will fully realize the difficulties in communicating something so visual as the dance through means so confined to words of many-faced values. Thus, dance criticism suffers from its own complexity which keeps it from being well written, convincing and brilliant.

Should we not ask ourselves what validity any criticism has and to what end the writing of reviews is pursued if not for the mere purpose of recording events for a posterity whose interest in all of them is rather questionable? I have heard it said more than once by established artists that they could no longer take critics seriously; but when unanimous raves haloed their endeavors they collected all the reviews to set them off in the nicest offset reprint. And I have always wondered whether it is really true—what I was made to believe—that dancers are only reading the pans of their colleagues.

I doubt that critics have the power to break or make an artist, even those critics who, due to their alignment with all-powerful papers, hold a trumpet-tongued position. True, they can sometimes slow down an artist's career, or they can become his unsalaried press agents and secure bookings and jobs. But I agree with Carlyle that if any artist can be killed by one or many critiques, the sooner he is so dispatched the better.

Every artist looks for recognition, and rightly so. If he is clever he will try to find out the predilections of the critic and then match the critic's response to what he intended to create in the light of these two different worlds that face each other. He should neither take praise nor fault-finding literally. Both should caution him, make him think and compare the mental notes of the critical reaction with the original visualization of his work, because both always fall short of their goal. For any criticism to be constructive, the artist must be willing to give the critic his due.

How very personal—and of the one-man's-poison-and-meat variation—criticism is proves the fact that not all critics have the same to say, not even if they basically are of one opinion in their praise or pan. Furthermore, it is at least as confusing and irritating for the critic as it must be for the artist if the critical reactions to one and the same piece are completely contradictory as to the whole work, or to any of its details. But as little as the critic must then despair in his integrity and judgment, neither should the artist despair in criticism as such nor in his own artistry. It only demonstrates that art is the intangible of something very tangible.

Since we live in a world in which art has become a property, a commodity and even an investment, a world in which the artist has to sell himself, the critic's role as the one who does the inadvertent selling was imposed on him by the artist and the public alike. And a public which relies on the critic for guidance in its judgment is eavesdropping on another person's heartbeat to gauge its own pulse. Both should memorize Lord Byron's lines:

> Seek roses in December, ice in June;
> Hope constancy in wind, or corn in chaff;
> Believe in women or an epitaph,
> Or any other thing that's false, before
> You trust in critics.

It was said Raphael would have been the same great painter he was even though he had been born without hands. I expect the critic to be such an artist, born as a sage and seer who developed all his perceptive and creative faculties without using them in that one particular field in which he functions as a critic. The dance critic will come closest to this far-set goal if he shows an unusual literary gift—as a matter of fact, if he himself is a poet, because only the immediacy and remoteness of the poetic image can picture the visual image of the rhythmic sweep of human bodies in space and time, can make us relive and remember the elusive quality of the dance.

The great writers on the dance were literary men who, if not practicing poets, were endowed with the power of poetic vision. From Stendhal and Gautier, from Baudelaire and Mallarmé to Cocteau and Marianne Moore, they all have caught the essence and the spirit of the dance with that intense subtlety of the word which gives lasting existence to the illuminated illusion of a moving reality. The Russian-French critic André Levinson is probably the most outstanding example of a non-poetic critic who had the ability to penetrate the heart of the dance and to present it with absorbing intensity. But he was a literary craftsman with an extraordinary vision; aided by a clear perception of the artistry involved, he developed, as no one else before him, a philosophy of the dance which makes his writings important. Only Edwin Denby's loose pieces written on the margin of time come close to Levinson's essays. But Denby has not only viewed the dance with the distant look of the philosopher, he is also a minor poet of major sensitivity.

When we speak of the obvious requirements of a critic as those of an intimate familiarity with the art he deals with and the craft enabling him to utter his criticism, we usually forget another feature which, in its self-evidence, is basic to both these aspects: namely, that the critic is only human. Therefore, he must have the right to be wrong and, what is even worse in the eyes of some people, to change his mind. His critical faculty grows—at least, we must hope so—and growth means change.

A crucial point is his integrity. As a critic he cannot afford to indulge in partisanship, but as a human being he cannot help having preferences. As we all do, he cannot avoid living in the narrow world of those whose interests he shares, and the dance world is particularly small. Will knowing the dancer and choreographer not warp his viewpoint, influence his judgment? It certainly will, if he is not strong enough to withstand the inner pressure of his infatuations or animosities. But then he runs the risk of giving himself away. His approach will be feeble or too forceful, his adjectives too glaring or underplaying the facts. If we know how to read, style unmasks the writer.

The critic's prejudices may be annoying. But are not all our preferences dictated by the secret of affinity, by those attracting and repelling forces embedded in our animalistic instincts over which we have no control? To demand that a critic be objective is to ask him to deny that he is human. On the contrary, I expect him to be very much involved, emotionally and intellectually, in what he is criticizing. If he is also deeply and honestly concerned with the art as such, then his devotion will keep him from failing his public as well as the artists.

I expect him to enter the theatre with a feeling of awe and the awareness that something of God lives in every creative attempt. There should be a sense of humility in him that something emerged into existence from non-existence. He must realize that the purpose of art is to be, its only function to give itself to whoever can see in it whatever this particular expression means to him.

The critic must try to feel his way into each work, to sense the artist's intention. With every curtain going up he will have to adjust himself to the object he criticizes. He should be guided neither by his emotions nor his intellect, but by all his faculties at the same time. It may, however, depend on the piece of art whether the stronger demands are made on his emotions or intellect. And a great deal of his judgment will depend on his ability to recognize this at once.

Ideally, the critic should have left the imprint of the day with his coat in the cloakroom, or shove both under the seat—more so than any other spectator. He should not sit there with his arms and mind crossed, but with eyes and ears open, with the attentive curiosity of a child and with the wisdom of the aged and experienced amateur (amateur in the original sense of the word, denoting someone who loves the art). He should want to embrace his object with absolute freedom and be completely free from any absolutes. He is out to explore what feeling qualities are embodied in form and content, what the work means to him and what it may mean to the man next to him. In trying to find this out, he should be guided by principles, but not by theories.

When the curtain falls the critic's total involvement ends, his first step into an undefinable state of detachment begins. He now faces the stupendous task of holding on to the last impression with which he was left and to think backwards in order to catch some vanishing images and to look down on the remaining design and movement sequences from those towering moments that seemed memorable.

The artist creates in response to an inner need and to outside stimuli. The framework within which he creates is his personality, circumscribed by its limitations, no matter how prolific and many-sided he may be. It is an infinitesimal segment in comparison to what the critic must respond to who is exposed to the expected and unexpected, to the possible and impossible. An artist mostly creates out of a certain experience. How wide has the range of the critic's experience to be to match those of each artist! Fortunately, man feeds his awareness with many vicarious experiences. Moreover, there may be as many different expressions as there are original artists, but all these expressions can be reduced to a few basic conscious events.

T. S. Eliot pointed out that the most important qualification of any critic is a "very highly developed sense of fact" and his task is to put "the reader in possession of facts which he would otherwise have missed." Eliot spoke of a literary critic, but the same—and in a far more drastic manner—holds good for any critic of the theatre, and particularly of the dance. Theatre as the performing branch of dramatic literature and even opera, as a part of the world of music, has always evoked criticism of a proven method with a sound tradition, with a technique and terminology. These two performing art forms demand an intellectual approach and permit an emotional identification. This is true of the dance in a far lesser degree. But the fact that the kinetic response is an added factor of great significance in the dance not only points to the strongly physical and elusive quality of the art, it also widens the scope of dance critique and, at the same time, narrows the critic's chance of grasping the intangible literally and literarily.

His knowledge must encompass all the theatre arts, since ballet as much as modern dance can only be viewed in conjunction with their close relation to music, within the frame of the stage décors and the costumes. Lighting, the use of projections, all this can easily change the quality of the moving body. Usually, the critic has to form his judgment after one seeing, and very few critics have the ability to hear the music with the same intensity with which their eyes absorb the visual image. Costume and stage architecture are totally real and constant in contrast to the flight of movement which, born of time and lost to space, ceases to be while it is.

The critic's mental burden while watching a dance performance makes comparison and analysis, the keystone of all criticism, rather difficult. His awareness of the theatre arts—as badly needed as it may be—is of little avail if not complemented by a broad knowledge of literature and a sense of history, because the dancer-choreographer leans heavily on mythology and on Biblical and literary material.

It seems to be a moot question—though often raised—whether the critic should have had some dance training, or will fare better if he were a dancer or choreographer. It is obvious that the experience of how the body moves and how it feels to move is a great help in sensing a movement quality. But was Nijinsky justified in saying angrily when, no doubt, his vanity was hurt, that "Svetlov had never danced in any of the ballets he wrote about and did not know what dancing means"? If Svetlov had danced in them and then became a critic rather than remained a dancer, should we not be more suspicious of a failure in his craft sitting in judgment on his peer? Does not frustration distort our responses? As an artist I would prefer a critic who approaches my efforts with innocence, an aesthetic and ecstatic feeling for what I am doing, rather than with a detailed technical knowledge out of his own experience and a hidden grudge against his fate. Since a vicarious knowledge of technique can be acquired, the non-dancing critic is in no way inferior to the dancer-turned-critic. However, the critic should have a clear concept of dance composition, of the ethnic roots of all rhythmic movement as well as of ballet tradition. Only then can he grasp and quickly coordinate the spiritual values and technical coherence the very moment movement unfolds.

Let us assume that the critic's mind plodded through comparison and analysis, that his visual memory successfully retained most of the highlights of what he saw and that he is now ready to translate his visual impressions into verbal imagery. It is only then that his greatest difficulty begins, his bout with semantics.

His troubles start with the adjective whose easy descriptive power of common provenience is most treacherous. He relies on it since it is pliant and pleasing and, above all, the next best to the only and ultimate word which often is trapped on the tip of his tongue. He then realizes that it is no longer a matter of his right judgment alone. A single word, a certain idiom or an uncertain phrase can give his pronunciation a different slant, a distorted meaning.

If we were to collect a critic's description of dancers as "radiant," "brilliant," "superb," or "breathtaking"—to choose four words of many recurring often in dance critiques—and would make the critic see at one and the same time the various dancers whom he adjectivized as radiant, brilliant, superb and breathtaking, he would neither believe his own eyes nor his words. Can we maintain that Anna Pavlova as well as Maria Tallchief could and can fit with equal justification these four descriptive words? And does not our own mental image of these two ballerinas give these words another quality?

> Her technique is of a sort to dazzle the eye. The most difficult
> tricks of the art of the dancer she executed with supreme ease . . .
> Grace, a certain sensuous charm, and a decided sense of humor are
> other qualities that she possesses. In fact, it would be difficult to

conceive a dancer who so nearly realizes the ideal of this sort of dancing.

This is a fair sample of better dance criticism. If asked who is thus described, we may easily find a dozen ballerinas—although Carl Van Vechten wrote these lines about Pavlova in *The New York Times* in 1910.

The critics' choice of words is as indicative of their personalities as their points of view expressed through them. Therefore, the editorial "we" is either a megalomaniac attitude assuming that everyone working for the magazine or newspaper would not shrink from sharing the same opinion, or it is a cowardly flight into a half-hearted anonymity. What their eyes see, only their "I's" can express. In one of his letters to his editor, Kenningale Cook, Oscar Wilde wrote in 1877: "I always say I and not 'we.' We belongs to the days of anonymous articles, not to signed articles like mine. To say 'we have seen Argos' either implies that I am a Royal Personage, or that the whole staff of the . . . visited Argos. And I always say clearly what I know to be true, such as that the revival of culture is due to Mr. Ruskin, or that Mr. Richmond has not read Aeschylus' *Choephoroe.* To say 'perhaps' sports the remark . . ."

John Martin once advocated the erasure of the word "grace" from the dance critic's dictionary. By the same token, one could successfully plead for keeping many a threadbare word out of the critic's vocabulary. Words such as "ease" and "grace" certainly have a timeworn, tired look vying in triteness with many adjectives. And yet they are indispensable. I feel they can be used with grace and ease when placed within a cliché-free image, or even in conjunction with an adjective of contrapuntal quality. No critic can completely escape the curse of the adjective. As a matter of fact, I find that "superb" can have a "radiant" power when superbly used, and "breathtaking" can be made to fit brilliantly a final descriptive exclamation that brooks no further superlative.

We must acknowledge a great deal of circumstantial evidence against the dance critic, an evidence accumulated through the decades. But we must also take into account his testimony that although the English language has 600,000 words of which a substantial part are adjectives, more often than not the only right word and the exact phrasing eludes him in describing a dancer or dance movement because of the inherent elusiveness of the art itself.

The least successful is the "schoolteacher" in the critic who cannot help grading a work instead of putting it into its right place by evoking images suggestive of the work itself. This is why only the "poet" in the critic can really do full justice to a dance piece. He works with similar tools as the dancer and choreographer, tools that create an illusion, the magic of illumination, the realization of something unreal. He can communicate the core of his experience. Since he can see and has the vision to see into the inmost within and far beyond the narrow strip of the horizon, he can make us see. He can awaken a feeling of expectation or heighten our sense of appreciation. He can quicken our sensual response to the sensuous brilliance of the dancers. His perception can conjure up and capsulize the dancers' movements—limb for limb, body in unison with or juxtaposition to body—in a sentence that has the verbal power, the rhythmic subtlety, depth and lightness to make us feel the inexpressible, the movement-woven wonder of the dance.

When thinking of a critic at a time when I myself did not yet belong to this privileged circle, I imagined him to be a kind of westernized Brahmin. Webster defines a Brahmin not only as a Hindu priest, a highly cultured person, but also as a supercilious or exclusive intellectual. The delightful novelist Aubrey Menen says of a Brahmin in his book *The Ramayana* that "any man could become a Brahmin provided he set himself up to know better than his fellowmen, and was sharp enough to get away with it." That the Brahmin are priests of a faith that extols anticipation of blessedness through extinction of desire and pleasure seems unfortunately applicable in some cases of professional—I had almost said, sacerdotal—criticism.

In my weirdest dreams I have imagined that the critic was born when one artist, whose egomania overlooked the scathing consequences of his deed, wanted to destroy his rival; or that the first critic must have been an artist who failed in his creative efforts, but felt he was able to criticize what he was unable to do. Whatever his genesis, he has become an unnecessary necessity in our complex society, and sometimes his trade has luckily been joined by artists whose creative genius functioned properly in one or another field of artistic expression.

I cannot believe that anyone could feel the desperate urge at an early age to become a critic. In spite of the fact that criticism is an art for which one must be born, one only discovers it after having reached a more or less mature stage. Most often the critic slips into this profession by a thousand coincidences and the one ability: to be a critic.

Being a good dance critic is a difficult task, but also difficult is *reading* criticism—good or bad. Accepting even a respected critic's opinion with no reflection is more distressing than being subjected to a poorly trained critic's opinion. It takes a certain degree of sophistication in reading dance criticism to recognize the humanness of the critic and the logical differences in taste and background between the reader and the critic. Miss Cass's article shows this graphically. Sophistication is also necessary in dealing with the dance critic as an intellectual, philosophical writer who, besides invoking his taste, will seek historical perspectives in his criticism.

THE USES OF CRITICISM

JOAN B. CASS

The printed word has a powerful authority. I have found myself reading dance reviews in the morning newspaper, with respectful attention, despite the fact that I, the writer, knew I left the concert hall the previous evening uncertain of my opinions. Therefore I can understand why so many in the audience make the mistake of seeking Olympian judgments, with absolute validity, from published criticism.

Please heed these printed words of caution: not only is the critic a fallible human being who may have been suffering from indigestion last night, but, even under the best of circumstances, for you to accept his opinions as your own, you would have to agree with him on all these questions and more: What is beauty? truth? decadence? the function of art in society? You can be sure he does not have universally satisfying answers on these points. In fact, unless your age, temperament, emotional, and artistic experiences are identical with the critic's, you probably ought to differ from him on individual works.

How do you think you would have responded to an evening such as this one? One January, shortly after a snow storm, a friend and I struggled up the icy hill to the Spingold Theater of Brandeis University where the Once Group of Ann Arbor, Michigan, was opening the dance series entitled "Expressions 67."

As he took our tickets, the doorman said, "Be sure to get your onion from the usher."

We entered the auditorium, where a lot of people were milling around—some in black tights and white tunics, some barefoot in bras and panties, and some dressed just average extreme. I think the latter were Brandeis students, although we never determined with any certainty who were performers and who members of the audience.

The stage looked provocative, with a silhouette construction of ladders and folding chairs, and a silent procession of black-clad bodies with flashing red lights. "Ah, it's a train," I thought, since the program listed the title of the piece as *Night Train*. Then the lights went brighter, and the dark figures sat down to play at a table. A voice came over the sound system:

"Do you want to see a dirty film? Anyone who wants to see a dirty film, take off your shoes and stand on your seat. Come on now, I see two people standing. Aren't there any more who want to see a dirty film? Don't be shy. Just stand on your seats."

I was confused, because soon there were over a hundred young people standing on their seats, and yet the monologue continued for at least ten minutes, pleading that more than two people respond. Finally, I realized that this must be a tape, the speaker having long since gone home in boredom. Even the stalwart seat standers began to hiss and clap to try to move the action along a bit. Then, indeed, a fuzzy, dim film was projected on a dark brick wall, and one could barely discern a nude female gyrating.

"Now," said Big Brother over the mike, "Everybody undress and change clothes with the person sitting next to you." This time there was less audience participation than before, although we did notice a tall boy exchanging several sweaters and boots with a tall girl on the side balcony.

A bottle of champagne was passed from row to row. Someone handed out chocolate and Italian bread. Prizes were distributed to two people at a time for them to share. "How do you share a picture?" asked the lady in back of me. "Rip it in half," I suggested, thinking of Solomon's advice to the two mothers who claimed one baby.

Then a balloon descended from the ceiling, swelled, and burst. All of this took well over an hour, punctuated by pretty but vacant-looking girls flashing spotlights in our eyes, and loud noises like bombs and jets erupting from the mike. I had sun glasses but no ear plugs with which to defend myself. We tore ourselves away and drove to the newspaper office, where I described what took place and characterized it as the childish mud pie that it appeared to me. A few days later a letter came from a high school senior (who composes electronic music) containing the following:

"I have noticed that you have criticized the Once Group performance as being 'inane . . . inept and slovenly.' The performance was of one piece, *Night Train,* in which the group interpreted such statements as 'The way they hear the things they hear' and 'Things feel the way they feel' with the intentions that the 'they' would not be defined and would be left to the observer to define.

"In this particular performance, the barrier between performer, participant, and observer was broken down. I myself, for example, felt that the salad that was prepared and distributed to some in the audience added to my personal 'absorption' of what went on that evening. The emphasis was on the interpretation of these statements, not necessarily on particulars. This is an emphasis on process rather than object.

"I would be quite interested to know just why a reviewer such as yourself finds it so hard to evaluate such a performance simply in terms of its value as a personal experience rather than as compared to traditional theatre productions."

The answer, of course, is that I did evaluate the performance as a personal experience, just as did my angry accuser. But although we both live in Massachusetts in the 1960s, in a sense we inhabit different worlds—not only because I am a woman and he is a man and I am older and he is younger, but because there were such sharp contrasts in the climate that surrounded our formative years.

Today's philosophy, of which he is a product, equates everything in value. His prophet is Marshall McLuhan, with his "medium is the message" slogan. Nothing is better or worse than anything else—its only significance is that it exists and that one experiences it. Fulfillment of self and perception of sensation are ultimate goals. Meaning and content lie only in the ephemeral process that occurs when the viewer is physically witnessing or taking part in an event. The ultimate expression is not an artistic object, but a "be-in"; not something that can be discussed, analyzed and returned to, but only something that can be felt at the moment.

I was raised in another era, when artists were expected to have a point of view, either intellectual or emotional; when human beings—and especially artists—were expected to care about ideas and their exact expression; and when form was considered to be a tangible, planned structure whose analysis during and after a performance added mental pleasure to aesthetic contemplation.

Will history prove the young man to have been right? It is possible that art will change its form completely, that increasingly larger groups will· desert the expensively ticketed concert halls and the too often snobbishly sterile museums to meet elsewhere and immerse themselves together in doing, feeling, perceiving activities—thus preparing society for whole new patterns of communal life.

Or, as he matures, will this musician and his contemporaries discover a need for more disciplined, discriminating modes of artistic communication, according to more traditional principles (proving me to have been the true owner of aesthetic verities)?

Interesting points for speculation, but in no case can they affect the actual, valid feelings one member of the audience experienced on that frosty January evening. How fine that he had a positive response. How much better than if he had waited, as too many people do, to read the reviews before deciding whether or not to enjoy himself.

Not only age and upbringing color aesthetic reactions. Even within the same school of art, a romantic personality will prefer a tender piece to a strident one; a restless type may demand more drama or energetic motion; and surely the amount of exposure one has had in the past to a given genre will determine whether it alienates through strangeness, appeals through familiarity, or bores through too much repetition.

If there are so many subjective factors at work, what, if any function, does the dance critic serve?

He is the dance specialist in our compartmentalized society. By virtue of devoting endless hours of observation and sometimes study in concert halls and studios, he has gained a body of knowledge about the major technical systems of ballet, modern dance, and ethnic dance. He has learned about the historical variations in choreographic approaches and has spoken to artists about their work. Hopefully, he has an interesting mind, honed by a broad orientation in the humanities.

Given this equipment, he is in a position to be a stimulating companion for you in the dance world, to enhance your enjoyment by imparting useful information, making perceptive comments analyzing the form of the dance, or illuminating its parallels with other arts. If you have found a particular critic fairly trustworthy, you can use him as a quick market guide when time and money do not permit you to attend all available dance events.

The critic is the intellectual, the philosophic member of the physical dance world. Where the best choreography evokes complex feelings, the best criticism should provoke thought—but always thought that leads back to the dances themselves. Remember, there is no such thing as a vicarious aesthetic experience. Criticism must always be used with dance—never instead of it.

The fellow who says he knows nothing about art but knows what he likes may seem foolish, but he has at least felt something. His more sophisticated neighbor who interposes the words of all the critics between himself and the work may be in the know, but he has missed the point of art.

REFERENCES, PART SIX

CHAPTER 26. Taste and Judgment

[1] Katherine Gilbert, *Aesthetic Studies* (Durham, N.C.: Duke University Press, 1952), p. 116.

[2] Robert Goldwater and Marco Treves (eds.), *Artists on Art* (New York: Pantheon Books, 1945), p. 408.

[3] R. H. Wilenski, *English Painting* (Boston & New York: Hale, Cushman & Flint, 1933), p. 124.

[4] Paul S. Wingert, in the Introduction to the catalog of *Prehistoric Stone Sculpture of the Pacific Northwest*, an exhibition at the Portland Art Museum (1952).

[5] James Thrall Soby, *Georges Rouault* (New York: Museum of Modern Art, n.d.).

[6] E. H. Gombrich, *The Story of Art* (11th ed.; London: Phaidon, 1966), p.70.

[7] *Esquire*, "Liquor Intelligencer."

SEVEN

The Dance Artist

The dance artist leads a life very much like any other artist, with certain notable exceptions. The dancer's art is a physical one and is based on a physical training that leads him to a high level of expression. Significant achievement in the art becomes at best an exhausting goal, at times an impossible one. But those who have achieved a great deal have also felt an enormous sense of accomplishment. Because dance is a performing art, the dancer, like other performing artists, spends most of his time preparing himself for the supreme moment that is theatre. He then goes back to the studio to prepare himself anew, to improve his abilities, and to examine himself introspectively.

A dancer is always a student. Even while performing regularly, he always takes classes with teachers he respects. He can never let his technique falter—and as long as he continues to perform he must believe that he can improve. The active life of performing can begin very young, and for some very special people can extend into late middle age—depending upon the physical demands of the person's special artistic focus. A choreographer usually begins later, after serving a kind of apprenticeship, and he can produce works as long as his mind is active and he can indicate his desires to his dancers.

Dancers, engaged in a non-verbal art form, are seldom noted for their words, but this does not mean that there has not been a great deal of thought put into the interpretation of a role or the concept of a new piece. Actually, the greatest personalities in dance today are most articulate and have tremendous verbal insights into dance, the other arts, and into life itself. Any dance artist today must be aware of today's society; that is, he must be well read and well educated. He must have a philosophy of art and life, must know the human body, music, stagecraft, lighting, acting, and must even have some insight into the technological achievements of science if he is to make art relevant to our fast-paced society. The knowledge, the dedication, the energy, and the sensitivity of the dance artist has combined many times to produce persons of great accomplishment.

But dance calls for a practical person too. A dancer cannot falsely believe he is great; he cannot *wish* his body to change; he cannot make a dance and have it presented in a flash. Producing a dancer and polishing a dance are both laborious. The dancer must work for everything; he may be endowed with a talent, but without the physical labor, his talent will never develop. The dancer must marry his art.

The dance artist develops skills that can be used in situations from concert work to commercial television. And if he wants to work, he should be prepared for any eventuality. Most serious dancers prefer the concert stage, where the individual fruits of their labors can be seen for what they are, not as a small fragment of a larger and sometimes gauche presentation. This is not to say that some very skilled dancers have not stayed in commercial work, only that artistic expression is not as limited in the concert field. The pay for concert work is small, and worldly rewards few and far between; yet, dancers stay with it for the mental and physical satisfaction found therein. Dance provides a total contact with life unlike any other field or any other art.

A dancer works in groups for the most part. Unlike a painter, the dancer usually studies, creates, and performs in group situations. Private lessons and solo concerts are rare. A dance is choreographed with living human beings who must cooperate to fulfill the demands of the choreographer. But dancers will often put in their ideas, sometimes vocally but more often by lending their particular movement characteristics to the finished work. The choreographer must deal with these living beings, create with and for them, and engender an attitude of discipline that will make the product compatible with his desires. A dance company is also an entity with a group character and a life of its own.

31

THE INFLUENCE OF THE ARTIST

Some dance artists, such as Isadora Duncan, Vaslav Nijinsky, Anna Pavlova, and Martha Graham, have been made into legends. These artists were not always in public favor, but certainly each made—and Graham is still making—their mark on dance history. Isadora Duncan left us a great legacy and is generally given credit for propelling the evolution into what finally became modern dance as Doris Humphrey spoke of it.

Although we are interested in the kinds of lives dance people live, we should also be interested in the impressions they make on others, since another's view may reveal facets of an artist's personality that might otherwise remain unknown. Isadora greatly appealed to the emancipation yearnings of women early in this century. She is not only responsible for giving impetus to modern dance; she also encouraged a concept of natural dance, that is, dancing that *everyone* could do. She "turned on" the imagination of many women and may also be partly to blame for "turning off" many men to the same idea. After Isadora others rejuvenated the more technical and powerfully compelling aspects that brought men back into dance, or at least back into modern dance.

Maria-Theresa's article, although written in 1959, takes a very old-fashioned look at Isadora's legacy. The aspects of Isadora's art that have had influence are her return to natural expressive movement and her regard for the classical Greek ideal.

THE SPIRIT OF ISADORA DUNCAN

MARIA-THERESA

When still a child, I had the good fortune to enter Isadora Duncan's school of the dance in Berlin, which she had founded there because of the classical climate that still prevailed in that city at the turn of the century. Indeed, all of Germany was still under the sway of classical thought and for that reason Isadora Duncan encountered deep understanding and a lively response to her art, which was steeped in classical ideas and ideals.

Believing that by this time everyone interested in the dance is familiar with the aims and achievements of this phenomenal artist, who at the beginning of this century appeared like a meteor over the horizon of the art world—a living symbol of beauty, spirit, grace and truth—I shall touch only briefly on her artistry, and try to answer the question "What is the significance of the ideas and ideals Isadora promulgated and the extent to which they might be carried out today?"

Isadora was, of course, more than a superb dancer. An artist, a visionary and a free spirit, not only did she raise the dance to its antique significance and to the highest level of art; she was the catalytic force that freed and quickened the minds of artists and public alike for the enjoyment of creative imagination in the dance.

Thus, one should never forget that it was she who first brought to the dance the new freedom of spirit and of movement and allied it with the fresh personal, imaginative, vital, triumphant and creative expression which the world has come to accept as "living" art, and which some narrow minds wish to consider a purely "modern" phenomenon.

The dance may be regarded as a medium for technical display or it may appeal to the intellect or to the emotions. It has many different aspects. As for the "classical dance," it is many things to many people, but it is profoundly artistic and its radius reaches out to many fields. One thing is paramount. It is not merely dancing or movement; it is a great and wonderful expression of the human spirit and an illumination of the human soul. As such it is an enlargement of experience.

Speaking of Isadora one can only chant a paean to her artistry and

Reprinted from *Music Journal*, XVII, No. 6 (September, 1959), 16 & 66, by permission.

to the visions and ideals that inspired her dancing. It would be impossible to do justice to her art in a brief discussion, but one may say that, although inspired by Greece in its obvious as well as in its deeper aspects, it had its roots in life itself. One may therefore call her art a form of "natural dancing" which, essentially, is also Greek, expressed in the simplest of terms and depending on the artist's deep feeling for the intangibles of truth and the mysterious essence of nature. It should also be stressed that although it was "natural," her dance did not lack in grace, life and power.

Therefore, a better term than "natural dancing" is, I believe, "classical dancing," because of its deep humanity, its unbounded free spirit and universality of expression, and because of its achieving a maximum of life without descending to the dismal trivialities of realism. All the more so because Isadora Duncan, perceiving the innate nature of music, specifically classic music, by a stroke of genius made it an integral part of the dance. In adding life, the music does not surrender its own, but ideally blended and inextricably woven together, both music and dance enlarge and enhance each other, take on new dimensions, become an integral art. Merging it into an indivisible unity that conveyed the atmosphere, the thematic bases, the moods and spirit filled with different and subtle shades of meaning, Isadora's dance offered the greatest stimulation for the alert and expectant eye and ear as well as for the mind and the heart.

Classical music, by its close bond and deep kinship, being imbued with every human experience from greatest joy to deepest tragedy, lent a profound humanity to her dancing—to the classical dance—and a sense of "universality" that no other type of dancing ever had to an equal degree. It offered too in some mysterious way a glimpse of perfection, of an ideal sought and found. Natural, and deeply musical, it thus was a truly classic art; it brought us closer to the sources of all exultation and to the central flame of art. Infused with a feeling of naturalness, poetry and beauty for mankind to turn to, to find an answer to their tortured quest for peace and beauty, a dreaming in the presence of nature, it thus had a specific and far-reaching significance.

The casual observer may think this classic dancing to be an imitation of Greek dancing or an archeological revival. Far from it! No pedantic or pedestrian effort to recapture the technical style, it is never mechanical; it is living art, embracing the human and the aesthetic rather than the academic quality—a shaping of art and dancing into the artist's own renaissance of the classic spirit.

A genius, a true artist, Isadora Duncan had a radiant personality. But she was no teacher in the ordinary sense. She did not explain. Isadora taught by inspiring. She danced or indicated by a gesture. She believed that art should be caught on the wings of genius. You could not learn it; you grasped it intuitively, spontaneously, or by a stroke of lightning. The spark within you must turn into flame. It was to be an inner unfoldment that could not be forced artificially. If you had the "eye" to see and the spirit to grasp it, her dancing offered to each beholder a waking dream of an aspiring, unsuspected self.

To dance in the classical style, then, is to be "natural," in the Greek sense—vital, flamelike, vibrant, spirited and radiant. Therefore, to dance in this classical style is never a mechanical or sterile imitation of Greek art; nor is it a mannerism or a specially contrived device.

Neither the "natural" nor the "classical" excludes the human, the tragic or the poetic, because they are encompassed by the human spirit. This "classical dance," then, is not without exultation and depth. It is an impassioned gesture, a movement of the soul—the exultant fervor of the spirit. It is an illumination.

Intuitive and improvisatory to a high degree, yet always creative and impassioned, subtle, sensitive in detail, the whole architecture of such dancing is based on the surge and mood inherent in the music and thereby becomes a wondrous synthesis, where all the deeply visionary and the dramatic and musical gifts of the artist come to the fore and shine and illumine everything. Lifted by enthusiasm and inspiration, yet creative and meaningful, such dances are more than merely a performance. Though ever evocative, they are also oracular, being expressive of the great and eternal themes of which the music speaks—expressive of beauty, poetry and truth.

32

THE BACKGROUND AND MOTIVATION
OF A DANCE ARTIST

Martha Graham is still the most celebrated personality in the realm of modern dance today. She, too, has been a great revolutionary and innovator of dance in theatre. Like many artists, she has gone through clear developmental periods, changing the focus and intention of her art. Martha Graham has developed a very disciplined technique that has produced many excellent dancers.

There is no student of modern dance who does not owe some part of his or her training to the work of Martha Graham, since it has influenced almost every modern dance teacher and performer in this country and the the world. Graham is very interested in the student, since she recognizes that every dancer is always a student of dance no matter how great he becomes. The following piece is not a formal essay; rather, it consists of excerpts from an extemporaneous address given by Miss Graham when accepting the Aspen Award at Aspen, Colorado, in 1965. It eloquently reveals the dedication, sense of responsibility, and love for her work of a great artist—and, indeed, of all great dance artists.

HOW I BECAME A DANCER

MARTHA GRAHAM

What can I say? You know, I speak without notes because I cannot read and look up and down, and besides I wear glasses, and I am very vain. So, the main thing is, of course, that I can always look into your faces. That's what I can do today, and when I do speak in a theatre I always ask that the lights be up enough so that I can see the eyes and the faces of those to whom I'm speaking. After all, they have made my life—they have shared in my life and anything that I have done is a construction really, helped by many, many, many thousands of people.

When I was approached by Dr. [Alvin C.] Eurich in New York, he asked if he could come to see me. He came to my apartment and told me of this honor. I was completely stunned. I could say nothing. There was one periodical, which is very famous but must remain

From *Saturday Review*, XLVIII, No. 35 (August 28, 1965), 54. Copyright 1965 Saturday Review, Inc.

nameless, that asked: "Well, what did you say when you got it?" And I said, "I don't believe I said anything." And the man said, "Didn't you say 'whoopee' or anything like that?" I said, "No. To begin with, it's a word I never use. And in the face of a sacred honor, such as this is, it would mean nothing." It is joy, yes, that I experience but it is also something far more than that. It's a renewal of a commitment.

A dancer's life is a strange one. It is not one of complete refusal to live life by any means. Just because I don't have children is no reason why the members of the company can't have children. And they do. They have quite a few, now—twelve or something like that.

People have asked me why I chose to be a dancer. I did not choose to be a dancer. I was chosen to be a dancer, and with that you live all your life. When any young student asks me, "Do you think I should be a dancer?" I always say, "If you can ask me that question, no! Only if there is just one way to make life vivid for yourself and for others should you embark upon such a career."

You see, to begin with, it takes about ten years to produce a dancer. That's not intermittent training; that's daily training. You go step by step by step. In ten years you'll be dancing—probably even before that time—but by ten years, if you are going to be a dancer at all, you will have mastered the instrument. You will know the wonders of the human body, because there is nothing more wonderful. The next time you look into the mirror, just look at the way the ears rest next to your head; look at the way the hairline grows; think of the little bones in your wrists; think of the magic of that foot, comparatively small, upon which your whole weight rests. It's a miracle. And the dance in all those areas is a celebration of that miracle. Sometimes, when it's very hot, as it was when I left New York, you see some of these poor creatures standing at the exercise bar, sweating—the hairs all down. They had come in looking lovely, and they leave looking rather purified—but in between it's very low, very low.

And then, of course, outside your classroom work, there are two areas which you have to embark upon. One is the cultivation of the craft in the school where you are working. The other is that something that is—and has to remain—entirely with you. This is the cultivation of the being from which whatever there is to say comes. It just doesn't come out of nowhere; it comes out of great curiosity. It comes out of a desire to be an image-maker, because that's what imagination means. It means only the ability to make images. But it means the ability to make those images, not as dehumanized things but as great figures. Take Clytemnestra—that angry, wild, wicked woman. In the ballet that I do, I take her from the end of the third play where she asks, after she is in Hades, "Why do I go dishonored among the dead? Others have killed, but I go dishonored among the dead." And not until she recognizes the fact that she killed—not out of why she said she killed, which was vengeance for the sacrifice of Iphigenia, her daughter, but out of lust for Aegisthus—could she become free to take the branches from Hades and to move.

It cost me a great deal of effort and a great deal of time, but every minute has been treasured. The main thing, of course, always is the fact that there is only one of you in the world—just one! You came from a certain background, you were born at a certain time—a certain instant in the history of the world. And as such, you are unique.

They say every snowflake is different. I can well believe it. But you are unique, and if that uniqueness is not fulfilled, then something has been lost. Ambition is not enough; necessity is everything.

I have nothing more to say except one thing. I have always loved St.-John Perse for giving me this line, which is in one of his poems: "We have so little time to be born to this instant."

Thank you.

George Balanchine is recognized as the foremost choreographer of ballet today. It is impossible to learn about the field of dance without referring to the work of George Balanchine. An artist who creates so many disciples as well as dozens of masterful ballets also arouses a great amount of animosity. No one can be cool about Balanchine; he is either respected as a genius or respected as a tyrant. But he is respected.

Balanchine's choreography has brought the classical traditions into the mainstream of American ballet, while he himself has built one of the finest companies in the world—the New York City Ballet. He has a significant knowledge of music, which lends his ballets a clear form, often like their musical counterparts. This is one important way dance and music can work together. Balanchine's scope has led him into the realm of plotless ballets, where the choreography is of utmost importance, but he has also undertaken many other choreographic ventures, including ballets with story lines, commercial works, and television productions. Balanchine is one of a kind—unique, a genius.

THE GENIUS OF BALANCHINE

BERNARD TAPER

George Balanchine's continued creativity must be reckoned one of the wonders of the ballet world. As a general rule, choreographers, like lyric poets, tend to do their best work when young. Several of the most noted choreographers of our time have started out meteorically, only to run out of inspiration or energy as they approach middle age. This may well be, as Agnes de Mille has written, because of the essential conditions of this craft: the choreographer is subjected to a nervous strain unique among artists in having to compose with human beings as his medium, rather than inert matter; he is forced always to work with live ammunition, so to speak.

From pp. 257-68 (excluding photos) in BALANCHINE, by Bernard Taper. Copyright © 1960, 1963 by Bernard Taper. Reprinted by permission of Harper & Row, Publishers, and Collins Publishers.

If Balanchine suffers from these conditions, he certainly does not show it. When he choreographs, he looks like a happy man. The ballets come cascading from him as happily and artfully as the play of Italian fountains. He will be sixty years old next January, and this last decade of his life has been his most prolific. During these past ten years he has choreographed more than thirty ballets for his New York City Ballet, as well as staged three operas—for Hamburg, the Met and the N.B.C.—and supervised the mounting of various of his works by ballet companies throughout the world, from Winnipeg to Milan. Lotte Lenya, who was in the 1933 performance of *The Seven Deadly Sins* and also in the 1958 production, which turned out to be virtually a new work in its choreography rather than a revival, commented after the later occasion, "It was breathtaking to work with Balanchine again after twenty-five years and find him so full of ideas and energy still. With other creative people I've known, the time always comes when you can say to yourself, a little sadly, 'Well, that's it—there'll be no more surprises.' But with Balanchine you can't say that. Who knows what he's still got up his sleeve!" Balanchine, himself, has commented, when asked how it happens that he seems to gain in vigor as he grows older, "That's nothing. Old people don't get tired—it's only the young who tire. Confusion exhausts them. I've got more energy now than when I was younger because I know exactly what I want to do."

What he wants to do most, of course, is to keep his company going, which is no small task, and to continue to make ballets in which the dance predominates, exploring new possibilities in his old art all the time. The two objectives are inseparable in his mind, since he cannot conceive of choreography except in the tangible, living terms of the bodies of the dancers who assemble, on call, before him at rehearsal time. "My dancers, you might say, *are* my choreography, at the moment of performance."

His most distinctive contribution to ballet, as has long been recognized, has been his bold assertion of the dance element. Other elements had held the limelight previously—the virtuosity of the individual ballerina, the décor, the plot; sometimes the dancing got lost altogether. Balanchine has been the first to make the choreography, in effect, the star of the show, evolving what has been called perhaps the purest kind of ballet, in which all the drama is in the dance itself—in the pattern of movement unfolding in intimate relationship with the music. These ballets of his are sometimes called "abstract" but he considers this a misnomer, since he is not trying to present any abstractions in his work, and prefers to call them "plotless" ballets. Plotless or not, there is always drama in them, and a recognizable attitude or outlook.

In addition to these pure dance ballets, he will generally, each season, do any of a number of quite different kinds of ballets, depending on what he thinks the repertory seems to need at the moment. In doing so, he describes himself as like a chef, or a restaurant owner, who has the obligation to present his patrons with a varied menu, so that they will be satisfied and well dined and will want to come back again. Among the long roster of ballets he has made in his lifetime are to be found acknowledged masterworks in a wide range of categories; narrative ballets such as *Prodigal Son* and *Orpheus,* which are reckoned among the most powerful dramatic pieces in the contemporary ballet repertoire; romantic evocations of mood and atmosphere, like *Liebeslieder Walzer* or *Cotillon;* amusing novelties on the order of *Western Symphony* and *Square Dance;* and strange visions of indefinable nightmare, such as *Ivesiana* and *Opus 34.* In all of these he has sought to convey his ideas not in a literal way but in terms of dance metaphors. As [Lincoln] Kirstein has said, "He has no interest in any effect that is not danced." When he chooses to do a ballet with a plot, he can tell a story with masterly clarity and economy. He thinks it should not be necessary for an audience to have to learn the language of pantomime in order to follow what is taking place on the stage, as did the St. Petersburg balletomanes in the old days, who used to attend regular classes in the subject. Nor should it be necessary to read an involved synopsis in the program. "The curtain should just go up, and if the spectators understand what's going on, it's good—if not, not," Balanchine says. In a narrative ballet, the relationships should be such as can be grasped at sight. He once compressed the essence of his years of consideration of this matter into a nutshell of wisdom he called Balanchine's Law, which went: "There are no sisters-in-law in ballet." Yet when, in 1962, he choreographed his first completely new, evening-long ballet, *A Midsummer Night's Dream,* he was able to make clear, with no apparent strain, that whole complex tangle of relationships, with all the humor, fantasy, romanticism and suspense one could wish—and to do it all through dance conceptions, not through mime.

Almost singlehanded, Balanchine has kept the classic tradition of ballet alive in our epoch. He carried out a revolt against the Fokine revolutionaries; but, as can be seen now, Balanchine's revolution was a new one, not a counter revolution. For if he kept classic ballet alive, it was not through idolatry and archaeology; but through constant innovation, experiment and discovery. Always Balanchine has thought of ballet as a living art, not as a relic of the past to be worshipfully or academically preserved. The company's repertoire is not a museum; the only two traditional works Balanchine has mounted for it—*The Nutcracker* and the second act of *Swan Lake*—have both been freely staged by him to suit his company's personnel and his own preferences. Balanchine's classicism is a contemporary classicism—designed to be seen by 20th-century eyes and make its effects on 20th-century nerves. The classic vocabulary of steps is employed in a different way from Petipa: extensions are higher, movements may be faster and more staccato, combinations are apt to be more complicated and intense. Aside from the obvious fact of having jettisoned the plot and dispensed with the pantomime, Balanchine will differ from Petipa's approach in such respects as his employment of several ballerinas in a work, dancing parts of equal importance, or in the importance he gives to the *corps de ballet* as an element of the total dance composition. In Petipa's ballets the *corps* danced very little, but was mainly used for pictorial effects. In Balanchine's ballets the *corps* is expected to dance a great deal and perform demanding feats of skill; a Balanchine *corps de ballet* member will swoop easily through a chain of steps that a Petipa ballerina would have thought impossible to do. The same thing has happened in nearly all fields of physical attainment; the mile is now run twenty or thirty seconds faster than it was at the turn of the century. But despite the differences in technique, Balanchine shares with Petipa—and with the other great exponents of classicism, in all the arts, throughout the ages—a common outlook as to the relationship of his art to society, and to humanity. "The secrets of emotion Balanchine reveals," [Edwin] Denby has written, in a discussion of Balanchine's classicism, "are like those of Mozart, tender, joyous and true. He leaves the audience with a civilized happiness. His art is peaceful and exciting, as classic art has always been."

Very different in appearance from his classic ballets have been Balanchine's ballets to contemporary music. In a line of ballets which begins with *Four Temperaments* in 1947 and whose high points have been perhaps *Ivesiana* in 1953, *Agon* in 1957, *Episodes* in 1959 and *Movements* in 1963, he has boldly explored realms of movement not seen before in ballet. These works have each been quite different from the other, in implicit content and spirit. *Agon* was pert, witty, a high-wire act, a contemporary comment on skill and danger, employing for effect in places a typically American kind of understatement, like that of the astronaut saying, as he emerged from the capsule in which he had just orbited the world, "Boy, what a ride!" *Episodes,* to the music of Webern, seemed to be about alienation and depersonalization, not in explicit terms of any plot, but in its very essence—in the way the dancers were manipulated, like so many manikins, as if devoid of all will. *Movements* was rarified, remote, beyond good and evil, with a cold, godlike serenity. But each of these works was hailed, as it appeared, as a landmark, a breakthrough—one of those rare productions that affect the course of dance history. How advanced Balanchine's explorations have been was revealed, whether the comparison was intentional or not, during the season of *Episodes* première, at which time it was danced in two parts, with the opening part choreographed and danced by Martha Graham and her company. The modern dance group, in handsome, ornate Elizabethan costumes, danced the story of the death of Mary,

Queen of Scots; the classical ballet company went through its grim, strange paces in stark, black-and-white practice clothes. The critics wrote what a curious thing it was to see the two companies together this way, and noted that it was the modern dancers who seemed old-fashioned, the classic ballet company which looked modern.

In regard to the Balanchine ballets in the novelty category, these lighter offerings, which are intended, one might say, to fill a place similar in the repertory to that occupied by perhaps a baked Alaska in a chef's menu, often take as their starting point some device or gimmick. In *Native Dancers* it was simply the conception of the girls as fillies, the boys as jockeys; in *Square Dance,* it was the perception of common musical forms in the country dances of today and the works of 17th-century classical composers; in *Western Symphony,* the amusement was in putting classical ballet steps to "Red River Valley" and "On Top of Old Smoky." Even in these, it will be noted that the gimmick is almost always a dance conception, not one imported from the world of mime; and it is also to be noted that Balanchine will often work more deeply than he sets out to do. In *Bugaku,* for instance, Balanchine goes beyond the Japanese setting, costumes and mannerisms, which are the superficial aspects of the ballet, and achieves in his choreography, through tempos as slow and alien as those of a deep-sea diver on the ocean bottom, a profound and powerful sense of a culture completely different from our own.

To some, all this seems perhaps illicitly easy and facile. Balanchine's ability to work in many styles is a trait he shares with certain other contemporary artists—with Picasso and Stravinsky, for example. Perhaps ours is the age of the great chameleon, of the quick change artist. Through all of Balanchine's works, though, no matter how diverse, a common thread runs. They all bear his strong stamp; it would not be possible to mistake them for the work of anybody else.

In all these ballets of his, whatever the genre, music has always been the platform for him—or better yet, the sustaining element in which he swims. A friend who went backstage to congratulate Balanchine after the première, in 1952, of *Caracole,* a ballet to the music of Mozart's *Divertimento No. ˙15,* remembers finding Balanchine off to one side, by himself, in a kind of rapture. "Oh, that Mozart—that music!" he kept saying and paid no heed to his admirer's compliments on the wonders of his choreography.

Even when the score that Balanchine choreographs for is not a masterpiece, it is always treated by him with affection and appropriate respect. This is not the same thing as being solemn about it. Some of the intellectuals in the City Center audience—the ones who flock reverently to the "twelve-tone nights" which in recent years have been a feature of every season, when all four ballets on the program will be to serial music and there will not be a single resolved cadence to be heard the whole evening long—were shocked when, in 1958, their admired Mr. Balanchine chose to do a ballet, *Stars and Stripes,* to the marches of John Philip Sousa. Boulez they would have been ready for, or Stockhausen—but *Sousa!* They decided finally that Balanchine must be spoofing, but he never said he was. His only comment was, "I like Sousa's music. It makes me feel good."

When Balanchine is engaged in making a ballet, he will sometimes offer prayers to the composer if he runs into difficulties. "Let us pray to Gounod," he was heard saying to some of the company when he was choreographing *Gounod Symphony;* "he will help us." This brought smiles to the lips of those who heard him. They assumed he was being whimsical, but he was not. He meant it—not symbolically, either, but simply and literally. He feels certain that the composers have often heard his prayers and have interceded to help him assemble the materials of his ballet in suitable style—"assemble," not "create." Creation is an act performed only by God, in his view. "God creates, woman inspires, and man assembles," he says.

Some critics have opined that Balanchine is actually too musical for his own good. They declare that what he does is closer to eurythmy than ballet, as they define ballet. The most distinguished of the critics who take this line is Cyril Beaumont. Reviewing *Ballet Imperial* in 1950, Beaumont wrote, "The relation between music and choreography is almost automatic. It seems to me to be less creative choreography than the literal reproduction in terms of the dance of the rhythm, texture, and pattern of the music. It is a mathematical process rather than a creative one." Beaumont is once reported to have commented, in a discussion with Anatole Chujoy, that Balanchine always repeats his choreography when the music repeats, and that this is a fault because it leaves the audience with the impression that the choreographer could not think of any other steps to put in that place. Aside from the fact that this is surely a curious observation to make in regard to a choreographer who has proved himself to be as facile as any who ever lived, it misses the intention completely. Balanchine often likes to show a dance motif or section twice, because he knows that audiences often fail to grasp what they are seeing the first time. His choreographic repeat frequently serves a parallel function to that fulfilled by the musical repeat in the score. He knows that in dance, as in music—and in life, too, for that matter—a repeat is not a repeat, in its effect. One cannot bathe twice in the same stream, as the Greek philosopher said. One experiences the same thing differently the second time.

Actually, there are to be found in Balanchine's ballets many instances in which the music repeats and the choreography does not. The most obvious example that comes to mind was *Opus 34,* a ballet of grim, nightmarish quality to the music of Arnold Schönberg. The ballet consisted of two parts. The score was played through twice. In the first part, the choreography was in what the critics would call

Balanchine's abstract style; the second part, to the same music, was a hallucinatory operation-room scene, with choreography of a strange dance-mime character. Sometimes in his ballets Balanchine follows the music more closely than those in the audience, including even perhaps Cyril Beaumont, might be aware of. In *Episodes,* for instance, there occurs an unusual moment when the girls are turned upside down and do *entrechats* while head down, feet in the air. When asked about this, Balanchine replied gravely, "Oh, I have to do that. That's where Webern inverts the theme. See, it's right here in the score." But one may be certain that Balanchine would not have choreographed it that way if the action had not, first and foremost, pleased him visually and been in accord with his palette of movement for that particular ballet. There are theme inversions in Tchaikovsky's *Serenade for Strings* and in Bach's *Double Violin Concerto* but no upside-down *entrechats* to be found in the ballets Balanchine choreographed to those scores. Similarly, in *Movements:* at the start Stravinsky exposes the sequence of notes in his tone row with great rapidity, and Balanchine deploys his dancers in the same way. Later in the piece, Stravinsky brings back the tone row sequence, but this time in very leisurely fashion; Balanchine repeats his earlier choreographic deployment, but in the new leisurely tempo.

Such turns and devices give Balanchine pleasure. They can be considered, since so few people in the audience are ever aware of them, the private games of a choreographer. Yet it is quite possible that such linking of dance patterns to the musical patterns works in subtle, subliminal ways on even an uncomprehending audience to convey the overall effect characteristic of Balanchine ballets—of appropriateness and harmony, of surprises that are seldom gratuitous, and of fulfilled expectations. In any case, he does not do what he does in order to illustrate some theory. He has no theories about this, and he hopes the audience will not bother itself with theories. One should not need to be aware of the inner workings to appreciate a ballet, just as it should not be necessary to have to read a ballet's plot beforehand.

In regard to the question of whether Balanchine's musicality operates restrictively on him as a choreographer, one can hardly do better than cite the judgments of Igor Stravinsky, who has concerned himself more with the ballet than any first-rate composer in history and who, in the course of his phenomenal half-century of composing for the ballet, has had his works staged by almost every choreographer of the age. Stravinsky, of course, has long since expressed his preference for Balanchine as collaborator. "I don't see how anyone can be a choreographer unless, like Balanchine, he is a musician first," Stravinsky has written. Unfortunately, he adds wryly, very few choreographers have been musicians. In Stravinsky's opinion, Balanchine's musicality actually enables him to free himself from the obvious constrictions of the music, particularly the tyranny of the beat (which, Stravinsky thinks, trapped Nijinsky inextricably in his choreography for *Le Sacre du Printemps*), and to construct dance phrases that have a life of their own yet are always subtly linked with the musical phrases.

THE DANCER AS ACTOR

Nora Kaye was prima ballerina of American Ballet Theatre when this short statement was written. The most important idea is that the ballerina today is not just a technician but an actress, over and beyond any technique. Just as much time and energy must be given to the portrayal of a role as to the problems of dance technique. The dancer must be a thinking, questioning performer.

THE AMERICAN BALLERINA

NORA KAYE

The whole point of view of the ballerina has changed. In the past she was concerned with the technical aspect of ballet whereas now she thinks primarily of portrayal. The ballerina, of course (whatever her era), must bring something of her own creative skill to bear upon her theatrical realization of those patterns of dance established by the choreographer. Not so long ago the ballerina tended to embellish the technical side of a given role, but today's truly contemporary ballerina, instead of adding virtuoso embroidery to her assignment, endeavors to extend and develop the dramatic lines of a role.

In *Swan Lake,* for example, after learning the choreography, I found that it did not consist merely of a series of *arabesques, pirouettes,* and other traditional steps, but that each movement itself, because of its application to a specific story line, had a specific meaning. My dancing ancestress was rarely aware of drama outside of the pantomimic sequences in her ballet. As her descendant, I am concerned with the drama of movement. In *Swan Lake,* there is a pirouette which follows that moment when the Prince gently lifts the Queen of the Swans from her position of low obeisance close to the floor. This pirouette, I feel, should represent not only a physical culmination of a movement phrase but also reflect the emotional fulfillment experienced by a woman who finds herself warm and secure in the arms of the man she loves.

There are other supposedly traditional movements in *Swan Lake,*

From *Theatre Arts*, XXXIV, No. 9 (September, 1950), 47-48.

each of which has, for me at least, a specific meaning. One might point to one arabesque which repels, another which invites, and yet another which represents the desire for escape, just as elsewhere in this ballet a sequence of supported turns in attitude also conveys the escape-urge. One might argue that realistic drama, the conveying of human emotion, has little place in a ballet predicated upon fantasy, but in rebuttal I will say that the Swan Queen or the Firebird or Giselle (in her aspect as a ghost-maiden) must, if she is to evoke the sympathy of an audience, demonstrate real, as well as fantastic, values.

As another example of the modern ballerina's approach to a classical role, I might point to *Giselle*. Naturally, this ballet must be presented in terms of its own dance period, but while some ballerinas of the past have been content to project it merely as a conventional "ballerina role," the modern interpreters are inclined to present the "real" Giselle herself, and not simply as a ballerina slumming as a peasant maid.

In all traditional roles, then, the modern American ballerina is dedicated not to the reproduction of past performances but to the renewing of great parts. In traditional roles as in new roles, she attempts to analyze and absorb the backgrounds of a character so that she comes to move as only that character could move. In other words—to go back to our original example—a pirouette is not simply a pirouette. It can convey an emotional value and that value will vary from Giselle to Hagar, from the Swan Queen to Lizzie Borden, and from episode to episode within each ballet in which these characters appear.

In *Pillar of Fire*, a modern work, we were faced with a play without words. The characters were explained to us by the choreographer, Antony Tudor, in the nature of life backgrounds. So clearly were these explained in biographical terms to us by Mr. Tudor that when we came to experience the actual choreography, we found that we could move only as those characters would move. This, in the main, is true of all contemporary ballets in that each movement, large or small, must express and be irrevocably allied to a specific character and his highly individual characteristics. Hagar, in this ballet, could not possibly move like Giselle, for, although the technique of ballet has remained comparatively unchanged for two centuries, our current awareness of the dramatic values and usages of traditional movement has become so personalized as to make some of these movements (on certain occasions) almost unrecognizable as the actions familiar to the classroom.

As an American ballerina, then, I never take anything for granted. I question each tradition, each interpretation, each movement. The answers I have found, sometimes right and sometimes wrong, constitute my contribution to the young American dancer of ballet: not to accept until you understand (at least to your own satisfaction), and not to dance any role, ancient or new, until you do understand. This urge to question and to discover is, I think, the trademark of American ballet.

Very few choreographers have assigned themselves to one specific company or one specific job, mainly because of the need to earn a living but sometimes because of the challenges in preparing dances in different mediums. Each medium has its own problems and its own hazards, but in all of them efforts are bent toward that moment of performance that can be a success when the dancers, other participating artists, and the choreographer have joined their best talents.

Commercial choreography, or even choreography for opera, is not the goal of most creative dance artists, although many great choreographers are invited to create for these mediums because of their past achievements. Concert dance would be the choice of John Butler for its creative freedom, but it is interesting to note how Butler brings his skills in the concert field to his other undertakings.

CONFESSIONS OF A CHOREOGRAPHER

JOHN BUTLER

It might be easier to duck the issue and answer with the cliché that each medium is different but equally satisfying, in the final analysis. But are they?

Ballet per se offers a notable contrast with choreography for opera or for television, in that the story line or the libretto usually comes before anything else—and sometimes out of left field. It may emanate from a certain texture of light or from a casual glimpse of a person. It may also be found in legend. When I first went abroad in 1949, I became familiar with an old Italian hand gesture that supposedly wards off the evil spell of a woman's eye. After haunting me for two years, this gesture of the index and small fingers formed the basis for the ballet *Mal Occhio. The Glory Folk*, which had its première last summer in Spoleto, Italy, is another case in point. An Alexander Calder mobile was the source of inspiration for this ballet, which deals with a simple man's faith in God and the vindication of his belief when the mobile begins to move and becomes the symbol of the Holy Ghost.

From *Theatre Arts*, XLII, No. 4 (April,1959), 69-72.

Of course, not all ideas originate with the choreographer, but he is able to adapt them to his own needs, nevertheless. When Gian-Carlo Menotti gave me the basic material for *The Unicorn, the Gorgon and the Manticore,* the poet was the central character. In its finished form, the poet had become a "spectator," and the countess, originally a relatively minor figure, had emerged as the protagonist. In other words, even within a given story line, the choreographer can establish his viewpoint. In all artistic creations, fluidity is the governing factor, though the degree of freedom varies according to the medium involved.

Ballet in opera is a more constricting proposition, since the story line and the characters of the opera predispose virtually everything a choreographer may wish to do. But some of us have the devilish desire to be radical at times. When I worked on *Aida* at the New York City Opera several seasons ago, I choreographed the entire triumphal scene as a duet between a woman and a man—"Egypt" and her "slave." Tullio Serafin, the dean of Italian maestros, who conducted the work, almost had a stroke when he first observed the ballet at the dress rehearsal. Accustomed to seeing the scene staged in Italy with a body of dancers numbering fifty to a hundred, with elephants, tigers and leopards, he could find no merit in this innovation, despite our explanations of economic factors and stage dimensions.

The big waltz that I choreographed for the City Opera production of *Die Fledermaus* during that same year was also a controversial affair and quite different from the real Viennese *divertissement* I have staged this season for the same classic operetta at the Metropolitan Opera. For the New York City Opera, the waltz was treated as a somewhat strange story idea within the framework of the actual operetta. The two principal dancers were coupled throughout the dance, personifying one bat (each was dressed as half a bat), until I had them split in two at the end. A national magazine offered the following comment: "Usually at this point ·in the operetta there is a cheerful waltz, but Mr. Butler saw fit to have a bat pulled in half and cast a pall over the entire proceedings." It is a review I have always cherished among my favorites. At the Metropolitan, of course, I used a much larger *corps de ballet,* dressed in tights and tutus, with Lupe Serrano as *prima ballerina* and Jacques d'Amboise as *premier danseur.* The two versions of the same ballet may be contrasted as "the slightly macabre versus the customary fireworks."

Radical though a choreographer may wish to be in opera, he must be mindful that the ballet should never destroy the overall mood that singers and other musicians have worked so hard to establish. I made a serious mistake once in a production of *Carmen;* on the day after the performance, the headlines over the reviews stressed the ballet instead of the excellent mezzo-soprano who was making her debut. It taught me the lesson that a choreographer must always consider himself a slave of sorts if he is to function properly in the world of opera.

In ballet per se, after the story line has been found, the concept of the structure is the next step. At this point the choreographer decides what he needs—a certain interval in which to establish atmosphere, more time to introduce his leading characters, and so on. Much less "so on" and definitely not *ad libitum* is the rule with regard to structural plotting in the world of television, whether one creates an interpolated dance for a televised musical comedy or a variety show, or whether one stages a complete ballet for a program like "Omnibus." The clock is the ever watchful ogre, and on more than one occasion a choreographer has found his inventiveness cramped by the remark "the shorter the better." Eventually one blocks out the form of the work to the very end—which, I might add, can be a stumbling block, or at least it can be for me. It has been said by critics and associates that my endings are often shockers, but I must confess that the conception of the endings is sheer torture. I can think of a beginning any time, but I am still looking, rather wistfully, for the ballet that has ten openings and no finale.

Once I have decided on the structure of the story, the composer enters the picture. Again we have something in contrast with the world of opera, where, in most cases, the composer entered the picture long before I was born. I prefer to work with a new score, but since a certain expenditure is required in the commissioning of a work, many a choreographer becomes a slave of the monster called "budget." In that case he is forced to fall back upon an established score. Sometimes this is not irrevocable. For *The Mask of the Wild Man,* I used 13th-century recorder music, with isolated percussion effects, when the work had its première. That was at Jacob's Pillow in 1952. But when the ballet was scheduled again at the Spoleto festival last summer, good fortune came upon me in the form of Peggy Glanville-Hicks, who composed special music for this same work and thus enabled me to redesign it.

Though economic considerations may often dictate the terms in the world of ballet, help sometimes comes from those with enthusiasm for an idea. Such "angels" are usually the great artists, persons like Alexander Calder, who gave of himself unstintingly when he designed the set for the Spoleto presentation of *The Glory Folk* at the very time he was creating the large revolving abstract sculpture for the American Pavilion at the Brussels World's Fair. And what of someone like the costume designer Karinska, who so frequently has placed her limitless imagination and vast resources at the disposal of the ballet? As a matter of fact, there is no end to the list of those who have contributed to the creation of ballet, and who receive in return only a fraction of what they might get in another, more lucrative medium.

Unless a choreographer is fortunate enough to have found a Maecenas, or works in a country where ballet is subsidized, he still must make sacrifices of some sort. He must either abandon his basic idea, in order not to compromise, or feed in some of the chips himself. In my case, on more than one occasion I have parted with some treasured possession. Many a painting in my collection has left my walls so that I could obtain a backdrop, a curtain or a set of costumes to fulfill an idea. Sacrifices of that sort would not be necessary if I worked solely in television or in big opera houses like the Metropolitan or Covent Garden. When you are employed in a field in which ingenuity becomes second nature, you can develop a few of the characteristics of a rogue. Last spring, when Menotti asked me to undertake the overall dance direction of the Spoleto festival, his budget permitted the engagement of only five dancers. Obviously I wanted more, and so I dropped a casual word about having stumbled upon two wonderful dancers who were twins. "Imagine what strange, exciting things we could do with twins," I said. Sensing some sort of coup, he responded immediately. "Get them! By all means, grab them!" he said. If Mr. Menotti happens to read this, he will learn the truth of the matter for the first time. I hadn't just come upon the twins when I spoke to him; I was practicing pure, premeditated chicanery. But I believe he will understand and forgive me.

Once the economic considerations have been eliminated, the actual work begins, which is the design of the movement. Some of my colleagues work in advance of rehearsals, a practice I do not adhere to. In my own case, too much depends on the music and the artistic characteristics of the dancers. Creating the movement to the highly personal talents of a dancer is, of course, a luxury, and that is especially true when the choreographer does not head his own ballet company. Sometimes the revival of a work may depend entirely upon the availability of a specific dancer. When that is not the case, the choreographer must change the movements to fit new personalities. The television performances of Menotti's *Amahl and the Night Visitors* during the past eight years provide an illustration. The three solo dancers in the première were Melissa Hayden, Nicolas Magallanes and Glen Tetley; the second year the cast included Mary Hinckson, Tetley and myself; and this season, for the eighth presentation, the dancers were Tetley, Carmen de Lavallade and Charles Saint Amant. Each cast demanded a slightly different treatment of the same dance.

In finalizing the actual pattern of the dance, I may ask the composer to change certain passages in his score. I may request that some bars be repeated, that others be eliminated, or altogether new ones be written. It is a freedom I also enjoy in television and on Broadway, but not in opera, for obvious reasons—unless we are dealing with modern opera. Bitter experience has taught me that only a neophyte among composers will consider his first score a finished product, in which every note is immortal. The experienced composer understands the problems of a choreographer. In preparing his score for *The Adventure,* Samuel Barber permitted repeats and other changes to facilitate matters for me. The same spirit of cooperation was shown by Aaron Copland when we worked on the barn dance of *The Tender Land,* and by Leonard Bernstein, who composed a "Dance of the Seven Veils" for the television presentation of Oscar Wilde's drama *Salome,* in which Eartha Kitt appeared. As a matter of fact, the final creation of a ballet is a matter of give and take. The choreographer needs cooperation to execute his ideas; at the same time he welcomes suggestions from all the participating artists.

We have seen that the actual structure of a ballet is governed by the libretto, economic considerations and the specific talents of the dancers. There is another factor: the dimensions of the stage. It stands to reason that choreography suitable for the vastness of the Metropolitan Opera House or Radio City Music Hall is not what one would create for the limited space of a small theatre.

A new problem, however, is encountered in television, where we tend to lose the sense of orientation because the camera cannot remain stationary. As an example, let us say that a woman performer is moved to dance by the memory of her departed lover. On stage we retain at all times the place from which the man exited; the place is clearly indicated, and all her concentration is directed toward that spot. In television such a procedure is almost impossible. Once the spot has disappeared from the screen—even if only for a moment—the audience has lost its sense of orientation. There are times when the camera is a valuable helper, however, for it has a selective function. Within the fraction of a second we can dispose of sixteen dancers and focus on a single hand in order to achieve dramatic and emotional impact. The camera also adds dimension; the audience can be transported from one point to another, from the top of the theatre to the stage, and from one wing to the other.

Television has often been accused of many things it is not guilty of. A choreographer is hardly ever the slave of the camera, and very seldom is he the slave of the sponsor. There are exceptions, of course. Arthur Murray was not the model of cooperation when I choreographed a ballet for his opening show this season. He was blunt, in fact: "I don't want anything original or creative on my program. I want to keep this a *nice* show." But, in contrast, there are the David Susskinds, the Steve Allens, and programs like "Omnibus" and "Look Up and Live." They all welcome originality and allow as much freedom as that important matter of time will permit.

The mediums are different, we may conclude, but each gives the choreographer the excitement that goes with work involving some degree of creativity. It may be found in a television show that stars a Bert Lahr or Kay Thompson, for even within such commercial confines there always comes that moment of magic during rehearsals when a thing works. Or it may be found in the rarefied atmosphere of the Metropolitan Opera and within the confines of a traditional field—again in rehearsal with a sensitized *corps de ballet* or with the concentrated talent of a Jacques d'Amboise at your disposal. The excitement also may occur within one's own ballet, where the confines are personal imagination and discipline. There is an atmosphere of dedication when one is working with a Janet Reed, Carmen de Lavallade, Glen Tetley or Buzz Miller. And from such an association of choreographer and artists there comes the supreme achievement—the moment that is dance, and theatre too.

Dance artists have to be, or appear to be, gregarious beings in their work. At times they are summoned by other artists to participate in inter-arts activities, but more often they are busy enlisting the talents of costumers, lighting technicians, composers, managers, and, of course, other dancers. It is difficult to have a deep understanding of a dance artist until he is seen working with and within a group whose every member is heading toward the goal that is theatre. One of the world's leading choreographers is Merce Cunningham, who, like many other artists, has struggled for recognition. Even now, when recognition is his, he has persistent financial problems.

A dance company takes a long time to develop into a working entity able to function in a choreographer's own special ways. Merce Cunningham has a unique and unorthodox approach to choreography, but, like all choreographers, his dedication to his new pieces is undeniable. The members of the company are willing to believe in the worth of the end result, even though the process might sometimes be difficult to understand. Merce Cunningham, after many years and aided by working relationships with geniuses—musicians John Cage and David Tudor, painter Robert Rauschenberg—has built a company that commands respect from within and inspires awe in its audiences.

AN APPETITE FOR MOTION

CALVIN TOMKINS

The first rehearsal of *Scramble,* one of three major new dance works created by Merce Cunningham during the last twelve months, took place at the Cunningham studio one afternoon last spring in the interval between two regularly scheduled dance classes. The fact that only three of his eight regular dancers were on hand that day did not bother Cunningham in the least. "I learned long ago that if I waited until everyone was available to rehearse, I'd never finish anything," he said later. "So I just evolved this system of choreographing for whoever's there." Carolyn Brown, the principal female dancer in the Cunningham company, had been teaching the intermediate class in the studio—a large room, thirty by forty-five feet, on the fourth floor of a dingy loft building in the East Thirties, with a high ceiling, worn linoleum on the floor, and windows at one end overlooking Third Avenue—and two other Cunningham dancers, Sandra Neels and Yseult Riopelle, had been in the class, along with a dozen other students; the three girls had stayed on afterward, exercising to keep their muscles limber, until Cunningham arrived, shortly after three o'clock.

Nodding cheerfully to the dancers, Cunningham took a position near a long mirror that runs the length of the studio's south wall and did a series of rapid, loose-jointed movements, turning and changing direction, breaking off abruptly, finishing the phrase with a hand gesture, and then going into another experimental sequence. As he approaches fifty, Cunningham still moves like no other dancer. He cannot jump as high or as far as he used to, but the years have not diminished his uncanny speed and elasticity or his fluid, restless animal grace. An inch over six feet tall, long in the torso but not particularly so in the legs, he has a physical presence that is oddly deceptive. Offstage, in ordinary clothes, he looks thin to the point of frailty; performing, or even moving about the studio in a drab green shirt and sweat pants, he is a powerful and supple athlete, a dominating figure. His face is endlessly expressive—gaunt, furrowed, large-featured, with arching brows and a high forehead framed by tight, archaic curls that are now touched with gray. The features convey a force that is not readily apparent offstage, where most people find him unfailingly courteous, informal, and yet somewhat withdrawn.

After ten minutes of self-absorbed experimentation, Cunningham signaled by softly clapping his hands that he was ready to start working on the new dance, which had not yet been named. He began with Carolyn Brown, his most accomplished dancer, a lean, dark-haired girl, who was wearing black woolen tights and a black sleeveless top. She watched him attentively, hovering a few steps behind him as he demonstrated in front of the mirror the rapid phrase that he had been sketching out by himself a few minutes before. She moved with him, picking up some of the motion as she went along, and when he demonstrated it a second time, she was able to follow him almost step for step. Her arms were wrong, though, and Cunningham stopped to show her what he wanted—a flowing, wavelike motion back from each shoulder, slower in tempo than the leg movements. Cunningham watched her try it out several times, nodded approvingly, and turned to Sandra Neels. Miss Neels, a long-legged brunette, wearing a white leotard with a blue velours overblouse, was to come in from the wings, pause, then spring vertically into the air three times, her arms rising and falling in countermotion to the jumps, the third jump bringing her to a point just behind where Carolyn Brown would be at the end of her phrase. When Miss Neels had mastered this, Cunningham proceeded to give Yseult Riopelle, the company's nineteen-year-old apprentice, a relatively simple walking-and-turning step that would bring her on from the other side of the stage and position her slightly behind and to one side of Miss Neels.

The three girls responded very differently to Cunningham's instructions. Carolyn Brown, a perfectionist, a brilliant and mature dancer at the peak of her career, seemed to want to understand every aspect of the movement that had been given to her, to have all the details clear in her mind, before she put them together. She practiced the arm motion over and over while Cunningham worked with the two others, watching herself critically in the mirror until she had it just right. When she did the whole phrase, though, the quality that she gave to it was her own and not Cunningham's; it was precise, poised, and under strict control. Sandra Neels, who is about the same height as Carolyn Brown but looks taller because of the length of her legs, preferred to absorb the phrase in its entirety; she tended to make her jumps a little more graceful and less emphatic than Cunningham wanted, but she responded with alacrity to his corrections. Miss Riopelle moved more stiffly, counting to herself and trying hard to remember the steps. There was no music to support the dancers. The only sounds in the room were the friction of bare feet on the linoleum floor, hard breathing, and the muffled sounds of traffic on Third Avenue.

After about twenty minutes, Cunningham went on to the next phrase, which the three girls were to do in unison. It was a sort of grotesque walk—a swinging of the legs out sidewise from the hips while the torso shifted from side to side and the head wagged in a stiff articulation, like a marionette on strings. The movement had a quality often found in Cunningham's work—a physical awkwardness that is disturbing at first glance but later, in the context of the dance, beautiful. It took the girls some time to get this, which Cunningham demonstrated over and over—teaching with his body rather than verbally. Very few words were exchanged throughout the session. In the time remaining that afternoon, Cunningham gave them two more phrases. The first was made up of very slow movements—extended turns and deep knee bends made while each dancer poised, heronlike, on one leg. They danced it together, in a circle, but not in unison, and at intervals one dancer would break into a swift measure and then return to the slow, turning motion. The other phrase was a strict-unison movement that involved large, space-devouring strides and ended with each girl bringing her arms forward over her head as she glided offstage. Since a phrase to be done in unison requires exact timing, Cunningham gave them a strong, steady beat by clapping his hands. Later, when they had learned the movement, they would do without the beat—just as they would do without the support of music throughout the dance.

No aspect of Cunningham's choreography—which, during the last decade, has been the most influential (and controversial) development in the world of modern dance—dismays lovers of traditional choreography so much as his complete dissociation of dance and music. Cunningham is not the only choreographer to dispense with storytelling and mimed emotion—the underpinnings of classical ballet and of most modern dance as well—but until fairly recently he was the only one to treat music and dance as distinct and wholly independent activities that simply occur in a common time and place. Most people tend to assume that there is a natural link between dance and rhythmic accompaniment of some sort, and a great many dancers consider Cunningham's denial of that link both arbitrary and self-defeating. Music can support a dancer—help him to jump higher and to move with greater precision—so why dispense with this useful and ancient relationship? Actually, as the ethno-musicologist Curt Sachs pointed out in his *World History of the Dance,* there is evidence that primitive man may very well have started dancing in response to certain inner promptings long before he danced to audible rhythms, and the supposed unity of music and dance may not be "natural" at all. In any case, Cunningham firmly believes that the independence of the dance from the music offers to both a higher degree of expressive freedom. "The result is that the dance is free to act as it chooses, as is the music," he wrote in a 1953 magazine article. "The music doesn't have to work itself to death trying to underline the dance, or the dance create havoc in trying to be as flashy as the music."

In Cunningham's work, the dissociation dates from the beginning of his professional association with the composer John Cage, who has served for the last twenty-five years as musical director of the Cunningham dance company. Cunningham and Cage met in the thirties at the Cornish School, an arts-centered institution in Seattle, where Cunningham was a student and Cage was on the faculty. They met again in New York in the forties, while Cunningham was dancing with the Martha Graham company. Cage had already evolved a method of composing music based on units of time, a method that afforded a complete break with the traditional theme-and-variations melodic structure of composition. Cunningham responded enthusiastically to this structural notion of Cage's, because it fitted in precisely with his own artistic leanings. "I never could stand the modern dance idea of structure in terms of theme and variations," Cunningham said recently. "That sort of A-B-A business based on emotional or psychological meanings just seemed ridiculous to me." From the start of their association, Cage and Cunningham have simply agreed on a certain time structure—for example, eight parts of two minutes each—and then gone off independently to compose the music and the dance.

In the spring of 1944, Cunningham and Cage gave their first joint New York recital, at the Humphrey-Weidman studio theatre. Cage played his own compositions on a "prepared" piano (nuts, bolts, bits of rubber, and other objects were inserted between the strings, thus converting the instrument into a sort of percussion orchestra), while Cunningham danced to rhythms that sometimes coincided with what Cage was playing and sometimes did not. "A lot of modern dance people in the audience liked one of my dances on that program—the one called *Root of an Unfocus*—because it seemed to them to be tied to an emotional meaning," Cunningham recalled not long ago. "They thought it had to do with fear. It had nothing directly to do with fear as far as I was concerned. The main thing about it—and the thing everybody missed—was that its structure was based on time, in the same sense that a radio show is. It was divided into time units, and the dance and the music would come together at the beginning and the end of each unit but in between they would be independent of each other. This was the beginning of the idea that music and dance could be dissociated, and from this point on the dissociation in our work just got wider and wider."

In the years since 1944, Cunningham has commissioned or composed dances to scores by many of the leading avant-garde composers in this country and Europe, including Pierre Boulez, Bo Nilsson, Morton Feldman, Christian Wolff, Earle Brown (who is Carolyn's husband), and, of course, Cage. As the new dance started to take shape in his mind last spring, he decided to approach Toshi Ichiyanagi, a young Japanese composer who four years earlier had done the score for Cunningham's *Story* and was now working in New York under a grant from the JDR 3rd (or John D. Rockefeller III) Fund. Ichiyanagi readily agreed to do a new score for Cunningham. He even came to several rehearsals, to get an idea of what the dance was going to be like—something he had not done in the case of *Story*. His score was not completed until shortly before the première, however, and the first time the dancers heard it was during their initial performance of the dance onstage.

Having begun with Carolyn Brown, Sandra Neels, and Yseult Riopelle, Cunningham continued to work with them exclusively for the rest of that week, at the end of which he went to California for a teaching engagement at Mills College. Several of the other dancers in the company had begun to wonder whether they would be in the piece at all. "They're all wondering about the new dance," Cunningham said wryly. "But then so am I." He had no clear idea of what the piece might become, except for a vague feeling that it would be a fairly long work—thirty minutes or longer—and quite complex. "I don't have ideas, exactly," he explained to a friend the afternoon before he left for California. "There's no thinking involved in my choreography. I work alone for a couple of hours every morning in the studio. I just try things out. And my eye catches something in the mirror, or the body catches something that looks interesting, and then I work on that. Of course, I know that when I give it to the dancers it's going to look different, just because their bodies are not the same as mine. But there's a point of balance—a point of tension—to any movement, and, with luck, I can transfer that to someone else. Sometimes it's not transferable—either their bodies won't do it or I can't translate it for them. But it's all in terms of the body, you see. I don't work through images or ideas—I work through the body. And I don't ever want a dancer to start thinking that a movement *means* something. That was what I really didn't like about working with Martha Graham—the idea that was always being given to you that a particular movement meant something specific. I thought that was nonsense. And, you know, I really think Martha felt it was, too. Once, when we were rehearsing *Appalachian Spring,* I had a passage that Martha said had to do with fear, or maybe with ecstasy—she wasn't sure which—and she said why didn't I go and work on it and see what I came up with. I did, and she was delighted; she even said it had solved some of her other problems. It's always seemed to me that Martha's followers make her ideas much more rigid and specific than they really are with her, and that Martha herself has a basic respect for the ambiguity in all dance movement. At least, that's my opinion. The ambiguity is always the interesting part for me, the getting to know each other in a new terrain—what we're doing now in this new piece."

The ambiguity in Cunningham's work has led some critics to call his dances abstract. This term is somewhat misleading, for—unlike the Alwin Nikolais dancers, who wear elaborate and enveloping costumes—Cunningham's dancers are never merely symbolic or decorative. "My feeling is very strongly that we are human beings engaged in certain situations," Cunningham has said. These situations may not be familiar, or even recognizable, but the dancers, whose simple costumes never conceal the body and whose movements are all based on the body's natural expressivity, are never more or less than human. Cunningham is often asked just what it is, in a dance that tells no story and delineates no psychological or emotional state of mind, that is being expressed. His reply is that he does not set out to express anything specifically. There is no "statement," no underlying idea or meaning. At the same time, he does believe that each of his dances produces a unique atmosphere, and, like many 20th-century artists, he invites the spectator to interpret that atmosphere in any way he wishes. Even a specific interpretation is all right with Cunningham. He wrote some years ago, "If the dancer dances—which is not the same as having theories about dancing or wishing to dance or trying to dance or remembering in his body someone else's dance—but if the dancer *dances,* everything is there. The meaning is there if that's what you want."

With a small company such as Cunningham's, in which everyone is to some degree a soloist, the look of each dance changes markedly as the company itself changes. (Two dancers have left the group since last spring, and two others have joined it. As a result, the company that is to perform *Scramble*—together with *Rain Forest* and *Walkaround Time,* the two other new works—at the Brooklyn Academy of Music this month will be dancing the piece rather differently from the day it was danced at its initial performance.) Cunningham welcomes and uses all individual variations. He chooses his dancers for technical ability and physical strength and also, one gathers, for intelligence. Carolyn Brown, the daughter of a dance teacher who had performed with the Denishawn troupe, claims that she tried hard not to become a dancer; she had been accepted as a graduate student in philosophy at Columbia when she started taking Cunningham's classes, in 1952. Gus Solomons, Jr., who joined the company in 1965, has a degree in architecture from M.I.T. Cunningham wants each of his dancers to develop and project a uniquely personal style, not a style that would be a mere reflection of his own. His training, which depends upon a natural and free use of the whole body, has the effect, he once said, of letting "the individual quality of each of the dancers appear, naked, powerful, and unafraid."

After attending a few rehearsals, one begins to understand what Cunningham means by this individual quality. It has·very little to do with "personality" in the commonly accepted sense, and nothing at all to do with the stage mannerisms of an actor or actress. Rather, it is tied up with a particular way of moving, which, in turn, bears a direct relation to the physical proportions of the dancer. Barbara Lloyd, whose small delicate body is attenuated from the hips down, moves with a delightful childlike spontaneity; of all the girls in the company she seems to be the most natural dancer, and critics often single her out, after Carolyn Brown, for special mention. Gus Solomons, a Negro, who is six feet four inches tall and whose legs are very long in relation to his torso, has a relaxed, springy buoyancy that is in striking contrast to the controlled precision of Albert Reid, a much more compactly built dancer. The personal quality of each dancer may be emphasized by the length of the neck, the way the head is carried, the relation of the arms to the torso. Valda Setterfield, who apprenticed briefly with José Limon before joining Cunningham in 1965, has an aristocratic hauteur that can change in a twinkling to its own comic parody. Peter Saul, trained in both ballet and modern dance, moves with an intensity that becomes even stronger during the stillnesses between movements. Yseult Riopelle is still working out her individual style. Sandra Neels, whose sole ambition when she came East from Seattle six years ago was to become a Cunningham dancer, made the breakthrough about two years ago. "I saw it start to happen," Cunningham said last spring. "I just caught something out of the corner of my eye, and said to myself, 'Well, now, that's beginning to be interesting.' Sometimes, you see, when a dancer works as hard as Sandra does, and has great concentration, she goes through everything and gets to this particular thing, this personal character that comes through the dance—not in spite of it but through it. For a long time, Sandra didn't have that, and people didn't notice her much. All you saw were those long legs and the short torso. Now it's all come together, and what you notice is herself. That's what makes watching dancers so fascinating."

Just before Cunningham went out to Mills College last spring, he gave Miss Neels a solo to do in the new dance. Characteristically, he did not tell her that it was to be a solo, and she did not know until some time later that she would be alone onstage when she performed it. She practiced the movement constantly, in spare moments between classes and during rehearsals. It was a slow phrase, with frequent changes of tempo and many points of stillness. (In Cunningham's dances, stillness is not just a pause between movements; like the negative volumes in a Henry Moore sculpture, Cunningham's still points have a distinct expressive power of their own.) Cunningham told Miss Neels to make the changes in tempo very clear, but he offered no other suggestions, and she was not at all sure that she was doing what he wanted. Soon after his return from California, she did the movement in rehearsal and heard him say, more or less to himself, "Oh, yes, it's going to work." But she had no idea precisely what she was doing to draw forth this comment. The dancers all learn not to expect direct praise from Cunningham, or anything very specific in the way of verbal direction. Miss Neels feels that without Carolyn Brown's help she could never have learned the repertory. "In spite of his being such a marvelous teacher, Merce is never completely precise about things," she explained once. "When he does something, you can see the whole shape of it beautifully, but often you're not quite sure about the direction—about whether you're supposed to face front or diagonally, or whether the back is supposed to be straight or curved." For his part, Cunningham maintains that he is too impatient to be able to enjoy teaching. He has said that the only sort of teaching he would find congenial is the teaching of the Japanese Zen masters, "who just go on doing what they do."

The individual quality of Cunningham's own dancing defies brief analysis. Any movement, he has said, can become part of a dance, and there are times during a performance when a movement of his looks so unstylized and natural or, conversely, so eccentric that he does not appear to be dancing at all. He frequently starts a phrase with no sense of preparation, no visible "attack"; he simply moves, as an animal moves, effortlessly and without tension, lending an impromptu, experimental character to the most complicated passages. In almost everything he does, there is a delicate balance between feral grace and awkwardness—the pleasing awkwardness of something done expertly but for the first time. "I think dance only comes alive when it gets awkward again," Cunningham once said. "I remember the only time I saw Ulanova. She was dancing *Giselle,* that old chestnut, and yet she managed to make it seem awkward and fresh again. That's what I admire." The critic Peter Yates has described as essential to the quality of Cunningham's dancing "the sensation of release, the prevailing relaxation, however elaborate or difficult the movement." Certainly the release is there, taking the forms, in astonishing variety, of wit, intelligence, strength, guile, tenderness, menace, and playful, openhearted curiosity. "I think basically it comes down to an appetite for motion," Cunningham said of his own dancing last spring. "Once, years ago, a student came to me and said she understood why I wanted to invent all these new kinds of movement but she didn't understand why I wanted to do them fast. My answer was 'Appetite.' It's as though you were going to get up and walk over to that door over there." He pointed to the door of the studio, through which students were just then entering for an advanced class. "You do it the normal way. Then you wonder how it would be if there were an obstacle in the way that you had to go around and still arrive in the same amount of time. And you do it with a lot more steps, and with fewer steps, and then you add some turning and jumping—all these other possibilities. You just have to be interested in motion for its own sake."

Merce Cunningham was born and brought up in Centralia, Washington, a small town fifty miles south of Tacoma. His father practiced law in Centralia, and his two brothers live there today—one practices law, and the other is a judge. Cunningham might conceivably have followed the same course if he had not started, at the age of twelve and by his own request, to attend private dance classes offered by Mrs. J. W. Barrett, a former vaudeville performer and circus bareback rider who imparted a rare theatrical zest to the Centralia social scene. Mrs. Barrett soon recognized that her new pupil was a naturally gifted dancer, with an extraordinary sense of rhythm. She accordingly arranged a dance program at the local Grange hall for Cunningham and her daughter Marjorie, who was about the same age, and the event was so successful that when summer came around she took them both on what she called a "vaudeville tour" to California and back. Cunningham still treasures the memory of one night during that tour, when the make-up bag got lost. He and Marjorie huddled in a broom closet, which served as the dressing room for the night club they were to perform in, while Mrs. Barrett searched for the missing bag. Suddenly Mrs. Barrett flung open the closet door, took one look at their forlorn expressions, and burst out laughing. "There's no make-up," she said, "so bite your lips and pinch your cheeks, and you're on!" Her spirit is something that Cunningham likes to recall during difficult moments on tour with his company.

Cunningham planned to become an actor when, after graduation from high school in Centralia, he went away to the Cornish School in Seattle in 1937. But he soon found himself getting more and more deeply involved in the dance department at Cornish. The head of the department was Bonnie Bird, a modern dancer who had worked with Martha Graham. At the end of his second year at Cornish, Miss Bird and John Cage, who played the piano for dance classes in addition to his other duties on the Cornish faculty, encouraged Cunningham to enroll in a summer program at Mills College, in Oakland, where the Bennington School of the Dance and a number of prominent figures in American modern dance—including Martha Graham, Doris Humphrey, Charles Weidman, and Hanya Holm—were to be in residence. Miss Graham saw Cunningham dance in a student program, and immediately afterward she suggested that he come to New York and work with her. Cunningham managed, not without difficulty, to persuade his parents, and two weeks later, in September, 1940, he arrived in New York and presented himself at the Graham studio. "Oh," said Miss Graham. "I didn't think you'd come." But she at once gave him an important solo part in the new dance she was then working on, called *Every Soul Is a Circus*. Cunningham was thus a soloist from the start of his professional career.

Martha Graham's immense and revolutionary contribution to the expressive language of dance was based, to a certain extent, upon a new relationship between the dancer's body and the floor. To the gravity-defying illusion conveyed by the ballet dancer *en pointe* Miss Graham opposed the sculptural dignity of a body drawing its strength and its expressive power from its contact with the solid ground. Her dancing, accordingly, possessed a monolithic quality, a heaviness of movement and gesture. It struck some people as odd that she should become enthusiastic about a dancer like Cunningham, whose natural gifts—bounce and lightness, and astonishing speed—seemed almost the exact opposite of her needs. Cunningham's own explanation is that Miss Graham's choreography was just then in the process of changing. "I think she had begun to be interested in the possibility of lightness," he said recently. "And, of course, she would always use the things that a dancer could do." In any event, Cunningham drew high praise from the critics for his athletic performance as the Acrobat in *Every Soul Is a Circus,* and for the next five years he was, with Erick Hawkins, one of the featured male soloists with the Graham troupe.

By the end of his first season with Miss Graham, Cunningham had started to wonder what else there was to do in the field of dance. He had been to see a great many dance recitals and performances in New

York that winter, and had found himself increasingly drawn to the ballet. "What appealed to me was the technical demands of ballet," he said. "Martha made great demands, of course, but not so much technically. Ballet's demands interested me: dexterity in the legs, speed, and, of course, air—jumping up and down." In spite of the deep and rather bitter schism dividing ballet and modern dance at that time—there was practically no communication between devotees of the two—Cunningham managed, with Miss Graham's help and encouragement, to enroll in the School of American Ballet, which had been founded in 1933 by Lincoln Kirstein and Edward M. M. Warburg, and of which George Balanchine was the director. Cunningham studied there for two years, on and off, while continuing to perform with the Graham troupe, and the training, he feels, was invaluable. It was certainly as important an influence as Miss Graham's in the development of his own style.

Cunningham also had a brief flirtation with the Broadway stage at about this time. Agnes de Mille, Valerie Bettis, and a few other modern dancers were just starting then to break into the musical comedy field, displacing the one-two-three-kick chorines of yore, and in 1943 Miss de Mille offered Cunningham a dancing role in *Oklahoma!,* for which she was doing the choreography. Cunningham turned it down. Six months later, though, he did accept a solo dancing part in another show that Miss de Mille choreographed, *One Touch of Venus.* He rehearsed and performed with the show for a week in Boston, and felt so ridiculous that he withdrew before the opening in New York, offering the somewhat lame excuse that Martha Graham needed him to rehearse for a tour that was about the begin. The Broadway musical stage has given employment to many modern dancers since then—it is still the only place they can earn what non-dancers would consider a decent living—but Cunningham was never tempted by Broadway again.

By this time, Cunningham had started to withdraw from the powerful influence of Martha Graham. Although he continued until 1945 to dance in certain works of hers and to tour with the company, he stopped taking her classes and spent most of his time working by himself, in a small loft studio on Seventeenth Street near Union Square. He lived on the money he made touring with Miss Graham, augmented by an occasional check from his parents, but in time he also started to teach a little. "I was just trying out everything I could think of," he has said of this period. "Probably the idea of having my own company was in my head, but I didn't really think in those terms. I'd always wanted to make dances, and I was just experimenting with different types of movement." The joint Cunningham-Cage recital at the Humphrey-Weidman studio in April, 1944, gave New Yorkers an opportunity to see the results of his experiments. Edwin Denby, in his review of the recital for the *Herald Tribune,* wrote of Cunningham, "His build resembles that of the juvenile 'saltimbanques' of the early Picasso canvases. As a dancer, his instep and his knees are extraordinarily elastic and quick, his steps, runs, knee bends, and leaps are brilliant in lightness and speed. His torso can turn on its vertical axis with great sensitivity, his shoulders are held lightly free, and his head poises intelligently. The arms are light and long, they float but do not have an active look. These are all merits particularly suited to lyric expression. The effect of them is one of excessively elegant and irreproachable sensuality." Of the program itself, Denby wrote, "I have never seen a first recital that combined such impeccable taste, intellectually and decoratively, such originality of dance material, and so sure a manner of presentation."

There has never been any question about Cunningham's natural gifts. Ever since 1944, though, there has been no end of dispute over the uses to which he has put these gifts, and the directions in which his explorations have led him. Some of Cunningham's dances—*Nocturnes,* for example, and the much acclaimed *Summerspace*—have been as lyrical, as elegant, and as irreproachably sensual as Denby or anyone else could have wished. Other dances have put lyricism very distinctly aside, however, in favor of grotesque distortions and eccentricities whose effect seems primarily comic, though in a few works, such as *Winterbranch* and the more recent *Place,* the whole purpose seems to be to create an atmosphere of grim devastation. Certainly the most amazing aspect of his work over the years has been its variety—its kaleidoscopic changes of tone and mood, not only from one dance to another but often within a single dance. As the London *Observer* noted in 1964, after the Cunningham troupe had had an extraordinary triumph in London, his dances "are so full of invention that they will be a mine for imitators for years."

Following the 1944 recital, Cunningham and Cage gave annual New York presentations of their new works. Their recitals, at the Y.M.H.A., the Hunter College Playhouse, and elsewhere, were attended mostly by painters and poets—rarely, in the early years, by musicians and dancers—and it took most of the next year for Cage and Cunningham to pay off the modest debts they had incurred for each recital, so they began casting about for performance opportunities outside New York. They found them by writing to colleges and universities, and from 1947 until fairly recently they rarely performed anywhere else. Their travels were sometimes complicated by Cunningham's rather sketchy sense of geography—he once booked them to perform in Phoenix and Seattle on the same day, thinking somehow that the difference in time zones would make the connection possible—but they covered a lot of territory and perplexed a sizable number of students. Confronted for the first time by prepared-piano music that incorporated many non-musical sounds and long silences, and by dancing that was neither interpretive nor programmatic, the audiences in the small colleges that Cunningham and Cage visited were usually dumbfounded. "People didn't yell or scream," Cunningham has said, "but there was a lot of nervous laughter, and, of course, a great many people walked out. If they happened to know anything about the modern dance—Graham and José Limon and people like that—they didn't like us at all."

The majority of established modern dancers did not look with much favor upon what Cunningham was doing, either, and it is worthy of note that his first major commission came from the rival world of ballet. Early in 1947, the newly formed Ballet Society in New York, which had grown out of Balanchine's School of American Ballet and was soon to become the New York City Ballet, commissioned Cunningham and Cage to create a work for its company of brilliant young dancers. Cage composed a score for an orchestra of forty conventional instruments. Cunningham worked independently with the dancers, among whom was the future star Tanaquil Le Clercq. Most of the dancers, Cunningham discovered, were much disturbed at first when they found themselves rehearsing without music, but then they caught on and did it beautifully. Isamu Noguchi designed the sets for the new work, which was called *The Seasons,* and which had its première at the Ziegfeld Theatre in May, 1947. Cunningham returned to the School of American Ballet in 1948 for two years, this time as a teacher, and in the summer of 1949 he put together a recital in Paris with Tanaquil Le Clercq and Betty Nichols, another young dancer from Ballet Society, whom he had happened to meet outside the American Express office. The recital took place in the atelier of the painter Jean Hélion, before a rather distinguished audience of artists and literati. Alice B. Toklas sat in the front row, and afterward she told Cunningham that she liked his dancing, "because it's so pagan." Cunningham has always enjoyed working with ballet-trained dancers, and as recently as the fall of 1967 he accepted an invitation to re-create his *Summerspace* for the Cullberg Ballet Company, in Stockholm. By 1949, though, he had begun to think more and more seriously of forming his own company.

"Forming a company," Cunningham said once, "means simply that you decide you want to do a piece with some other people instead of alone, and so you start to look around." He had already made a few pieces in which his students at the Seventeenth Street studio danced, but in those days his students were mostly dancers who had received their fundamental training elsewhere, and their physical and intellectual attributes did not always satisfy Cunningham's requirements. Following his return from Europe in 1949, he began to get a number of pupils with little or no previous training. The most talented of these students—Marianne Preger, Remy Charlip, Jo Anne Melsher, Marilyn Wood, and, later on, Paul Taylor, Viola Farber, Judith Dunn, and Carolyn Brown—became the nucleus of an informal Cunningham company. Performance opportunities were rare. Leonard Bernstein invited them to dance at the Brandeis University Festival of the Performing Arts in 1952, and in 1953 they appeared at the Alvin Theatre, in New York, in a program with the Martha Graham and José Limon companies. The Cunningham group did not really begin to function as a unit, however, until the summer of 1953, when it was invited to Black Mountain College, in North Carolina. Cunningham and Cage had been going to this militantly experimental institution since 1947, to perform and to teach; the faculty and the students were hospitable to their work, and the previous summer they had put on Cage's *Theatre Piece #1,* a mixture of dancing, music, poetry, motion pictures, slide projections, and other activities, planned and unplanned, that is now generally considered to have been the real beginning of the trend in this country toward Happenings and multi-media shows of all kinds. In 1953, the Cunningham dancers were in residence at Black Mountain for six weeks. They worked together every day, and acquired a repertory of new Cunningham dances that included *Collage* and *Suite by Chance*—the latter having an electronic score, the first of its kind written for a dance, by the young American composer Christian Wolff.

Like Cage in his music, Cunningham at this time was experimenting with various chance methods of composition, in an effort to go beyond his personal taste and his own physical memory of dance motions. He drew up elaborate charts for different aspects of the dance—tempo, direction of movement, kind of movement (leaping, running, turning, and so on), single or group movement—and then tossed coins to determine the order in which these would go together. For one dance, *Untitled Solo,* Cunningham drew up charts for specific movements of his head, back, shoulders, arms, hands, legs, and feet; to his great surprise, the dance turned out to be intensely dramatic. Unlike Cage, whose interest in chance was in part a reflection of an interest in Oriental religions and in recent developments in mathematics and science, Cunningham considered chance simply a tool for practical use—one method among others. "If you use chance, all sorts of things happen that wouldn't otherwise," he said once. "I found my dances becoming richer and more interesting, so I continued using chance methods. That's the only reason." Cunningham is a far more traditional artist than Cage in some ways; he will use chance when he thinks it may be useful, but he also depends on his own powers of conscious invention, his personal taste, and at times his memory, and he refuses to be bound by any system, even one of his own devising. At Black Mountain in that summer of 1953, for example, he abrogated the dissociation of music and dance long enough to choreograph a work, which he called *Septet,* for a particular piece of music—the *Three Pieces in the Form of a Pear,* by Erik Satie. It was because Cunningham liked the music so much that he decided to make a dance to go with it—though there was not the strict, beat-for-beat relationship that ballet lovers would recognize. He did the same thing three years later with Satie's *Nocturnes.*

The Cunningham dancers had their first major New York engagement in December, 1953—a one-week stand at the off-Broadway Theatre de Lys. They performed all the new works they had rehearsed that summer, played to a full house each night, and were totally ignored by the press. "But we had started to be a company, and that was something," Cunningham has recalled. "My idea was just to go on making pieces, and I felt it was silly to make a piece and then wait for an opportunity to do it, so I continued writing letters all the time to colleges and universities. We got a few dates. I remember once, at Notre Dame, there was a prom the same night and the only people in the audience were priests and nuns. But that's the way it happened—the company just sort of evolved."

The Cunningham company continued to evolve for the next decade, in spite of the desperate economics of the modern dance. In 1965, the Rockefeller Panel Report on the Performing Arts estimated that the total public for dance of all kinds in this country was less than one million regular attendants, and pointed out that, for economic reasons, even Martha Graham "has not toured in her own country for fifteen years." Although the Cunningham company traveled light—for several years they managed to get everything, including costumes and sets, into Cage's Volkswagen Microbus—the expense of transporting and feeding even a small company of dancers usually exceeded the modest fees that colleges could offer them, and, as a result, Cunningham could rarely pay his dancers anything at all beyond their expenses. The dancers supported themselves between engagements, usually by teaching, and considered themselves well rewarded simply to be associated with Cunningham. Naturally, some dropped out. Paul Taylor, a brilliantly gifted dancer, left in 1954 to form his own company, and several of the girls stopped dancing to get married or to have babies. By and large, though, that first "classic" Cunningham troupe functioned, far more than most repertory companies, as a tightly knit family. Its members all got along, in spite of the cramped quarters and the other recurrent miseries of the touring life. They saw a great deal of each other in New York between engagements, they shared the same ideas and interests, and they approached their work in the same state of intense stimulation, as a result of Cunningham's creative vision. Judith Dunn, who left Cunningham's company in 1963, to create dances of her own, has recalled that once, when the dancers trooped into a roadside diner after traveling all day, a waitress asked if they were members of some religious group. This spirit carried over into their dancing, and helped to create the strong impression of unity and physical inter-relatedness that in Cunningham's dances takes the place of the precise correlation of music and dance in the formal ballet.

Like the other members of the company, Cunningham supported himself mainly by teaching. Although he rarely performed in New York, young dancers heard about him and came to study with him, drawn by the belief that he was breaking new ground in the dance. The followers of Martha Graham, generally speaking, were continuing to work the psychological-symbolic vein that she had first mined thirty years earlier. Cunningham's work had less in common with the modern dance choreography of Graham and José Limon than it had with the dazzling neo-classicism of George Balanchine, who had made the New York City Ballet into the most advanced and most exciting ballet company in the world. Both Cunningham and Balanchine have always been interested in movement for its own sake, and Balanchine's ballets are often as plotless as Cunningham's pieces. The movement, however, is fundamentally different. Out of the so-called contraction-and-release technique of Martha Graham, Cunningham developed an articulation of the back and torso that is large and free—something not found in the ballet, where the torso is held relatively rigid at all times. Nor is it found in the Graham choreography, with its tense and dramatically contorted bodies. Cunningham's students are taught that the body operates from a central point of balance in the lower region of the spine; once this center of balance is fully recognized, he has written, the spine "acts not just as a source for the arms and legs, but in itself can coil and explode like a spring, can grow taut or loose, can turn on its own axis or project into space directions." Cunningham took "dexterity in the legs" from ballet technique and transformed it into a means of spatial expression. Instead of moving primarily up and down and in long leaps, as ballet dancers do, the Cunningham dancers tend to make large lateral movements; they cover a great deal of stage space, and make frequent use of everyday, non-stylized motions, such as walking and running. The difference between the Balanchine and the Cunningham companies became very clear in 1966, when, at Balanchine's invitation, Cunningham restaged his *Summerspace* for the New York City Ballet. Marvelously trained as Balanchine's dancers were, they found it extraordinarily difficult to move in the large, sweeping manner that is natural to the Cunningham company, and they could not do everyday things like running without making them seem slightly artificial. The New York City Ballet's performance of *Summerspace* struck most of the critics as interesting but not quite successful (when Viola Farber, then one of Cunningham's dancers, saw it she burst into tears), and Balanchine has not kept the work in the company's active repertory.

Many of the young dancers who sought out Cunningham were interested in doing choreography themselves. A class in experimental music and dance composition at the Cunningham studio in 1960, conducted by Robert Dunn, with Cunningham's cooperation, and made up almost entirely of Cunningham students, led directly to the formation of a new dance avant-garde that became associated with the Judson Memorial Church, on Washington Square. Taking as their starting point Cunningham's idea that any movement can be part of a dance, Yvonne Rainer, Judith Dunn, Steve Paxton, and other members of the Judson group arrived at a sort of non-dance aesthetic that could dispense with such rudimentary requirements as dance training and physical technique. Cunningham himself has never been willing to dispense with technique, and as a result he is looked upon by some of his former disciples with a respect that is slightly tinged with condescension. He has remained firmly committed to dance as dance, although he acknowledges that the concept is difficult to define. "I think it has to do with amplification, with enlargement," he said recently. "Dancing provides something—an amplification of energy—that is not provided any other way, and that's what interests me." It might be added that in Cunningham's case an innate and nearly infallible sense of theatre underlies all his experiments, and makes the final result interesting whether or not one is aware of the aesthetic that produced it.

Cunningham's ideas have always had much in common with those of his contemporaries in the visual arts, and for this reason some of his most loyal admirers and supporters have been painters and sculptors. His dances have been compared to the canvases of Jackson Pollock, in which there is no fixed center but, rather, an all-over relatedness of shifting movement. His feeling that any movement can be part of a dance has its echo in the assemblages and combines of Robert Rauschenberg, among others. Both Rauschenberg and Jasper Johns, the two most influential artists of the post-Pollock generation, have been associated directly with the Cunningham company—Rauschenberg for several years was its costume and stage designer, and Johns last summer became its artistic adviser. Rauschenberg was at Black Mountain during the summer of 1952, and he took part in *Theatre Piece #1*, projecting slides of his paintings onto a screen and playing a wind-up Victrola. For ten years, starting in 1954, he designed the costumes and sets for virtually all the new Cunningham dances, and from 1961 to 1964, having taught himself the rudiments of theatrical lighting, he traveled with the group as its lighting designer and stage manager. Rauschenberg's fertile imagination contributed to some of the most striking works in the repertory: *Summerspace,* for which he and Johns painted a huge pointillist backdrop that the dancers, who wear costumes of the same pointillist pattern, seem to disappear into whenever they stop moving; *Antic Meet,* a marvelously loony piece that at one point has Carolyn Brown, in a nightgown Rauschenberg found in a thrift shop, step through an onstage door and sit down in a chair strapped to Cunningham's back; *Story,* the indeterminate work for which Rauschenberg devised costumes and props out of whatever he found backstage on the day of the performance, and *Winterbranch,* a dark and powerful work that has been variously interpreted as being "about" nuclear war, concentration camps, Vietnam, and a shipwreck (as a sea captain's wife once suggested).

The collaboration of Cage, Cunningham, and Rauschenberg was an immensely stimulating experience for all three, and it also attracted the attention of people who might not normally have interested themselves in modern dance. In the late fifties, Cunningham began to receive more and more invitations to perform abroad, in Europe and even in the Far East—invitations that had to be turned down in most cases, because he lacked the money to get there. Cunningham did perform in Europe in 1958 and 1960, together with Cage, David Tudor, and Carolyn Brown, who had by this time become his principal dancer; in order for him to take the entire company along, someone would have had to put up the money for air transportation. The State Department, which regularly sends performing groups on foreign tours, considers Cunningham's work "controversial" and has consistently withheld its support.

Early in 1964, the company received a number of invitations to perform at European summer music festivals, and at the same time the wealthy family of Gita Sarabhai, an Indian musician who had studied with Cage, renewed an offer it had made once before to arrange a series of performances in India. The State Department refused to pay any travel costs, as usual, but this time Cunningham's admirers among New York artists came to the rescue. In 1962, a number of artists had contributed paintings to a benefit sale at the Allan Stone Gallery, which had been organized by the Foundation for Contemporary Performance Arts in order to make it possible for the Cunningham company to have a one-week "season" in a Broadway theatre. The Broadway season had not come about, for various reasons, so now the entire proceeds of the sale—slightly more than seventeen thousand dollars—were made available to Cunningham for travel expenses around the world. A grant of twenty thousand dollars for payroll expenses while in the Far East was subsequently obtained from the JDR 3rd Fund, and this, together with some additional grants from private sources, plus the sales of a sculpture by Richard Lippold and a painting by Rauschenberg, seemed to provide nearly sufficient funds for the undertaking. In June, 1964, therefore, the Cunningham dance company, with its various assisting artists and attendants (eighteen people in all, including ten dancers and Barbara Lloyd's two-year-old son), embarked on a world tour.

The tour lasted six months. The company gave seventy performances, starting in Strasbourg and Paris, where its reception was mixed, moving on to Venice, Vienna, and London, where it caused such a sensation that a one-week engagement at Sadler's Wells was extended by three more sold-out weeks at the Phoenix, and then going on to Scandinavia, Czechoslovakia, and Poland, and eventually to India, Thailand, and Japan. There were some casualties en route. Shareen Blair, a very pretty blond dancer, married an admirer in London and left the company forthwith. Viola Farber, who shared feature billing with Carolyn Brown, strained the Achilles' tendon in her left heel during a performance in Paris but continued to dance throughout the tour, despite medical warnings, and aggravated the injury to such a degree that she was obliged to withdraw from professional dancing soon after the company returned to the United States. (The loss was keenly felt. "She was unlike any other dancer I've ever seen," Cunningham said not long ago. "She always looked as though she were off balance, but she was always *on*. We used to do a duet called *Paired*, in which we'd come out at one point with our hands smeared with paint from cans we kept in the wings and daub it on each other; a certain color gave the cue for a certain kind of movement, and the movements were extremely hazardous. I don't think I could have done it with anyone but Viola. And that body! At Connecticut College once, a friend of mine in the audience heard a lady say, 'If that blond girl were my daughter, I'd snatch her right off the stage!' ") Also, to everyone's sorrow, friction arose between Cunningham and Rauschenberg during the tour and led to Rauschenberg's severing his ties with the company that fall. Rauschenberg had won the grand international prize for painting at the Venice Biennale in June, and this made him the most publicized painter in Europe; the friction, friends of both men believe, was a matter of artistic temperaments and was almost certainly unavoidable.

Although the company came home heavily in debt, the world tour proved to be a watershed in its development. The London success was a large factor. Dance critics, theatre and film directors, painters, musicians, and young aesthetes of all kinds had flocked to see the Cunningham dancers in London and had been enchanted by their ability to combine freedom of movement with classical precision. Being taken seriously in London, it seemed, was the key to being taken seriously in New York. The company was scheduled to dance twice at the Hunter College Playhouse that fall, and the demand for tickets was so great that a third performance was added. Appearances followed at the New York State Theatre, at the Brooklyn Academy of Music, and, in 1965, at Philharmonic Hall, where the Cunningham-Cage *Variations V* had its première. This is a multi-media work in which radio antennas mounted about the stage respond to the motion of the dancers' bodies, thus creating an electronic score anew each time, while in the background a huge screen shows fragmented images from television and movie films by

Stan VanDerBeek; the piece ends with Cunningham riding a bicycle onstage.

Invitations also came in from other parts of the country. In the fall of 1965, the company gave a week of performances at the Harper Theatre Dance Festival, in Chicago, during which they presented the latest Cunningham-Cage work, called *How to Pass, Kick, Fall, and Run.* This immediately became the company's most popular offering—an irresistible combination of joyous athletics by the dancers, who wear bright sweaters and white ankle socks, and a "score" made up of droll stories read, one a minute, by Cage, who sits at a table at one side of the stage and sips champagne while reading. For this and other numbers, the company could now count on a lively reception everywhere it went, and Cunningham's reputation grew rapidly. He had been discovered by a new and predominantly youthful audience, which had perhaps not been previously interested in dance and responded to Cunningham's dances as a new form of theatre. But when the Cunningham company was invited to represent America at the highly esteemed Paris International Dance Festival in November, 1966, the State Department once again refused to put up any funds, arguing that, as one government official blandly put it, "there was not much interest in Cunningham's kind of thing in Europe." The Cunningham dancers made the trip anyway, thanks largely to the generosity of the Spanish painter Joan Miró, who had seen them dance two years before, and who donated a painting to be sold for the purpose of paying their travel costs. In Paris, where they were in competition with state-subsidized dance companies from Cuba, the Soviet Union, and other countries, Cunningham took the major prize—the golden star for choreography. The award was received in Cunningham's absence (he had already flown home) by a U.S. Embassy official, who then refused to turn it over to Cunningham's business administrator, explaining that he preferred to send it to Washington. The award reached Cunningham in New York two weeks later, by mail, in a package on which there was forty cents' postage due.

For a modern dance company, international success can be ruinous. Cunningham's debts, covering the accumulated losses of two foreign tours, the costs of moving to his new studio, on Third Avenue, and a sizable sum in back taxes due to the government, amounted to something in excess of seventeen thousand dollars by last spring, at the time he was starting to work on *Scramble.* He did not seem to be seriously troubled by this burden, which is a fairly typical one for a small dance company in America. "I try not to think about money anymore," he confided to a friend at the time. "If I think about it at all, I get too nervous." Some practical thinking about the problem *was* being done, however—by Judith Blinken, the booking agent for the company, and by the directors of the

Cunningham Dance Foundation, a tax-exempt organization formed in 1964 to cope with the economic consequences of Cunningham's expanded activities in various fields. Mrs. Blinken, an attractive and resourceful young woman who also serves as Cunningham's business representative, and Wilder Green, a curator of the Museum of Modern Art, had organized a benefit for the Cunningham company to be held on June 3rd at the estate of the architect Philip Johnson, in Connecticut. They hoped to raise enough money this way to pay off at least a portion of the debt. In addition to working on the new dance, therefore, Cunningham was preparing a one-hour dance program for the company to present at the benefit. They would be dancing outdoors, and Cunningham planned to use sections from several of his dances, including the new one.

When Cunningham got back from his week of teaching at Mills College, he scheduled daily rehearsals for the entire company. With the exception of Peter Saul, who had injured his back during a performance earlier in the season, everybody would be dancing in the new piece. Saul came to the studio now and then to watch the rehearsals, which were sandwiched between two afternoon classes. Valda Setterfield and Barbara Lloyd frequently brought their small sons, who played together, sometimes quite noisily, during rehearsals. Gus Solomons, Albert Reid, and Barbara Lloyd all had outside teaching commitments that obliged them to miss some rehearsals, and on those occasions Cunningham tried to work on parts of the dance in which they did not appear. By this time, he had pretty well decided to call the new dance *Scramble*—a word that suggested to him the kind of coming together and breaking apart in interweaving movements that he was working out for it. Cunningham likes ambiguity in his titles, and in this case, he has said, he also had in mind the "scrambling" of codes and messages, the Air Force slang expression for getting planes off the ground in a hurry, and, prosaically enough, the method of cooking eggs.

Scramble took shape slowly at first, and by June 3rd, the day of the benefit at Philip Johnson's, the dancers had learned only about six minutes of the new material. They danced this much of it at the very end of the one-hour program, which also included portions of *Field Dances, Variations V, Rune, Suite for Five Nocturnes*, and *How to Pass, Kick, Fall, and Run*. They performed on a specially constructed outdoor stage, before a large and fashionable audience seated in a meadow, to the accompaniment of a largely electronic score created spontaneously by John Cage, David Tudor, Gordon Mumma, and Toshi Ichiyanagi. It had been Cage's idea to make of the occasion a sort of aural "picnic," with each musician bringing whatever sounds and sound-producing equipment he favored, and the rural welkin was rent by the amplified sounds of creaking automobile doors, engines, windshield wipers, and radios; a giant amplified tam-tam; a small Audubon birdcall (also amplified); a

French horn; and a good deal of miscellaneous electronic feedback. Usually, the Cunningham dancers say, they are so absorbed in the movement that they do not really hear the music being played, but this time the sheer volume commanded attention. Carolyn Brown complained later that the noise had affected her inner ear and, consequently, her balance, so that for a moment during the performance she came close to fainting. The company danced superbly nevertheless, and the six minutes of *Scramble* at the end impressed the audience as particularly brilliant. Dusk was falling over the meadow by this time, and Miss Beverly Emmons, the company's lighting designer and stage manager, had turned on some improvised stage lights—two spots mounted on a pole, plus the headlights of a Ford ranch wagon. During Carolyn Brown's first solo, a lovely sequence in which her undulating arm movements suggest a swimmer under water, one of several big helium balloons that had been tethered behind the stage was cut loose from its moorings; it rose swiftly above the trees and into a violet sky, where it cut across the white vapor trail of a passing jet—an effect that seemed perfectly in keeping with the atmosphere of the dance.

The Johnson benefit was a phenomenal success. Nearly four hundred invited guests—far more than had been expected—paid seventy-five dollars apiece to attend, and they stayed on after the performance for an elegant picnic supper, provided by Mr. and Mrs. John de Menil, who were co-sponsors of the event with Philip Johnson. The party ended somewhat abruptly at eleven-thirty, when a local policeman, acting on complaints from neighbors, silenced the Velvet Underground rock group just as it and the more enthusiastic amateur dancers among the guests were getting into action on the outdoor stage. No one seemed to feel particularly ill used, however, and Judith Blinken had excellent news to report at the next board meeting of the Cunningham Dance Foundation. The benefit receipts, after all expenses were subtracted, came to nearly twenty-four thousand dollars—enough to wipe out the debt and leave a surplus for future activities.

After a day off to recover from the benefit, Cunningham and his dancers began to work intensively on *Scramble*. The summer schedule went into effect at the studio on the same day, June 5th, which meant a considerable increase in the number of students attending classes. There were three classes every day—starting at ten-forty-five in the morning—and more than a hundred students. Cunningham taught five classes a week—three advanced, and two repertory classes for students who wanted to go further and master a specific Cunningham work (in this case *Rune*). Carolyn Brown and Sandra Neels taught the intermediate and elementary classes, and Albert Reid taught a new class in fundamentals for beginners (the dancers called this the zoo class). Lewis Lloyd, Barbara's former husband, who had been working part-time as an all-purpose business-and-office manager, was hired on a full-time basis by the Cunningham Dance Foundation early in June, and this freed Cunningham from a number of managerial chores and enabled him to devote most of his time and attention to the new dance.

As *Scramble* progressed, it made increasing demands on the dancers. It was clearly going to be "a real *dance* dance," as Gus Solomons put it—full of active, strenuous movement. Carolyn Brown, Sandra Neels, and Yseult Riopelle had been given a very fast and intricate passage in which they wove in and out of an interlocking, constantly shifting circle; the passage required perfect timing, and for several days they collided with each other every now and then, and dissolved in laughter each time it happened. There was also a sequence in which all the dancers ran the length of the room four times, leaping and pirouetting as they ran, and trotted back each time to start off in a different order. The continuity of the dance had not yet been established. Cunningham often uses chance operations—coin tossing—to determine such factors as the sequence of movements in a dance. So far, though, it appeared that deliberate choice had been a far more important factor than chance in the evolution of *Scramble*. Cunningham carefully gave each dancer the steps and the body movements that he had worked out in advance, and these figures became the raw material of the dance. He would change the movement if it did not seem to work well, or if the dancer felt uncomfortable doing it, and sometimes he would see something unexpected that he liked and would incorporate it—pausing to jot the new movement down in a spiral notebook that provided a rough, partly verbal and partly visual shorthand record of the choreography. Cunningham watched his dancers closely, alert for any new shape or movement that he might use. With *Scramble,* though, every movement, once accepted, was scrupulously plotted and rehearsed.

The whole question of chance in Cunningham's work is frequently misunderstood, even by some of his most ardent admirers. Chance sometimes (but not always) enters the choreographic process as a means of determining the kinds of movements used, the order of the movements, the tempi, and other specific aspects of the dance; Cunningham uses it to arrive at certain decisions, which are then permanent. Indeterminacy, a wholly different concept, enters when the dancers are allowed to make certain choices of their own *during* the performance. One occasionally hears people in the audience at a Cunningham recital say knowingly that the dancers "do whatever they like" onstage—a feat that, in view of the complexity and intricate timing of the choreography, would be astonishing indeed. Actually, there is only one piece in the current repertory, *Field Dances,* that allows the dancers any freedom of choice during performance. *Field Dances,* which dates from 1963, was designed to be performed by any number of dancers, in any space, over any length of time. Cunningham's method was to devise and give to the dancers a series of relatively simple movements, some of which could be done solo and others in conjunction with one or more people. Each dancer has a different gamut of movements, and each is free to do these in any order and in any part of the performing area, and the dancers are also free to leave the stage at any time. *Field Dances* is performed to Cage's *Variations IV*—a collage of recorded sounds—and the dancers simply stop when the music stops. The dance changes from performance to performance and is thus "indeterminate," but the degree of indeterminacy is confined within strict limits. The same used to be true of *Story,* in which the range of movements was somewhat more complicated. Cunningham sometimes talks of experimenting further in the direction of indeterminacy, but he worries about injuries that might result from dancers colliding with one another at high speed, and he also suspects that more indeterminacy might turn out to be less interesting. "The trouble is, we all tend to fall back on our old habits," he said one afternoon in his studio. "Dancing is very tiring, and when you're tired you're likely to just do the easy thing, the thing you know. Whereas when you know what you have to do, you can usually jump the fatigue, go beyond it." Several of Cunningham's dancers tend to question his basic tolerance for any degree of indeterminacy at all. "Every time we did *Story,* Merce was furious with us afterward," Sandra Neels said once. "He always said, 'We're never going to perform *that* again.' " Finally, he did drop it from the repertory.

Scramble was certainly not indeterminate, nor did chance play much of a role in its creation. Cunningham kept experimenting with the order of its various parts. By the middle of June, he had blocked out three main sections of the dance. There would be four sections in all, and his idea was that each one would be complete in itself. The longest section was the one that began with the whole company running four times across the stage. The fourth time across, Sandra Neels and Gus Solomons fell to the floor and remained there while the others went off; then, rising slowly, they began a sinuous, erotic duet, which led into the solo by Miss Neels. This section also included the Carolyn Brown solo with the swimming movement and a Brown-Cunningham duet, which began with her taking extended positions while he scrambled (literally) under her outstretched arm or leg. The duet then erupted into a very active series of rapid leaps and pirouettes, crisscrossing the stage and ending when she made a startling head-first leap into the wings, where she was caught by Gus Solomons and Albert Reid. One of the other sections centered on an athletic male trio, somewhat violent at times, for Cunningham, Solomons, and Reid. Cunningham was currently devoting his attention to the third section, which began with six of the dancers locked in a tight huddle that kept shifting as they changed positions, while Cunningham hovered on the periphery; the whole group then moved crablike across the floor and suddenly disintegrated as the dancers broke free and scattered, regrouped in pairs or threes, and went running and leaping across the floor in recurrent flurries of activity. Because the movement was so complex and so strenuous, the dancers were exhausted at the end of each rehearsal. During the brief breaks, they would collapse on the floor, or lie propped against the wall with their legs above their heads. They all downed vast quantities of vitamin pills, and taped and retaped their bare insteps against floor burns. The weather had grown warm and humid, and the sweat poured off them; wherever a dancer's body touched the floor a damp patch remained. Cunningham said that the new dance had started to take its own shape and life, and that his job from now on was to avoid interfering with it. He hoped to have it finished in time for their next engagement—a two-day appearance, on July 24th and 25th, at the Ravinia Music Festival, in Illinois—but he was not committing himself to that.

As the pressure increased, so did the emotional intensity of the dancers. One day, Cunningham was working on a new, extremely complicated phrase, to be done by all the dancers in unison, that occurred in the fourth section. Barbara Lloyd, who teaches a dance class at the Fine Arts Workshop, in Carnegie Hall, twice a week, had missed the previous rehearsal, at which Cunningham had taught them the new phrase. Sandra Neels coached her while the others waited for Cunningham to start the rehearsal, but the movement was too difficult to learn in a few minutes. When the company rehearsed it, Mrs. Lloyd could not keep up; each time they reached a certain point, she dropped out and stood against the wall. Cunningham asked her to try it alone. She got about halfway through the phrase, lost it, and walked back to the wall with her head down, fighting tears. Miss Neels hurried over to reassure her, and Cunningham went on to rehearse the men's trio. Later, he returned to the difficult unison phrase, and rehearsed it over and over while Mrs. Lloyd watched from the sidelines. By the end of the rehearsal, everyone was gasping with exhaustion. Miss Neels, who had developed new uncertainties of her own about the difficult phrase, began to question Carolyn Brown; when Mrs. Brown replied irritably, Miss Neels burst into tears. Later, though, in an East Village bar where the dancers gathered, they all seemed relaxed and in good spirits again. For half an hour after the rehearsal, Cunningham had worked alone with Mrs. Lloyd, coaching her in the new phrase.

No one at this point had a clear idea of what Cunningham himself would be doing in *Scramble*. There were a few passages—his duet with Carolyn Brown, the male trio, the "huddle" of six—that he danced with the others in rehearsal, but until the end of June he concentrated for the most part on what the others did and simply sketched in his own movements, taking a few steps and then indicating the rest with hand motions. As a result, the whole shape of the dance was never apparent. "Merce never talks about a piece, or lets you know what he's thinking about it," Mrs. Brown told a visitor in the studio. "And we never know what it's going to look like, because we don't know what *he's* going to be doing. All the time we were learning *Place,* for example, we weren't even sure he was going to be in it. I had a completely different idea about that dance, and then when we performed it the first time and saw him we all reacted in a completely new way." *Place,* which was added to the repertory just before *Scramble,* is also full of very lively movement, and while the dancers were learning it they came to think of it as a light and high-spirited piece of choreography. In performance, however, the combination of Gordon Mumma's harsh electronic score (entitled "Mesa"), Beverly Emmons' dimly lit stage, and Cunningham's strange wanderings and slitherings produced an atmosphere that was far from cheerful. Cunningham has conceded that his own part—he is onstage through virtually the entire dance—did in fact change the weight and the general tone of *Place* in a way that was unforeseen by him as well as by the dancers. He did not feel that his part in *Scramble* would have this effect, but one could never tell what a Cunningham dance was really going to look like until it had been performed at least once, with costumes, lighting, set, and music all contributing independently to the total effect.

The set and costumes for *Scramble* were being designed by Frank Stella, a young New York painter known for his severe, geometrically striped and shaped canvases. Stella had never designed a stage set before, and when Cunningham suggested the project to him, early in July, there was very little time remaining. By then, Cunningham had definitely committed himself to presenting *Scramble* at the Ravinia festival, so the set would have to be designed and built in two weeks. Stella nevertheless agreed to do it, and came to the studio on July 5th to see a rehearsal. He sat on the floor of the studio smoking a substantial cigar and watching the dancers attentively. Afterward, he asked some detailed questions. How tall was the tallest dancer when his arms were raised above his head? What were the dimensions of the Ravinia stage, and how high was the ceiling there? Would Cunningham object if part of the stage was blocked off? Cunningham said they would be dancing *Scramble* in the outdoor pavilion at Ravinia, on a stage that was used mainly as an orchestra shell; Beverly Emmons had been trying for three days to get the exact dimensions of the stage, but no one out there seemed to know them. "You understand, nothing about the dance is fixed yet," Cunningham said. "The order of things can be changed, the timing—we can stop and start again at any point. I've kept it that way on purpose."

What Stella had in mind was a set consisting of several broad horizontal bands of colored canvas of varying lengths, each to be mounted at a different height between vertical supports. The dancers would move in and out among these overlapping color bands, which would sometimes conceal parts of their bodies from view; he spoke of the horizontal lines' functioning as a contrast to the rapid lateral movement of the dance. Cunningham asked him if the individual bands, with their supports, could be moved about during the performance, and Stella said he didn't see why not. He said he would work something out and come back in a few days.

Stella came back on July 12th, with a scale drawing on lined yellow paper. The drawing showed six colored bands—red, orange, yellow, green, blue, and purple—ranging in length from four to twenty-four feet and mounted from floor level to eighteen feet in the air. Stella said that the vertical supports holding the frames of canvas would be on casters, so they would be easy to move about. He wanted these supports to be made of the heavy cast-iron pipe used in the garment district for clothes racks; the homely solidity of the pipe appealed to him. For the costumes, Cunningham had settled on six ordinary stretch-fabric leotards for the girls and jump suits for the men dyed the same colors as the canvas. The other two costumes would be black (Cunningham) and white (Carolyn Brown). Gus Solomons and Lewis Lloyd, who had been looking on while Stella explained his ideas to Cunningham, expressed some doubts about the set. Lloyd felt that the vertical supports would take up too much floor space and get in the dancers' way. Solomons thought it was going to look like "a real old-fashioned stage set—cumbersome." Cunningham said he thought the whole idea looked very beautiful.

Toshi Ichiyanagi, the composer, whom no one had seen for several weeks, came to the rehearsal on July 14th. Small, neat, and faultlessly attired (in contrast with Stella, who rarely appeared in anything but paint-spattered khakis and an undershirt), the composer sat quietly on a hard chair for two hours while the dancers rehearsed *Scramble* and also worked on *Nocturnes.* John Cage had come in that afternoon to play the Satie piano score for the rehearsal of *Nocturnes,* and when he finished Ichiyanagi opened a large manila envelope and showed him a page of the score for *Scramble.* The score was on white drawing paper, and it had no notes or clef signs or other conventional musical marks. Ichiyanagi had invented his own form of notation for the piece, consisting of exquisitely drawn symbols that referred to various kinds of sound and sound characteristics. Cage said that it looked difficult and very challenging. "It's as though one had to be intelligent in order to play it," he said, beaming.

As the day of the Ravinia première approached, the afternoon rehearsals lasted longer and longer—sometimes until six-thirty or seven o'clock. Fortunately, the dancers did not require a great deal of rehearsing for the other pieces they would be doing at Ravinia; they were scheduled to perform for two nights there, and in addition to the new work they would be dancing *Suite for Five, Place, Nocturnes, Winterbranch,* and *How to Pass, Kick, Fall, and Run,* all of which were in the current repertory and fairly fresh in their minds. Each piece required several rehearsals, though, and *Scramble* was only just beginning to take its final shape. Cunningham went through the entire dance at each rehearsal, timing each of the four major sections and experimenting, even now, with different sequences. Not until July 20th, just a few days before the performance, did he settle on the order that he would use at Ravinia. *Scramble* would begin with the section that the dancers had learned most recently, in which they came in very slowly, one by one, from the wings, each with a different sort of sinuous movement, until they formed a tight group at the center of the stage. Cunningham then sprang into the quick, complex phrase that had given Barbara Lloyd trouble earlier, and, one by one, they followed him until all of them were dancing the phrase in unison. This was followed by a new Cunningham solo, which the dancers now saw for the first time. The solo progressed through odd crouchings and twistings of the body to a passage in which Cunningham seemed to be making karate motions with his arms (he had seen an exhibition of karate and judo at Town Hall in the spring, and it fascinated him), and then he began a loose, loping, circling movement about the stage. As he was finishing the circling movement one day, he suddenly shouted—an angry roar that sounded more animal than human. The dancers thought for a moment that he had hurt himself. When he continued to dance, unperturbed, they realized that it must be part of the solo.

Cunningham also added several new and extremely difficult passages for Carolyn Brown in the second section of the dance. "I'm very happy about it," Mrs. Brown said afterward, "and I won't have it right for at least a year." In the third section, Sandra Neels' solo was developing beautifully. Her long, supple body looked strangely vulnerable during the intervals of stillness, and she was making the shape of each movement very clear. The fourth section began with the interlocking sextet of dancers, who broke apart to go flying singly and by twos and threes across the stage in waves, and then changed, at the very end, to a stealthy slow movement, with the dancers meeting and making brief contact—knee pressing into partner's hip joint—then sliding past. Cunningham said that the dance was "shaking down," but no one knew whether or not he was pleased with it. As the day of the performance approached, he became increasingly withdrawn and thoughtful.

The Ravinia festival runs from the end of June to the middle of September, and is one of the oldest and most distinguished of America's summer music events. Virtually all the great opera stars of the world performed there during the early years of the century, when it was primarily an operatic festival, and since 1936, when concerts began again after a four-year Depression blackout, Ravinia has been the summer home of the Chicago Symphony and has attracted prominent guest artists of all kinds. The festival is held in a pleasant, old-fashioned park twenty-five miles from Chicago. Many of its devoted patrons arrive early and picnic on the well-kept lawn under ancient leafy oaks, and if the concert is being given in the open-air pavilion they sometimes do not bother to buy tickets. The Cunningham company was to give its first performance, on July 24th, in Murray Theatre, a traditional theatre with a capacity of nine hundred and fifty; the world première of *Scramble* would take place the next night in the outdoor pavilion, which seats four thousand.

The company flew out to Chicago on July 23rd, a Sunday, arriving around noon and proceeding in rented cars to the Holiday Inn at Highland Park, about three miles from Ravinia. There were eighteen in the group—nine dancers (including Peter Saul, who would not be performing in *Scramble*), four musicians (Cage, Ichiyanagi, the pianist David Tudor, and the young composer Gordon Mumma), one child (Benjamin Lloyd), a business manager (Lewis Lloyd), an assistant business manager (Theresa Dickinson, who was soon to become the second Mrs. Lloyd), a lighting designer and stage manager (Beverly Emmons), and Gary Zeller, a young off-Broadway set builder, whom Lloyd had engaged to build Frank Stella's set. Although Zeller's firm, the New Century Studios, was charging the company less than it would have had to pay to have the set built by an uptown theatrical contractor, Lloyd said that it and the costumes were still going to cost more than three thousand dollars—enough to wipe out the remaining surplus from the Philip Johnson benefit and put the company in the hole again financially. The set would also necessitate many minor changes and readjustments in the choreography, but none of this bothered Cunningham. "If it works, it could be rather magnificent," he said. "The scale of the thing is immense, you know, and it *is* flexible—at least, I hope it's flexible. We'll know tomorrow anyway."

Later that afternoon, Cunningham, Cage, Tudor, Mumma, and several of the dancers drove over to Ravinia Park for an orchestral concert in the pavilion. The program, an all-contemporary one, included *Available Forms I,* a work by Earle Brown, Carolyn's husband. Cunningham stayed on after the concert to inspect the stage and the backstage area of the pavilion. The stage itself was large, but because it had been designed for use by a symphony orchestra and not for theatrical performances, its lighting and staging facilities were limited. Cunningham spent a long time in silent contemplation of the space, visualizing how his dancers would fill it. In a large ballet company, the *corps de ballet* creates guidelines for the eye and focuses attention upon the principal dancers; to fill a stage with eight or nine dancers and to sustain patterns of individual movement that do not lose themselves in isolation or conflict with others going on simultaneously requires not only a different form of choreography but a different concept of the performing space. For Cunningham, the stage is a continuum, an Einsteinian field in which the dancers relate not to fixed points (as even the Balanchine dancers do) but to one another. "Every point on the stage can be interesting, can be used," Cunningham has said. For an hour or more that afternoon, he studied the Ravinia stage, thinking how he would use it for *Scramble.*

The Monday evening performance in Murray Theatre was sold out. Cunningham started the program with *Suite for Five* (the five were Cunningham himself, Carolyn Brown, Barbara Lloyd, Sandra Neels, and Albert Reid), a dance that he once described as "very sparse, and largely about being still." The dance has an Oriental delicacy of movement, and the music (Cage's *Music for Piano 4-84*) is quiet. The audience, which was predominantly middle-aged and well dressed, applauded with what seemed like a sense of relief, as though, having braced themselves for uncompromising modernism, they had received a pleasant surprise. *Place,* which came next, quickly restored the mood of apprehension. A few couples left the theatre soon after it began, and a larger number covered their ears whenever Gordon Mumma's electronic score reached a certain volume. On the dark stage, the girls looked naked and defenseless in transparent-plastic costumes; the men, in dark leotards, had a furtive, menacing air. *Place* tends to engulf the spectators in a grim atmosphere of urban devastation, just as the dancers in it seem to be engulfed in the harsh roaring of sound. The ending is somewhat hair-raising. The girls fall and lie motionless while the men dance over and around them and finally drag them away; then Cunningham, lying at stage center, climbs into a large plastic bag and, with violent thrashing motions, propels himself offstage. The audience applauded the piece respectfully when it was over and returned, following the intermission, with surprisingly few desertions for the final work on the program, the Satie *Nocturnes.* They were rewarded by what is probably the most alluring work in the Cunningham repertory—a dance that many Cunningham admirers feel is almost *too* beautiful, in the classic, balletic sense. The dancers are all in white. Rauschenberg designed their costumes to resemble "inhabited seashells," and his cool blue-white lighting and simple set—a white gauze curtain across half the stage, making a separation between movement seen clearly and movement seen as though at a distance—create a dreamlike, moonlit space for the dancers to inhabit. The dance itself is a sequence of rendezvous. The dancers meet and part—come together, touch, follow, relinquish contact—moving sometimes with the delicate Satie piano music and sometimes independently of it as the music and the dance hold rendezvous of their own. Throughout the dance, there are moments of unexpected humor and moments of sudden beauty (as when

Carolyn Brown, whirling across the stage, at each turn sends shards of reflected light flashing from a mirror-glass tiara), and at the end Cunningham, kneeling behind the gauze curtain, seems to be waving a spectral, though friendly, farewell. The audience loved it.

As soon as he could manage to do so politely, Cunningham excused himself from the throng of well-wishers backstage, changed into street clothes, and hurried over to the pavilion to see how Gary Zeller was getting along with the set for *Scramble*. Zeller had started to assemble the various elements that afternoon, with somewhat grudging assistance from the Ravinia stagehands. The vertical support pieces were made of polished aluminium, broken down into lengths that fitted together ingeniously. (The cast-iron pipe that Stella originally wanted to use had turned out to be far too heavy.) The strips of colored canvas, eighteen inches wide, were each to be attached to two horizontal aluminium supports with Velcro tape fasteners, and the horizontal supports were then to be attached to the uprights at the desired heights. Two of the six elements had been assembled so far—a four-foot red one, standing eighteen feet high, and a twenty-four-foot purple one, standing at floor level. Cunningham shoved the long purple strip around the stage with one foot, testing its maneuverability. It moved fairly easily on its casters. He stood on the stage for nearly an hour, chin in hand, eyes narrowed, and from time to time he made notes on a scrap of paper. He also conferred with Zeller and Beverly Emmons, both of whom planned to work through the night—Zeller to finish building the set and Miss Emmons to oversee the installation of a special lighting boom.

The rest of the company had gone for a late supper (the dancers do not eat before a performance) at a restaurant near their motel, and Cunningham joined them there shortly after eleven. In contrast with their high spirits—the post-performance euphoria that is one of the few visible rewards of the dancer—Cunningham seemed, if anything, more withdrawn and reserved than usual. He had wrenched a knee quite painfully during the performance of *Place*, but nobody else knew this at the time. By midnight, the dancers had all gone to bed.

Most of them were in the motel dining room at nine the next morning. Over breakfast, they discussed the Detroit riots, which were front-page news in all the Chicago papers that day, and read the reviews of the previous night's performance, which were generally favorable (they had "held the audience rapt throughout some extremely bizarre happenings onstage," according to one reviewer). David Tudor and Gordon Mumma had already gone over to the pavilion to see about some rented sound equipment for that evening's performance. Beverly Emmons and Gary Zeller, who had worked until 3 A.M., hurried back to work immediately after breakfast. Cunningham remained in his room. He had awakened to find his knee swollen and painful, and he wanted to give it as much rest as possible. It was a perfect summer day, clear and warm and still, with none of the humidity that had made the rehearsals in Manhattan particularly trying.

At the pavilion, Beverly Emmons was having her problems with the stagehands. They were not accustomed to coping with theatrical demands, for the Chicago Symphony and its guest artists did not require much in the way of stagecraft. Miss Emmons, an emphatic young woman dressed that day in a very short tan miniskirt, was trying to get the orchestra's equipment removed from several dressing rooms, and she was also trying to get somebody to clean and, if possible, sand the stage, which was rough and splintery. She was not having much luck. Mumma and Tudor, on the other hand, were delighted with the sound equipment that the festival had provided for them. The Cunningham company owns very little sound equipment, so it usually sends a list of its electronic requirements to the management wherever it is going to perform and hopes for the best. The Ravinia festival's general manager, Marshall Turkin, had come through magnificently, with four eight-inch loudspeakers, all the amplification circuitry required, and two local sound engineers to help in assembling it. The sound men spent the morning mounting and hooking up the speakers at either side of the stage, while Mumma and Tudor built themselves electronic control nests on the stage itself, one at either edge. Most of the wiring was for Ichiyanagi's score.

The Ichiyanagi score had turned out, as Cage predicted, to be extremely difficult. The notation called at certain points for an instrument to be played by another instrument; Ichiyanagi left it up to the performer to decide just what the instruction meant and how it was to be carried out. All morning, Mumma, whenever he had a free moment, practiced his French-horn part. He is a virtuoso French-horn player, and he solved the "instrument plays other instrument" problem by using a bassoon reed and an oboe reed in place of the horn's regular brass mouthpiece. The sound he got with the bassoon reed was mournful and sonorous; with the oboe reed it was wavering and a trifle shrill.

The dancers arrived at ten-thirty and spent the next hour warming up onstage, oblivious of the stagehands and of the sound equipment, which occasionally emitted earsplitting squeals and buzzes. Each of the dancers had a different sequence of exercises for stretching and limbering the muscles. They worked in silence, totally absorbed in their individual routines. One leg and then the other would swing back and forth twenty times, lightly brushing the floor as it swept through its arc; then twenty times out to the side, then twenty times in a circle. Gus Solomons, who looked casual and relaxed even when rebounding from a great leap, took less time to warm up than Albert Reid or Peter Saul, who would appear in the two works that were to make up the evening's program along with *Scramble.* Among the girls, Barbara Lloyd, Valda Setterfield, and Yseult Riopelle worked for a while, rested, then started again. Carolyn Brown and Sandra Neels worked more or less steadily, scarcely pausing for breath, until Cunningham summoned them at twelve-fifteen to start rehearsing *Scramble.*

Cunningham, whose warmup gave no indication that his knee bothered him, had spent a large part of the morning experimenting with the set, moving the six elements in accordance with a group of charts he had drawn up the night before in his room. The blue canvas, which was in the middle range in respect to both length and height, had developed a slight but noticeable sag. Zeller did not want to add a vertical center brace without consulting Frank Stella, but nobody seemed to know for certain whether Stella was coming out for the première.

The fresh, strong colors of the Stella set had an extraordinary effect on the movement of the dance. The set seemed to change the scale of the piece, containing and interacting with the dancers and defining the shape of their movements in unexpected ways. Cunningham wanted the positions of the various elements to be changed after each of the major sections of the dance, and the dancers had to adjust their movements and their cues accordingly. At certain points, they had to step over the bases of the aluminum supports, which were difficult to see under any circumstances and would be even more of a hazard under stage lighting. Entrances and exits had to be reworked. Instead of wings, the stage had four small doors, one at each side and two at the rear. A dancer would go out one door and run along a dark and narrow passageway backstage to get into position for the next entrance; there were moments of confusion when a dancer found the exit partly blocked by one of the vertical supports. When Carolyn Brown first rehearsed her flying leap off the stage, her head almost grazed the low lintel of the doorway. She did it four more times, practicing a lower trajectory, while the other dancers held their breath. It was nearly two o'clock before Cunningham finished with *Scramble.* The dance seemed to have grown enormously in the Stella set, and it was clear that the strange centrifugal and centripetal relationships of the dancers as they came together and separated on the big stage would add up to a large-scale and infinitely complex work.

While the dancers quickly rehearsed *Winterbranch* and *How to Pass, Kick, Fall, and Run*—the two works that would be performed after *Scramble* on the evening's program—Ichiyanagi and Cage held a conference with two percussionists from the Chicago Symphony who had been added to the performing ensemble for *Scramble.* The newcomers stared in some perplexity at the pages of the score, with their beautifully drawn but totally unfamiliar notation. Ichiyanagi, whose English is excellent but halting, explained, with Cage's occasional assistance, the meaning of each symbol. There was a symbol for pitched sounds, another for noises, and another for sounds electronically produced; there was a symbol specifying when an instrument was to be played by another instrument, and a symbol for when a pitched sound was to "hit" a noise, or vice versa. The degree of loudness or softness was indicated by the position of the symbol above or below a horizontal line. Almost all the sounds were to be sustained for as long as possible, and they were to be produced without emphasis or stress, so that the effect would be of sounds with no beginning or end. Each performer had a wide range of choices both in the instruments he could use and in methods of sound production, and for a while the two Chicago Symphony men could not quite grasp what was expected of them. They wondered how a pitched sound could "hit" a noise. By letting a triangle strike against the back of a chair? Ichiyanagi nodded. Gradually, with Ichiyanagi's and Cage's encouragement, the idea that these sound problems were theirs to solve began to appeal to the two men. They became visibly enthusiastic.

Cunningham finished rehearsing *Winterbranch* and *How to* at two-thirty. The dancers collapsed on the stage, exhausted and dirty after four hours' work, and watched the musicians setting up their percussion instruments in the space between the stage and the front row of seats. Mumma and Tudor were still wiring their apparatus together, and the loud crackle of electronic feedback periodically shut off conversation.

"Are we going to hear any of the music before we dance?" Carolyn Brown asked Ichiyanagi.

Ichiyanagi said he hoped there would be time for a music rehearsal that afternoon.

"Is it very loud?" Sandra Neels inquired.

Mumma said that the speakers were mounted outside the stage area, one on either side, and therefore the sound would not be loud at all for those onstage. "It's going to be a mixture of live and electronic sound," he added.

"We know," Miss Neels murmured, a trifle glumly.

The company had a late lunch at the motel and rested for an hour or so, and then, at five-thirty, Cunningham and several of the dancers drove back to Ravinia. The others followed half an hour later. In the car going over, Cunningham seemed surprisingly relaxed and peaceful; the withdrawn, preoccupied manner of the preceding days had largely disappeared, and he chatted amiably with the dancers about inconsequential matters that had nothing to do with the new dance or the performance. The evening was clear and cool, and the setting sun, slanting through the oaks in Ravinia Park, bathed the lawn in pools of light and shade. The dancers went backstage to put on their make-up. For the next forty minutes, the only sign of activity was a teen-age boy methodically dusting every seat in the pavilion while totally absorbed in a transistor radio that was belted to his waist and plugged into his left ear.

Shortly before six-thirty, Cunningham, wearing an ancient striped dressing gown and slippers, emerged from his dressing room and began once more to shift and rearrange the elements of the set. In the fading light onstage, his theatrical make-up gave him an unearthly look: huge, shrouded eyes and livid cheeks. He consulted his charts, moved the blue canvas, studied it for a while, moved another. After a few minutes, he went back into his dressing room and closed the door. One after another, the dancers came out and began to warm up. Yseult Riopelle was first, and then came Sandra Neels (face chalk white, eyes dark), then Gus Solomons (crouching and stretching like some giant mantis). Two teen-age girls, early arrivals, came to stand by the stage and stare in wonder at Solomons, who took no notice of them. The dancers wore practice clothes; they would not put on their costumes until the last moment.

By seven-thirty, the space on the lawn outside the pavilion proper was beginning to fill up with non-paying members of the audience. Families with young children staked out choice spots, spread their picnics, and trained binoculars on the practicing dancers. A diminishing patch of sunlight fell across the middle rows of seats inside the pavilion. Backstage, it was getting dark. In the passageway, Sandra Neels stood holding on to a pipe while she did slow knee bends. "I always feel as though I'm about to fall apart when we're doing a piece for the first time," she confided to Barbara Lloyd. "I only wish the stage were more friendly." The floor of the stage was even worse than it looked. During rehearsals, the dancers had worn ballet slippers to guard against splinters, but during the performance itself they would be barefoot.

Just before eight o'clock, Frank Stella appeared backstage. He had on his customary undershirt and khakis and, as usual, was smoking a cigar. "I wasn't going to come," he explained, "but then I decided I'd hate myself too much if I didn't, so I just dropped what I was doing and went out to La Guardia." He needed two dollars to pay the taxi driver, who had brought him over from O'Hare Airport. Stella and Gary Zeller went out onstage to look at the set. The artist seemed pleased. "The green one sags a little, but it's not too bad," he observed. "The little red one looks great up there." Zeller had put an aluminium strut in the blue canvas to remove most of its sag. Stella approved, but soon he and Zeller were deep in a discussion of how the set could be improved technically and made less cumbersome; Stella thought it might be possible to devise a system of overhead cables. Lewis Lloyd, who had joined them, went away shaking his head.

Cage and Ichiyanagi were checking the equipment that the men from the Chicago Symphony had procured for them. Each of the four percussion players (Cage, Ichiyanagi, and the two newcomers) had his own ensemble of instruments. The Chicago Symphony men were stationed just to the right of the stage, where they had surrounded themselves with drums, triangles, gongs, a vibraphone, marimbas, and various other conventional or improvised instruments. Ichiyanagi, in the center, would perform mainly on the piano and the celesta. Cage was off by himself at the left, with more drums, a glockenspiel, wood blocks, and a battery of electronic sound-making devices. David Tudor and Gordon Mumma were up on the stage itself—Mumma at the far left, with his French horn and his electronics, and Tudor at the far right, with an all-electronic console, which he would use to modify and mix the sounds that the others were making. Mumma was very excited about the score, which he said was by far the most difficult he had ever had to perform for a dance concert. When the Chicago Symphony men tried to explain their parts to three of their colleagues who had dropped by, one of the visitors remarked that Ichiyanagi's score would make the previous Sunday's avant-garde program sound like Mozart. (After the performance, many people remarked how surprisingly gentle and "musical" the score had been, and how Japanese.)

It was almost completely dark backstage now, and very quiet. The dancers were putting on their costumes. The paying audience started to file in at about eight-fifteen. It looked to be the same sort of audience as the previous night's, but considerably larger; two-thirds of the four thousand seats were occupied by eight-thirty. A bell rang backstage, and the dancers assembled quietly in the dark passageway. The five girls stood very still in their new skin-tight leotards (Carolyn Brown in pure white, the others in yellow, green, orange, and purple); Albert Reid and Gus Solomons (Reid in a red jump suit, Solomons in a blue one) seemed to be barely suppressing an urge to be in motion. Cunningham joined them; it was the first time anyone had seen him in nearly an hour. He wore a black jump suit. His manner was calm and gently paternal, and for the last few moments, as they whispered and joked in the dark passageway, the company seemed like an affectionate family on the eve of some pleasant celebration. Beverly Emmons came up and said that the music was going to start very soon. "They'll play for two minutes while I dim the house lights," she said. "When I put the stage lights up, you begin. O.K.?" There was a last-minute question about curtain calls—should they go offstage and then come back, or just stay onstage at the end? Cunningham said to go off and then come back. The music started quietly, with some long, isolated sounds from the celesta and the glockenspiel, and the house lights began to dim. The dancers all cupped their hands and blew kisses to one another. "Have a good time," Cunningham whispered as they scattered to their various entrance points. The stage lights came up, and the dance began.

EIGHT

Problems in Dance

Every field is beset with problems, and dance is no exception. In the performing arts, where people must work together toward the common goal of a well-executed performance of high quality, time is a great factor. Therefore, organizations are often run by a highly authoritarian figure. Unfortunately, this is often the only way to put on performances. Someone has to lead—some one person must inevitably take the responsibility. The opera director, the conductor, the play director, or the choreographer must often be like a commander leading his troops into battle; very few performances can be created by the democratic process. Although responsibility must be assumed by many—set designers, electricians and carpenters, costumers, house and box office managers, musicians, and in dance, ultimately, the choreographer—in the end one person has to say "yes" or "no." This person might be a choreographer, a producer, an impresario, or a company director. It can be said that theatre is an art with a love for crisis, for every performance has its share of minor or major tragedies. Perhaps this very excitement draws people to theatre.

Dance is a constant competition with oneself. After every performance begins the struggle to make the next one better; every artist continues to attempt to make a unique and personal statement about life through his art. Sometimes the performing arts seem to become stagnant or repetitious. When the great artist recognizes that such a thing is taking place, he becomes a protester, usually through his new works although sometimes by writing about his art. This section includes a short piece by the choreographer Jean Georges Noverre, showing this same problem in dance in the eighteenth century. This question of stagnation and rejuvenation will always be with us.

Because of the need for leadership and sometimes complete control or domination, those in control are under constant scrutiny. These people command respect, sometimes from love, sometimes from fear, and sometimes from hatred, but respect nevertheless. Since the performing arts focus so clearly on the moment of theatre, the leader may be ruthless in his quest for talent, time, and, inevitably, money. Those people who accumulate the time, talent, and ways to finance their operations must become thick-skinned and quite oblivious to any criticism which would wish to diminish the authority they have earned. On the other hand, the critic's voice may be important to the dance field as a whole; it might point out stagnation and should be considered in many instances. George Balanchine must be given credit for building a great ballet company respected throughout the world. His name will go down in history, owing in part to his unfriendly critics. The article on "Balanchineballet" illuminates some by-products of the Balanchine empire that Douglas Turnbaugh and many other dance experts have criticized.

The problems of dance in the universities become the problems of the entire field of dance when we consider that the universities have supported modern dance in this country and have engaged most of our ballet companies through concert series. The following quote from *The Performing Arts: Problems and Prospects* illustrates the relationship between dance and the universities:

> University concert bureaus are generally free from commitment to the star system and have provided young, relatively unknown artists with opportunities to establish their reputations. Indeed, without them, the modern dance could not exist at all in this country. In many parts of the country, the university is the only agency capable of organizing programs of high quality in all the arts.[1]

Several views of dance are presented that indicate relationships that dance in the universities has built up within departments of women's physical education. Many universities have moved their dance units to areas of the fine and performing arts, but these moves have often become a reality only after years of negotiation to achieve independence, not so much from physical education as from an administrative structure not suited to the creation of significant art. Physical educators have used very intelligent arguments to defend the inclusion of modern dance in their curriculums, but the situations that are uncovered in this working relationship seem to indicate the irrelevance of *any* arguments to promote its continuance.

Dance has long been a shunned field of human endeavor in the

Christian world. Some of the caution is well founded, since dance and the performing arts can be a haven for the outcast from society who finds his skills accepted regardless of his personal traits. This has caused a certain ease with regard to traditional mores within the performing arts professions, but these mores are not a part of the performance—they are not in that mainstream of activity that funnels its energies toward a performance. Dance has a special problem of being inseparable from the human body. Our Puritanical heritage has taught a disdain for the activities of the flesh, and, naturally, since dance as an art has this frame of reference, it is believed—perhaps unconsciously by some—fraught with the devil. Prostitution, homosexuality, drug addiction, etc., have been associated with dance, and with other arts as well. Dance does not create vices. Nevertheless, attention can be drawn to the fact that homosexuality in particular *does* exist in dance and the arts. This problem is a thorn in the side of the field, and it is hoped that with education, beginning in the schools and extending to mature audiences, dance will be recognized as a beautiful human activity for man and for mankind.

The last problem, which is not dealt with in this book, is money. The editors could see no reason for emphasizing a problem that nearly everyone has. Dance costs money, but so does just about everything else. Dance companies need money, but so do all performing artists. Dance students need financial help, but so do medical students. The situation is summed up quite well in the Rockefeller Panel Report:

> Most major dance groups in the United States fall far short of meeting their expenses from the sale of tickets. Although dancers are generally the lowest paid of the performing artists, company budgets run high. Dance companies usually have a large number of performers, require extensive rehearsal, need music and scenery, and have the continuing expense of mounting new productions. The audience for the dance is still small, and this, too, adds to the difficulties at the box office.
>
> A major segment of the dance world has no institutional support whatsoever. It consists of small companies organized by individual choreographers to give performances whenever money can be gathered together to rent a hall, provide some sort of basic musical accompaniment, and print tickets. This method of doing business almost guarantees box office failure.[2]

Government grants have helped, but there is no guarantee these will continue; private foundations have helped, but their future support is equally unpredictable. The best hope is in education, that is, in making *all* the arts, including dance, such a vital part of our well-being and such an important part of the life of the educated man in society that the need for the arts will be expressed by the public. In the past ten years or so a great deal of progress has been made in this direction. When our society is ready to pay for a quality of life as represented in part by the arts, then financial problems will not be so great.

CHANGING THE PRESENT STRUCTURE:
AN EIGHTEENTH-CENTURY VIEW

Jean Georges Noverre (1727-1810) was an important dance innovator and, indeed, a revolutionary in his day. Like other artists before him, and many after, he condemned the styles of his time and sought to make dance something different. Noverre represents historically a problem that has always existed: where do we go from here? Art cannot be mass produced; each article is an original. Noverre attempted to put his stamp of disapproval on the goings-on of 1760 by naming the situations and giving some suggestions for improvement. He did have an effect on ballet for years to come, and, in fact, many of the ideas Noverre describes were embraced by others and held sway for more than a century—until the rebellion of Michael Fokine.

The problems described in the editors' introduction and "Letter I" of Noverre's *Letters on Dancing and Ballets* are indicative of only a few of the many that can and do exist in dance. Noverre was interested in the use of technique for human expression, not as an end in itself. He also was intrigued with the idea of faithfully blending all the arts in ballet, the problems of combining music with dance, the transient nature of a ballet, ballet as story or pure dance, and the use of symmetry. Artists in both ballet and modern dance continue to be concerned with these questions. They will never be solved; there are no answers to what dance should be, only opinions. Noverre's ideas are the valid opinions of a sensitive artist looking at the ballet of the eighteenth century.

AUTHOR'S PREFACE

JEAN GEORGES NOVERRE

When I decided to write on an art which is the continual object of my studies and reflections, I little foresaw the success and effect of my letters on dancing when they appeared in 1760. They were welcomed with interest by men of letters and persons of taste; but, at the same time, they were received with spite and ill humor by those for whom they were primarily designed. They aroused the indignation of nearly all the dancers of Europe, and especially those attached to the Opéra at Paris, which was, is, and will continue for a long time to be the first and most magnificent of the temples of Terpsichore, but the votaries of which are the most pretentious and ill-humored. Anathemas were hurled at me, I was treated as a reformer, and regarded as a man so much the more dangerous since I attacked the principles held in veneration owing to their antiquity.

When one has grown old in an art, whose laws one has followed and practiced from childhood, it is difficult to go back to school again: idleness and self-esteem are both opposed to it; it is as difficult to forget what one has acquired as to learn something new. The bitterness and disgust evoked by revolutions, of whatever kind, are always felt by persons of a certain age. The succeeding generations are always the ones to enjoy their useful and agreeable consequences.

To break hideous masks, to burn ridiculous perukes, to suppress clumsy paniers, to do away with still more inconvenient hip pads, to substitute taste for routine, to indicate a manner of dress more noble, more accurate and more picturesque, to demand action and expression in dancing, to demonstrate the immense distance which lies between mechanical technique and the genius which places dancing beside the imitative arts—all this was to expose myself to the ill-humor of those who respect and venerate the ancient laws and customs, however barbaric and ridiculous they might be. Again, when I received the praises and commendations of artists of all kinds, I was, on the other hand, the butt of the envy and satire of those for whom I wrote.

However, as in all arts, observations and principles drawn from nature always end by conquering. My opponents, although

From *Letters on Dancing and Ballets,* trans. Cyril W. Beaumont (New York: Dance Horizons, 1966), from the revised and enlarged edition published in St. Petersburg, 1803, pp. 1-14.

exclaiming that I was wrong, and rebutting my ideas, yet adopted them gradually. They came over more and more to my way of thinking, and unconsciously carried out my reforms, and soon I saw myself seconded by artists who, with taste and imagination rising superior to their art, were far above sentiments of envy and jealousy.

M. Boquet, who had comprehended and adopted my views; M. Dauberval, my pupil, who struggled continually against prejudice, custom and bad taste; M. Vestris himself, who in his turn was struck by the truths which I had taught when he first saw them put into practice at Stuttgart; all these artists since become so celebrated, yielded to the evidence and ranged themselves under my banner. Soon, opera took a new line in regard to the costume, pomp and variety of its ballets, and the dancing in this style of entertainment, which, although still capable of further perfection, has become nevertheless the most brilliant in Europe, at last emerged from its long infancy; it learned to speak the language of the passions which before it had not even lisped.

If one reflects on what opera was in 1760 and on what it is today,* it will be difficult not to recognize the effect produced by my letters. In fact they have been translated into Italian, German and English. The glory of my art, my age, and my numerous brilliant successes permits me to state that I have achieved a revolution in dancing, as striking and as lasting as that achieved by Gluck in the realm of music. The successes even by imitators today are the greatest testimony of the value of the principles which I have laid down in this work.

My letters were but the first stone of the monument which I desired to erect to that form of expressive dancing which the Greeks called pantomime.

Dancing, according to the accepted definition of the word, is the art of composing steps with grace, precision and facility to the time and bars given in the music, just as music itself is simply the art of combining sounds and modulations so that they afford pleasure to the ear. But the gifted musician does not confine himself to so limited a circle, and the distance he traverses beyond is much greater than the circle itself. He studies the character and accents of the passions and expresses them in his compositions. On the other hand, the *maître de ballet,* striking out beyond the customary limits of his art, seeks in these same passions their characteristic movements and gestures; and binding with the same chain those steps, gestures and facial expressions to the sentiments he desires to express, he finds, in bringing together all these elements, the means of producing the most astonishing effects. It is well known to what degree the art of moving an audience by gesture was carried by the ancient mimes.

In this regard I shall even permit myself a reflection which comes

*That is, in 1803.

naturally here, since it arises from the subject under discussion; I submit and leave it to the judgment of those learned persons who have made a study of analyzing our feelings.

At the performance of a play the feelings of each spectator are aroused in strength and intensity proportionate to his greater or lesser power of being affected. Now, from the least sensitive to the most sensitive spectator there is a multitude of shades of feeling, each of which is applicable to one of them, so that a quite natural conclusion must be reached. That is, that the author's dialogue must rise above or fall below the average responsiveness of the majority of the spectators. A cold and unemotional man will nearly always find the author's expressions exaggerated and even absurd, while the emotionable and excitable spectator will often find the action slow and tedious: whence I conclude that the playwright's thoughts seldom accord exactly with the responsiveness of the spectator; unless the charm of the diction does not lay all the spectators under the same spell, an effect which I find difficult to conceive.

Pantomime, in my opinion, has not this drawback. It is only necessary to indicate by the steps, gestures, movements and facial expression the sentiments of each person; and it leaves to each spectator the task of imagining a dialogue which is ever true since it is always in accord with the emotions received.

This reflection has led me to examine with scrupulous attention all that takes place both at the performance of a pantomime ballet and at that of a play (supposing them to be of equal merit in their respective spheres). It has always seemed to me that in pantomime the effect is more general, more uniform and, if I may say so, more in consonance with the total feelings aroused by the performance.

I do not think that this thought is a purely metaphysical one. It has always appeared to me to express a truth easily comprehensible. There are, undoubtedly, a great many things which pantomime can only indicate, but in regard to the passions there is a degree of expression to which words cannot attain, or rather there are passions for which no words exist. Then dancing allied with action triumphs. A step, a gesture, a movement, and an attitude express what no words can say; the more violent the sentiments it is required to depict, the less able is one to find words to express them. Exclamations, which are the apex to which the language of passions can reach, become insufficient, and have to be replaced by gesture.

After reading these remarks one will realize the angle from which I looked at dancing from the moment I considered the subject, and how far in advance were my first ideas on that art in comparison with those then current. But, like the man who climbed to the summit of a mountain and saw the horizon stretch away before him, as I advanced in the career upon which I had just entered, I saw the path grow longer, as it were, at each step. I felt that dancing allied to action could be associated with all the imitative arts, and itself become one of them.

Since then, before selecting melodies to which I could adapt steps, before studying steps to make them into what was then known as a ballet, I sought subjects either in mythology, history or my own imagination which not only afforded opportunity for the introduction of dances and festivals, but which, in the course of the development of the theme, offered a graduated action and interest. My poem once conceived, I studied all the gestures, movements and expressions which could render the passions and sentiments arising from my theme. Only after concluding this labor did I summon music to my aid. Having explained to the composer the different details of the picture which I had just sketched out, I then asked him for music adapted to each situation and to each feeling. In place of writing steps to written airs, as couplets are set to known melodies, I composed, if I may so express myself, the dialogue of my ballet and then I had music written to fit each phrase and each thought.

Thus I explained to Gluck the characteristic air of the ballet of the savages in *Iphigénie in Tauride:* the steps, gestures, attitudes and expressions of the different characters, which I outlined to him, gave to this celebrated composer the theme for that fine piece of music.

My ideas did not stop there. Pantomime being more of a performance for the eyes than for the ears, I thought that the arts which most please the sight should be brought in alliance with it. Painting, architecture, perspective and optics became the object of my studies. I composed no more ballets in which the laws relative to those different arts were not scrupulously observed, each time there arose an opportunity of employing them. It cannot but be realized that I must have made many reflections on each one separately, and on the general principles which unite them to one another. I set down on paper the thoughts born of my studies; they were the object of a correspondence* in which I reviewed the different arts which are allied to dancing with action.

This correspondence gave me the opportunity to speak of the players who have enriched with their talents the different theatres in Europe. But this material entrusted to friends would certainly have been lost to the public and the arts if a circumstance, both worthy and unforeseen, had not permitted me today to bring it together and make it public.

Like those intrepid navigators who brave storm and tempest to discover unknown lands from which they bring back objects to enrich science and art, commerce and industry, but whom insurmountable obstacles oppose in the midst of their travels, I

*A reference to Noverre's *Lettres sur les arts imitateurs* included in the *Collected Works*, published in St. Petersburg, 1803, and for which the above Preface was written.

confess that I have been forced to suspend mine. My sallies and efforts have been in vain, I have been unable to cross that barrier raised by impossibility and on which was written: *Thou shalt go no farther.*

I shall speak of these obstacles, and I shall prove that they cannot be vanquished. They are to the art of ballet with action what in former times the Pillars of Hercules were to navigators.

LETTER I

Poetry, painting and dancing, Sir, are, or should be, no other than a faithful likeness of beautiful nature. It is owing to their accuracy of representation that the works of men like Corneille and Racine, Raphael and Michelangelo, have been handed down to posterity, after having obtained (what is rare enough) the commendation of their own age. Why can we not add to the names of these great men those of the *maîtres de ballet** who made themselves so celebrated in their day? But they are scarcely known; is it the fault of their art, or of themselves?

A ballet is a picture, or rather a series of pictures connected one with the other by the plot which provides the theme of the ballet; the stage is, as it were, the canvas on which the composer expresses his ideas; the choice of the music, scenery and costumes are his colors; the composer is the painter. If nature has endowed him with that passionate enthusiasm which is the soul of all imitative arts, will not immortality be assured him? Why are the names of *maîtres de ballet* unknown to us? It is because works of this kind endure only for a moment and are forgotten almost as soon as the impressions they had produced; hence there remains not a vestige of the most sublime productions of a Bathyllus and a Pylades.† Hardly

---

*As a general rule, whenever Noverre uses the term *maître de ballet*, he employs it in its old sense of meaning the person who composes the dances in a *divertissement*, or ballet. Nowadays, such a person is termed the *chorégraphe*, while the designation *maître de ballet* is applied to the individual responsible for the training of the dancers and the maintenance of their technique at the requisite standard of efficiency.

†Bathyllus and Pylades were two celebrated mimes famous about 22 B.C. Bathyllus of Alexandria, the freedman and favorite of Maecenas, together with Pylades of Cicilia and his pupil Hylas, brought imitative dance (termed *Pantomimus*) to Rome, where it became one of the most popular public amusements until the fall of the Empire. Bathyllus excelled in the interpretation of comic scenes, while Pylades was unsurpassed in the representation of tragic themes. At first, the two actors gave performances together, then, becoming jealous of each other's fame, they quarreled and established rival theatres. Each

a notion has been preserved of those pantomimes so celebrated in the age of Augustus.*

If these great composers, unable to transmit to posterity their fugitive pictures, had at least bequeathed us their ideas and the principles of their art, if they had set forth the laws of the style of which they were the creators, their names and writings would have traversed the immensity of the ages and they would not have sacrificed their labors and repose for a moment's glory. Those who have succeeded them would have had some principles to guide them, and the art of pantomime and gesture, formerly carried to a point which still astonishes the imagination, would not have perished.

Since the loss of that art, no one has sought to rediscover it, or, so to speak, to create it a second time. Appalled by the difficulties of that enterprise, my predecessors have abandoned it, without making a single attempt, and have allowed a divorce, which it would appear must be eternal, to exist between pure dancing and pantomime.

More venturesome than they, perhaps less gifted, I have dared to fathom the art of devising ballets with action, to reunite action with dancing, to accord it some expression and purpose. I have dared to tread new paths, encouraged by the indulgence of the public which has supported me in crises capable of rebuffing one's self-esteem; and my successes appear to authorize me to satisfy your curiosity regarding an art which you cherish, and to which I have devoted my every moment.

From the reign of Augustus to our days, ballets have been only feeble sketches of what they may one day become. This art, born of genius and good taste, can become beautiful and varied to an infinite degree. History, legend, painting, all the arts may unite to withdraw their sister art from the obscurity in which she is shrouded; and it astonishes one that *maîtres de ballet* have disdained such powerful assistance.

The programs of the ballets which have been given, during the past century or so, in the different courts of Europe, incline one to believe that this art (which was still of no account), far from having progressed, is more and more declining. These kinds of traditions, it is true, are always strongly suspect. It is with ballets as with entertainments in general: nothing so grandiose and so alluring on paper, and often nothing so dull and ill-arranged in performance.

I think, Sir, that this art has remained in its infancy only because

founded a school and each had a numerous band of followers whose fierce partisanship led to many brawls and sometimes bloodshed.

Some account of these actors will be found in Castil-Blaze, *La Danse et les ballets* (Paris: Paulin, 1832), Ch. 1. For a description of their performances, consult W. Smith, *A Dictionary of Greek and Roman Antiquities* (2 vols., 1891), vol. II, p. 334, *Pantomimus*.

*The first Emperor of the Roman Empire. Born, September 23, 63 B.C.; died, August 29, A.D. 14.

its effects have been limited, like those of fireworks designed simply to gratify the eyes; although this art shares with the best plays the advantage of inspiring, moving and captivating the spectator by the charm of its interest and illusion. No one has suspected its power of speaking to the heart.

If our ballets be feeble, monotonous and dull, if they be devoid of ideas, meaning, expression and character, it is less, I repeat, the fault of the art than that of the artist: does he ignore that dancing united to pantomime is an imitative art? I shall be tempted to believe it, because the majority of composers restrict themselves to making a servile copy of a certain number of steps and figures to which the public has been treated for centuries past; in such wise that the ballets from *Phaéton,* * or from another opera, revived by a modern composer, differ so little from those of the past that one would imagine they were always the same.

In fact, it is rare, not to say impossible, to find genius in the plans, elegance in the forms, lightness in the groups, precision and neatness in the tracks which lead to the different figures; the art of disguising old things and giving them an air of novelty is scarcely known.

Maîtres de ballet should consult the pictures of great painters. This examination would undoubtedly bring them in touch with nature; then they should avoid, as often as possible, that symmetry in the figures which, repeating the same thing, offers two similar pictures on the same canvas. That is not to say that I condemn in general all symmetrical figures or to think that I claim to abolish the practice entirely, for that would be to misinterpret my views.

The abuse of the best things is always detrimental; I only disapprove of the too frequent and too repeated use of these kinds of figures, a practice which my colleagues will feel to be vicious when they essay to copy nature faithfully and to depict on the stage different passions with the shades and colors which appertain to each in particular.

Symmetrical figures from right to left are, in my opinion, only supportable in the *corps d'entrées,*† which have no means of

---

*A lyrical tragedy in five acts and a prologue, with libretto by Quinault and music by Lully. It was first played before the court on January 6, 1663. The first public performance was given at the Académie Royale de Musique, on April 27 of the same year. It had an immense success due to its many charming airs and the wealth of the mechanical effects introduced. Its theme was the return of the Golden Age, and it was intended as a panegyric in honor of Louis XIV.

† An *entrée* is a *divertissement* executed by a number of dancers. Compan, in his *Dictionnaire de danse* (Paris: Cailleau, 1787), gives the following definition: "The usual division for all kinds of ballets is five acts. Each act consists of three, six, nine, and sometimes twelve *entrées*. The term *entrée* is given to one or more bands of dancers who, by means of their steps, gestures and attitudes, express that portion of the whole theme which has been assigned to them."

expression, and which, conveying nothing, are employed simply to give the *premiers danseurs* time to take breath; they can have a place in a *ballet général* which concludes a festival; further, they can be tolerated in *pas d'exécution, pas de quatre, pas de six,* etc., although, to my mind, it would be ridiculous, in these fragments, to sacrifice expression and feeling to bodily skill and agility of the legs; but symmetry should give place to nature in *scènes d'action.* One example, however slight it may be, will make my meaning clear and suffice to support my contention.

A band of nymphs, at the unexpected sight of a troupe of young fauns, takes flight hurriedly in fear; the fauns, on their side, pursue the nymphs with eagerness, which generally suggests delight; presently, they stop to examine the impression they have made on the nymphs; at the same time the latter suspend their course—they regard the fauns with fear, seek to discover their designs, and to attain by flight a refuge which would secure them against the danger which threatens; the two troupes approach; the nymphs resist, defend themselves and escape with a skill equal to their agility, etc.

That is what I term a *scène d'action,* where the dance should speak with fire and energy; where symmetrical and formal figures cannot be employed without transgressing truth and shocking probability, without enfeebling the action and chilling the interest. There, I say, is a scene which should offer a ravishing disorder, and where the composer's art should not appear except to embellish nature.

A *maître de ballet,* devoid of intelligence and good taste, will treat this portion of the dance mechanically, and deprive it of its effect, because he will not feel the spirit of it. He will place the nymphs and the fauns on several parallel lines; he will scrupulously exact that all the nymphs be posed in uniform attitudes, and that the fauns have their arms raised at the same height. He will take great care in his arrangement not to place five nymphs to the right and seven to the left, for this would transgress the traditions of the Opéra but he will make a cold and formal performance of a *scène d'action* which should be full of fire.

Some ill-disposed critics, who do not understand enough of the art to judge of its different effects, will say that this scene should offer two pictures only: that the desire of the fauns should express one, and the fear of the nymphs depict the other. But how many different gradations are there to contrive in that fear and that desire; what oppositions, what variations of light and shade to observe, so that from these two sentiments there result a multitude of pictures, each more animated than the other!

All men having the same passions, differ only in proportion to their sensibilities; they affect with more or less force all men, and manifest themselves outwardly with more or less vehemence and impetuosity. This principle stated, which nature demonstrates every day, one should vary the attitudes, diffuse the shades of expression, and thenceforth the pantomimic action of each person would cease to be monotonous.

It would result in being both a faithful imitator and an excellent painter, to put variety in the expression of the heads, to give an air of ferocity to some of the fauns, to others less passion, to these a more tender air, and, lastly, to the others a voluptuous character which would calm or share the fear of the nymphs. The sketch of this picture determines naturally the composition of the other: I see then the nymphs who hesitate between pleasure and fear, I perceive others who, by their contrasting attitudes, depict to me the different emotions with which their being is agitated. The latter are prouder than their companions; the former mingle fear with a sense of curiosity which renders the picture more seductive—this variety is the more attractive in its likeness to nature. You must agree with me, Sir, that symmetry should always be banished from dances with action.

I will ask those who usually are prejudiced if they will find symmetry in a flock of stray sheep which wish to escape from the murdering fangs of wolves, or in a band of peasants who abandon their fields and hamlets to avoid the fury of the enemy who pursues them? No, without a doubt; but true art consists in concealing art. I do not counsel disorder and confusion at all; on the contrary, I desire that regularity be found even in irregularity. I ask for ingenious groups, strong but always natural situations, a manner of composition which conceals the composer's labors from the eyes of the spectator.

As to figures, they only deserve to please when they are presented in quick succession and designed with both taste and elegance.

I am, &c.

LEADERSHIP OR CONTROL?

One clear and present danger in the performing arts is one of control. This element takes many shapes simply because of economics and people. In the graphic arts, such as sculpture and painting, artists work alone, and although there are the realities of public opinion and patronage to contend with, certainly an individual artist is quite free to create and exhibit his wares, even if he must consign himself to a life of poverty. Often, he will create the forms only from materials he can afford. In the performing arts, many people are involved: dancers, musicians, stagehands, etc. The expenses must be met by wealthy patronage and large organizations, and thereby varying degrees of freedom may be lost.

In countries where dance is supported by the state, such as England, Denmark, and Russia, the traditions have been well preserved, although innovation is very slow. This is also a problem of control, as the condition represents a kind of monopoly that must exist if the traditional expensive ballet is to exist. But where experimentation is also to occur, more daring leadership must be exercised, and then friction can result. Artists want to have creative freedom, yet they need money to produce. The reconciliation of these two needs will always be a problem.

America has been hard pressed in preserving the European tradition because of lack of money, particularly a general lack of government support and lack of state-supported dance schools to train dancers in the old forms. In addition, there is not an overwhelming need to preserve European tradition, especially when one jet airliner can bring a complete production here in a matter of hours.

The strongest organization in America today seems to be the New York City Ballet. Its home is in the Lincoln Center of the Performing Arts, and its principal choreographer and director is George Balanchine. It is a fine organization because it has fostered much great work, but there are other great organizations. Balanchine has been able to spread his leadership to several other regional ballets partly because of a large Ford Foundation grant, and particularly through the influence of his School of American Ballet and his excellent company. Some dance people love his leadership, others are concerned about the possibilities of one-man control over *all* ballet in America. In the performing arts, jealousies will often show up, especially when an organization becomes powerful—meaning it has money, or the ability to acquire necessary monies.

The Balanchine organization has definitely created a stir, and several views should be noted in order to understand the problems. The Bernard Taper article (Ch. 33) extols Balanchine's virtues, while the following is not favorable to "Mr. B." Important people such as Mr. Balanchine will inevitably create controversy over their style of leadership and the extent of their dominance.

A NEW LOOK AT BALANCHINEBALLET

DOUGLAS TURNBAUGH

This spring marks the end of a big year for George Balanchine and the New York City Ballet. It was a year in which they and their affiliate School of American Ballet became the recipients of the Ford Foundation's bounteous $6,000,000 grant, the largest sum ever dispensed in culture give-aways. The company moved into princely and highly publicized quarters at the New York State Theater, and further solidified its position as the best-endowed ballet establishment in the country by winning a power struggle in the Lincoln Center front office to gain complete control over the Theater. Yet at the very moment when they are at a pinnacle of power, Balanchine and company may be able to detect some faini whisperings from the rear of their sumptuous hall, whisperings that could signify merely the stirring of a faintly restless audience, or that could warn of some structural adjustment more serious than the normal settling of a new building.

The dance world's initial outrage at the Ford Foundation's exclusivity has spent itself. The dire predictions have all been made and the sour grapes have been eaten. Now is a good time to begin examining the company which has had so many riches showered upon it, and the artistic qualities of the man whose personality pervades it, George Balanchine. What endorsement established Balanchine's company as the ultimate in the American field, and what accomplishments are likely to result from its now pre-eminent position?

First of all, politicians in New York City in 1948 gave him the facilities of City Center. Prior to 1948, Balanchine's participation in ballet on a national level, since his arrival here in 1934, had been the creation of three works for the Ballet Russe de Monte Carlo and two works for the Ballet Theatre,[1] although some of his other works were in their repertoires also. He supplied the repertoire for a group based at his school which called itself the American Ballet. This name had not much justification considering the company's parochial nature and Russian motor force, but it frankly indicated Balanchine's ambitions. More impressive to politicians was Balanchine's long list

From *Dance Scope*, I, No. 2 (Spring, 1965), 28-34. Copyright © The National Dance Teachers Guild, Inc. Reprinted with permission.

of credits on Broadway and in Hollywood. This meant he had been employed by the Big Money and had proven himself.

Balanchine was on the New York scene with powerful patrons at the right moment. Politicians as well as merchants felt the stirrings after the war of what would erupt into the culture boom. The Ballet Russe de Monte Carlo had played City Center, and the Ballet Theatre had climaxed its 1946-47 season there with a record-breaking engagement. The politicians had that old theatre, a tax forfeit, and they cannily decided to experiment. Balanchine moved in and called his company the New York City Ballet. As the boom expanded, the success of the gesture paid off handsomely. New York City was praised for its support of culture. The resulting publicity was national, tremendous, and free. The phenomenal success of this experiment was undoubtedly a factor in the later decision to group all the city's cultural totems in one acropolis of temples at Lincoln Center. When a resident ballet company was needed to complete Lincoln Center's array of glittering talent, the NYC Ballet was the obvious one for the assignment.

What happened to the competition? If they were more deserving, why did they lose out? In 1948, the year Balanchine moved into City Center, the leading American companies, the Ballet Russe de Monte Carlo and the Ballet Theatre, were, in a sense, locked out of New York City. These companies had played City Center, but had had no permanent home in New York. They were forced to exist by constant touring, an agony the NYC Ballet has never known. Their situation was further aggravated by being outside the powerful influence of Sol Hurok, who had the organization and apparatus to successfully promote the expensive and cumbersome groups that ballet companies must be. So the two oldest American companies found themselves in competition both in New York City and on tour with the companies Hurok brought from abroad, who generally had further support from their respective governments. Furthermore, the New York City press, with its national influence, particularly in theatre, took a chauvinistic interest in New York City's own company, as well as a respectful attitude to anything imported. The Ballet Russe de Monte Carlo and the Ballet Theatre not only had to find suitable temporary theatres in Manhattan, and pay tremendous rents, and charge correspondingly higher prices, and face correspondingly shorter seasons, but also they could not be at their best after months of grueling tours by train and bus. Lack of enthusiasm from the press and New York-based glamour magazines eventually undermined their position with their audiences on the road. It became a demoralizing situation which these companies bravely withstood. The Ballet Theatre survived partly through patronage of the State Department in the form of overseas tours. The NYC Ballet also benefited from this exporting of American culture, but the Ballet Russe de Monte Carlo was damned by its name.

This company, after 25 years of regularly touring the United States, was as familiar an institution throughout the continent as the NYC Ballet is on Manhattan Island. The Ballet Russe de Monte Carlo gave to its audience and to its company of artists a comprehensive education in every aspect of ballet, through a broad selection of works from classics to contemporary. It utilized and developed American talent—painters, musicians, choreographers, and dancers—as well as European and South American artists. The company was unique in that it did not attempt to create a national or regional or one-man image, but assembled the best from the international scene. In 1942, this company produced Agnes de Mille's revolutionary *Rodeo,* a ballet which almost instantaneously changed the history of theatrical dancing. When the Ballet Russe de Monte Carlo finally was obliged to cease operations there wasn't a murmur of regret from the national, New York City-oriented press.

The Ballet Theatre continues its precarious life. Its appearance this season was awaited with great anxiety by balletomanes because in this company rests the last hope for a rival of significant stature to compete with the Balanchine monopoly, and because this company's incomparable repertoire of American ballet exists only as long as the company exists. The reorganized Robert Joffrey Ballet has recently received $115,000 from the Ford Foundation, but that will hardly allow it to rival the NYC Ballet. The Harkness Ballet, although it has announced itself as a challenger to Balanchine's position, has yet to be seen here. The triumph of the Ballet Theatre this spring is a demonstration that American ballet can still be vital and dynamic, much to the surprise of many. Unfortunately this triumph has not secured the company the basic necessities of a home theatre and financial stability. At the close of its season Walter Terry called it "America's best ballet company," but its future is still an unsolved question.

Balanchine's determination to dominate the ballet scene manifested itself early in his career. In 1923, at the age of nineteen, he gave a program designed to show the evolution of ballet in Russia from Petipa through Fokine "to my own ideas of movement."[2] This program could be put over in New York City 42 years later, but not in Russia in 1923. The evening was not a success and he soon left Russia, apparently carrying a distaste for any work not his own which remains with him today. "He was asked this spring who was creating good choreographic works today. His answer was a flat, impartial, definitive, 'No choreography exists in the world today.' What about the work of some of the younger choreographers he has presented? 'Not very interesting.' "[3] It is hard to believe that anyone as deeply involved in dance as Balanchine could be unaware and unappreciative of the choreography of John Butler, Kenneth MacMillan, Jerome Robbins, Alwin Nikolais, Martha Graham, just to cite some obvious examples. Such innocence would indicate either a tremendous preoccupation with one's own work, or a deliberate avoidance of the work of others. A review of the NYC Ballet's repertoire over the years gives surprising support to both these assumptions.

From Oct. 11, 1948, through Jan. 26, 1964, not counting entire seasons of his *Nutcracker* production, the NYC Ballet gave 3,356 performances of 68 Balanchine works. The closest any other choreographer came to this was Jerome Robbins, with 674 performances of ten ballets. Next was Todd Bolender with 163 performances of seven ballets; Lew Christensen with 131 performances of four ballets; Frederick Ashton with 107 of two ballets. Nobody else topped 100. Antony Tudor rated only 37 performances of four of his ballets.[4]

Balanchine's own career had at its inception every advantage and assistance from Diaghilev, who engaged him immediately after he had left Russia in 1924. He was twenty years old and a product of Soviet ballet. He met Diaghilev at an opportune moment, when a new choreographer was needed. Diaghilev wanted to replace Nijinsky; Massine, eight years older than Balanchine, was no longer exclusively with the company; Dolin, Balanchine's own age, was launched as a dancer; and Lifar, a year younger than Balanchine, was still developing as a dancer. Grigoriev, the company *régisseur* during its entire existence, has noted that Diaghilev was disappointed to find Balanchine's ideas, at the age of twenty, "already, so to speak, crystallized."[5] However, Balanchine was given Nijinsky's position and in the next five seasons (1924-29) he worked as choreographer in the creation of ten ballets. Some of these were successful, notably *Apollon Musagète* (1928) and *Le Fils Prodigue* (1929), and are the source of his reputation today. These two ballets are in the repertoire of the NYC Ballet, although altered and infrequently performed.

It is essential to remember that at this time ballets were not considered to be the sole achievement of the choreographer. Stravinsky, Prokofiev, Rouault, de Chirico, Derain, Utrillo, Lifar, Woicikowski, Doubrovska, Danilova, Nikitina . . . these were a few of the artists Balanchine worked with, and their contributions must not be minimized. Russia's tremendous artistic revolution was obscured by her political revolution, which in the end suppressed the arts to political use. But before that catastrophe, in theatre, cinema, music, painting, dance, there were innovations which changed the current of Western tradition. Diaghilev thrived in this environment. He was a catalyst for genius, and his company's appearance in Paris in 1909 electrified the entire artistic world. The classic ballet in Russia had been a showcase for favorites. Kschessinska had been *prima ballerina assoluta* and the Czar's mistress besides. Fokine, influenced by Stanislavsky's ideas, created ballets with coordinated scenarios, or *mises-en-scène* would be a safer term today, with a high level of dancing demanded as integral to the structure, not merely as divertissement. In this same sense, Fokine's ballets introduced ensemble playing, a Stanislavsky technique used today, which means everybody on stage is relative to the *mise-en-scène,* just as Chekhov's plays made rhetorical speech backed up by static tableaux obsolete. Dancers used a form of Stanislavsky's method in preparation of roles. They were interpretive artists, rather than gymnasts to music. These ideas were never accepted or comprehended by Balanchine and his work ever since has been isolated from the development of the art of dance. "George Balanchine, whom many consider the greatest living ballet choreographer, was no revolutionist. He worked in the direct line of development from a classic premise."[6] It follows that Balanchine *"était le seul chorégraphe de son temps à ne pas avoir subi l'influence de Fokine, c'était un héritier direct de Petipa."*[7]

Who was Petipa anyway? He was a Frenchman, born in 1822, who became *maître de ballet* at the Imperial theatre in St. Petersburg in 1851. He created formula ballet productions on a huge scale, and controlled Russian ballet for over 50 years. He died in 1910, having created over 50 ballets. Mme. Karsavina has remarked that by the time she was beginning her career his work was considered extremely old-fashioned and out of touch with modern developments. Regarding his influence on movement, Lifar wrote: "Marius Petipa in Russia enriched, if only slightly, our technique. This he achieved by developing virtuosity to its utmost within the bounds of the technique already accepted, making use of academic movements evolved long before his time."[8]

The same can be said for Balanchine. His idea of the *mécanique* of the dancer as being of sole interest is not new or revolutionary. We presume today that a ballet dancer will be accomplished in the technical requirements of his art, whether he is with the NYC Ballet or the Kirov or Ballet Theatre. What we hope to see is something accomplished with that technique. Few students of ballet sweat at the *barre* with purely athletic ambitions. Surely it is a thrill to do a beautiful *double tour en l'air,* but most students aspire to become interpretive and/or creative artists. The rare dancers who follow Balanchine's philosophy can at best achieve the position of smooth-working automatons, but more often seem awkward puppets. Already young dancers with creative drive, with more than athletic ambition, ignore American ballet as a sterile backwater. Where within the present U.S. ballet world could a creative dancer or choreographer hope to find an outlet? The new generation is often obliged to turn to other dance forms.

It is Martha Graham who has created a new language of dance, given it a new vocabulary. It is she who significantly uses all kinds of theatrical possibilities, coordinated efforts of *mise-en-scène,* embodying the artistic and intellectual tempers of our day. Strange as it may seem, it is her ideas which succeed Fokine's. It is she who has gone forward and given further impetus to other choreographers.

Balanchine, except when his early experience with Diaghilev physically forced him into contact with significant talents, remains aloof, completely out of the contemporary artistic world. *Episodes I and II*, presented by the NYC Ballet in 1959, might seem an exception to this, but is not. Martha Graham did Part I which was performed by her own dancers and Balanchine did Part II which was performed by his dancers. It was not a collaboration at all. Thus Graham's influence never touched the NYC company, and her portion of the work was never, could never be, in the repertoire. It was meant to be a pedagogic lesson to Balanchine's audience, but the force of Graham's talent undoubtedly converted more to her side than otherwise.

Balanchine's Complete Stories of the Great Ballets, by George Balanchine (published 1954), contains descriptions of 132 ballets. Of these 132, more than a quarter are his own. Such an exaggeration of one's own importance has apparently gone unnoticed. His audience maintains an emperor's-new-clothes attitude seldom refuted by the critics. Within the dance profession who would be so insane as to risk banishment from, or forever be denied entrance to, the only place in the U.S.A. where a dancer has any financial security? Lois Bewley, formerly a member of the NYC Ballet, and before that the Ballet Theatre and the Ballet Russe de Monte Carlo, dared to rebel and with three other courageous dancers formed the First Chamber Dance Quartet. They perform their own works in the best chamber style, and give witty parodies of the Master's work. But few people have the kind of guts and organizational sense to strike out alone.

The most pleasant Balanchine ballets are the rare ones which involve serious collaboration: *Liebeslieder Waltzer* (1960) is memorable for its lovely gowns; *Seven Deadly Sins* (reworking of the 1933 ballet) had unusually contemporary-looking costumes and décors; *Western Symphony* (1954) used a commissioned score by Hershy Kay, and through its music, costume, décor and dance achieved a charming mood. But of all the works created for this company the only really impressive ones are *Orpheus* (1948), with fantastic décor by Noguchi, and *Firebird* (1949), a reworking of a ballet for which Fokine created the book and choreography in 1910 with original scenery and costumes by Golovine. The Balanchine version has stunning décor and costumes by Marc Chagall. As is to be expected, these ballets are the result of more than the choreographer's work. One senses in them the possibility of the hand of Lincoln Kirstein, General Director of the NYC Ballet and since 1934 a Balanchine patron. As artistic director of the New York Pro Musica, he has demonstrated his own impeccable taste in their beautiful productions of *The Play of Herod* and *The Play of Daniel.* Why then hasn't he exercised more influence over the NYC Ballet's productions, which desperately need a controlling hand?

The last time I saw Balanchine's version of *Firebird* I noticed first of all that Chagall's name was missing from the credits. Second, the curtain opened on Chagall's forest scene which was so incompetently or perversely lit that it resembled a ghostly cinemascope screen. The décor's initial effect of creating a mood was ruined. Third, the Monsters' costumes were in colors entirely out of keeping with Chagall's delicately coordinated palette, and these distracting dyes served only to point up the banal movements of the dancers wearing them. It seems that the costumes are not Chagall's and he will not allow his name to be used when such a travesty is made of his work. Ideally, leading contemporary painters might be delighted to work in the medium of stage décor—Rauschenberg and Rivers are certainly interested in theatre, but their names aren't seen at Lincoln Center.

In an attempt to justify his success with Ford and Lincoln Center, Balanchine said: "If other companies could produce, they too would have shared. The NYC Ballet has a set-up. We can produce."[9] A set-up indeed: from its inception the company had the physical facilities and advantages of performing in City Center. But the allusion is false. The Ballet Russe de Monte Carlo produced, the Ballet Theatre produces (132 ballets between 1940 and 1960) without benefit of set-up. On Balanchine's basis, Leon Leonidoff at the Radio City Music Hall should have gotten the New York State Theater—he has a ballet company, too, and a set-up, and he really produces, four times a day every day year after year.

Balanchine's production record, like Leonidoff's, smacks of formula. He unabashedly repeats himself. This last season is a perfect example. The two "new" works were announced as *Harlequinade* and "Untitled." "Untitled" was finally titled *Pas de Deux and Divertissement.* Why there was such a to-do about its title is a mystery, unless it was to disguise the fact that this work is a reworking of his *Sylvia pas de deux* presented in 1950. The other "new" work, *Harlequinade,* was choreographed by Petipa in 1900. It was later in the repertoire of the Ballet Russe de Monte Carlo with choreography by Boris Romanoff. Balanchine's version was presented in 1952. The fact remains that these two ballets are not new, although perhaps some choreography was altered. Even the décor for *Harlequinade* was second-hand, consisting of scenery originally designed for the New York City Opera's *La Cenerentola.* This décor uses the Victorian toy theatre designs published by Pollock which were the basis of the décor and costumes of Lord Berner's *The Triumph of Neptune,* choreographed by Balanchine in 1926. The only item of dance interest in *Harlequinade* was the pleasant surprise of seeing Deni Lamont dancing a principal role. Although one of the best dancers in the company, he has been held for several years in a minor position in the *corps,* perhaps as purgatory for having once been a soloist with the Ballet Russe de Monte Carlo, where his extraordinary stage presence was counted an asset. Also conspicuous among the stage movement was the spectacle of stagehands behind an ill-masked flat, unconcernedly moving about and chewing gum or chatting in full view of everyone in the audience above the orchestra level.

The season before last, *Ballet Imperial,* a work created in 1941 (see pages 34-36 of *Balanchine's Complete Stories of the Great Ballets*), was presented as a new work with choreography by Balanchine but staged by Frederick Franklin, who must have danced it many times when it was in the Ballet Russe de Monte Carlo repertoire. This company presented it in 1945 at City Center. It was also performed by Sadler's Wells Ballet and by the ballet of La Scala.

To regard this situation dispassionately is not easy for anyone who cares about ballet. But, for a moment, not even considering aesthetics, is it not clear that to present reworked standards as new works is patently dishonest? And if production was the key to winning Lincoln Center and the Ford Foundation grant, how is it explained away that Balanchine did no new works for two seasons at Lincoln Center?

People who care about dance have long ago written off Balanchineballet. There is, of course, a threat that ". . . American audiences may end up believing that there is only one style of choreography, one style of repertoire, one style of dancing."[10] But I don't think so. Dance will always have its audience, and this audience will just as soon sit on the floor at the Judson Church, or make the trek to the Kaufmann Auditorium or the Henry Street Playhouse, because they are not passive. They are looking for something special, something creative, something provocative and exciting, which they have learned will not be found with the New York City Ballet.

39

PHYSICAL EDUCATION OR AN INDEPENDENT ART?

Great dance is accepted as art by the general public, although it involves not only aesthetic considerations but unusual expenditures of physical energy as well. However, no one puts dance reviews on the sports page of newspapers, since the enormous physical virtuosity associated with dance is only part of the story.

On the other hand, administrative politics in universities, the idea of dance and the arts for everyone, the possibility of superficially looking at skills without the art, the open spaces in gymnasiums; the relationship of modern or "expressive" dance to the emancipation yearnings of women early in this century, the inclusion of an aesthetic view of the human body, the scientific correlations and needs in terms of anatomy and other body sciences—all have led to a departmental structure in many universities in which dance is a part of women's physical education.

This structure was, and is, handed down to secondary and elementary education, since the universities are responsible for teacher education. However, due to the increasing number of colleges offering dance in their fine and performing arts departments, the problem is beginning to level out. The following article defends the alignment of dance and physical education. Note, however, that Mr. Beiswanger wrote it back in 1936.

PHYSICAL EDUCATION AND THE EMERGENCE
OF THE MODERN DANCE

GEORGE BEISWANGER

One of the problems which concerns those who are responsible for the physical education programs of high schools and colleges today is the relationship of that program to the dance, and in particular to that contemporary movement which is called the modern dance.* Is the modern dance an expression of the basic values and ideals of physical education, or is it a fad, a passing mode of reaction against older and more solid forms of dance? Are its physically demanding techniques fundamentally sound? Are they within the range of the average college and high school girl, or do they strain the body beyond the precepts of a sane kinesiology? To what extent can the reaction of the average audience against the modern dance be discounted as a natural response to a new form of art, destined in time to be changed into enthusiastic appreciation as the art becomes more familiar? What bonds of relationship are there between the aims of physical education and the purpose of the modern dance which justify the promissory note that a director of physical education gives when she engages an instructor to teach it and extends her cooperation and support?

The interest with which these questions are being asked is characteristic of the alertness of the physical education movement to developments which promise an enrichment of its fundamental program. It is also, in the judgment of the author, an indication that even those who are most doubtful about the ultimate value of the modern dance have unconsciously felt the vigor and quality of a significant art. The reason for this is that the modern dance is, at least in part, an outgrowth of the impulses which have given rise to

*The term "modern" is obviously only a convenient tag. Every art is modern in its own day, *if it is alive*. The author uses the term because it serves to remind one of the truth just stated, and also because there is at the present time no more satisfactory term.

From the *Journal of Health, Physical Education and Recreation*, VII, No. 7 (September, 1936), 413-16 & 463.

Note: This article was presented as a paper before the Dance Section of the American Physical Education Association Convention, St. Louis, Mo., April 17, 1936.

the physical education movement. It is the kind of dance which results when the goals of physical education are clarified and communicated on a conscious and artistic plane. The modern dance puts into art form the meanings and the philosophy of life for which physical education stands. It is physical education's own dance, its own art.

Its origin attests that. In its inception, the modern dance stems from Isadora Duncan. The ideas which led her to free the dance from outmoded forms and outgrown ideals was an intuition of the body and its capacity for free movement identical in principle with the basic idea underlying the modern physical education movement. As Elizabeth Selden says in her recent book, *The Dancer's Quest,* Isadora Duncan "succeeded in freeing the body; the dance took off its slippers and corsets." With her the dance returned "to dignity of motion and to a common-sense treatment of the body; by its simplicity and naturalness, it endeared itself to modern educators and made its way into the educational system, especially in America, where the Greek ideals of physical education found a ready echo."[1] She felt the same need for a more natural approach to the human body as a means of expression that was enlarging and transforming the drills of traditional gymnastics into the free and creative body activities that characterize the present approach.

This impulse, as it was felt in physical education and the dance alike, was romantic at first. That is to say, it relied upon spontaneous, emotionally charged movement, without extended consideration of a science of body techniques or of ultimate aims and goals. In both cases, there was only a hope for and a promise of real education and vital art, a promise that waited upon the scientific study of body capacities and the intensive development of body skills to bring forth either a mature philosophy of physical education or an adult art. This promise is now being fulfilled, and in both fields. Those who are primarily interested in physical education know how substantially founded a science the profession has become. Those who are primarily teachers of the dance know how the intensive study of the body as an art medium has transformed the romantic dance of Isadora Duncan and her followers into the modern dance. The important thing to note is that teachers of physical education and teachers of the dance alike have been responding to the same necessity for maturing the original insight common to both, by grounding each pursuit in a study of technical means and by clarifying the original, confused purposes of each into clear-cut educational and artistic goals. Following not divergent but parallel courses of development, touching each other at countless points on the way, interacting to the mutual advantage of each, physical education and the modern dance face each other not as opponents but as partners, as mature products, one in the field of education, the other in the field of art, of the same basic need to free the body for the fullest realization of its own human capacities.

The more one examines physical education and the modern dance in relation to each other, the more is one impressed with the truth of the thesis that has just been stated. The most apparent point of union is the desire to cultivate the experience of satisfying movement. Elizabeth Selden has said that the modern dance is vitally related to "the American passion for movement for its own sake."[2] So is physical education. Americans are a people who love the exhilaration of free, expansive activity. That love is rooted in the experiences of frontier life. It is reinforced by the breadth of the American land and by the new means of increased mobility that have been developed by machine civilization. It has led to the creation of such movement arts as the motion picture and the present social dance. It has transformed the character of American architecture and painting. It is today finding expression in an intense love of sports, an extraordinary development of physical education, and the modern dance.

But the relationship is an even closer one. The types of movement stressed in the modern dance are native to, if not actually derived from, our activity experiences. Whether the teachings of the dance or its programs are studied, the similarities are apparent. Reduce the movements of basketball or baseball or football on the slow-motion film, and they become the sustained movements of the dance. The wind-up is the swing; the delivery a percussive stroke. The pivot is the turn. From the track come leaps, widespread and irresistible. Football men use the fundamental pattern of the fall; they learn the wisdom of quick tension, quick release, and complete relaxation. The pole vault marshals and releases energy like a dance. Percussive, sustained, and swinging movements in activities and sports all display in the quality of their modes of action the method of gathering and expending energy that characterizes the modern dance.

Underlying these likenesses is an identical conception of the nature of movement. One of the fundamental tenets of the modern dance is the principle that the torso is the center of energy, and that movement must be initiated therein, even if the ultimate points of discharge are the body extremities. This will not sound like strange doctrine to any teacher of physical education, nor the correlative principle that energy can be most efficiently gathered and expended in the form of rhythmic alternations of flexion and extension, tension and release. The complete and smoothly coordinated integration of body energies which skilled coaching brings is precisely the aim of this new type of dance on the technical side.

In the light of this relationship, one may say that the modern dance uses and directs for expressional purposes the natural body movements which physical educators teach. Instead of movement for the sake of some extrinsic goal, such as the winning of a game, the purpose is now intrinsic, the expressive realization of the qualities of movement in their own right and for their own sake. The immediate satisfyingness of movement which sports incidentally give in connection with the endeavor to develop "good form" is brought to the fore in the dance. In the game, it is form for the sake of skill which is stressed; in the dance it is skill for the sake of form—for the creative quality of movement which skill brings. This is not to say that the modern dance starts with athletic movements as such and superimposes upon them a pantomimic kind of art. The dance may make use of game motives in an occasional composition, but it starts with movement itself. It gives conscious fulfillment to the experience of movement by revealing its qualities for what they are in experience, so that the dancer may feel them and receive thereby an access of meaning and joy.

It is natural for such a dance to stress vigor and largeness of movement. The American is large, tall, built for broad, sweeping movement, well-fed, a glorier in the experience that activity gives. Therefore he has little use in the dance for the mincing steps of the traditional waltz or the delicate patterns of the ballet. Bare feet, broadly planted; strong movements gathering force and yet retaining lyrical elegance: these are the qualities of American movement and for that reason shape the contemporary dance. It is not strange to find that high school and college girls (and boys as well) take to the modern dance, once they overcome a natural feeling of strangeness and begin to try its movements. For these movements are theirs, the ones with which they have become familiar during all the years of sports experience.

The belief in the creative value of movement is basic, whether one examines the philosophy of physical education or that of the modern dance. Experience itself, at its best, is rhythmic movement. Life when it is fine is not passive but active. It is dance. Get men and women to move rightly, in harmony, with vigor, and toward valid goals, and the educational problem is on the road to solution. This is what Plato meant many centuries ago when he made music and gymnastic the two fundamentals of ideal education: music—the movement of feet, sounds, and sight in harmony with right values; gymnastic—the trained body moving at the behest of the dance.

Along with a belief in the importance of movement is the preoccupation of both physical education and the modern dance with form. As far as the dance is concerned, those who are unused to its particular type of movement are apt to think that the modern dance is artificial and highly abstract. Usually, however, one does not view the insistence of a good sports' instructor upon "good form" in the same light. And yet the purpose is the same. The demand for effective coordination and efficient rhythm in sports is merely given an artistic aim and outlet in the dance. When the physical education teacher stimulates in students the desire to learn how to exert energy at the proper point with economy of effort, when he or she insists upon examining all the possibilities of movement until just the right skill is discovered and learned, when disciplined practice is demanded until a high degree of expertness is reached, the teacher is preparing students for a dance which makes the same kind of demands in its art.

The ideal of form is, as a matter of fact, deeply imbedded in the philosophy of physical education. A movement which achieves a desired end and therefore has form is the only right and ultimately natural one to make. There must be insistent and scientific search for more perfect means of movement. The modern dance, feeling the same ideal of perfection in form, has simply accepted the implications of these principles of art. Any movement of which the body is capable has value for expression, and can be given its own quality of perfection. When that value is made explicit by selecting and perfecting the best means for making it manifest, the value has aesthetic quality. The range of the vocabulary of movement is thus as unlimited as the range in human activity itself; in fact, the dance enlarges the boundaries of movement in its search for deeper meanings and more effective modes of communication.

Much of the vocabulary of the modern dance seems distorted and grotesque to the average person. The dance today does use distortion, as must any contemporary art which desires to make a vital comment upon the disturbed and chaotic world in which we live. But there is less distortion in that sense in the modern dance than is customarily supposed. Most of the so-called grotesqueness is a result of a free study of the expressional possibilities of movement. Even the unusual vocabulary which Martha Graham uses in her dance, and which often seems unnatural to the average individual because it violates certain accepted but totally irrelevant canons of modesty or beauty, appears on longer acquaintance to be the discovery of a faithful student of the human body who has found the intricately varied and thrillingly expressive patterns that the body can make, once it is conceived of as a free medium of art. The movement vocabulary of the modern dance enlarges the range of experience, perfects the sense of form, and, even more importantly, speaks intimately to values already implanted by everyday experiences of movement.

In connection with the vigor of form that characterizes the modern dance, there is the experience of joy-in-movement which it communicates to dancer and spectator alike. Here is another interest which the dance possesses in common with physical education. The old gymnastics missed the experience of joy in its stress upon drill. No educator worthy of his name today fails to regard this value as the most important which physical activity can generate. The same thing is true of the modern dance. The search for patterns of movement which will call forth the organic energy of human beings in the most vital form is also a search on the subjective or conscious side for the sense of mastery that skilled movement brings. The words, exhilaration and joy, are used advisedly. For what both physical education and the dance seek is not a subjective and emotional happiness but a quite objective awareness of the power and surge and recreating value of the body in motion. The modern dance is a Nietzschean one in which man stretches to the limits of his cosmos and takes it in unto himself. The quality of exhilaration that permeates active living is brought to the fore. Physical education becomes art. It is not surprising, therefore, that the modern dance should appeal to the adolescent today, when it is rightly and carefully taught.

Physical education and the modern dance also meet in the respect which each feels for the fact of individual differences. There is no need to remind the reader how important the consideration of individual capacities and limitations has become in the modern physical education program. The same concern appears in the philosophy of the modern dance (if not always in its practice). The old dance required a certain uniform type of bodily perfection. Only a few individuals could hope to be real dancers; there was only one Pavlova or one Nijinsky. The technical demands of the ballet were insurmountable to all except the privileged body. This selectivity was suitable to an essentially aristocratic art. The modern dance, as an expression of democratic ideals, takes the individual into account. Its techniques are adapted to the particular body with which each person must work. Each dancer is led to explore and to cultivate the movements that are peculiarly suitable to her, after a general approach to movement has freed the body from the inhibitions of inactive and unimaginative living. Any one can learn to dance who can move and who has, besides, a modicum of imagination, a sense of values, artistic integrity, and the will to persist at the creative task.

The desire to release the artistic potentialities of each individual, no matter what type of body he or she may possess, accounts in part for the difficulty which audiences experience in adjusting to performances of the new dance. It is somewhat of a shock, perhaps, to see bodies that according to the accepted ideal were never meant to dance. A norm of beauty, itself highly artificial and aristocratic, is brought into play, whether one is aware of it or not, a norm that is inconsistent with the genuine ideals of physical education itself. Those who bring to the dance a sense of the right of each person to find aesthetic fulfillment in movement will begin to see how expressive and truly beautiful even the most unlikely body can become when allowed and encouraged to develop a dance that is suited to its own limitations and capabilities. The modern dance, by declaring its faith in the creative capacity of the individual, whoever he or she may be, is thus exemplifying not only a basic principle of physical education but a fundamental aspect of the democratic venture and ideal.

There is still a fifth important similarity in practice and outlook, the emphasis which is placed upon group activity and expression. Perhaps more significant for the future than any other aspect of physical education is its stress upon the socializing value of group play. That, too, is part of the American tradition. American games are typically mass games: football, basketball, baseball. As mass games, however, they are not regimented in drill formation as gymnastics was—many thousands of persons going through exactly the same activity in precisely the same way. Rather, these games involve the intricate cooperation of many different kinds of skill in one complicated activity, the skills varying from individual to individual. They use the developed specialties of many kinds of people and weave them into a communal pattern. We sense important value in this type of group activity, in which there is perfection of individual attainment and yet a cooperative working-together toward a common end.

Exactly the same conception of group movement characterizes the modern dance, and is producing a kind of group composition that, in a sense, has never before been created in the history of the dance. One needs to witness the intricate interweaving of individual dance patterns into an organic whole that characterizes the larger compositions of the Graham or the Humphrey-Weidman groups to sense the quality of this new type of group dance. It is significant that dance leaders are using the word, "group," as sharply distinguished from the ballet "chorus," in which a mass of individually indistinguishable dancers accompany a solo artist, and also from the Greek "orchesis," a body of dancers fused into one voice and expressing one emotion in which the sense of individual participation is lost. In the group compositions of the modern dance, as in our most typical games, each individual has something special which is hers to do, and yet the movements work together into an organic and social whole. Nothing is quite so exciting about the modern dance as this fact. And it grows consciously out of the philosophy that has underlain the movement from the start. For Isadora Duncan, dance was a communal art. Martha Graham insists that those who see her in solo performance alone miss the greater share of what she has to give; she says that she herself cannot feel the complete depth and power of her own message unless it is reinforced by the group, for what she is trying to say is essentially a group thing.

It is extremely interesting at this point to note that the emphasis in physical education for women has been turning lately from group sports toward those individual and dual sport activities which have social utility for post-college living. The group sports have not been an altogether ideal means for adequate socialization. For women especially, the importance of the competitive element and the responsibility of playing well in order that the team might win have fallen heavily upon the poorly equipped and socially backward girl. By adding to her sense of physical inferiority while highly stimulating her social sensibilities, team sports have often run the danger of increasing rather than removing maladjustment, at the same time tending to develop attitudes of superiority in the more skilled girls with at times antisocial results.

40
DANCE IN PHYSICAL EDUCATION:
AN ADMINISTRATIVE SET-UP REVEALED

The fact that dance is generally moving out of women's physical education departments into schools of fine and performing arts indicates a definite swing toward the viewpoint that dance has more to do with aesthetic education than with any other discipline. For years battles have raged in academic circles over the place of dance, propelled mainly by those crusading teachers who believed dance warranted better than an in-service status in its adopted field. These crusaders search for independence, not because of a dislike for physical education but for a love of dance.

The following article presents arguments against the inclusion of dance in physical education. It is based on figures gained by a recent survey that was recognized by the State of Wisconsin's Department of Public Instruction and led to a state-wide certification for dance teachers at the elementary and secondary levels. Although the information obtained reveals the situation in the high schools and elementary schools of Wisconsin, it indicates the grave situation in dance education throughout America that has resulted from the inclusion of dance in women's physical education programs. Those educators who have become responsible for dance in the public schools are only applying the methods they learned in teacher-training institutions.

Only parts of the survey and its conclusions are given here.

EXCERPTS FROM "A SURVEY OF DANCE EDUCATION IN THE ELEMENTARY AND SECONDARY SCHOOLS IN THE STATE OF WISCONSIN"

MYRON HOWARD NADEL

Information on the situation in dance education in the Wisconsin public schools at the elementary and secondary levels was gathered through the use of a twenty-five point questionnaire, covering the kinds of dance taught, the amount of dance taught, and the background of the teachers. The main concern was with the dance arts, more specifically modern dance and ballet.

The foremost problem was finding those people responsible for dance education, since much information was hidden in physical education files, following the traditional linking of dance with physical education in the schools and colleges. Indeed, the Wisconsin Arts Council Survey of the Arts came out with the statement that no figures were available for dance education because of its burial within physical education departments.[1] This could have been interpreted to mean that no dance was taught in Wisconsin public schools, which was clearly erroneous even at the time of the survey.

Questionnaires were sent to 1,971 public schools: 395 to junior and senior high schools and 1,576 to elementary schools with more than four faculty members. Of the 1,971 questionnaires sent, 691 were returned answered, a return of 39 percent, or nearly four out of ten.

The returns revealed that 205 schools have teachers who say they teach modern dance. For the rest, the reasons given for disinterest in, or the inappropriateness of, dance as an educational tool fell into the following three categories: religious factions in the school opposed dance, time limitations, insufficient staff.

There seems to be a disproportionate amount of dance education at the secondary school level compared to the elementary school level. From the ages of 6 to 11, when creative work in the arts could be so well used, it is most neglected, but the elementary schools are not limited so much by space as by personnel. As shown in some Manhattan schools, classrooms can be easily converted for creative dance activities.[2] Certainly films, slides, and discussions on dance and the other arts can take place in any classroom. It is heartening to note that at least 160 out of 395 schools, or over 40 percent of the secondary schools, have modern dance. But since all but two of the teachers surveyed were female, the school system says in effect that modern dance is performed and taught by women because it is located in girls' physical education programs.

Ballet has a very low incidence for several reasons:

1) Most colleges (where the teachers are trained) do not offer it.
2) It is usually considered a highly specialized area for achievement and instruction.
3) Quite often the goals of ballet training are to produce a professional dancer; more divergent goals are attainable through the study of modern dance.

In attempting to obtain minimal information about modern dance activities in the schools, a statement of goals in teaching seemed pertinent. The teachers were given the following category choices of goals: physical, recreational, creative, aesthetic, and other. They were asked to rate their goals. In the papers of the 188 teachers who did this, the creative and aesthetic goals ranked 200 times as one of the top two choices, while physical and recreational goals ranked only 174 times. To further examine the activity in dance, it was thought valuable to know if the teachers thought that modern dance activities should be offered to boys. All 205 answered this question with a yes; that is, 100 percent felt that boys would benefit from these classes. One teacher had some reservation, but answered yes. It is strange, then, to note that only two percent of the students were boys, and that this mean number was mostly due to a male teacher in Menomonee Falls, Wisconsin, 50 percent of whose students were boys. Only 10 schools listed *any* percentage of boys.

Fifty-one of the schools had a modern dance club, and 51 of the teachers supported and prepared dancing for musical and dramatic productions. The mean number of performances by these schools is 1.2 performances per year. The range of performances per year in the 60 schools that either have clubs or give performances with no official club is from zero to four performances a year.

The purposes of any dance club, besides its social and recreational aspects, should include the following:

1) Extra work in the skills required in modern dance
2) Extra opportunity for the creative aspects of dance:
   —self-enjoyment and fulfillment
   —additional or initial performance opportunity
3) Provisions for groups of capable students who can perform when called upon
4) Teaching dance through its most important function—as a performing art.

It would then be supposed that in order to insure these goals, the average backgrounds of those responsible for these extracurricular clubs and performances would be more intensive in the area of dance. The survey did not show a greater intensity.

It would take a careful study of live situations in high school dance classes to make any valuable judgments about what actually happens in them. The cost and time invested in such a study, to be thorough, would be extremely high. The facts of the survey tend to show the teachers' views on their teaching assignment rather than any success or failure they might have. However, it will be instructive to review some basic facts of life within physical education classes, especially at the secondary-school level:

1) A class of less than 30 students is difficult to find. In fact, classes of 40 or 50 students are tolerated.
2) Gymnasium floors are invariably covered with a gym primer, a very hard, shiny floor sealer designed for maximum protection of the floor and maximum non-skid reaction with tennis shoes.
3) Volleyball nets, basketball backboards, mats, and other paraphernalia necessary to sports, games, and the body skills developed in physical education programs are usually set up, ready for activity or visibly seen in the room.
4) Gymnasiums are large and acoustically bad for voice carriage, demanding loud instructions from teachers and inviting inattentiveness from the large number of students.
5) It is difficult to require the normal dance class costume of leotard and tights for financial reasons, although this is, in fact, obligatory in many instances. Therefore, dance is often studied in gym uniforms.

Even with the most noble intentions and the finest teachers in the world, it is difficult to achieve the potential of the dance arts in situations of this type. Twenty students in a room of *any* size is a medium-to-high figure for meaningful student-teacher contact. In order for techniques to be fully taught and for freedom of movement in bare feet, floors need to be stripped down to the bare wood. Floors covered with sealers are too slippery in ballet shoes, and either restrictively sticky or extremely slippery with bare feet, depending upon the moisture-oil level of the student's skin. Techniques and free exploration of movement cannot function well under these limitations, to say nothing of the possibilities for injury that such circumstances involve. Tennis shoes are not the answer, for the freedom here is even more severely restricted.

It is difficult to see how the creative and aesthetic goals in dance, for which the majority of the teachers are striving, can be achieved in the physical plant of the gymnasium. For the dance to be creative and aesthetic, one must begin in a room uncluttered by paraphernalia and focused on the moving body, not on equipment. Unnecessary clutter takes the student's mind off the very essence of dance-body awareness. The size and acoustics of the room also make subtleties in gesture, expression, and teachers' voices somewhat incomprehensible, or, at best, imperceivable. It is in this context that the study examined the teacher's ideas of her role.

Modern dance has often been the standard bearer for creativity and individuality in education. In order to understand why the teachers chose creative and aesthetic goals over recreational and physical ones, it is necessary to understand the "standard-bearer syndrome." Although modern dance can at best be loosely defined, in the early twentieth century it represented, in part, a revolt against the artificialities and virtuosities of ballet—an individual recital art as contrasted with the more formal ballet spectacle. Although there are some small instances of male dominance in modern dance, in general the female educators, such as Margaret H'Doubler at the University of Wisconsin in Madison, saw this art as having great potential in education. Women's physical education departments opened their facilities to these pioneer women, and programs developing teachers in this field were begun. Dance spread quickly and permeated into uncountable numbers of colleges and secondary schools. Rather than a special field, it became a sideline of physical education, as easily accessible to the female physical education student as were volleyball and mass games.

The nature of classwork in modern dance took the shape of simple movement patterns, usually analyzed and taught from a highly scientific base (because of the relationship of the physical education field to kinesiology and other body sciences), and improvisation or studies—sometimes called the creative approach. The creative part of these classes became so important that most of the defenses for dance in the curriculum rested on the ideas of the mind-body realization (kinesthetic awareness), so necessary for aesthetic appreciation of movement. These ideas, though not strange to actors, poets, and composers, were inherently exciting and stimulating for physical educators. That creative and aesthetic goals can flower within physical education departments has been demonstrated positively in some college programs (although many of these have now been transferred to colleges of creative and performing arts). The tremendous proliferation of dance as a creative art activity has been made possible by the emphasis on creative teaching in all areas and the importance of physical fitness. However, as standard bearer for these concepts, modern dance has been disseminated and prostituted to a point where it is often unrecognizable as an art form or even an entity.

It is because of this background that the creative and aesthetic goals out-ranked the normal physical and recreational goals inherent in the physical education field. The question is, are these truly the goals, or have the teachers been swayed by the standard-bearer syndrome?

It might be assumed that if teachers are to teach a special area, they should have had some background in that subject as a student. If they have had no background, they should have, at least, consulted the methods and materials available for presenting their subject. In dance this assumption has been proved incorrect, since nearly two out of five teachers have had one semester (one credit) or less of modern dance technique, and a bold 14 percent have not taken any technique. This is as unthinkable as the mathematics teacher who has never solved a problem, or the industrial arts teacher who has never worked a lathe. Even the mean average of 2.2 semester hours interpolated into 90 actual class hours hardly approaches one-half the amount of studio work required of elementary students in the other arts.

It is somewhat heartening that eight percent of the teachers took more than four semesters of technique, or proceeded to an equivalent of junior level college work. But it should be kept in mind that the actual number of credit hours totaled by these teachers in dance technique is the same as their number of semester courses (in other words, one credit hour per course), since the skill or studio nature of technique courses yields fewer credits per class hour than the standard academic course credits.

We remember that the creative goals of the teachers topped the list of chosen goals, although upon examination of the teachers' own creative experience with dance, as indicated by their composition studies, we find a great discrepancy. (Even if "creative" work has been lumped into some other dance area in these teachers' course work, it is of little significance here, since it would tend to further cut down figures in the area of techniques and/or materials.) Since participating in the creative act is at the very essence of knowledge about creativity, it is hard to reconcile that 62 percent of the teachers have had only one semester course in composition, when there is such a great emphasis on creativity in their teaching. The major question raised about the reconciliation of stated goals with actual background is: Can the teacher who has never created his own dance adequately guide a student in this process?

Dance is a creative and performing art. If the teacher has had one semester of composition, is it possible to assume that she has had any significant breadth of experience in creating, perfecting, and performing dance? In short, there is little chance that all but a very small portion have had the experience necessary to guide their students in the full creative act. Even if the focus is on process alone, not product, the small amount of background course work indicates little knowledge of the process.

Methods and materials courses are at the core of most physical education curricula. Because of the broad nature of the field, which covers a multitude of activities, this is a necessary situation. It is expected, therefore, that the teachers would be strongest in dance methods courses, since dance is most often treated as one of the activities under the physical education aegis and within the general framework of methods and materials courses. This was not the case, since the mean average of methods courses was less than one semester-hour. The lack of methods courses would be entirely understandable if a great deal of attention had been paid to the other dance areas. Since this has been shown not to be the case, it is clear that the dance background of the teachers can be described as weak to negligible.

The survey examined the idea that those teachers who say they are teaching modern dance are actually strongest in recreational dance, to see if their weaknesses in the dance arts could be balanced by strengths in the folk- and square-dance forms, but the facts could not support such a view. To be realistic, the scope of the subject makes it difficult for the general physical educator to cover the field without being weak in nearly all individual areas. In addition, the large number of areas to be studied in the preparation of the teacher of dance within the already over-taxed physical education situation makes specializations within dance no more than a sentence in a catalog description, not an educational reality.

Incredible as it is, the average number of courses the teachers had taken in technique was 2.2 semesters, usually worth one credit per semester. Any similarity between this low figure and analogous statistics in technical training in any other field would be minute. Music studies should be the dance teacher's strongest auxiliary field, yet only 15 percent of the teachers polled had had more than one semester course in basic materials of music.

Since 17 percent of the top two goals were aesthetic, it seems ominous that only five percent of the people had taken any course in aesthetics. This could lead one to believe that a good number of the 17 percent derived their aesthetic goals from dance philosophy courses and their general arts experiences. This again is a dubious premise, considering the mean average of courses in dance history and philosophy combined was less than one-third of one semester. Perhaps aesthetic goals connote other meanings to these teachers.

Regardless of course work in aesthetics and the creative process of dance, the teachers felt disposed to state their goals as creative and aesthetic. This, then, should be strong evidence of involvement with dance as a theatre art either as performer or viewer, especially since performing experiences can easily supplant course work to enrich the backgrounds of dance teachers.

Again, this was overwhelmingly not the case, and, in fact, the teachers' perception of what constitutes professional performing experiences showed a lack of understanding of dance as an art form. The backgrounds of the 51 teachers who have dance clubs and the nine more who guide student performances in dramatic and musical shows indicate that they are ill-equipped to impart a basic understanding of the process of preparing for the art of theatre. For how can this process be taught well where it has not been experienced? How can teachers who have not performed in musicals or studied music be expected to produce dances for these productions that will serve any educational goals or be valuable in any way? How can concerts and recitals be run efficiently by teachers who have not studied or experienced the elements and mechanics of the theatre? The hope that course work and experience in theatre supplanted the lack of course work in dance was shown to be ill founded.

Reading journal articles and reviews and comradeship in professional and lay dance organizations are other methods for broadening the teacher's dance experience, but only one belonged to a local dance council and only one to the state dance council. To embarrass the situation further, only eight percent of the teachers subscribe to and regularly read *Dance Magazine* or *Dance News*, and only one reads *Dance Scope*, the publication of the National (now American) Dance Guild. None read the two highly respected journals *Impulse Annual* or *Dance Perspectives*.

It is of merit that 63 percent read the *Journal of Health, Physical Education and Recreation (JOPHER)*, but equally distressing that 37 percent do not. This has gloomy implications for the straight physical education responsibilities of the teachers. It is also praiseworthy that each month a column on some phase of dance is printed in this journal. Although these articles are brief, they do present the views of some of the country's prominent dance educators. Unfortunately, there is little or no contact with the professional dance world, and current events in the dance arts are not published here, since *JOHPER* is not a news magazine but a professional physical education journal.

Reviews, articles on the professional dance world, and current events are most easily accessible through *Dance Magazine* and *Dance News*. Since only eight percent read these news magazines, it can be assumed that 92 percent of the teachers do not know what is happening in the dance world. The incidence of those teachers who read the reviews in *The New York Times* was not studied.

The best thinking of dance critics, historians, philosophers, professionals, and educators is represented in the more scholarly dance journals *Dance Scope, Impulse Annual,* and *Dance Perspectives.* Since only one teacher reads *Dance Scope,* there is little hope that these teachers have much interest in the scholarly side of dance. Perhaps they do not know about these journals, or in their function as educators we might assume they would read them.

For the three-year period preceding the survey, the total attendance at professional dance concerts for all 205 teachers equaled only 475 seats—less than one performance a year. And when we consider that nearly 30 percent have seen *no* professional dance concerts, we may diagnose a serious lack of interest in the field.

One hundred and ninety-seven of the modern dance teachers rated their qualifications in the following four categories: highly qualified, fairly well qualified, minimally qualified, not qualified. Sixty-four percent of the teachers felt they were either highly qualified or fairly well qualified to teach modern dance. Thirty-one percent felt they were minimally qualified, and five percent felt they were not qualified. When asked to list their areas of highest qualification, 35 teachers (or 18 percent) indicated modern dance.

As we have seen, there are very few teachers with strong qualifications derived either from their experiences, courses, or current interests. One can only conclude that, in addition to their lack of background in all areas of dance, the teachers display a preponderant lack of interest in all phases of the dance world and a general lack of understanding of the teacher's role, the values of dance, and the importance of studying the field.

To sum up: The average modern dance teacher at a senior high school is in the girls' physical education department and is responsible for teaching other areas in the girls' physical education curriculum. Her teaching (of dance) averages four hours a week, with slightly more than two hours devoted to modern dance and the rest to folk and square. All her students are girls, but she feels both boys and girls should be required to study dance. Her first goal in teaching is creative, and her next important goals are both physical and recreational. She does not direct a modern dance club.

She holds a bachelor's degree in physical education. Her studies included two semesters in modern dance technique in a college department of physical education, and one-half a semester of dance composition. In addition, she had one semester of methods in modern dance. This is the extent of her background in the dance arts. She also had a course in folk and square dance, but no methods course in recreational dance.

She has had no college courses or background in theatre arts, music, dance history or philosophy, nor did she belong to, or perform with, her college orchesis group or have any outside performing experience. She does not belong to a professional or regional dance organization, but reads a brief article on dance in the *Journal of Health, Physical Education and Recreation* every month or so. Unfortunately, she does not read *Dance Magazine* or *Dance News* and is unaware of the scholarly dance publications. Although she has been to no ballet performances, she did see one professional modern dance concert in the last three years. She thinks of herself as fairly well qualified to teach modern dance!

The survey revealed a depressing picture of dance education in the Wisconsin public elementary and secondary schools, which the state is attempting to rectify. We must assume the situation is much the same in other states, since no study has been published that shows a better situation anywhere else in the country. Regardless of any philosophical relationship of dance to physical education, the realities are dismal.

That the field of dance and the field of physical education have certain underlying connections is self-evident. But they are no more related than dance and medicine or psychology or other sciences relating to the needs of the human body. Both fields are concerned with human movement; therefore, after the administrative ties that have bogged down both fields in the past are severed, dancers may realize some real needs that the field of physical education might serve.

It was mentioned that breaking the ties comes from a love of dance, not a dislike of physical education; therefore, it should be of concern to the educated dance artist that the administrative battles within physical education find a solution, so that research and education in truly related subject matter can commence.

MAJOR SHORTCOMINGS OF PHYSICAL EDUCATION

MYRON HOWARD NADEL

The field of physical education is beset with shortcomings, such as fuzzy definitions of its boundaries and responsibilities, but it is generally an area that is making major attempts to re-evaluate its existence and so clearly define its role in the educational system. This has been a great aid to dance.

A new direction in thinking is somewhat clarified in articles such as the Redfern article, "Physical Education as an Academic Discipline."[1]

Although I am an outsider to the working problems of physical education, it seems to me that one of the greatest difficulties of physical education involves the search for a body of knowledge unique to the field—in other words, a search for an academic discipline. If physical education lacks the respect it should have, it may very well be because it is resting on "borrowed" knowledge. It borrows from anatomy, physiology, physics, medicine, etc.; in fact, it may very well be a kind of collaborative laboratory for using knowledge from other fields. I don't suggest that this stop, but the field must search for an underlying discipline, or be unrespected and perhaps pushed out of the educational system altogether. Much literature in physical education communicates the unrest, but articles on the field as "academic discipline" lead my thoughts to a possible outlet that could lead to a solution.

It is well agreed that movement keeps us alive and that movement may well be the essence of life. I cannot see a limit to the importance of movement, and can envision some sort of science based on movement. Kinesiology can be a large part of this science, which would also include the recording of movement, the analysis of movement in behavioral terms, the meaning of gesture, and the control of bodily expression and communication. I can envision research on movement similarities and differences between countries and races, between centuries, and between men. This research may lead to a whole new understanding of communication.

In this realm, the work of Rudolf Laban is most noteworthy.* He has given us two complementary systems of notating human movement, one dealing in the analysis of position in space and time and another dealing in the analysis of effort and the shape of movement.[2] The former is called Labanotation in America and Kinetography Laban in Europe, and the latter is generally called Effort-Shape writing. Labanotation has given dance a literature and made dance a literate and academic art within the educational framework. There is now a concrete way to analyze and compare dance forms.

Dance is not the only area where Labanotation and Effort-Shape is being used. During World War II, Rudolf Laban was employed by the British government to analyze and improve the output in factories. By notating the effort pattern of workers, he was able scientifically to judge the effort-accomplishment ratio and thereby suggest better ways to channel the effort or energy to improve the ratio. One of Laban's students, Irmgard Bartenieff, has applied effort observation in physical therapy and has worked with psychiatrists at a New York mental hospital recording movement and effort patterns along with the psychiatrists' observations. She is using Laban's analysis. Physical education students at Ohio State University have studied Labanotation with the aim of recording and better understanding movement in sports. Anthropologists have become extremely interested in recording human movement for their purposes. A dancer-anthropologist from Hungary, Csaba Palfi, has been hired by anthropology departments to lecture on Kinetography and its relation to anthropology. I have been involved in a seminar in

*The work of E. Metheny, in *Connotations of Movement in Sport and Dance* (Dubuque: Wm. C. Brown, 1965), is also giving the concept of a movement science great validity. The importance of the "kinestruct," "kinescept," and other discoveries cannot be overemphasized. Miss Metheny's work is also at the core of my idea of a movement science.

ethnography in which I gave participants a means of recording gesture and showed how this could best be done.

The point is that activity is at the heart of what physical educators do. No quantitative or qualitative judgment need be of concern yet. Activity (movement), then, may be where the discipline lies, and an international language for the understanding of movement, the improvement of movement (if that is a purpose), and communication through movement must be concrete before it can indeed be called a discipline. Whether Laban's work and the work of the Dance Notation Bureau (also called the Center for Movement Research and Analysis) will satisfy the requirement of a discipline is questionable. But certainly the scientific thought that is involved in the system provides the tools for academic soundness.

Labanotation is not a difficult system, because it is based on a logical series of symbols. Basic assumptions are used in Labanotation that are always taken to be true—somewhat like the most basic notions in mathematics I (i.e., one plus one equals two is no more true than that the I symbol divides the body into left and right halves). The basic assumptions deal with levels of the center of gravity, the point of analysis in limbs and torso, division of the left and right sides of the body, placement of symbols in columns, and symbols for directions. Although Labanotation is a very sophisticated device for recording rhythmic patterns, it can also be used without a staff to indicate generally the timing of actions, if this is desired. Labanotation is particularly sophisticated in rhythmic notation because the length of symbols is directly proportionate to the length of time a movement lasts. In addition, it can graphically record simultaneous differences in timing of different parts of the body.

The complimentary system of Effort-Shape is likewise a simple and logical system based on only sixteen symbols, eight contrasting effort elements and eight contrasting shape elements represented by varying combinations of horizontal, vertical, and double diagonal lines. Indicators for parts of the body are taken from Labanotation. A need for Effort-Shape Notation arose after the system of Labanotation had crystallized. It became apparent to Laban and his co-worker, Warren Lamb, that even after structural and rhythmic details were clearly recorded, the quality of movement needed to be captured. The difficulty arose not in the system, but in the accurate observation of the many extreme and subtle shades of movement expression. Thus, if Effort-Shape is to be used for recording the dynamics of movement behavior and assessing the functional and expressive vocabulary of people, Effort training must include visual observation and the analysis thereof for its recording.

There are, of course, other ways to record movement, some unique to dance, some more usable in other fields. It is thought that the ancient Egyptians had a simple method for the annotating of movement, and the Romans used some form of movement notation in recording salutatory gestures, but the first significant attempt to record movement—in this case, dance—was by Thoinot Arbeau in the sixteenth century. His method of recording the pre-classic dance forms used word abbreviations with musical notes and is described in his book *Orchésographie.*[3] Not only don't the words tells us enough, but the interpretation is now—400 years later—extremely vague. A system of track drawings devised by Raoul Feuillet was used quite extensively in the court dances of the seventeenth and eighteenth centuries.[4] This was fine for the simple gestures of the upper bodies in those dances, but could not begin to record something like a jackknife dive or wrestling postures. Attempts have been made at stick-figure drawing along with musical notation, but problems of three-dimensional rendering, the impossibility of telling what happens between stick-figure poses, and the size of stick figures make these systems nearly useless.[5] Systems using symbols derived from musical notation are too limited to notate complex movement, and musical symbols that describe subtle rhythmic variation are already too complicated to be added to. Systems of writing movement as plotted in space, such as the Benesh system that is used in many ballet companies, have the greatest possibilities where movements are codified. The transfer of Benesh to scientific analysis of movement in industry would be a difficult task. Film, of course, is a good method for recording movement in all fields, but the sheer bulk makes it very difficult to handle, and it still must be carefully analyzed for any meaning to come from the recording. The best results in reconstruction of a dance work have been obtained through use of film *and* Labanotation.

If a sort of movement science can be derived from Laban's work, it can serve as the foundation of movement education. Physical education can then have its own body of knowledge. The language of movement may very well be the concrete foundation for the field.

For organizations such as the American Association of Health, Physical Education, and Recreation and departments of physical education to rebuild from their present foundations may well be impossible, but an effort must be made. A science that furthers knowledge of physical sensitivity and increases the awareness of non-verbal communication that constantly accompanies verbal expression and interaction between people may be the answer to solving a major substantive shortcoming in the field of physical education. The importance and need for understanding movement has been given a big thrust by the social sciences, psychiatry, and dance, but there is clearly a need for years of research, as well as proliferation and use of the knowledge, that physical educators can answer. If need be, the field might change its name to "movement science." There is no reason, then, why the applied movement scientist couldn't use his knowledge in many forms of human movement, such as sports, industry, and communication. This restructuring might mean the complete disintegration of health, physical education, and recreation into separate fields, but what could be more useless than retaining an organization housing everything from trainers and physiologists to playground leaders, folk dancers, lacrosse coaches, dance educators, and driving teachers? My suggestion, which is likely to be scorned as subversive, is to make a new organization of movement sciences and a *separate* organization of athletics and recreation, and, if need be, a third organization of health and safety.

Educational methods may be temporarily dislocated during such reorganization, but one should realize that sports and recreation have existed since time immemorial; they are, and have been, a part of humanity, and their very durability attests their worth. In short, a firm foundation should be built that can then be translated, as in mathematics, music, etc., into the educational framework to serve the needs of humanity more directly. Let's build a believable foundation from movement science. Let's foster sports and recreation, which are inherently important to mankind. Then, let's allow the purposes of education to direct teaching methods in the educational institutions. And let the new restructuring of the massive old field of physical education promote dance from afar, because both fields need information from the separate field of movement science.

Erick Hawkins offers us some insight into why dance has traditionally been a field for women. He suggests that an approach to dance as an art, with a sincere philosophy of its immediacy and meaning as art and life, will make it a place for women *and* men. A particular distaste for what ballet has been is shown here, and Mr. Hawkins pins part of the blame on the traditional ballet for the position of men in dance.

The philosophy of Mr. Hawkins is closely related to Eastern ways of thought regarding what dance should be. He thinks of the art as one of subtlety and one that exists for the moment, as something very spiritual and beautiful. Mr. Hawkins' answer to the problem of men in dance is not to display a virile "he-man" or a man's physique and temperament; the answer, he says, lies more in the whole man as mover, thinker, and artist.

WHY DOES A MAN DANCE, AND WHAT DOES HE DANCE, AND WHO SHOULD WATCH HIM?

ERICK HAWKINS

After I had started my first dance training in New York, for two years I did not write to my family what I was doing. When a young man has arrived at his vocation and is put in the terrible position that his vocation in the world's eyes is a questionable one for a man, you can see what trouble he is in.

After a couple of more years of training, I took a summer off to settle this question for myself. I was born on the New Mexico-Colorado line very close to the oldest dance culture in America, that of the Seven Cities of Cibola, Zuni, and of the Rio Grande pueblos, of the Hopis and Navajos, but I had never seen any of their dance ceremonies. So I spent the summer traveling around in an old Model A Ford, ferreting out news of every dance given that summer in New Mexico and Arizona. I had to see and feel whether a grown man could dance without being a fool.

That was a wonderful summer for me, for it set my soul at rest. I

From *The Dance of Choreographer Erick Hawkins* (New York: Guinn & Co., 1964). Copyright Erick Hawkins.

saw beautiful Corn dances at Zia pueblo where two men, then two women, then two men alternated down the dance line from the older men at the head to the kids four and five. Sometimes the older men danced with their beautiful black straight hair hanging down their backs to their waist. I saw once at the Hopi village of Mishongovi the chief of the Snake clan lead the line of men into the plaza limping with his hurt knee. He was ninety-two.

The summer told me that I had seen men use dance as part of their worship, part of their way of coming into harmony with their own life and the lives of all the other centers of the world around them. I saw how the men singers and the Mudheads, the clowns, watched with great care and hovered over the sacred dancers in their Katchina masks. That through the dancing the people were protected, and the young men initiated into manhood and knowledge of divine and inner power and harmony among the people.

This summer made me know that I would never be happy until I found a way to make the dance for us Americans part of a concept of totality. I knew that dance would never be for me only entertainment. I knew I could never again make the distinction between sacred and profane. At the end of a two-day ritual Rain dance at Zuni with 44 men in masks, I had seen the Mudheads make the Indian crowd roar with laughter in ritual comedy like a comedy at the beginning of the world.

Once the dance of men in our theatre is not partial, piecemeal, a triviality, mere virtuosity, mere Romantic daydream, mere narcissistic display, mere exhibitionism of private neurosis, mere adjunct to the display of women's charm, it would be honored and would be a worthy vocation among all of men's worthy vocations.

It is the specialization in our dance in which it is not demanded of men dancers that they be complete men and complete artists, carrying on their art in relation to everything else in the world, that has given dancing for men its bad name and its insignificance.

Dance for men in America has no prototypic underlying ritual and myth such as the matador in the Spanish bullfight has to give him his challenge, his commitment, his worth and his honor. But unless something equivalent to this is finally created in the soul of the American people a man's dancing will always be inconsequential.

A man dancing will have to go far beyond entertainment. A man dancing somehow will have to stand for what a man can become. He will really have to be a hero, in his body, his mind, his spirit.

I say that when President Kennedy has to admit to the world in a public speech that seven young American men have to be drafted into the army in order to weed out two worthy to be soldiers, something is wrong. When three of the five rejected fail to meet normal physical standards, and two of the five fail those in mental health, something is wrong, and the deep excitement of living a full human life is denied these young men through inadequate ways of developing our human potential.

Where is the image of a man fully developed in mind and body, integrated into reality, to be found ideally more than in the purposeless rhythmic play of the dance?

For

Dance is the most beautiful metaphor of existence in the world.

The absence of this knowledge will have to be corrected in the Western world. Sport will not suffice, no matter how marvelous it is. But even in sport the more rhythmic, the closer to a dance, the more purposeless it becomes.

The great image of the path of purposelessness in the East is the dance of Shiva, Nataraja, lord of the dance, in the construction, maintenance, and destruction of the world. It is not accident, and not inconsequential that the Western world has no equivalent.

The man dancing in America no matter how long it takes will have to find this archetypal image: *that the man dancing in the theatre is showing man becoming man.* The man dancing in the theatre is the image of man as he performs the rite of being a man for all men in the audience, as "in each corrida the entire country is watching the reflection of its hope . . . At each triumph the matador, once more, is unfurling the map of his country. Eternally, in sacrificial blood, rises the country of Spain, the country of men."

That is not our way, but we shall have to find another way to come to the same place.

Our present conception of why a man as dancer is lightweight is a hangover, in large part, of the position of the man in the ballet of Europe, and it is a great pity that it was ever imported to pollute the possible development of a dance art in America. For something is wrong when the men dancing in ballet are often in the public press called "the boys." Somehow, then, they are not psychologically fulfilling the function of men in the art.

This great distortion which was inherent in the beginnings of ballet was that the *person* of the dancer was exhibited and *not the art,* the inner art, as seen through the dancer. It is part of the cult of personality of the West. Just as the woman in our culture was looked upon in the words of Simone de Beauvoir as "object," so her place as "object" was transferred to the stage. Since in real life the woman was accepted and approved as "object," so she was approved by the male audience as "object" on the stage. When the man entered upon the stage as dancer with its emphasis on charm and physical display, he too was regarded as "object." But in our culture a man with a man's work to do cannot be an "object." So here was the impasse. He was tolerated because he could lift the woman and display her. If she was a princess, then for appearance's sake you had a cardboard prince. Sometimes this rather superfluous "prince" drops his role of prince and becomes an acrobat and does some air turns and *pirouettes* and *grands· jetés*. Naturally the man can do some virtuoso stunts that a woman can't.

But a grown-up woman doesn't want to see only little boys dance. Ask any psychologist about the woman's dreams of Spanish men and satyrs.

Not until the men in our dance find not a copied passion but their own flesh and blood passion will our dance be good enough, and our women take their rightful place as awakened women.

INTRODUCTION

[1]*Performing Arts: Problems and Prospects—Rockefeller Report on the Future of the Theatre, Dance, Music in America* (New York: McGraw-Hill, 1965), p. 180.
[2]*Ibid.*, pp. 60-61.

CHAPTER 38. Leadership or Control?

[1]Hope Sheridan, "Check List of Balanchine Ballets, 1923-62," *Ballet Today*, Vol. XIII, No. 18 (Oct. 1962).
[2]George Balanchine, *Balanchine's Complete Stories of the Great Ballets* (Garden City, N.Y.: Doubleday, 1954), p. 493.
[3]Rosalyn Krokover and Harold C. Schonberg, "Ballet in America: One-Man Show?" *Harper's Magazine* (Sept. 1964).
[4]*Ibid.*
[5]S. L. Grigoriev, *The Diaghilev Ballet, 1909-1929* (London: Constable, 1953), p. 208.
[6]Agnes de Mille, *Dance to the Piper* (Boston: Little, Brown, 1952), p. 235.
[7]In English, "was the only choreographer of his time not to have come under the influence of Fokine; he was a direct descendant of Petipa." Boris Kochno, *Le Ballet* (Paris: Hachette, 1954), p. 339.
[8]Serge Lifar, "The Technical Evolution of Academic Dancing," in Arnold Haskell (ed.), *Ballet Decade* (London: A. & C. Black, 1956), p. 114.
[9]Krokover and Schonberg, *op. cit.*
[10]*Ibid.*

CHAPTER 39. Physical Education or an Independent Art?

[1]Elizabeth Selden, *The Dancer's Quest* (Berkeley: University of California Press, 1935), p. 20.
[2]*Ibid.*, p. 77.

CHAPTER 40. Dance in Physical Education: An Administrative Set-up Revealed

[1]"Arts in Education: Wisconsin Arts Resources Study Documentation for Report of Task Force III," Department of Public Instuction, Madison, Wisconsin (1967), pp 6-8.
[2]"An Awareness of Dignity," *Dance Magazine*, XLI, 2 (Nov. 1967), 40-41.

CHAPTER 41. Dance and Physical Education: A Relationship Clarified

[1] Betty Redfern, "Physical Education as an Academic Discipline," *The New Era*, XLVI (Feb. 1965), 37-40.

[2] Albrect Knust, *Handbook of Kinetography Laban* (Hamburg: Das Tanzarchiv, 1958).

[3] Thoinot Arbeau, *Orchésographie* (New York: Dance Horizons, 1966; originally published, 1588).

[4] Raoul Feuillet, *L'Art de décrire la danse,* originally published, 1700; copy at Lincoln Center, Library and Museum of the Performing Arts, New York.

[5] Arthur Saint-Leon, *Stenochoréographie,* originally published, 1852; copy at Lincoln Center, Library and Museum of the Performing Arts, New York.

NINE

Facets of Dance Education

The closing section deals with the education of the layman and the aspiring professional in dance. At the root of dance education is the study and activity of movement, for the purpose of gaining a kinesthetic understanding of the art. As it would be senseless to study music or art without dealing directly with the materials, so is it uselessly academic to study dance without experiencing movement as doer and/or viewer. Naturally, much of the emphasis, for someone intending to broaden his knowledge of dance, must be based on his own physical capacities. Therefore, older people can become dance appreciators by seeing a great deal of the art in performance, while those with more willing bodies should attempt to experience some of the physical agonies and glories of studying movement and the accomplishments of creating dances of varied magnitude. There are many places to study: the universities, privately, and with local dance groups.

The aspiring professional cannot avoid physical training, but both the lay appreciator and the dance student must recognize the purpose of movement study: it is simply to develop an instrument that can express an expanding artistic sensitivity and the intellectual and spiritual growth of the individual. Any person can relate to this goal; therefore, many of the first problems faced in dance education can be faced with great reward by the aspiring professionals and lay people. This section deals with the study of movement and its goals; it is not a manual for the technique class. There are plenty of those, and for every manual of techniques there are contradictory ideas; for every teacher of movement, there is another whose approach is different.

Any artist must broaden his knowledge of the humanities and social and natural sciences with an appetite for discovering the world we live in, so that he can give us a vision of ourselves—and perhaps a better vision. The anti-intellectual dancer is not the dance artist. The artist has expanded his vision of the world so that when his instrument is ready, he can create the new dance, the new art, his own significant statement.

Noticeably lacking in this book is the entire field of dance history. This oversight is purposeful, because the field is too large to condense into a part of a book. Indeed, the history of dance deserves, and has inspired, its own books. An educated dancer knows his history and knows his place in the development of dance to the present, for without this knowledge he cannot create a new statement. An old statement may be worthy when the artist knows the background and worth of his statement, but to paint another *Mona Lisa* or do another *Dying Swan*, thinking it is new, is naive. The educated dance artist is not naive.

The preceding parts of this book have dealt with correlated areas of the dancer's knowledge—those areas of dance education where awareness is important and where the dance appreciator can better understand the scope of the field. This section deals more with the philosophy behind the active part of experience in movement. All are facets of dance education.

Dance as a creative art activity should be as basic to the education of the human being as any creative art, and its force should be recognized for its potential in human development. Dance in education cannot be an opiate for society. But the fact that education heads toward an *integration* of human capacities in terms of cognitive knowledge, physical control, and the total ability to express one's unique ideas gives dance (in which these qualities are inherent) a very important place in education.

Nor can we question the value of time spent expanding our taste and ideas in all the arts, when the creative arts have held such an important role through history. Some societies have measured their greatness by their culture, and certainly the quality of life we all seek is partly dependent on our aesthetic potential both as contributors and appreciators. For our educational system to overlook deep aesthetic experiences would be to neglect a very basic need of man. Since dance embodies a harmonious intertwining of mental and physical activities, the totality of the art gives it educational value. To contribute to the larger aims of education then, dance embodies intellectual, spiritual, and physical qualities. Margaret H'Doubler also stresses the emotional contribution of dance.

EDUCATION THROUGH DANCE

MARGARET H'DOUBLER

If dance is to function again as a vital experience in the lives of our people, it must be the responsibility of our educators. The inclusion of dance in the general education program is the one means of giving free opportunity to every child for experiencing the contributions it can make to his developing personality and his growing artistic nature.

In considering such a plan we should be able to answer such questions as these: What do we mean by dance? What are its ultimate values and justifications? Of what importance is creative art activity in the development of the mind? And, finally, what is its value for the individual? Such a search into the nature of dance

From Margaret H'Doubler, *Dance: A Creative Art Experience* (2d ed.; Madison: University of Wisconsin Press; © 1967 by the Regents of the University of Wisconsin), 59-66.

yields a philosophy based on a fundamental belief in the artistic and aesthetic capacities of human nature and in the values of expression through some creative art activity. From this philosophy must be formed a theory that will be an expression of the aims for which dance should work as well as a formulation of the underlying principles. An example of such a formulation is the insistence that dance be experienced as an adequate means of expression, so that, when the movements of the intellectual, emotional, and spiritual natures are coordinated with the activities of the body, there will result an expression that is vital and dynamic.

To work toward this end we must build a theory on a knowledge of the structure of the body and the laws of bodily movement. And to appreciate and understand the relation between feeling and action we must know the psychology of the emotions and the part they play in the urge to expression in movement. This carries us over into the science of dance: the systematized knowledge that tells us how to go to work—how to adjust our efforts to attain the desired ends. These ends will depend upon the view we hold for art, its social and individual values. Also, we must develop a technique that will result in forms that are in accordance with this artistic intention.

Education should be a building toward the integration of human capacities and powers resulting in well-adjusted, useful, balanced individuals. The desire to find peace within ourselves and to bring about an adequate adjustment to the life around us is the basis for all mental and physical activity. From birth to death life is a series of changing behavior patterns because life itself is an unfolding process. Just as the growth of man in civilization is the growth of man in consciousness, so is the educated, cultured, individual life dependent upon the growth and function of the mind, upon its capacity to know, will, imagine, create, and execute.

Everywhere educators are realizing that what is needed more than pedagogical preaching is intelligent stimulation to self-activity. There are, and always will be, many different theories of education. Often the education defined as "a preparation for life" has been so interpreted as to make it no more than a means of bettering one's economic condition. On the other hand, some critics seem to feel that the aim of education is success in living—quite a different matter. For this reason some thinkers and writers, especially those not in intimate touch with the actualities of education, have questioned the importance of creative activity and give but little place to the appreciation of beauty or the cultivation of artistic values. The reply to such attacks lies in a knowledge of the nature of the arts and in recent advances in educational theory.

No one who understands the relation of the arts to human personality can question their values in education, nor can those who have followed educational science during recent years fail to see that provision for the arts must be made in any adequate educational plan. If we go to one of the first masters of educational theory, Plato, we are told that "the purpose of education is to give to the body and soul all the beauty and all the perfection of which they are capable." This definition of purpose still holds, but today we would qualify Plato's statement in some such manner as that suggested by Spencer in his definition of life as "the conscious adjustment of internal relations to external." Both views, it is clear, focus upon the development and growth of the individual, and both imply self-activity, which we may take as the keynote of current educational speculation. The higher aim of education today is the development to the fullest extent of the growth of the individual, based upon a scientific understanding of all his needs and capacities. In so doing we try to attune our own thinking to harmonize with the student's particular interests because we realize that in his interests lies the key to his needs and capacities. Education cannot supply individual capacities—these must be inborn; but it can stimulate and aid in their growth; it can educate the student by giving him the opportunity to develop himself.

There are two aspects to education: one, the capacity to take in, to become impressed; the other, the capacity to give out, to express. To receive impressions informs the mind, but to express its reactions to these impressions requires coordination and cooperation of all the mental powers. Power to perceive and to evaluate experience is a high faculty, but of little use unless put into execution. Mere perception and comprehension of knowledge are not sufficient for the fullest development of the mind. To know is the essential first step, but it is the expression of what we know that develops character and a sense of values. It is through perception, intuition, feeling, and conception that our personalities assimilate experience and work it up into our own substance and the world of thought, emotion, and will.

Without this metabolism of experience damage is done to the emerging personality. It is likely to become overburdened and disorganized with undigested and unassimilated information, and inner spontaneity becomes hampered. If dance education is to contribute to this psychic integration, it is essential that the student experience movement in forms characteristic of human responses; that he be led, consciously, from the more natural movement types determined by structure to those responses that are variable and individually modifiable and under the control of higher associative processes; and, finally, it is essential that he experience and evaluate, as he progresses, the accompanying feeling tones of emotional enrichment.

In other words, dance education must be emotional, intellectual, and spiritual, as well as physical, if dance is to contribute to the larger aims of education—the developing of personality through conscious experiencing. It should capitalize every possible resource, selecting and integrating the contributions into a totality.

If we accept the belief in the organic wholeness of man, it is evident that the development of his energies must be interdependent. Our emotions and desires need intelligent selection and guidance, and to be carried to their fullest expression they demand skillful execution.

In such a concept of human development the body should be considered as the outer aspect of personality, for it is the agent through which we receive impressions from the external world and by which we communicate our meaning. Thus the body should be given as careful a study and as high a perfection of technique as the associated processes of thought and feeling. The most completely developed person is the one who has trained all his powers with equal dignity and consideration, in order that he may be physically, intellectually, and emotionally integrated. We may restate the meaning of education as the disciplining and training of our powers and the attainment of skill in execution.

The very nature of the arts makes them especially adapted to this ideal of education, for it is only in art that all the aspects of man's complex nature are united in expression. In art, as in reality, the drives are of the emotional nature; when subjected to the restraint and directions of the intellect and executed by the physical, they result in a fusion of all our energies with the focal point centered in the personality.

The place of dance in developing such individual growth is understood if personality is defined as the expressive total of all our physical, emotional, intellectual, and spiritual energies. These energies are in a constant state of reacting to and being acted upon by the social order in which we live. Of all the arts, dance is peculiarly suited to such a fulfillment of the personality. It serves all the ends of individual growth; it helps to develop the body; it stimulates the imagination and challenges the intellect; it helps to cultivate an appreciation for beauty; and it deepens and refines the emotional nature.

In the teaching and studying of dance we should not be concerned whether or not students develop into professional or recital dancers. The concern should be to develop the power of expression through the study of dance. It may be asked whether the expression of ordinary people has any particular value. It is true that expression is of special interest in professional art. We go to the works of the greatest artists for the wisdom and beauty and emotion they can communicate to us. But expression, execution, and sharing also belong to general education, and they are needs felt by all normal people.

Too often the tendency is to center dance education in performance, with the emphasis on technical skill, instead of studying the subject as a whole and using creative motor experience as the basis of instruction. In considering dance as an educational and creative art experience and not as performance, we should take care that students know dance as a special way of re-experiencing aesthetic values discovered in reality. Everyone has within himself the same potentialities as the artist dancer, but perhaps to a lesser degree. Everyone has intellect, emotion, spirit, imagination, ability to move, and educable responses. Every normal person is equipped with power to think, feel, will, and act. Anyone can dance within the limits of his capacities. To bring this to the realization of our youth necessitates an approach that is based on these fundamental human capacities. One of our problems is how to keep the creative impulse alive through the maturing years and how to help carry this impulse over into the realities of adult life with heightened power and more enlightened purpose. The basic forces underlying all living forms must be realized as the source of the creative impulse which impels to expression.

If dance is to realize these educational possibilities, it must take upon itself a form that is suited to them. It should base its movement forms on the laws of bodily motion, and the study of motion should include movement in all the forms characteristic of human responses. At the same time its techniques should be simple enough to afford the amateur student sufficient mastery of the body as his instrument of expression, and complex enough to prove interesting and valuable to those who wish to make dance their chosen profession. The rhythmic scope of dance will need to be sufficiently broad to include the varying personal rhythms of the students, and its forms and content will need to be flexible enough to provide opportunity for widely different expressions of widely different individuals.

Although such an approach to dance does not insist on artistic perfection from the professional critic's point of view, it can insist on high amateur standards and, in so doing, build a foundation for the development of a keen artistic integrity and appreciation. From such a background of study will arise those who are destined by original endowment to become our artist dancers. Our first concern is to teach boys and girls and men and women by means of dance, to teach dance as an experience that contributes to a philosophy and scheme of living.

It is to be expected that not everyone will be a great dancer, and that dancing, of course, will be experienced as a complete art form more by some than by others; but, as every child has a right to a box of crayons and some instruction in the fundamental principles of drawing and in the use of color, whether or not there is any chance of his becoming a professional artist, so every child has a right to know how to achieve control of his body in order that he may use it to the limit of his ability for the expression of his own reactions to life. Even if he can never carry his efforts far enough to realize dance in its highest forms, he may experience the sheer joy of the rhythmic sense of free, controlled, and expressive movement, and through this know an addition to life to which every human being is entitled. If the interest in giving instruction in dance is to produce dancers only, dance as a creative and pleasurable art experience, possible to all, is doomed.

It is because of this tendency that those who are convinced of the value of dance are striving to restore to society a dance that is creative, expressive, communicable, and social, a dance form that in every way will qualify as art.

BUILDING THE INSTRUMENT FOR DANCE

It is generally assumed that dance classes are based on physical activities. Although true, the assumption gives little recognition to the relationship of mind to body, which is fundamental both in lay dance education and in the education of the professional. Learning the vocabulary of movement in ballet or the varied movement terms and patterns that have developed in contemporary techniques is important, but not as important as studying *how* they are done.

The instrument for dance is the human body, and we all possess it, while we may not all own violins. Most of the dancer's life is spent perfecting his instrument so that it will be his willing medium for expression. Dr. Lulu E. Sweigard has spent the greater part of her life helping dancers and others concerned with human movement understand their instrument regardless of their intention. The goal for building an instrument for artistic expression is to achieve efficiency in movement. Briefly, this means getting the greatest results with the minimum amount of effort. Any dancer's plan to achieve perfection must recognize this goal. The instrument that obeys commands of the mind, from the most miniscule movement to the greatest bound, from the most subtle allusion to the most intense impulse, from the creation of simple lines to intricate weavings, or from very slow motion to that so quick as to be nearly unseen, is an efficient instrument.

The lay student of dance can strive toward efficiency of movement for the most obvious reasons of conservation of energy, but the professional must direct his entire basic training in technique toward this goal. Style and expression are rarely separated from the dancer's physical training as discussed here.

PSYCHOMOTOR FUNCTION AS CORRELATED WITH BODY MECHANICS AND POSTURE

LULU E. SWEIGARD

The term "psychomotor," separated into its parts, means mind and movement. It suggests that activity of the mind is accompanied by movement in and of the human body. Movement, initiated in the body itself, is produced by the action of muscles, mainly on bones. Hence, we may say that activity of the mind is accompanied by muscle action, or that thinking has its motor components. Experimental work substantiating such statements has been done mainly in the field of psychology, since the time of William James, who first placed emphasis on the theory.

Because of preconceived and frequently inaccurate ideas regarding body mechanics and posture, especially posture, the meaning of each, as used here, must be defined. Consider body mechanics first. Physics defines mechanics as that branch which treats of the motions of bodies and the causes of changes in these motions. Body mechanics, then, must be defined, similarly, as treating of the movement of the human body and the causes of changes in its movement. Causes of changes in motion of the human body are no different from the causes of changes in motion of inanimate bodies. Hence, we cannot logically escape the fact that physical laws apply to the balance and movement of the human body, just as to any other structure. Failure to recognize this fact has led to illogical and unscientific reasoning regarding body alignment and movement. Further, it has decreased the value of a number of experimental studies by its interference with a scientific approach to problems.

Consider next the term "posture." Some authors speak of "postures," thus implying that each individual can have more than one posture. In view of the results of experimental work, this is not true. Perhaps the erroneous idea that a person can have "postures" is due to failure to distinguish between the two terms, posture and position. Position means the manner of being placed or arranged, as in standing, sitting, or stooping. Posture, in contrast, means the *relative* position of the various parts of anything. In the human body it is the relative position, or pattern of relationship, of the parts, of

From Transactions of The New York Academy of Sciences, Ser. 11, VII, No. 7 (May, 1949), 243-48. © The New York Academy of Sciences, 1949; reprinted by permission.

the body. A pattern of relationship of body parts, or posture, tends to exist in each and every position the body may assume.

The meaning of posture may be clarified further by turning to the results of research on body alignment. One study was made by means of radiographs of the skeletal framework in the standing position; another study was made by means of photographs of the nude body, likewise in the standing position. Each of these studies indicates: (1) that in every individual there is a consistent and persistent pattern of relationship in the alignment of the various parts of the body as its equilibrium is maintained in the upright position; (2) that there is similarity in the pattern of alignment of the majority of individuals; and (3) that the nearer the parts of the body are to its center of gravity, the less variable the pattern of relationship of parts tends to be. The latter is logical from the standpoint of physical laws.

The posture pattern also influences the manner in which all movement activities are performed. To some extent this can be verified by observation. Characteristic postural idiosyncracies are noticeable in friends whether they are standing, sitting, or moving. The degree of influence, however, of the postural pattern on movement must be determined through experimental study. One such study of the influence of the posture pattern on the movement of walking will be completed in the near future.

Having defined body mechanics and posture, there is need for consideration of *how* ability to maintain equilibrium and to move is established and *why* patterns of postural alignment and movement tend to be consistent and persistent, even to grow worse. The human being is a self-directing mechanism through the action of his muscular system on his skeletal framework. Muscles, however, do not contract to produce movement unless and until they receive motor messages from the central nervous system. How are these messages instigated? What determines their muscle destiny? Is the motivating force a thought or idea? If so, is the thought concerned with muscle action; or is it concerned with movement only?

To answer such questions briefly, the development of ability to move must be considered. The body is the only means of expressing one's self. For expression there must be movement. Expression is sought from birth, and movement, to accomplish this, must be learned slowly by trial and error methods until adequate muscle coordination is established.

The individual is born with certain primary reflexes which he is unable to control, or change but briefly, if at all. Beyond primary reflexes, other reflexes make it possible at birth to move arms and legs and to squirm the trunk, but without specific direction. Neuro-muscular coordination toward directed and effective movement has not yet been established. But it can be and is, in the early years of life. The learning process takes place through building S-R bonds—muscle responses to specific stimuli. These are slowly established and, more frequently than not, the initial motivating force which activates many and complicated S-R bonds is the idea or thought of movement. Thus neuro-muscular action patterns are conditioned so that movement can be directed effectively toward the accomplishment of purpose.

Many influences play on this conditioning process: inherited structure, especially skeletal, muscular, neurological; mechanical, such as toys, furniture, clothing; pathological, as disease or sickness of any kind; injury, even though it thwarts only temporarily the ability to move; nutrition, with its general effects on growth and health; sociological, in its adjustment to others of society; and psychological, which are of great variety. Within the realm of psychological influences occur some of the most detrimental. The child imitates the posture and movement of those he admires and loves. He unconsciously absorbs and tends to live imposed ideas about posture and movement, whether they are good or not. He is influenced by the emotional stability of his parents, teachers and others about him. Discipline, or its lack, also has an important influence on the degree of muscular strain created in his body.

Thus, through trial and error methods, influenced by innumerable factors, neuro-muscular reflexes concerned with balance and movement of the body are conditioned; they become a matter of habit. Habits exist in the neural pathways traveled by motor messages through and from the central nervous system to the muscles. Continued use over the years sets more firmly the habit patterns of neuro-muscular action. Beyond their use required by the usual activities of life, few people are fortunate enough to escape the habit-setting effects of time-honored postural admonitions and of exercises for different parts of the body. As they are practiced, conditioned reflexes are used, habits are intensified, and muscular strain is added.

It may be concluded then that conditioned neuro-muscular action accounts for and is the *main cause* of the consistence and persistence of a postural pattern and manner of movement; also, that it limits both the ability to assume a good posture at will and the ability that may be attained in the performance of a skill, whether this skill be one used in work, play, or recreation.

With an understanding of the reason for postural pattern and manner of movement, attention can be turned to the possibility of their change, whether change is worthwhile, and how it can be brought about.

No one can deny the fact that that which has been conditioned in the human being can be reconditioned. Just as surely as Pavlov conditioned dogs so that their mouths watered at the sound of a bell, so can the human being be reconditioned in his muscular responses to stimuli. Toward what end, is the important consideration.

To determine logical and worthwhile goals in the reconditioning process, reasoning should proceed along mechanical lines. The established goal which has led to the construction of increasingly better inanimate mechanisms is a greater degree of efficiency—a better ratio of useful work to energy used. Granting that this is a worthy goal in engineering, economically and otherwise, the important factors influencing efficiency in inanimate structures should be noted. They are, primarily, a well-balanced supporting framework, ease of movement of parts of the structure in the performance of their work, and movement of all parts in accord with physical laws and principles of mechanics.

The fundamental aim in education and training for better body mechanics and posture likewise should be a greater degree of efficiency. This aim cannot be attained in the function of the human body without consideration of the same primary factors which influence the degree of efficiency in other mechanisms. In terms of the human body they are: alignment of the supporting skeletal framework in accord with principles of balance; flexibility of all joints in accord with their architecture and with principles of muscle function; and good mechanical use of all parts of the body, especially of the upper and lower extremities.

Before any procedure can be employed effectively to increase efficiency in the operation of the human mechanism, one must have (1) a clear concept of *ideal* body alignment, and (2) knowledge of deviations from the ideal which are typical of the majority of individuals.

To consider the ideal first, alignment of the skeletal structure would conform in so far as its architecture would allow, with the simple principles of balance. These principles are concerned with the adequacy of the various bases for support of weight throughout the structure, and the distribution of the weight of structure so that it is near the central line and near the base. Conformity with these principles determines the degree of stability of equilibrium. Logically, the true base of the human structure is the pelvis, since the center of gravity is located in that area. Recognition of this is essential to scientific reasoning in regard to both body alignment and movement.

As the concept of good skeletal relationships and alignment is built, accompanying muscle action and body contour can be studied and interpreted in terms of the internal framework. The latter is simple as a statement; actually, it is difficult and complicated—never ending and never fully known. It must be taken into consideration, too, that structural builds are different; hence, body contours are different, even when bones are well balanced. Aesthetic preference of a type of human figure must not be allowed to confuse scientific thinking.

Study of the deviations from ideal alignment indicates that there is, in general, a typically poor posture pattern found in the majority of individuals. The familiar postural difficulties, as forward head, round back, prominent abdomen, etc., should be interpreted in terms of poor skeletal relationships. In the majority of individuals, to a greater or less degree, interpretation shows that the following faulty relationships tend to occur. The trunk is too short in back, too long in front, and asymmetrical laterally. The lower extremities assume a backward and laterally different slant toward the feet. There are few, if any, spinal columns without lateral deviations of more or less degree, and few whose natural forward-backward curves are well balanced for weight support. Both the ribs and the shoulders are invariably supported at a higher level from the pelvic base than their bony attachments indicate. Finally, but not to complete the picture, the head tends to be too far forward, as well as rotated and tipped laterally.

All these deviations from good alignment imply a pattern of overwork, or hypertonicity, in muscle action. It must be so, since individuals, by means of muscle action, maintain their equilibrium in a consistently poor pattern of alignment.

As a concept of typically poor skeletal alignment is built, relative muscle action and distortion of body contour occurring with it must be interpreted. There are a few experimental studies which aid in this. They do not give a solution, however, to the intricate problem of muscle action; they serve mainly to point the way to better reasoning on a problem which seems unending in its complication.

Posture teachers are indebted, primarily, to neurologists and psychologists for the scientific support of changes now occurring in their teaching. Such changes are supported by the principle: thinking influences muscle action. It can influence it detrimentally or beneficially. Its detrimental influence is within the experience of most people, notably that of continuing the work and battles of the day after going to bed at night, thus building greater strain in the body instead of releasing it. Its beneficial influence is demonstrated especially in the work of Mabel Elsworth Todd[1] and Sister Kenny, and to some degree in the work of many others in both medicine and education.

Mental activity, then, especially that in which the thought of movement is involved, is the most effective means employed thus far to recondition neuro-muscular action patterns in the body. Such mental activity can be encouraged in a variety of ways. The key to each, however, is mental imagery, that is, visualization of an imaginary situation. Teaching can and should proceed in a manner which will lead the student to think in terms of concrete images. As this is achieved, image-directed muscular responses tend to occur. When no voluntary aid is given by the subject, concentration on a mental image promotes a coordination of muscle action whose resultant is the line of action of forces at play in the imagined situation.

In order to obtain the best results, especially when working with a group, the teacher should first help students gain the ability to change muscle action through concentration on mental imagery, without giving voluntary aid, and to recognize and interpret the kinesthetic experience accompanying such change. As this ability is attained, voluntary movement may be added to promote greater power in the newer muscle patterns and to speed up change. Since time does not allow detailed consideration of movement, suffice it to say that it must be carefully chosen, and that its effectiveness is controlled to a large extent by simultaneous use of appropriate mental imagery.

Of great importance to effective results in teaching are the answers to the following questions. What mental images shall be used, where in the body, and what shall be the direction of visualized movement? The answers are determined from the typical deviations of skeletal structure from ideal alignment, and from the principles governing muscle action.

Through comparison of typically poor with ideal skeletal relationships the writer determined eight "lines-of-action" needed to produce better body alignment and greater freedom of movement. Each line-of-action extends from one part of the skeleton to another. Along each line, distance between bones either increases or decreases. Such change is promoted by visualized action, without voluntary movement. The mental images on which the individual concentrates to promote the line-of-action are so designed that the resultant of the action in the image will be identical with the desired line-of-action. It may require recoordination of as many as fifty or one hundred muscles to produce this resultant.

Briefly, the lines-of-action, stated according to their purpose and direction of movement, are as follows: (1) to lengthen the back downward; (2) to widen across the back of the pelvis between the great trochanters of the thighs; (3) to narrow across the front of the pelvis; (4) to produce alignment of the knee with the thigh joint; (5) to shorten the inside of the foot toward the heel; (6) to narrow the rib-case; (7) to shorten from the mid-front of the pelvis to the top of the forward lumbar curve; and (8) to shorten (or lengthen) from the top of the breast bone to the top of the forward cervical curve.

Thus, the lines-of-action determine the location and direction of movement in the body, which is only to be visualized. Images that may be used to promote lines-of-action are many and variable. However, they should seldom, if ever, be created in terms of muscle action which is so highly complicated. Furthermore, the student does not need actually to know a thing about muscles to change his posture and movement.

Presenting movement to be visualized is not the only way to promote thinking in terms of mental images. Another way lies in the educational procedure itself—the presentation of pertinent facts in an interesting and challenging way, leading the student to think in terms of concrete imagery in his own body. It should be remembered, also, that people tend to be visual, kinesthetic, or auditory minded. This requires some modification in procedure to make it equally effective for all.

To summarize the primary qualifications of one who might be termed an engineer of the human body, they include the following: a clear mental picture of ideal skeletal alignment, supported by knowledge of physical laws and principles of mechanics; ability to visualize within body contour the existing faulty alignment of bones and to interpret the interrelationship between this and existing muscle action; knowledge of change needed in bony relationships to promote greater structural stability and freedom of movement; and finally, logical aims by which proposed change in skeletal alignment may be evaluated.

To avoid possible misinterpretation of some of the statements that have been made, it seems advisable, before completing this discussion, to clarify the difference between two terms, efficiency and relaxation, which too often are used interchangeably.

Dr. Edmund Jacobson, in his report,[2] states "muscular relaxation (conceived as a limit) can be regarded as freedom from effort, physical and mental." If this definition is accepted, there is only one way to attain relaxation to the greatest degree, and that is during rest of the body in a specified lying position and with minimum mental activity. Increased efficiency, on the other hand, means the accomplishment of purpose in any activity and in any position with the least expenditure of energy.

To increase the degree of relaxation, muscle work is decreased, but it is not recoordinated for the purpose of changing skeletal relationships. Hence, relaxation would tend to occur in accord with established patterns of neuro-muscular action, changing them but slightly, if at all. Whatever change may occur in muscle coordination will be undirected and in response to the need to maintain equilibrium and to move while trying to relax. Such automatic and undirected change may be for the better; or it may be for the worse, especially in certain postural deviations, such as lateral curvature of the spine or sacroiliac strain.

To increase the degree of muscular efficiency, in contrast to relaxation, there must be better alignment of the skeletal framework. This is attained only as muscle action is reconditioned to produce it. As the mechanics becomes better, the total result is less muscle work.

It seems logical, then, to state that relaxation means less work in muscles. But it is not necessarily accompanied by an increased degree of efficiency, even though the metabolic rate may be lowered. On the other hand, an increased degree of efficiency means neuro-muscular recoordination, and it *is* accompanied by less muscle work.

To summarize, the development of the subject has dealt with: (1) the meaning of the terms "psychomotor," "body mechanics," and "posture"; (2) the significance of conditioned reflexes in the self-direction of the human mechanism; and (3) how conditioned reflexes may be reconditioned toward the production of those mechanical considerations which promote decrease of strain in all human activities.

The purpose of studying techniques in dance is to perfect the human instrument to the point where it is a willing instrument for the chosen artistic expression. This book does not include discursive descriptions of the techniques of ballet and modern dance, because such descriptions would only slight the techniques themselves. The dance appreciator is advised to study some terminology and some movement ideas and to try some formal or informal movement study for a kinesthetic appreciation of the art. This cannot be taught in books. The dancer gets his technique in class, but he must review the purpose of technique constantly. We must never forget that the struggle against the imperfections of the body leads finally to freedom of expression. A virtuoso's trick may be regarded as a circus stunt unless it is vital to the expression of the artistic structure. Technique is not an end in itself.

The idea of discipline should not give illusions of rigidity or externally enforced rules. Instead, self-direction, understanding, and control are what an artist must develop to create his wares. There are many ways to build self-discipline.

FREEDOM THROUGH DISCIPLINE

ROBERTA MEYER

It was not so many years ago that teachers of modern dance forbade their students to study ballet technique. Within the past few years, however, the trend has changed. Not only are modern dance students seeking ballet training on their own, but teachers of modern dance are providing ballet classes in their studios, and choreographers are insisting on proficient ballet technique from their performers.

As a ballet teacher who has worked with modern dancers under these circumstances, I have been asked to express my thoughts on the meaning of this current trend, and, if possible, to shed some light on the seemingly conflicting practice of many of these same dancers who, upon reaching a level of development which enables them to

Reprinted from IMPULSE: *The Annual of Contemporary Dance,* 1966, pp. 9-10, by permission of Impulse Publications, Inc., 160 Palo Alto Ave., San Francisco 94114.

create and perform their own works, appear almost studiously to avoid anything which choreographically might be referred to as "balletic" in structure.

It is my belief that there is no conflict between these apparently opposing developments, but, rather, that they are the logical outcome of a sequence of events which have taken place during the past half-century. The arts in many ways reflect the social, political, and ethical standards of the society of which they are an integral part. At the risk of sounding like a pseudo-sociologist, I shall outline some of the ideas which I believe may have contributed to the shaping of these current trends.

The twentieth century has brought vast changes. New theories in many fields have led us to challenge much that was accepted without question before the turn of the century. The process of breaking away from the stranglehold of tradition resulted in the destruction of ideas and values which were judged to be hypocritical, unrealistic, and inapplicable to the changing world. Within the art forms we can easily trace the many breaks with tradition which accompanied the attempts of musicians, painters, sculptors and dancers to explore new ways of depicting the emotional, mental, political and spiritual climate of the world in which they lived.

This artistic rebellion was originally led by people educated in the "old school" under the masters of the day. However, this was less true in the dance world than it was in the other art forms. The leaders in the rebellion against ballet did not attempt an evolutionary growth out of the established technique, but, rather, sought to establish a technique wholly independent of those characteristics which had come to be thought of as balletic clichés. The fact that some of the "clichés" served a purpose for efficient movement was disregarded by many of the "new" dancers, though some of them, having had training in the classical tradition, showed the results of such efficiency. Some artists were what might be termed "natural dancers." Expressiveness rather than virtuosity was their major concern. Therefore, they did not suffer from lack of a defined and disciplined technique; but unable to pass on their expressive gifts, many of their followers did!

Certain principles of movement apply to all normal human bodies, and those principles provide the tools which enable a dancer to move with maximum range and efficiency. Contrary to the belief of many dancers, differences in body structure do not preclude classic training. They are, in actuality, the very stuff of which our individuality is made; and, therefore, should be given the most effective and broad technique possible in order to provide a foundation upon which they achieve full expression. As the present generation of dancers is discovering, classic ballet training is capable of providing that foundation; *but,* some changes have had to take place within the attitudes of all concerned in order to make this possible.

It should be remembered that at the time of the first movement away from classic technique, ballet had reached a somewhat fallow period in choreography. The apex of neo-romanticism, under the influences of Petipa and Ivanov, had passed and, in spite of the reforms introduced by Fokine, many artists felt the need of a dance form more expressive of the times. Somehow, ballet, with its flowing tutus, pointed shoes and fairy tale themes, did not seem to be providing this expressive outlet, or was it even capable of doing so. It is true that some choreographers were experimenting with new movement and modern music, but these changes were too mild for those who felt the need to express themselves in a more "down-to-earth" way. The approaches they used, many of them based on primitive and oriental influences, were bound to draw the scorn of the classicists; the disdain was mutual, and so was born a conflict which has not been fully resolved.

Nonetheless, a beginning has been made. Fusion has begun to take place, and through it is coming much that is of value to both dance forms. Much of the recent trend toward a return to classical training seems to be the result of an increased understanding of the true nature of ballet technique as a means of building a foundation which, contrary to old ideas, is neither rigid, limiting, nor confining, but is capable, when correctly taught, of preparing the human body for technical virtuosity. It is not an end in itself, but, rather, a means to an end; that end, as many modern dancers are now discovering, to be determined by the artist.

In my discussion with modern dancers, it has become clear to me that many of them now feel that evolution of modern dance was hindered rather than helped by the many and varied techniques which had erupted on all sides. Dancers trained in one school found it difficult to adjust to another, and many dancers found it difficult to adjust to another's choreography. Individuality was fine, but it became obvious that 20 dancers using 20 different techniques could produce little that was cohesive, and that the resulting disparate effect could soon become as tedious and overworked a cliché as the swans and princes of which the modern dancers had once so heartily complained! Many of these dancers have overcome the idea that ballet technique is stereotyped, regardless of what they may think of ballet as an art form. They realize that it gives them a solid foundation and provides them with a common technical basis. I believe technique is learned primarily for the purpose of providing a foundation for experimentation, so one need not expect balletic structure within the framework of modern dance choreography. But, as the old adage states, "you cannot break the rules until you know them."

It is my belief that the experimentation which is now taking place and which, to many of us, seems utterly devoid of form and meaning, will lead to new forms. Equally important, however, is the fact that more dancers are becoming aware of the freedom which is the result of constructive discipline.

We are on a two-way street, and I do not wish to imply that benefits are to be found solely in the modern dance world. Ballet has received a tremendous and needed impetus from the present trend toward an exchange of ideas in concepts of movement. That, however, is another story! Suffice it to say that there are undoubtedly many reasons why modern dancers are studying ballet, and ballet dancers are studying modern dance. The main point is that out of this growing knowledge of what the human body can accomplish, if it is not hindered by closed minds and old ideas, is bound to come a dance form more exciting than we have yet seen. Perhaps there will always be a division between that which is called modern dance and that which is referred to as classical, but it is my feeling that the current techniques will, in time, become meshed, resulting in a technique that is capable of endless development, and that those forms which might still be clinging to the distinction between "modern" and "ballet" will have become archaic and limited.

More than ever, in many areas of our lives, it is necessary to expand our ideas, to increase our comprehension of what is taking place around us, to draw upon the many constructive forces with which we come into contact, to get rid of our old prejudices, and to overcome the contempt we often feel for that which we simply don't understand. The best way to do this is to open our minds and investigate.

This willingness to search and learn is becoming the current trend in dance. There will, of course, always be those who are unwilling to subject themselves to discipline in their haste to express themselves, and in periods of experimentation it is often difficult to separate the wheat from the chaff. Nonetheless, I believe that out of the great variety which is evident today, something of value will come; for experimentation, when built upon a solid foundation, is bound, eventually, to produce quality. We don't have to sit by and accept all that we see as work of integrity, but I do believe that it is in our own best interest to encourage the establishment of an efficient and workable technique, and to continue to investigate avenues which will lead to the evolution and development of the art of dance.

REFERENCES, PART NINE

CHAPTER 44. Building the Instrument for Dance

[1] Mabel Elsworth Todd, *The Thinking Body* (New York: P.B. Hoeber, 1937).
[2] Edmund Jacobson, "Theory of Hypertension in Man," trans. *New York Academy of Sciences*, 11, No. 2 (1948), 49-50.

CONTRIBUTING AUTHORS

ABEEL, ERICA

A former dancer, Mrs. Abeel is presently a lecturer in French literature at Barnard College and is completing her doctorate in French at Columbia University, New York. She has reviewed dance for a number of New York weekly newspapers and for *Saturday Review.*

BARTENIEFF, IRMGARD

Born in Germany, Miss Bartenieff is now closely associated with the Center for Movement Research and Analysis (Dance Notation Bureau) in New York. She is widely known as an authority on Laban's Effort-Shape system of movement analysis and has recently been involved with recording and analyzing the movement patterns of mentally disturbed patients in a New York hospital.

BEISWANGER, GEORGE

George Beiswanger is Professor Emeritus of Philosophy and Aesthetics at Georgia State College and dance critic of the *Atlanta Journal.* In the 1930s he began to write on the modern dance movement, and later became dance critic of *Theatre Arts Magazine* (1939-44). He has also been a contributor to *Dance Observer, Dance Magazine,* and *Dance News,* concentrating on the aesthetics of the performing arts. He has taught dance history and aesthetics at the Connecticut College School of Dance, conducted a seminar on 20th-century American dance at the Salzburg Seminar of American Studies, and served on the Dance Panel of the State Department Bureau of Cultural Presentations; he is presently a member of the Dance Panel of the American Council on the Arts. Mr. Beiswanger is an accomplished pianist and organist. Experience in depth in one or more of the arts seems to him requisite for genuinely relevant work in analytical aesthetics.

BOWERS, FAUBION

Mr. Bowers is an alumnus of Juilliard School of Music, New York, who gave up a career as a concert pianist to go to Japan. During the Occupation he was civilian censor of Japanese theatre. A prolific author, Mr. Bowers centers his writing on theatre and dance. His books include *Japanese Theatre, Dance in India, Theatre in the East,* and *Broadway USSR;* and his articles have appeared in *Saturday Review, Harper's Magazine, New Yorker, Dance Magazine, Esquire,* and *Holiday.* Mr. Bowers speaks five languages.

BURTNER, ELIZABETH

Professor Burtner directs the dance program at George Washington University, Washington, D.C. For many years she was a performing member of the Dance Playhouse Concert Group in Washington, D.C., for which she did much choreography. She has done staging for the Arena Stage, also in Washington. Her background includes a master's degree with emphasis in dance, and modern dance studies at Bennington College, Bennington, Vt., and the Humphrey-Weidman and Graham Schools in New York. In Europe, she studied at the Mary Wigman School in West Berlin and the Laban Art Movement Center in England, and attended ballet and mime classes in Paris. She has taken advanced seminars in Labanotation and Laban's Effort-Shape theories. Her wide-ranging interest in the field of dance has also led her to study Indian dance.

BUTLER, JOHN

A former soloist with Martha Graham's company, John Butler decided to make choreography his chief concern while still a young man. He formed his own company in 1953, but it did not last. Mr. Butler has been praised for inventive choreography for the New York City Opera and Metropolitan Opera, although, as a successful free-lance choreographer, he is now as at home choreographing for ice shows and TV as for ballet companies. Some of his recent concert works are the violent *Ceremony* for the Pennsylvania Ballet, the stirring *After Eden* for the Harkness Ballet, and the erotic *Carmina Burana* for the Netherlands Ballet. He often works with the modern dancer Glen Tetley.

CASS, JOAN B.

Miss Cass is presently dance critic of the *Boston Herald Traveler* and drama critic of the *Jewish Advocate.* She was associate editor of the *Dance Observer* (1947-52), and director of the Dance Department at Bowling Green State University, Bowling Green, Ohio (1948-50).

COHEN, SELMA JEANNE

Editor of the important journal *Dance Perspectives,* Miss Cohen also teaches dance history and criticism at the Connecticut College School of Dance and is an adjunct professor at the Institute of the Performing Arts, New York University. Miss Cohen received her doctorate in English from the University of Chicago. A former student of ballet and modern dance, she has developed into one of the major dance critics and historians of the day. She has been a staff member of *The New York Times* and *Saturday Review* and continues to write for periodicals. She is a member of the Advisory Dance Panel for the National Foundation on the Arts and a former director of both the National Association for Regional Ballet and American Society for Aesthetics.

EGAN, CAROL

A graduate of Juilliard School of Music's Dance Department, Miss Egan is equally at home in modern and ballet technique. She has performed with the Joyce Trisler company, Jack Moore, and the Juilliard Dance Ensemble. After teaching at Smith College, Northampton, Mass., for a year, she spent two seasons in Poland studying and performing with the Polish Mime Theatre. While in Europe, she choreographed *The Music Man* in East Berlin. The years 1967-69 were spent at the developing Dance Department at the University of Wisconsin-Milwaukee, where she also worked closely with the Theatre Department. She is now teaching with Paul Draper at the new Dance Department at Carnegie-Mellon University, Pittsburgh, where, in addition to her dance classes, she helps with movement for actors.

GENAUER, EMILY

For many years art critic for the *New York World Telegram* and the *New York Herald Tribune*, Miss Genauer now writes for *The Post*. She is the author of *The Best of Art, 1948* and the Metropolitan Museum monographs on *Toulouse-Lautrec* (1954) and *Chagall* (1956). She contributes regularly to national magazines. Among her many awards is the 1960 citation for distinguished service to journalism from the Columbia University School of Journalism.

GRAHAM, MARTHA

Internationally recognized as the high priestess of modern dance, Martha Graham left her first professional home, the Denishawn company, in 1923, to develop a technique training (based on the contraction) and choreographic style that were unique. The Martha Graham dance company is acclaimed throughout the world. Her choreography ranges from Americana in *Appalachian Spring* to the heroic in *Clytemnestra* and *Night Journey* and the farcical in *Acrobats of God*. The Martha Graham School of Contemporary Dance has educated many dancers and teachers and has generated similar schools in Tokyo, Tel-Aviv, and London. Now in her seventies, Miss Graham still occasionally performs important dramatic roles.

HALL, FERNAU

Mr. Hall is a British writer and critic. Raised in Canada, he specialized in theatre during his university years, then worked as an actor and stage manager in Europe, where he became drawn to the dance, particularly ballet. Subsequently, while pursuing a dance career, he wrote criticism for *The Dancing Times* and began research in dance history. His books include *Modern English Ballet* and *World Dance.*

HAWKINS, ERICK

One of the leading modern dancers of the 1930s and 1940s in Martha Graham's company, Mr. Hawkins continues to perform, now at the head of his own group. Imbued with a very personal sense of the beauty of movement, he seldom choreographs literally. His work (with the exception of *John Brown*) is abstract and features "choreographic sound" by his associate Lucia Dlugozewski. His best known pieces include *8 Clear Places, Early Floating,* and *Geography of Noon.* Mr. Hawkins is director of the New School of Dance Technique and Art in New York.

H'DOUBLER, MARGARET

After a long and distinguished career in dance education, Miss H'Doubler is now Professor Emeritus of the Department of Physical Education for Women, University of Wisconsin. She began as a physical educator, but was persuaded to initiate dance studies and succeeded in offering the first dance major in the country at the University of Wisconsin in 1926. Her texts, *Dance: A Creative Art Experience* and *Dance and Its Place in Education,* are widely used. Hers was the first "orchesis"—a performing group that was the model for many high school and college dance clubs. By spreading her philosophy that the dance should be enjoyed by all as a creative and educational experience, Miss H'Doubler had a great influence in bringing dance into all levels of the educational system.

HUMPHREY, DORIS

From the Denishawn company and school, Miss Humphrey, like Martha Graham, went out on her own to formulate a personal technique, based on the body's reaction to gravity. She and Charles Weidman toured extensively with their Humphrey-Weidman company in the early days of modern dance. In her later years, until her death in 1960, Doris Humphrey was on the faculty of the Dance Department at Juilliard School of Music, New York, where she founded and directed the Juilliard Dance Ensemble. She also served as artistic director of the José Limon company. Her text, *The Art of Making Dances,* is a useful tool for beginning choreographers.

JESSUP, BERTRAM

Presently Professor of Philosophy at the University of Washington, Seattle, Mr. Jessup has also taught at the University of California at Berkeley, University of Southern California, Sophie Newcomb College, and Case-Western Reserve. He spent a year in Heidelberg, Germany, as a research scholar and served on the Oregon Governor's Committee on the Arts and Humanities (1966-67). He regularly lectures on art at universities here and abroad. He has published *Relational Value Meanings;* translation of Goethe's *Faust,* Part I; *Philosophy in Shakespeare;* and numerous articles on aesthetics, theory of value, and philosophy and literature.

KAYE, NORA

Trained by Fokine and Antony Tudor at the Metropolitan Opera Ballet School, New York, Miss Kaye became the finest dramatic ballerina of her time. She joined American Ballet Theatre for its first season in 1940 and stayed until 1951, when she left to work with the New York City Ballet for three years. She then returned to American Ballet Theatre, whose repertory offered greater scope for her dramatic gifts. Antony Tudor used her talents in leading roles for his ballets *Pillar of Fire* and *Lilac Garden.* Now retired, she lives in California with her husband, choreographer-director Herbert Ross.

LANGER, SUSANNE K.

Mrs. Langer is presently Professor Emeritus of Philosophy and Research Scholar at Connecticut College for Women. She received her A.B., M.A., and Ph.D. degrees at Radcliffe, where for fifteen years she was Tutor in Philosophy. Later she taught at Columbia University. She has written several books on philosophy and logic; her widely known *Philosophy in a New Key* stimulated the aesthetic theory that emerged in *Feeling and Form.*

LIMON, JOSÉ

Mr. Limon's proud bearing and high cheekbones reveal his Mexican Indian parentage. At the age of 20, after arriving in New York to study art, Mr. Limon found he could better express himself in dance. He began his studies with Doris Humphrey, danced in the Humphrey-Weidman company, and formed his own company in the late 1940s with Humphrey as his artistic director. *The Moor's Pavane* (1949) established him as a choreographer. Mr. Limon is an accomplished organist, and music plays an important part in his creative work. He has tried the light and satirical, but he is at his best when his choreography is "the celebration and affirmation of human grandeur, dignity and nobility." Mr. Limon, now in his late fifties, has only recently relinquished his roles to younger dancers. He is remembered as a powerful, dignified, dramatic performer. He has been associated with the Dance Department at Juilliard School of Music since its inception. *

MACKINNON, DONALD W.

Mr. MacKinnon is director of Personality Assessment and Research at the University of California, Berkeley.

MARIA-THERESA

The last of the famous pupils of Isadora Duncan, Maria-Theresa bears a striking physical resemblance to her teacher and, spiritually, is a sincere disciple of Isadora's teachings. In 1959, Maria-Theresa gave a series of programs on the classic dance in New York City.

METHENY, ELEANOR

Miss Metheny is a physical educator at the University of Southern California, Los Angeles. A professional lecturer, she had a TV series entitled "Odyssey: Health and the Active Body" from 1965 to 1966. She was assistant editor of the *Journal of Health, Physical Education and Recreation* (1947-51) and president of the American Academy of Physical Education (1963-65).

MEYER, ROBERTA

Miss Meyer has been a member of both the New York City Ballet and the San Francisco Ballet companies. She has been on the faculty of the San Francisco Ballet School and now teaches at the Ziceva Ballet School in San Mateo, California. She is a contributor to dance periodicals.

NIKOLAIS, ALWIN

Teacher, choreographer, dancer, composer, painter, sculptor, writer, choreographer—this is the many-faceted Alwin Nikolais. He began to choreograph in 1939, embracing the new "modern dance" after training as a musician. Since 1948, he has been co-director of the Henry Street Playhouse, New York, which he has made into a recognized dance center. The Alwin Nikolais dance company was formed in 1956 from students trained by him. His choreography has been called "an exuberant kinetic theatre form." Each work emerges as the total product of Nikolais. He composes the music and movement and designs the elaborate set pieces and costumes as well

* José Limon died in 1972, but his company continues under the direction of Ruth Currier.

as the lighting. His dancers appear as the motor energy and design-makers for his compositions, rather than as human beings. Mr. Nikolais received the 1968 Dance Magazine Award. He is a consultant to arts councils and a past president of the Association of American Dance Companies.

NOVERRE, JEAN GEORGES (1727-1810)

French dancer, choreographer and teacher, Noverre attempted to change the form, costuming, and conventional nature of the ballet of his day. His pleas for reform were not to be fully realized until the ballets of Michael Fokine, more than a century later. Noverre advocated unity and logical plot (which would cut out dramatically meaningless solo work by "star" dancers), elimination of masks and stiff costumes, clear characterization and pantomime, and expansion of the rigid movement vocabulary. As a choreographer, his greatest works were performed in Stuttgart, London, and Vienna, where he worked with Gluck and Mozart. He wrote *Lettres sur la danse* in Stuttgart in 1760.

PORTNOY, JULIUS

Professor of Philosophy at Brooklyn College, Mr. Portnoy is author of *A Psychology of Art Creation, The Philosopher and Music, Music in the Life of Man*, and the forthcoming *The World Man Created*.

SHEETS, MAXINE

Maxine Sheets is a graduate of the University of Wisconsin, where she received her Ph.D. in Dance. She now teaches in the Department of Health, Physical Education and Recreation at the University State College of Buffalo, New York. Her book, *The Phenomenology of Dance*, looks at dance from a viewpoint very close to existentialist philosophy.

SORELL, WALTER

Mr. Sorell has written criticism and essays on the dance for *Dance Magazine* as its contributing editor, for *Dance Observer* as its editor for five years, and for other dance periodicals. A member of the faculty of the departments of Music at Columbia University and the New School, Mr. Sorell has contributed poetry, essays and fiction to national magazines. However, his main interest is dance theatre. His publications include a translation of Mary Wigman's *The Language of Dance, The Dance Has Many Faces* (editor), and *The Dance Through the Ages*.

SWEIGARD, LULU E.

Miss Sweigard received her Ph.D. in Anatomy at New York University, where she taught with Mabel Elsworth Todd. Her teachings are based on Todd's work as described in *The Thinking Body,* yet go further. Her work in posture was recognized for its potential value to dancers, and she has helped professionals and student dancers at Juilliard School of Music for many years. Concerned with correct alignment of the skeleton, Miss Sweigard's goal is efficient use of the body. She tries to eliminate unnecessary tensions that throw the bony structure out of alignment by using mental processes—by suggestive images that result in corrective lines of action.*

TAMIRIS, HELEN

Originally trained as a ballet dancer, Helen Tamiris became a leading figure in the development of the American modern dance. In 1930, she organized the Dance Repertory Theatre and then formed her own company. She was known for her many dances to the accompaniment of Negro spirituals. However, she is best remembered for her success in choreographing for musical comedy. She worked closely with her husband, modern dancer Daniel Nagrin. Miss Tamiris died in 1966.

TAPER, BERNARD

Mr. Taper is a well-known biographer. He is also a staff writer for *The New Yorker* magazine.

TOMKINS, CALVIN

Mr. Tomkins worked at *Newsweek* before joining the staff of *The New Yorker,* to which he has contributed many articles on a variety of subjects. In addition to *The Bride and the Bachelors,* his books include *Lewis and Clark Trail* (1965), *Eric Hoffer: An American Odyssey* (1968), and *Intermission* (1951), a novel.

TUDOR, ANTONY

English by birth, Tudor began his ballet studies in London at the age of 19 under Marie Rambert. His talent as a choreographer was revealed by his early works for the Ballet Club, London, among which was *Lilac Garden.* He formed his own company, the London Ballet, in 1938, performing often with Agnes de Mille. Miss de Mille helped to bring him to America to work with the new Ballet Theatre. For Ballet Theatre he created his best ballets and established himself

*Her book *Human Movement Potential* was published in 1974. Since Dr. Sweigard's death in 1974, her course at Juilliard, Anatomy for Dancers, has been taught by her husband, Dr. Fritz Popkin.

as one of the most brilliant choreographers of our time. Among his dances are *Pillar of Fire, Romeo and Juliet,* and *Undertow.* His ballets are based on social and psychological themes, and he generally does not use a *corps de ballet.* Mr. Tudor now teaches at the Juilliard School and is associated with the Metropolitan Opera Ballet. He also travels throughout the world setting his most respected works for ballet companies.

TURNBAUGH, DOUGLAS

Mr. Turnbaugh has contributed articles on dance to *New York Magazine,* the *Atlantic Monthly,* and the encyclopedia *North American.* Executive director of the Fine Arts Workshop, Inc., a private school for children in New York, he recently completed a five-month world tour lecturing on American dance. He is director of a survey on the use of notation in the Dance Theatre for the National Foundation on the Arts and Humanities and has served as executive director of the Dance Notation Bureau, the Center for Research on Movement and Analysis.

WOLMAN, BENJAMIN B.

Professor in the graduate program at Long Island University, a practicing psychoanalyst, and Dean of Faculty of the Institute of Applied Psychoanalysis, Dr. Wolman is also chief editor of the *Handbook of Clinical Psychology,* associate editor of the *American Image,* and chief editor of the series *Psychoanalysis and Contemporary Civilization.*

YOURLO, YOURY and ELIZABETH

Mr. and Mrs. Yourlo were co-authors of a long-running series called "Question & Answer" in *Dance Magazine,* in which they researched and answered readers' questions on all aspects of the art of dance. They now teach at Ballet Arts School of Bethesda, Maryland.

THE EDITORS

The Dance Experience is a first book for Myron Howard Nadel and Constance Nadel Miller, although Myron Nadel has been a frequent contributor to dance journals. The book evolved from the pioneering introductory dance course developed by Professor Nadel at the School of Fine Arts, University of Wisconsin, Milwaukee, where he is chairman of the Dance Department. Since his graduation from the Dance Division of the Juilliard School of Music, New York, and his attaining a graduate degree from Teachers College, Columbia University, Professor Nadel has been a professional performer, choreographer, and college teacher in the United States and abroad and has staged original works for television. In addition to his many other duties, he is an executive officer of the American Dance Guild and serves as resident choreographer of the Milwaukee Ballet.

Mrs. Miller also studied at Juilliard and received her degree from the University of Wisconsin, Milwaukee, where she later also taught. In Milwaukee, she founded and directed the Conservatory of Dance Education, worked for the state arts council, performed on local and nationwide television, with the Fine Arts Dance Theatre, and with the Milwaukee Ballet Company. While living in New York, 1970–75, she received her M.A. degree from Teachers College, Columbia University, taught technique and choreography for Adelphi University's Department of Performing Arts, served as vice chairman of the American Dance Guild, and directed and taught at the Jacob's Pillow school. After a year as head of dance at Mount Holyoke College, where she helped form a Five College Dance Department, marriage took her to New Jersey, where she teaches at Brookdale Community College in Lincroft.

Index

Abeel, Erica, 116, 373
Abstraction in dance, 19, 106
Absurd, Dance of the, 110
Académie Royale de Musique et Danse, L', 94
Acrobatics and theatre, 175, 176
Adventure, The (Butler-Barber), 255
Aesthetics, 3–14, 197, 198, 208–11
Agon (Balanchine-Stravinsky), 10, 243
Aida (Verdi), with choreography by Butler, 252
Ailey, Alvin, 133
Amahl and the Night Visitors (Menotti), with choreography by Butler, 254
American Association of Health, Physical Education, and Recreation, 340
American Ballet Theatre, 99, 168, 311, 314
American Dance Festival, 193
American Dance Guild, 334
Antechamber (Louis), 119
Antic Meet (Cunningham), with costumes and sets by Rauschenberg, 273
Apollon Musagète (Balanchine-Stravinsky), 313
Appalachian Spring (Graham-Copland), 262
Arbeau, Thoinot, 340
Armitage, Merle, 20
Arpino, Gerald, 122
Art et le geste, L' (D'Udine), 20, 55
Art of Making Dances, The (Humphrey), 105, 123
Artaud, Antonin, 176
Ashton, Sir Frederick, 180, 313
Australian Ballet, 141

Bach, Johann Sebastian, 80, 120, 132, 192, 246
Balanchine, George, 5, 10, 84, 90, 99, 129, 165–68, 240–47, 267, 272, 296, 309–17
Ballet, 93–100, 164–70, 180, 228, 251, 304, 329; classical, 14, 103; modern, 95, 97–100; romantic, 94, 95–97
Ballet d'action, 306–7
Ballet Folklorico of Mexico, 103
Ballet Imperial (Balanchine-Tchaikovsky), Franklin production of, 317
Ballet Rambert, 141
Ballet Society, 269
Ballets Russes, 99, 311, 315–16
Balletti, 94
Barber, Samuel, 192, 193, 255
Bartenieff, Irmgard, 151, 338, 373
Batsheva Modern Dance Company, 141
Baumann, Arthur, 122
Bayanihan of the Philippines, 103
Beaumont, Cyril W., 123, 245
Beethoven, Ludwig van, 20, 21, 68, 70, 159
Being and Nothingness (Sartre), 37, 55
Beiswanger, George, 82, 83, 318, 373
Benesh, Joan, 135, 140, 142
Benesh, Rudolph, 135–44
Benesh Notation, 135–44, 340
Bennington School of the Dance, 266
Berliner Ensemble, 175
Bernstein, Leonard, 180, 255, 270
Bettis, Valerie, 267

Billy the Kid (Loring-Copland), 104
Bird, Bonnie, 266
Birds, The (Aristophanes), 128
Black Mountain College, 270, 273
Bolender, Todd, 313
Bolshoi Ballet, 95, 144
Boquet, Louis, 301
Borodin, George, 28, 55
Boulez, Pierre, 245, 261
Bournonville, August, 93
Bowers, Faubion, 110, 373
Brandeis University Festival, 270
Brecht, Bertolt, 175
Britten, Benjamin, 191
Brook, Peter, 178
Brooklyn Academy of Music, 263, 275
Brown, Carolyn, 118, 258, 259, 261, 263–90
Brown, Earle, 261, 285
Bugaku (Balanchine-Mayuzumi), 244
Bunyan, John, 202, 205
Burtner, Elizabeth, 127, 374
Butler, John, 251, 312, 374

Cage, John, 117, 119, 122, 257, 260, 261, 266–71, 274–77, 280, 283, 285, 288–92
Calder, Alexander, 22, 80, 251, 253
Calligraphy, "lecture" danced in, by Santoro, 112
Capricorn Concerto (Barber), Limon's working to, 192
Caracole (Balanchine-Mozart), 244
Carmen (Bizet), with choreography by Butler, 252
Cass, Joan B., 225, 374
Chagall, Marc, 164, 167, 316
Chamber Symphony (Limon-Schönberg), 193
Chance in choreography, 83–89, 117
Changes and New Developments in Labanotation (Topaz, ed.), 130
Chaplin, Charlie, 175
Character dancing, 103
Charles Weidman Theatre of the Expression of the Two Arts, 112
Charlip, Remy, 269
Chicago Symphony, 285, 288–92
Choephoroe, The (Aeschylus), 223
Chopin, Frédéric, 21, 69, 70, 99, 159, 192
Chopiniana (original title of *Les Sylphides*), 98
Choreographers, 1, 6–14, 74–75, 85–89, 98, 108, 181, 184, 191–93, 213–15, 251–56
Choreography, 74–81, 82–89, 98–100
Choreology, 129, 135–44
Choroscript, 129, 145–50
Christensen, Lew, 313
Chujoy, Anatole, 245
City Center Joffrey Ballet, 100, 122, 312
"Classical dancing," 235, 236
Clowns (Arpino), 122
Clytemnestra (Graham-El Dabh), 6, 238
Cohen, Selma Jeanne, 3, 374
Collage (Cunningham), 270
Communication: art and, 72; dance and, 47; means of, in dance, 106–7
Complete Book of Ballets (Beaumont), 123

384